Keynesian Macroeconomics Beyond the IS-LM Model

Chandana Ghosh · Ambar Nath Ghosh

Keynesian Macroeconomics Beyond the IS-LM Model

Springer

Chandana Ghosh
Economic Research Unit
Indian Statistical Institute
Kolkata, West Bengal, India

Ambar Nath Ghosh
Economics Department
Jadavpur University
Kolkata, West Bengal, India

ISBN 978-981-13-7890-4 ISBN 978-981-13-7888-1 (eBook)
https://doi.org/10.1007/978-981-13-7888-1

JEL Classification: E, G, H

This Springer imprint is published by the registered company Springer Nature Singapore Pte Ltd.
The registered company address is: 152 Beach Road, #21-01/04 Gateway East, Singapore 189721, Singapore

Dedicated to the memory of
Professor Amitava Bose,
a great inspiration, an excellent teacher,
a brilliant mind with a golden heart.
We will never cease to miss him.

Preface

The major capitalist powers of Western Europe and the USA colonized the whole world before World War I had begun. Then, they fought two world wars for a larger share of the colonies. The two world wars weakened them considerably. World War I dealt such a devastating blow to the Tsar, the emperor of Russia, that the Bolsheviks in a bloodless revolution overthrew him and usurped power giving birth to the first socialist state in the world. The socialist state of Russia eventually grew into the Soviet Union and became a superpower after World War II. Threatened by the emergence of socialism, the capitalist powers after World War II became united and started building arms at a frantic pace to destroy the Soviet Union. The latter also had to invest heavily in defense for survival. Thus, a fierce arms race began between the Soviet Union and the capitalist powers led by the USA ushering in the era of the Cold War. Capitalist powers had to devote so much resources to arms building and to the reconstruction of their economies following the devastation wrought by World War II that they had no more resources left to contain the rising nationalist movements in their colonies. Hence, they granted them independence. Many of the newly independent colonies including India followed the Soviet model of planned economic development and resolved to develop their societies on the socialist path. During the Cold War, both the capitalist powers and the Soviet Union tried to spread their respective influences all across the world. However, the era of the Cold War eventually came to an end with the defeat and collapse of the Soviet Union. The capitalist powers came into dominance again and started colonizing the whole world once more both by waging war and through economic means. A capitalist society has multiparty democracy, where every adult citizen has one vote. At the same time, a capitalist society has a very high degree of inequality, with a handful of giant capitalists owning most of the non-labor resources of the country. Coexistence of extreme inequality and democracy is a puzzle. Democracy does not pose any threat to the enormous wealth of the giant capitalists or to capitalism. The major objective of the book is to suggest a solution to this puzzle and to show how capitalism works in the twenty-first century. It illustrates the working of capitalism taking up the cases of India, Greece, and the USA. Since mainstream economics does not even recognize the coexistence of capitalism and democracy as a puzzle, the book fills up an important gap in the literature. In fact, it is not possible for one to comprehend how capitalism works unless one has a satisfactory solution to the puzzle.

The book uses Keynesian tools and techniques to analyze how capitalism works. However, the IS-LM model or the IS-LM-based models have major shortcomings. The interlinkage between the real sector and the financial sector in these models is so inadequate and unsatisfactory that they cannot be used for any meaningful analysis of capitalism. This book, therefore, builds an alternative to the IS-LM model removing all its deficiencies that have survived repeated attempts at mending them. This constitutes a major contribution to Keynesian macroeconomics.

Kolkata, India

Chandana Ghosh
Ambar Nath Ghosh

Contents

About the Authors

Dr. Chandana Ghosh is Assistant Professor in the Economic Research Unit, Indian Statistical Institute, Kolkata. She has written four books (coauthored with Ambar Nath Ghosh) all published by Prentice Hall of India: “Economics of the Public Sector” (2008), “Public Finance”, 2nd ed. (2014), “Macroeconomics” (2011) and “Indian Economy: A Macro-Theoretic Analysis” (2016). All of these books are frequently used at many prominent universities and colleges throughout India.

Dr. Ambar Nath Ghosh is Professor at the Department of Economics, Jadavpur University, Kolkata. In addition to the books mentioned above that he has co-authored with Chandana Ghosh, he has also co-edited (with Asim Karmakar) the book “Analytical Issues in Trade, Development and Finance,” published by Springer in 2014.

Chapter 1
Introduction

Abstract This chapter delineates the salient features of capitalism and, in the process, introduces the theme and the plan of the book. In a capitalist society, a small section of giant capitalists own the bulk of the country's wealth and have in their command the lion's share of the country's income. At the same time, a capitalist society is characterized by multiparty democracy where every adult citizen has one vote. It is extremely puzzling that the political equality granted by democracy does not pose a threat to the enormous wealth and business empire of the giant capitalists or capitalism. This chapter seeks to explain this puzzling coexistence of extreme economic inequality and political equality in a capitalist society. The major capitalist powers conquer different countries of the world directly by waging wars and also through economic means and, thereby, help the giant capitalists expand their business empire all across the world. The objective of the book is to illustrate the working of the giant capitalists by analyzing the recent major policies and events in three countries, namely India, Greece, and the USA. This chapter gives a glimpse of how the book seeks to proceed with the task. The book carries out the analysis using Keynesian tools and techniques. However, the IS-LM model or the IS-LM-based Keynesian models have important shortcomings that make them unsuitable for our analysis of capitalism. The book has, therefore, developed a Keynesian alternative to the IS-LM model removing all its deficiencies. This chapter briefly summarizes the major shortcomings of the IS-LM model that have survived repeated attempts at mending them and points to the way in which the book seeks to resolve them.

1.1 Capitalist Societies and Common Man

The objective of this chapter is to introduce the theme of this book. The book focuses on capitalism. Capitalism refers to a form of society where production is carried out with hired labor. In such a society, a small section of people own all the material means of production (stocks of capital and natural resources), while the rest of people have only their capacities to work. The former are referred to as capitalists and the latter as workers. Workers have to sell their labor to the capitalists for survival. The book seeks to analyze how capitalism functions. It strives to show how developing

C. Ghosh and A. N. Ghosh, *Keynesian Macroeconomics Beyond the IS-LM Model*, https://doi.org/10.1007/978-981-13-7888-1_1

and developed countries perform under capitalism. Capitalism persists and dominates overwhelmingly even though it has very little to recommend itself. It is characterized by a high degree of inequality (see, for example, Stiglitz (2012) and Picketty (2014) in this context). Quite a large section of the people in capitalist countries such as the USA, which is the leading capitalist power in the world, do not have access to higher education and health care. Many of them do not have adequate access even to the basic necessities of life such as basic quality food, clothing, and shelter. United States Department of Agriculture (2018) estimated that 11.8% of US households were food insecure in 2017 and 4.5% of US households had very low food security in 2017. They also reported that over a period of five years from the day the survey began, 51.5% of US households were food insecure for some period in at least one year. US Department of Housing and Urban Development (2018) reported that in 2017, 17 people experienced homelessness on a given night per 10,000 people in the general population in 2016 and 65% of the homeless people lived in emergency shelters and the rest in unsheltered locations. However, this estimate of homeless people grossly underestimates the number of homeless people in the USA. The reason is the following. Many of the homeless people in the USA are homeless only temporarily due to unemployment or low-paying employment. They cease to be homeless as soon as they get employment or better jobs. Therefore, people who are homeless on a given night in a given year are likely to be largely different from those who are homeless on some other given night in the same year. Hence, the number of people who were homeless for at least some short period of time in a given year is likely to be substantially larger than the official estimate reported above. In fact, a study carried out by Reischauer (2000) estimated that between 2.3 million and 3.5 million people in the US experienced homelessness at least for some short period of time in 1999. US Department of Health and Human Services (2016) reported that 10.3% of people under age 65 did not have any health insurance in the second quarter of 2015. Given the very high cost of healthcare services in the USA, a person without health insurance does not get any access to healthcare services. The data given above are indicators of extreme poverty and deprivation. From these indicators, one may reasonably guess that most of the people live in considerable poverty and misery even in the most powerful of the capitalist countries. Even in underdeveloped capitalist countries like India, the degree of inequality is staggering. According to a report (Oxfam India 2018), only 1% of India's population own 76% of India's total wealth. Moreover, the incidence of malnutrition and hunger in India is one of the highest in the world (see Concern Worldwide 2018). The existence of extreme inequality and acute deprivation of the masses are a puzzle in capitalist economies in view of the kind of political framework within which they operate. Capitalist economies without exception operate within a framework of multiparty democracy, where every adult citizen has one vote. The political party that gets the majority of the votes usurps power and forms the government. It is, therefore, natural that the political parties should work for the masses, who sell their labor to earn a living and live a poverty-stricken miserable life. We should, therefore, expect the political parties to tax away all the surplus income of the rich and distribute them among the poor. We should also expect the political parties to take away all the wealth of the rich and use it for the benefit of the poor. However, no political party in a capitalist society behaves that way. In fact, they seek to do just the opposite so that inequality in the distribution of income and wealth widens over time and the poverty of the masses perpetuates. In what follows, we shall seek to resolve this puzzle.

1.2 Capitalism, Democracy, and Common Man

People in a capitalist society, as we have already pointed out, are divided into two classes: the capitalists and the workers. The former own all the material means of production consisting of all the capital stock and the natural resources. The latter own only their capacity to work, and they sell it to earn their living. In a capitalist country, a small section of giant capitalists carries out the major part of production. (In India, for example, TATAs, a business family/house, monopolizes production of salt, commercial vehicles, watches and just a handful of giant Indian capitalists and multinational companies produce most of the goods and services.) This small section of giant capitalists own most of the wealth of the country and have in their command the major part of the country's income. Their greatest challenge is to protect their enormous wealth from the rest of people, who constitute more than 99% of the total population. Obviously, they need state power to protect their wealth. To usurp state power, just like their business enterprises, they set up and run political parties. A political party has to make its programs and views known to people and make them popular among the masses. For this purpose, it needs a very large number of workers covering the entire country, has to hire services of media, organize meetings, rallies, etc. Thus, it requires an enormous amount of fund to set up and run political parties. Only the giant capitalists have the resources to set up and run political parties. The giant capitalists, therefore, set up and run political parties and through them usurp state power. In a multiparty democracy, political parties compete with one another for power. Their competitive strength depends crucially on the amount of fund at their disposal. If a political party disobeys the giant capitalists, they will divert their fund from the errant political party to other political parties weakening the former and strengthening the latter. Thus, all political parties in a capitalist society have to work for the giant capitalists and have to abide by their dictates.

The giant capitalists have to keep the workers under control. They do so in two ways, namely, by using state power and by reducing their dependence on workers. To achieve the latter, they invest on a massive scale in R&D to continuously incorporate labor-saving technological and managerial changes. This process creates a large pool of unemployed workers ruining the bargaining strength of the workers. With the loss in the bargaining strength, wages become low, jobs become insecure and informal, and work conditions deteriorate. In India, for example, employment in the organized sector (the modern sector consisting of large production units) did not increase at all during the period 1994–2017, while real value added in the organized sector increased approximately at the average rate of 6% annually. The organized sector in India employed 6% of the labor force in 2005, and this percentage is falling continuously, since employment is stagnant and labor force is growing (see Table 6.3). Thus, most of the workers in a capitalist society live in unemployment or insecure employment with low wages. This explains why most of the people even in the richest of the capitalist countries live a poverty-stricken miserable life.

To obfuscate the real cause of poverty and misery of the masses, the giant capitalists facilitate the spread of religion by promoting and funding religious institutions. Religion attributes the poverty and misery of the masses to their misdeeds either in their present incarnation or in their past incarnations. Religion asks people to lead a peaceful, hardworking, and truthful life dedicated to God and to worship God to attain salvation.

In a capitalist society, economists are workers and the giant capitalists hire workers to work for them. The giant capitalists want the government to keep direct tax rates at the lowest possible levels for the rich. They also want the government to give them a free hand in running and controlling the economy in accordance with their interest. Economists in capitalist countries, being hired by the giant capitalists, develop the kind of economics, neoclassical economics to be more precise, that vindicate these policies. Neoclassical economics recommends a non-interventionist laissez-faire policy, with a small government so that the ownership of the economy's non-labor resources and the control of the economy rest principally with the giant capitalists. Neoclassical economics also justifies low direct tax rates on the rich.

Capitalist economies are subject to trade cycles. Phases of high growth (of real GDP) and low growth alternate with one another. The phase of high growth is referred to as boom and that of low growth is referred to as recession or bust. Evidences (which we have cited in Chap. 9) suggest that giant capitalists through their speculative activities in the asset market create booms and busts to suit their interest. Giant capitalists, using their enormous financial might, start buying assets on a massive scale and, thereby, create stupendous bubbles in asset prices. Asset prices begin to rise at rates higher than the interest rates on loans. Through the media and the cadres of political parties, which are fully under the control of the giant capitalists, the giant capitalists generate the expectations among the masses that the high rate of inflation in asset prices, which is much above the interest rate, will continue in future. The masses, therefore, begin to consider it enormously profitable to buy the assets with loans to sell them off at a later date. The banks and other financial institutions, which are also owned and controlled by the giant capitalists, make loans available in plenty on extremely easy terms to anyone who asks for it for buying the assets. Thus, ordinary people and firms get caught in a mass speculative frenzy. They start borrowing on a massive scale to make speculative purchase of the assets for resale at a later date. Once this speculative purchases of the assets begin, the rate of asset price inflation moves to an even higher level turning the expectation of a high rate of inflation in the asset prices self-fulfilling. This gives a further boost to speculative activities on the part of the masses. The soaring asset prices and the speculative euphoria give a tremendous boost to the morale of both the consumers and investors. Both consumption and investment spending begin to rise ushering in a phase of boom in the economy. Once this mass speculative frenzy begins, the giant capitalists start dishoarding their stock of assets, which they had to build to make the asset prices soar before the mass speculative frenzy had begun, at a huge profit. Then, at an opportune moment suddenly offloads all their remaining stock of the assets to burst the bubble. As asset prices crash, the ordinary people and firms, who made speculative purchase of the assets with loans, make huge losses and become bankrupt. The large-scale loan default on the part of the heavily indebted ordinary households and firms drives the financial institutions to bankruptcy or on the verge of it. Financial institutions fail to or find it difficult to meet the depositors, or policy holder's claims. People lose faith in the financial institutions and supply of credit to financial institutions, firms and households dry up. As a result, morale of both the consumers and investors takes a massive beating. Consequently, both consumption and investment expenditure decline substantially driving the economy into a deep recession. The central bank and the government of the country intervene with a battery of stabilization measures to rescue the financial institutions and to prevent the economy from sliding into a deep depression. However, evidences (which are available in Chap. 9) suggest that these stabilization measures are designed in such a manner that the economy does not get out of the recession completely, but remains in a desired state of recession indefinitely. We have exemplified this sequence of events in the case of the USA (since the mid-nineties) in Chap. 9. The reason why the global capitalists behave the way specified above may be explained as follows.

Capitalists secure two things from the workers, their labor, and their savings. Workers park their savings with the banks and other financial institutions. Through their speculative activities described above, the global capitalists get a part of the savings of the workers transferred to them in the form of speculative gains. The reason why the giant capitalists want to keep their economy in a desired state of recession is the following. The central bank of the country uses the recession as an excuse to take steps so that the interest rate falls to the minimum possible level. This makes savings of the workers available to the giant capitalists at the minimum possible price. However, even though interest rates faced by the giant capitalists fall to the minimum possible level, interest rates faced by small and medium producers go up sharply with the onset of recession following the collapse of the asset price bubble. This happens because banks and other financial institutions tighten credit standards, as their risk perception regarding lending to not so financially strong borrowers deteriorates sharply (see in this connection Mishkin (2009, 2011) and Bernanke et al. (1999)). This substantially erodes the competitive strength of the small and medium producers. As a result, they lose out to the giant capitalists, who grab their market shares. The recession and the consequent large-scale increase in the unemployment rate weaken considerably the bargaining strength of the workers. This enables the giant capitalists to dilute labor standards, cut wages, and incorporate labor-saving technological and managerial changes. Thus, recession enables the giant capitalists to increase their market shares, their share in total income by weakening considerably the rest of the population. In sum, the recession enables the giant capitalists to consolidate their position and dominate over and control the rest of the people fully. The recession continues until the global capitalists launch again their aggressive speculative operations in the asset market.

Capitalism has been expansionist right from its birth (see Hunt and Lautzenheiser (2014), Chap. 13 in this context). The giant capitalists of Western Europe and the USA conquered and colonized the whole world before World War I. At that time, the giant capitalists were divided in accordance with their nationalities. They fought two world wars among themselves for larger shares of the colonies. These two world wars weakened them considerably. World War I dealt such a fatal blow to the Tsarist empire of Russia that the Bolsheviks overthrew the Tsar and usurped power in 1918. Thus, the first socialist state was born. The giant capitalists felt threatened, and the capitalist powers (USA, Europe, and Japan) sent troops to defeat the revolutionary government. However, the Bolsheviks won and their empire grew into Soviet Union. The allied forces during World War II defeated Germany with the help of the Soviet Union. Soviet Union emerged as a socialist superpower after World War II. The giant capitalists felt threatened. They feared the advent of socialism. They threatened to attack Soviet Union and had it caught in an arms race. Thus, following the conclusion of World War II, the era of Cold War began. Cold War refers to the arms race between the capitalist powers led by the USA and Soviet Union, the threat of attack that it involves and the efforts on the part of these two superpowers to spread their respective influences in the other countries of the world. World War II left the capitalist powers devastated. Reconstruction of the countries required an enormous amount of resources. Cold War also made substantial demand on their resources. The capitalist powers found themselves in a position where it was no longer possible for them to spend any resources for containing the rising nationalist movements in colonies and, thereby, retain their control over the colonies. Hence, they granted them independence. Many of these colonies including India adopted the Soviet model of planned economic development and declared socialism as their goal. The giant capitalists threatened by Soviet Union shed their differences and got united to fight the Cold War. They eventually won it and Soviet Union disintegrated in 1991. With the weakening of the Soviet Union in the eighties, the global capitalists regained control over many of the colonies not only through physical conquest (such as Afghanistan, Iraq, Libya, among others), but also through economic means (such as India, East Asian countries). We have discussed the strategy of conquest by economic means in detail in the case of Greece in Chap. 8. Through this strategy, the global capitalists get the targeted country caught in an external debt trap. They drive the country into a situation where it finds that it is not in a position to meet its external debt service charges. To avoid defaulting on its external debt obligations, the country under attack has to surrender to the IMF and seek its assistance. The IMF, in turn, makes the country under consideration give up its own economic policies and accept the economic policies of the IMF. The IMF designs the policies in such a manner that the country becomes completely dependent on large-scale foreign investments. In other words, it becomes dependent on the bounties of the global capitalists for survival and has to abide by their dictates at every step.

1.3 Capitalism at Work: India, Greece, and the USA

The objective of the book is to analyze the features of capitalism delineated above taking up the cases of different countries of the world. We start with the case of India first. Chapters 5, 6, and 7 deal with the case of India. We present the theme of Chap. 5 first. After gaining Independence, India adopted the Soviet model of planned economic development and wanted to develop itself into a socialist state. The Indian version of the Soviet model of planned economic development is called the Nehru–Mahalanobis strategy of development (NMSD). The objective of NMSD was to achieve self-reliance (which meant elimination of dependence on imports), and to provide the masses with the basic necessities of life at low prices and health care and education free of charge. Despite its eminent suitability in Indian context, India could not pursue the strategy for long. It had to give it up in 1991 following a severe external debt crisis or BOP crisis. There are two major reasons for the failure. First, India did not make any effort at developing its own independent knowledge and technological base. Second, from the beginning of the eighties, India started borrowing heavily from foreigners at market-determined interest rates. Both of these phenomena are puzzling. Without an independent base of knowledge and technology, it is never possible to devise ways and means of eliminating import dependence. Both Soviet Union and China, two major socialist powers, right from the very beginning invested heavily in the knowledge and technology sector to be independent in the spheres of knowledge and technology. They also achieved their goal. Hence, India's lack of effort in gaining independence in these two crucial areas was a puzzle. Since India produced with imported technology, which was never state of the art, India's export potential was extremely limited. Under such circumstances, borrowing on a large scale from external commercial sources was a sure recipe to get caught in an external debt trap and, thereby, surrender to the foreign financiers. Hence, the suicidal external borrowing spree on the part of the Government of India in the eighties is also a grave puzzle. India is, thus, a classic case of conquest by the global capitalists using economic means. In this chapter, we have presented a hypothesis explaining these two puzzles. To get out of the external debt trap, India sought help from the IMF and IMF made India give up its Nehru–Malanobis strategy and follow in its place the New Economic Policy (NEP). The NEP recommends a policy of free market, with the restrictions on production, investment, import, etc., of the NMSD era completely removed, and a small government with extremely low direct tax rates on the rich and stringent restrictions on government's fiscal deficit (borrowing). These restrictions severely curtail government's ability to provide public services. The government has to confine its activities principally to public administration and defense and depend on the private sector for the provision of all other goods and services. This chapter shows how NEP deepens substantially India's dependence on foreign investment and, thereby, makes India lose completely its policy-making autonomy and drives it hopelessly in a state where it has to abide by the dictates of the foreign investors (global capitalists) at every step. It also shows how NEP continuously widens inequality in the distribution of income and wealth, creates an extremely small island of unbelievable opulence in the midst of abysmal poverty, and makes India again a colony of the global capitalists.

Under NMSD, most of the institutions were social organizations. Profit making was not their driving force. They, instead, strove to achieve the goals of self-reliance and providing the masses with the basic necessities of life in adequate quantities at low prices. Financial institutions were no exceptions. Their goal was to provide everyone with completely safe avenues of saving yielding returns high and stable enough to see the savers through in their old age. They used the savings mobilized to meet all the legitimate credit needs of the society (i.e., the credit needs emanating from the goals set in the Five-Year Plans) at low interest rates specified by the planners. Under NEP, all the institutions including the banks and other financial institutions have become commercial organizations. Profit making has become their driving force. At the present, the banking sector in India is in deep trouble. In accordance with their common evil practice, global capitalists (foreign investors) started pumping in very large amounts of funds in India's stock market creating a huge stock price bubble since 2003–04. The soaring stock prices gave a huge boost to investors' morale and, thereby, brought about a phase of unprecedented high growth rate. This phase lasted till 2010–11. The stock price bubble burst and India plunged into a recession since 2011–12. The onset of recession led to the emergence of large-scale excess capacities, substantial reduction in the profit of the firms, and a spate of bankruptcies. This brought about a sharp increase in default rates giving rise to a large and rising stock of non-performing assets of the banks. Government of India has taken alarm and adopted a slew of measures to arrest the growth of non-performing assets of banks. The government/central bank has taken such measures as asking banks to tighten lending norms, raise capital adequacy ratio (since riskiness of their assets has gone up), etc. Chapter 6 develops a simple baseline model to examine the implications of this kind of policies. It shows that the policies noted above deepens recession, increases inequality, and exacerbates the problem of non-performing assets and low profit. It also shows that, instead of taking the banks and the defaulting firms to task for a factor that is completely beyond their control, the best way of tackling this problem is to adopt appropriate stabilization programs to counter the recession. It chalks out the stabilization policy that is appropriate for tackling the banks' and the economy's woes.

The large and growing non-performing assets of banks in India also point to another deep malaise of capitalism, namely corruption. Many large industrialists borrowed on a large scale from banks with a view to stealing the fund and defaulted on the loans with the onset of recession giving the excuse of recession-driven bankruptcy. They had close political links, and some of them fled the country and found asylum abroad. We have already pointed out that giant capitalists deliberately create recessions and one of the objectives is to rob the banks and other financial institutions of the workers' savings deposited with them. At the present, the Central Information Commission is pressurizing the RBI to disclose the names of the 'willful defaulters,' i.e., defaulters who borrowed with the intention of stealing the fund. Many large corporations became bankrupt following the onset of recession. The bankruptcies may also be a way of stealing banks' funds (workers' savings). Let us illustrate with an example. Suppose a giant capitalist borrows Rs. 20,000 crore from banks and also Rs. 20,000 crore from the stock market, sets up a company using Rs. 10,000 crore, fraudulently gets the value of the assets of the company recorded as Rs. 40,000 crore on paper, and steals Rs. 30,000 crore. He runs the company for some time and, as recession sets in, declares his company bankrupt, and delivers it to the creditors. This kind of strategy is quite plausible. The spate of bank frauds that occurred following the onset of recession in India since 2011–12 takes us to the issue of corruption. We address this issue in Chap. 7. This chapter argues that the system of private funding of political parties has put them completely under the control of the giant capitalists, who have in their command the major part of a country's income and wealth. As you should be able to recall, the giant capitalists need state power to protect and increase their wealth. Hence, they form, fund, and run the political parties just like their other business enterprises to usurp state power through them. Since the competitive strength of political parties depends upon the amount of fund at their disposal, they compete with one another for the donations of the giant capitalists and work feverishly to help them increase their command over the society's income and wealth both legally and illegally. On the illegal side, political parties allow giant capitalists to evade taxes, invest their savings in foreign assets in tax havens, and defraud the public sector banks, among others. We have shown in this chapter that these illegal favors or corrupt practices generate strong recessionary forces and slow down drastically the rate of growth of output and employment. In the wake of recessions and bank frauds, which lead to a sharp increase in the non-performing assets of banks and other financial institutes, the political parties pass laws or seek to pass laws such as Financial Regulation and Deposit Insurance (FRDI) Bill in India that empowers the financial institutions to confiscate the savings of the people held with them to tide over the crisis. We have shown in this chapter that such a measure is likely to bring about a collapse of the financial institutions and the economy.

Of the legal favors granted to the capitalists, we have considered two in Chap. 7. Government and the central bank often specify lending norms of banks and other financial institutions in such a manner that they favor the giant capitalists at the expense of the small and medium producers. They also often confiscate land of the small and medium producers and give it away to the giant capitalists. To examine the implications of these legal favors, we have divided the economy into an organized sector and an unorganized sector. The former consists of large firms owned by the giant capitalists, while the latter consists of firms owned by small and medium producers. We have shown in Chap. 7 that the legal favors mentioned here will in all probability lead to a cumulative expansion of the organized sector matched by a cumulative contraction of the unorganized sector. Both of these will bring about a sharp deterioration in the standard of living of the workers.

The latest conquest of the global capitalists through economic means is Greece. In Chap. 8, we explain how in 2010, the IMF, European Central Bank, and the European Commission took control of Greece on behalf of the foreign investors (global capitalists). Speculative activities of the global capitalists in the asset markets of the USA and Europe and large-scale inflow of capital into Greece since 2003 brought about a phase of unprecedented boom during 1996–2007 in Greece. We have explained in detail how it happened in Chap. 8. However, global capitalists burst the asset price bubbles and, thereby, plunged USA and Europe into a deep recession since 2008. At the same time, they stopped investing in Greece since 2008. These two factors drove Greece into a deep depression, and the Greek economy began to contract since 2008. The contraction of the Greek economy since 2008 drove the Greek Government into a sovereign debt crisis in 2010. The Greek Government sought the assistance of the European Commission, European Central Bank, and the IMF, henceforth referred to as the troika, to service its debt. The troika obliged, but in exchange imposed on Greece stringent austerity measures. The objective of Chap. 8 is to explain the above-mentioned booms and recessions in the Greek economy and the cause of the sovereign debt crisis in Greece. It also carefully analyses the implications of the austerity measures and attributes the perpetuation and deepening of the depression in the Greek economy since 2010 to them. It also suggests the measures that would have raised Greece's growth rate to a high level and resolved Greece's sovereign debt crisis.

A huge house price bubble formed in the US economy in the late nineties, and it collapsed in 2006 plunging the economy into a deep recession. The objective of Chap. 9 is to identify the causes of the formation of the house price bubble and its collapse. After carefully analyzing the available evidences, it concludes that the giant capitalists who control the giant financial institutions created the bubble and burst it. They did it to have the workers' savings parked with the financial institutions to themselves in the form of speculative capital gains. Policies of the US Government and Fed also facilitated the plan of the giant capitalists and helped them keep the economy under their control. More precisely, neither the US Government nor Fed took any steps to stop the formation of bubbles even though data revealed their existence right from 1998. They did not try to stop the common people from taking the plunge in a speculative purchase of houses. Obviously, the factors that drove the common people into the mass speculative frenzy must have also come into the notice of the US Government and Fed. Finally, the stabilization measures they adopted kept the economy in a desired state of recession instead of lifting it completely out of recession. This also, as we have pointed out earlier, served the interest of the global capitalists.

Our analysis suggests that the capitalists' iron hold over state power and their compulsion to keep in their control the rest of the people are at the root of the extreme inequality in the distribution of income and wealth and abysmal poverty of the masses in a capitalist economy. To make the political parties truly represent the masses, private funding of political parties in every form should be made completely illegal. The government should create infrastructure and facilities so that all political parties get equal opportunities to express their views free of cost. This is possible only if the workers are able to identify the real cause of their plight and unite to demand the kind of political reform suggested above. Without mass awareness and unity of the masses, there is no hope for them under capitalism.

1.4 Method of Analysis: Keynesian Macroeconomics

We have chosen Keynesian tools and techniques for our analysis of capitalism. Keynesian theory constitutes a critique of capitalism, as it regards a capitalist system to be inherently unstable. Contrary to neoclassical economics, it is of the view that a capitalist economy has no mechanism that automatically establishes full employment equilibrium. It postulates that government intervention is necessary to keep a capitalist economy stable. It suggests policies, called stabilization policies, that the government in a capitalist economy should adopt to counter recessions and inflation. It emphasizes on fiscal policy in the main as the instrument for countering recession. More precisely, it regards an increase in government expenditure financed by money creation as the most effective policy for countering recession.

Keynesian theory emphasizes on uncertainty and market imperfection as the major factors leading to rigidities in interest rates and wages that bring about a breakdown of the neoclassical mechanism that automatically generates full employment equilibrium. We fully subscribe to this view. We think that in a capitalist economy, most of the goods and services are produced by large corporations owned by the giant capitalists. Hence, most of the markets are oligopolies, where firms wield considerable market power. They set prices, a la Kalecki (1954), on the basis of cost and their competitive strength vis-à-vis their rivals and produce the level of output that meets the demand that comes forth at the prices set. Thus, the Keynesian theory which states that aggregate output is demand-determined is eminently suitable for our purpose. More precisely, the IS-LM model augmented by a price setting formula that makes price a function of the major determinants of cost of production may be the most suitable basic model of our analysis. But, we cannot use the IS-LM model, since it has many major shortcomings (see Rakshit (1993) in this connection). We discuss them below.

1.4.1 *The Shortcomings of the IS-LM Model*

To discuss the shortcomings of the IS-LM model, we describe the model first. It is given by the following two key equations:

$$Y = C((1-t)Y) + I(r; E) + G \tag{1.1}$$

and

$$\overline{M} = P.L(r, Y) \tag{1.2}$$

Equations (1.1) and (1.2) represent the goods market and money market equilibrium conditions. In (1.1), Y denotes GDP. The expression on the RHS gives aggregate planned demand for produced goods and services. We consider a closed economy here. Hence, aggregate planned demand has three components, namely aggregate planned consumption demand (C), aggregate planned investment demand (I), and government consumption (G). In the expression on the RHS of (1.1), the first term is the consumption function. C is made an increasing function of disposable income $(1 - t)Y$, where t denotes the tax rate. I is made a decreasing function of interest rate denoted by r and an increasing function of investors' expectations regarding the future prospect of their business denoted by E. E is exogenously given. G is a policy variable of the government. (1.1) states that aggregate output or GDP is determined by aggregate planned demand for produced goods and services. In (1.2), $\overline{M}$ is the given stock of money supply. It is a policy variable of the central bank. The expression on the RHS gives the demand for money. P denotes the price level, and $L(\cdot)$ is the demand for real balance function. Demand for real balance is made a decreasing function of r and an increasing function of Y. Besides the goods market and the money market, there is a bond market or credit market also. However, the bond market is not taken into account explicitly. The bond market is relegated to the background using Walras' law. Let us explain briefly. The IS-LM model assumes that there are only two types of financial assets, money and bond. Economic agents in the given period have a given stock of money and a given stock of bond in their wealth. The rest of their wealth consists of physical assets. The aggregate stock of wealth of the economic agents is given in the short run and so is the sock of wealth held in the form of physical assets. However, economic agents can change the composition of the stock of wealth held in the form of money and bond in the given short period. They may plan to hold more money, but they can do so only by reducing their holding of stock of bond by an equal value. Thus, the following aggregate wealth budget constraint holds for all the economic agents taken together:

$$\overline{M} + P_b B^s = M^d + P_b B^d \Rightarrow \left(M^d - \overline{M}\right) + P_b\left(B^d - B^s\right) = 0 \qquad (1.3)$$

In (1.3), P_b denotes price of bonds, B^s denotes the amount of bonds in the possession of the economic agents, M^d denotes the amount of money people want to hold, and B^d denotes the amount of bonds people want to hold. From (1.3), it is clear that if the money market is in equilibrium, so must be the bond market and vice versa. Hence, the bond market or the credit market is relegated to the background. Equations (1.1) and (1.2) contain two endogenous variables r and Y. We can solve them for their equilibrium values. We show their solution in Fig. 1.1, where equilibrium values of Y and r correspond to the point of intersection of the IS and LM representing (1.1) and (1.2), respectively. We are now in a position to describe the major shortcomings of the IS-LM model one by one.

Coexistence of Stocks and Flows within the Same Framework

From the above, it is clear that the IS-LM model conceives the real sector (market for produced goods and services) in terms of flows and the financial sector in terms of stocks. Flows are defined for a given short period of time, say a year or a quarter. Thus, for example, Y refers to GDP of a given year or a given quarter. Similarly, C refers to planned personal consumption expenditure of a given year or quarter and so

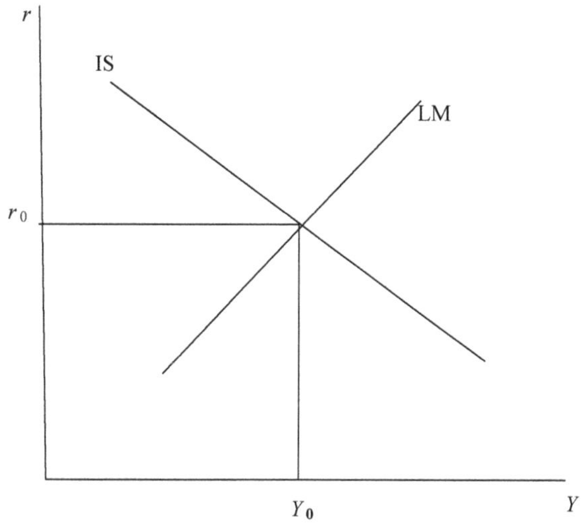

Fig. 1.1 Determination of Y and r in the IS-LM model

on. However, stocks refer not to a given period of time but to a given point of time. The IS-LM model reconciles this problem in the following manner. It defines stocks as quantities in the possession of the economic agents on the average at every point of time during the given short period under consideration or as quantities, economic agents plan to hold on the average at every point of time during the period under consideration. Thus, the stock of money supply, for example, is defined as the stock of money held on the average at every point of time by the economic agents in the given period and money demand refers to the stock of money that economic agents plan to hold on the average at every point of time during the given period. Demand for bond and supply of bond are defined in the same manner. This way of marrying the real sector and the financial sector gives rise to a few important problems. We have discussed all these problems in detail in Chap. 2. Here, we shall touch on some of them. One serious drawback of the IS-LM model is that it does not show how different components of aggregate expenditure are financed. The major part of I and large parts of G and C are financed by borrowing (i.e., by selling bonds in the IS-LM model). A part of G may be financed by money creation also. Hence, stocks of money supply and bond supply should be linked to G, C, and I. But, this linkage does not exist in the IS-LM model, where stocks of money and bond are taken as given and are, therefore, independent of G, C, and I. Since investment is a decreasing function of interest rate in the IS-LM model, it is clearly financed by issuing bonds. Hence, the stock of bond cannot be independent of the level of investment in the IS-LM model. Had the financial sector been conceived in terms of flows, i.e., in terms of changes in the stocks of money and bond, the link between different components of aggregate demand and changes in the stocks of bonds and money could have been clearly established and the issue of financing different components of aggregate expenditure could have been satisfactorily resolved. Clearly, if a model does not and cannot show how different components of aggregate expenditure are financed, one cannot use it to analyze real economic situations. Thus, in the IS-LM model, the interlinkage between the real sector and the financial sector is non-transparent, inadequate, and weak.

To illustrate how weak and unsatisfactory the interlinkage between the real and the financial sector is in the IS-LM model, we shall carry out a comparative static exercise. Let us consider the impact of an increase in E for exogenous reasons. (The IS-LM model does not address how the increase in I induced by the improvement in investors' expectations is financed.) This will bring about a rightward shift of the IS schedule in Fig. 1.1 and leave the LM curve unaffected. Therefore, equilibrium values of Y and r rise. How does it happen? Let us explain the adjustment process. Following the increase in E, investment goes up bringing about an excess demand for goods and services at the initial equilibrium (Y, r). Producers respond to it by raising Y. The increase in Y raises r. Let us explain how. The increase in Y raises (transaction) demand for money by PL_YdY. To meet this additional demand for money, economic agents in the IS-LM model try to sell bonds giving rise to excess supply in the bond market. This drives down the price of bonds, which implies an increase in the interest rate, since bonds pay their owners fixed sums of money at regular intervals over a given period of time. This process of adjustment is, however, extremely unsatisfactory at every step for the following reasons. First, focus on the first step stated as follows. 'As Y increases, people get more income. Hence, they want to make more purchases. They need additional amount of money to carry out these transactions. To secure this additional amount of money, they try to sell bonds.' Obviously, this sequence of events does not make much sense. We elaborate this point as follows. Note that as Y increases, people get the additional income in the form of money. They will spend a part of it for purposes of consumption and save the rest. If they want to save in the form of money, they can do that. If they want to save in the form of bonds, there will emerge an excess demand for bonds. In that case, however, bond price will rise lowering interest rate. Clearly, following an increase in income, there is no need for economic agents to secure money by selling bonds to make the additional purchases that the additional income induces. This happens in the IS-LM model because the flow of income and the stock of money in the possession of the income earners are not related to one another as they should be and as they actually are. Now, come to the next step stated as follows. 'To augment their stock of money, economic agents try to sell off bonds lowering bond price and, thereby, raising the rate of interest.' This sequence of events is also unsatisfactory for the following reasons. Here, everybody tries to sell bonds and no one tries to buy bonds. Hence, bond price goes down without any actual purchase or sell taking place. Economic agents, therefore, continue to have their same old stock of bonds purchased at prices that prevailed in the past. No one, therefore, has purchased any bond at the new lower price of bonds. Hence, the interest rates faced by the economic agents remain unchanged. Interest rates have not risen for any economic agent. The IS-LM model, therefore, cannot explain why interest rate will rise following an increase in Y, when stock of money remains unchanged. Thus, the link between the real sector and the financial sector in the IS-LM model is extremely weak and unsatisfactory. In reality, processes of generation of saving, credit and money, expenditure and income are inextricably linked together. Unfortunately, the IS-LM model fails to capture these intimate interrelationships completely. In the IS-LM model, for example, we do not know what people do with their saving. Normally, it should increase demand for financial as well as physical assets. Saving in reality is the most important source of new credit. However, IS-LM model fails to capture that. Clearly, the IS-LM model cannot provide us with a basic framework for analyzing capitalism.

Financial Intermediaries

IS-LM model does not have any financial intermediaries such as banks. Banks play a major role in mobilizing savings of the workers and making them available to the capitalists. Global capitalists use banks and other financial institutions as instruments for creating asset price bubbles. Omission of financial intermediaries is a major shortcoming of the IS-LM model and makes it unsuitable for analyzing capitalism. Bernanke and Blinder (1988) sought to incorporate banks in the IS-LM model. However, their effort did not produce the desired outcome. To be consistent with the rest of the financial sector in the IS-LM model, they conceived the banking sector in terms of stocks: stock of total bank credit and demand for the stock of total bank credit. As a result, they could not link the flows of expenditures to the demand for bank credit nor could they relate saving to the supply of bank credit. Since new bank credit finances quite a large part of aggregate expenditure and saving plays a major role in generating new bank credit, failure to incorporate these links makes their work as unsatisfactory as the IS-LM model.

Interest Rate Rigidity

Banking sector in all capitalist economies is an oligopoly, and bank interest rates display marked rigidity. The phenomenon is so well-known and pervasive that many writers such as Stiglitz and Weiss (1981) made elaborate efforts to explain it. Since other financial instruments such as bonds are close substitutes of bank credit as credit instruments and close substitutes of bank deposits as instruments of saving, interest rates on other financial instruments should have a close relationship with bank interest rates and rigidity of the latter should make the former rigid too. The IS-LM model, however, cannot handle the case where the interest rate is rigid. If we make interest rate rigid in the IS-LM model, the financial sector ceases to play any role in the determination of GDP. The simple Keynesian model suffices in explaining trade cycles, and the IS-LM model becomes redundant. However, this is inconsistent with reality. If interest rate is rigid and there is, for example, credit rationing, which is normally the case and which writers such as Stiglitz and Weiss (1981), Blinder (1987) et al. have modeled, the availability of new credit will determine aggregate spending and, thereby, GDP. Hence, even when interest rates are rigid, financial sector plays an important role in the determination of GDP. The IS-LM model cannot accommodate this scenario. For this reason also, IS-LM model cannot serve as a basic model for analyzing the major features of capitalism.

1.5 Keynesian Macroeconomics Beyond the IS-LM Model

We have developed in this book a model alternative to the IS-LM model. It has sought to remove all the shortcomings of the IS-LM model noted above. We have incorporated financial intermediaries and institutions in the model. We have shown how each and every item of expenditure is financed, how people hold their saving, how saving creates new money and new credit and how credit finances expenditure, and finally, how expenditure generates income. More precisely, the model brings out clearly how processes of generation of income, saving, new credit and money and expenditure are closely and inextricably linked together. We first incorporated only banks in our model. We, then, extended it to incorporate bonds. We have shown that incorporation of bonds does not affect our results in any way so that it suffices to consider banks only. In Chap. 2, we have developed the model for a closed economy and extended it to the case of an open economy without capital mobility. In Chap. 3, we have extended the model to the case of an open economy with perfect capital mobility. Chapter 4 first explains why imperfect capital mobility is the general case and perfect capital mobility is a special one. Then, it extends the model developed in Chap. 2 to the case of an open economy with imperfect capital mobility. Thus, the book makes a significant contribution to Keynesian macroeconomics.

1.6 Conclusion

The book makes significant contributions in two areas, namely analysis of capitalism in the twenty-first century and Keynesian macroeconomics. We have, accordingly, divided the book into two parts, viz. Part I and Part II. Part I consists of three chapters, Chaps. 2, 3, and 4, where we have developed the basic Keynesian models that are free from the shortcomings of the IS-LM-based models. In these models, the financial sector is adequately developed and the interlinkage between the real sector and the financial sector is transparent, realistic, and adequate. Part II of the book consists of the rest of the chapters, Chaps. 5–9, where we have illustrated how capitalism works taking up the cases of India, Greece, and USA using Keynesian tools of analysis developed in Part I of the book. We have shown how capitalism sets a small section of giant capitalists against the rest of the people and how the capitalists protect their empire from the masses and expand it causing immense misery and suffering to the masses. The book presents the analysis in a language that is comprehensible to the students and practitioners of mainstream economics. The book argues that democracy under capitalism is a farce and the giant capitalists run the political parties just as their other business enterprises. Hence, the political parties fall over one another to serve the interest of the giant capitalists. To resolve this problem, radical political reform is needed. As a first step toward giving political parties a chance of representing the masses, all kinds of private funding of political parties must be made illegal and the government should create infrastructure and facilities so that all political parties get equal and adequate opportunities for making their programs, policies, and views known to the people free of charge. To accomplish this, workers have to be made aware of the actual cause of their plight. They have to be united, and they should make the demand for making the necessary political reforms mentioned above.

References

Bernanke, B., & Blinder, A. (1988). Credit, money and aggregate demand. *American Economic Review, 78*, 435–439.

Bernanke, B. S., Gertler, M., & Gilchrist, S. (1999). The financial accelerator in a quantitative business cycle framework (Chap. 21). In *Handbook of macroeconomics* (Vol. 1, Part C, pp. 1341–1393).

Blinder, A. (1987). Credit rationing and effective supply failures. *The Economic Journal, 97*, 327–352.

Concern Worldwide. (2018). 2018 World Hunger Index Results. https://www.globalhungerindex.org/results/.

Hunt, E. K., & Lautzenheiser, M. (2014). *History of economic thought: A critical perspective* (3rd ed.). Delhi, India: PHI Learning Private Limited.

Kalecki, M. (1954). *Theory of economic dynamics: An essay on cyclical and long-run changes in capitalist economy*. London and New York: Routledge.

Mishkin, F. S. (2009). Is monetary policy effective during financial crises? *American Economic Review, 99*(2), 573–577.

Mishkin, F. S. (2011). Over the cliff: From the subprime to the global financial crisis. *Journal of Economic Perspectives, 25*(1), 49–70.

Oxfam India. (2018). India Inequality Report 2018. https://www.oxfamindia.org/sites/.../himanshu_inequality_Inequality_report_2018.pdf.

Picketty, T. (2014). *Capital in the twenty-first century*. Belknap Press, World.

Rakshit, M. (1993). Money, credit and monetary policy. In T. Majumdar (Ed.), *Nature, man and the environment*. Delhi: Oxford University Press.

Reischauer, R. (2000). *A new look at homelessness in America*. Washington, DC: Urban Institute Publications.

Stiglitz, J. E. (2012). *The price of inequality: How today's divided society endangers our future*. W. W. Norton and Company.

Stiglitz, J. E., & Weiss, A. (1981). Credit rationing in markets with imperfect information. *The American Economic Review, 71*(3), 393–410.

U.S. Department of Agriculture. (2018). Food Security in the US. Economic Research service.

U.S. Department of Health and Human Services. (2016). 2015 National Health Care Quality and Disparities Report and 5th Anniversary Update on the National Quality Strategy. Agency for Health Care Research and Quality.

U.S. Department of Housing and Urban Development. (2018). Annual Homeless Report (AHAR) to Congress. Office of Community Planning & Development.

Part I
Beyond the IS-LM Model

Chapter 2
Interaction Between the Real Sector and the Financial Sector: An Alternative to the IS-LM Model

Abstract The IS-LM model has many flaws. It puts together both stocks and flows in the same framework and, thereby, creates a serious problem of interpretation of the interest rate it determines. It also does not show how expenditures are financed. It does not incorporate financial intermediaries, which play an important role in mobilizing saving into investment and generating money and credit. This chapter develops an alternative model that seeks to resolve all the deficiencies of the IS-LM model mentioned above. The model does more than that. It shows that equality of demand for money and supply money cannot be a distinguishing feature of equilibrium, as the two should be equal always. Unlike the IS-LM model, which one can apply only to the case where the interest rate is flexible, the model developed here is applicable not only to the case of flexible interest rate but also to the case where the interest rate is rigid. In fact, the model shows that the classic Keynesian results hold in the case where interest rates charged by banks are rigid, which is the case in reality. We have extended the model to the case of an open economy also.

2.1 Introduction

The IS-LM model is yet to lose its relevance. Recent efforts by Blanchard (1981) and Romer (2013, 2000) to extend it bear ample testimony to that. However, one major weakness of the IS-LM model is its financial sector, which it conceives in terms of stocks of supply of money and demand for money. The real sector, however, is characterized in terms of flows. Flows refer to a period of time. Thus, the real sector determines output per unit of time such as daily output, weekly output, monthly output, or annual output. Stocks on the other hand are defined at every instant of time. At every instant of time, there is a stock of supply of money and a stock of demand for money, and these determine an interest rate at every instant of time. This obviously raises a problem of interpretation. Suppose the flows in the real sector are quarterly. The real sector thus determines quarterly output, quarterly consumption, etc. Stocks of demand for money and supply of money should determine the interest rate at every instant. Note that, even if the stock of money supply remains the same at every instant during a given period, money holding of the public will vary from

C. Ghosh and A. N. Ghosh, *Keynesian Macroeconomics Beyond the IS-LM Model*, https://doi.org/10.1007/978-981-13-7888-1_2

one instant to the other. Thus, interest rates of different instants during the given period are likely to be different. In the IS-LM, demand for money refers to the average of these instantaneous money holdings during the given period. What does the stock of demand for money defined in the above sense and the stock of supply of money determine in the IS-LM? Do they determine the average of these instantaneous interest rates? Will the average of the interest rates of all the instants during the given period really be equal to the interest rate that the demand for money and supply of money in the IS-LM determine? These issues are obviously unresolved.

Even if we ignore this problem, there are other more serious problems that emanate from the way the financial sector in the IS-LM model is characterized. Quite a large part of private and public consumption and investment expenditures are financed with credit. Thus, the process of generation of credit and that of demand should be closely related to one another. Again, we know that the process of generation of money and that of bank credit occur simultaneously. Thus, they are also intimately linked. Moreover, savers lend out quite a large part of their saving to the financial intermediaries such as banks, insurance companies and also to the government. Thus, the process of generation of saving and that of credit are also intimately connected. To sum up, the processes of generation of saving, credit, money, expenditure, and income are actually very closely interrelated. In other words, the multiplier process that takes place in the real sector in the IS-LM model and the money multiplier process must occur together. However, the IS-LM model fails to capture these interrelationships. In fact, the IS-LM model does not consider the financial intermediaries. Nor does the IS-LM model show how the expenditures are financed. In this paper, we shall develop a model that seeks to redress the problems noted above. Bernanke and Blinder (1988) and Blinder (1987) addressed some of the above-mentioned issues, but they could not resolve all the major problems of the IS-LM model specified here and present a workable framework that can be applied to explain the major short-run macroeconomic events. Bernanke and Blinder (1988), for example, incorporated commercial banks in the IS-LM model. However, it did not seek to resolve the other problems of the IS-LM model. Thus, in the aforementioned paper, the financial sector, just as in the IS-LM model, has been conceived in terms of stocks: supply of aggregate stock of money, demand for aggregate stock of money, supply of aggregate stock of bank credit, and demand for aggregate stock of bank credit. But, the commodity market, just as in the IS-LM model, has been presented in terms of flows. Accordingly, it fails to show how different components of aggregate expenditure are financed. As a result, the link between the real sector and the financial sector remains ill-developed. Just as in the IS-LM model, it becomes difficult to interpret the meanings of the interest rates determined in the Bernanke–Blinder paper. In the model we have developed, both the real sector and the financial sector, which includes the commercial banks, have been conceived in terms of flows. Hence, we have succeeded in showing how different components of aggregate expenditure are financed. Since the financial sector has been conceived in terms of flows, the equilibrium interest rate in our model is the one that equates the planned demand for and planned supply of new credit in the period under consideration. Thus, it resolves all the major problems of both the IS-LM and the Bernanke–Blinder model. Blinder (1987) has also incorporated banks.

It also shows how different components of expenditure are financed. However, it is a dynamic model and focuses only on the case where interest rates are rigid and there is rationing of credit. It, therefore, fails to become an alternative to the IS-LM model.

2.2 The Model for a Closed Economy

We shall develop first a very simple model that completely resolves the problems noted above. This model is derived from Rakshit (1993). We can easily extend this model to more general cases whenever needed. The model divides the economy into two sectors, the real sector, and the financial sector. We shall characterize the financial sector first.

The Financial Sector

The economy consists of the government, central bank, commercial banks, firms, and households. The government takes loans only from the central bank, and the central bank in its turn lends only to the government. Only firms take loans from the commercial banks and commercial banks receive deposits only from the households who hold their entire wealth or savings in the form of bank deposits and currency. Households are the ultimate lenders and do not take any loans. These assumptions can be easily generalized without any change in the results drawn. Let us now focus on the supply of loans in this economy.

Supply of Loans

The source of supply of new commercial bank loans is the new deposits they receive. The new deposits in turn come from the part of the saving that households hold in the form of bank deposits. We assume for the present that the households hold all their saving in the form of bank deposits and it is the only source of bank deposits. Households' saving is given by

$$S = (1 - c)Y = dD = dm \tag{2.1}$$

In (2.1), *S denotes saving, dD* and *dm* denote increase in bank deposit and increase in money supply, respectively, since there is no currency holding by assumption, c is the fixed average and marginal propensity to consume. Given our assumptions, the supply of new commercial bank loans denoted L^S is, therefore, given by

$$L^S = (1 - \rho)(1 - c)Y \tag{2.2}$$

In (2.2), ρ denotes the reserve–deposit ratio of the commercial banks. We assume it to be an increasing function of r_c, which denotes the interest rate at which the central bank lends to the commercial banks. r_c is a policy variable of the central bank, and we shall regard it as fixed.

Interest rate on commercial bank loans may be fixed or flexible. Our model can accommodate both cases. The assumption of a flexible market clearing interest rate is appropriate for a perfectly competitive credit market. However, the banking sector in most countries is dominated by just a few banks, and it is an oligopoly. In such a scenario, it is best to assume the interest rate to be rigid. We shall consider both the cases here. We shall take up the case of the flexible interest rate first to make the comparison of our model to the IS-LM model sharper.

Let us now focus on the real sector.

The Real Sector

We assume that in the real sector aggregate output is determined by aggregate final demand for goods and services. The price level is fixed, and it is taken to be unity. Aggregate planned consumption demand is given by

$$C = cY \quad 0 < c < 1 \tag{2.3}$$

We assume for simplicity that consumption is financed from income and not with loans. Aggregate planned investment demand is given by

$$I = I(r) \quad I' < 0 \tag{2.4}$$

where $r \equiv$ nominal interest rate. We assume, again for simplicity, that investment is financed entirely with loans taken from commercial banks. We assume further that investment is the only source of demand for commercial bank credit. Hence, the credit market is in equilibrium when

$$I(r) = \left(1 - \rho(r_{c_+})\right)(1 - c)Y \tag{2.5}$$

Government consumption, G, is, as we assume here, financed with loans from the central bank. Thus,

$$G = \mathrm{d}L_{\mathrm{gc}} = \frac{\mathrm{d}H}{P} \tag{2.6}$$

In (2.6), $\mathrm{d}L_{\mathrm{gc}}$ denotes new loans taken from the central bank by the government. We assume for simplicity that the increase in the stock of high-powered money denoted $\mathrm{d}H$ is solely due to the new loans taken by the government from the central bank.

The goods market is in equilibrium when

$$Y = cY + I(r) + G \tag{2.7}$$

The specification of our model is now complete. It consists of two key Eqs. (2.5) and (2.7) in two endogenous variables r and Y. We can solve them as follows. Substituting (2.5) into (2.7), we rewrite it as

$$Y = cY + \left(1 - \rho(r_{c_+})\right)(1 - c)Y + G \tag{2.8}$$

Fig. 2.1 Derivation of the equilibrium values of Y and r

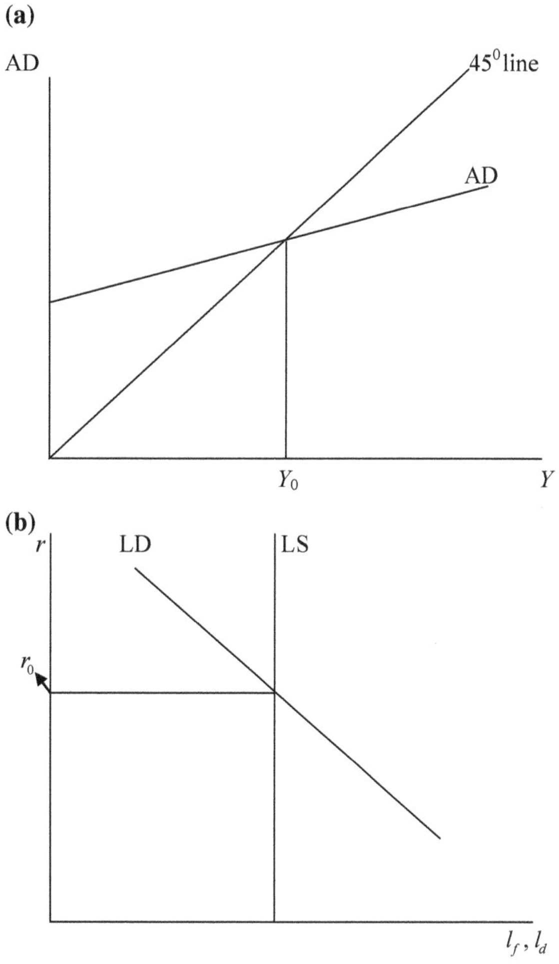

We can solve (2.8) for the equilibrium Y. Putting it in (2.5), we get the equilibrium value of r. The solution of r and Y is shown in Fig. 2.1a and b. In Fig. 2.1a, the AD schedule represents the RHS of (2.8). It gives the value of aggregate planned demand for goods and services (AD) corresponding to different values of Y. The equilibrium Y corresponds to the point of intersection of the AD schedule and the 45° line. The equilibrium Y is labeled Y_0. In Fig. 2.1b, r is measured on the vertical axis, while the supply of new loans of commercial banks and demand for new loans from commercial banks denoted by l_f and l_d, respectively, are measured on the horizontal axis. The vertical LS schedule gives the value of l_f, as given by the RHS of (2.5), corresponding to different values of r, when Y is fixed at its equilibrium value. The LD schedule on the other hand gives the value of l_d, as given by the LHS of (2.5), corresponding to different values of r. The equilibrium value of r corresponds to the point of intersection of LD and LS schedules. The equilibrium value of r is labeled r_0. We shall now carry out a few comparative static exercises to explain the working of the model.

2.3 Fiscal Policy: Government Expenditure Financed by Borrowing from the Central Bank

We shall here examine how an increase in G by $\mathrm{d}G$ financed by borrowing from the central bank affects Y and r. We shall first derive the results diagrammatically using Fig. 2.2a and b, where initial equilibrium values of Y and r correspond to the points of intersection of the AD schedule and the 45° line in Fig. 2.2a and the LD and LS schedules in Fig. 2.2b, respectively. These initial equilibrium values of Y and r are labeled Y_0 and r_0, respectively. Let us first focus on the AD schedule representing the RHS of (2.8) in Fig. 2.2a. Corresponding to every Y, G is larger by $\mathrm{d}G$. The AD schedule, therefore, shifts upward by $\mathrm{d}G$. The new AD schedule is labeled AD_2. The equilibrium value of Y will, accordingly, be larger. It is labeled Y_2.

In Fig. 2.2b, the new LS schedule representing the RHS of (2.5), corresponding to the new higher equilibrium value of Y, should be to the right of the initial LS schedule. The new LS schedule is labeled LS_2. The LD schedule, however, remains unaffected. Hence, the equilibrium r goes down. We shall now derive these results mathematically.

Mathematical Derivation of the Results

Taking total differential of (2.8) treating all exogenous variables other than G as fixed, and then, solving for $\mathrm{d}Y$, we get

$$\mathrm{d}Y = \frac{\mathrm{d}G}{1 - c - (1-\rho)(1-c)} = \frac{\mathrm{d}\left(\frac{\mathrm{d}H}{P}\right)}{(1-c)\rho} \tag{2.9}$$

Hence,

$$\mathrm{d}S = (1-c)\left[\frac{\mathrm{d}G}{(1-c)\rho}\right] = \frac{\mathrm{d}\left(\frac{\mathrm{d}H}{P}\right)}{\rho} = \mathrm{d}m = \mathrm{d}D \tag{2.10}$$

In (2.10), $\mathrm{d}S$, $\mathrm{d}m$, and $\mathrm{d}D$ denote increases in saving (S), money supply (m), and bank deposit (D) respectively.

Taking total differential of (2.5), substituting for $\mathrm{d}Y$ its value given by (2.9) and solving for $\mathrm{d}r$, we get

$$\mathrm{d}r = \frac{(1-\rho)(1-c)\left[\frac{\mathrm{d}\frac{\mathrm{d}H}{P}}{(1-c)\rho}\right]}{I'} = \frac{(1-\rho)\frac{\mathrm{d}\left(\frac{\mathrm{d}H}{P}\right)}{\rho}}{I'} \tag{2.11}$$

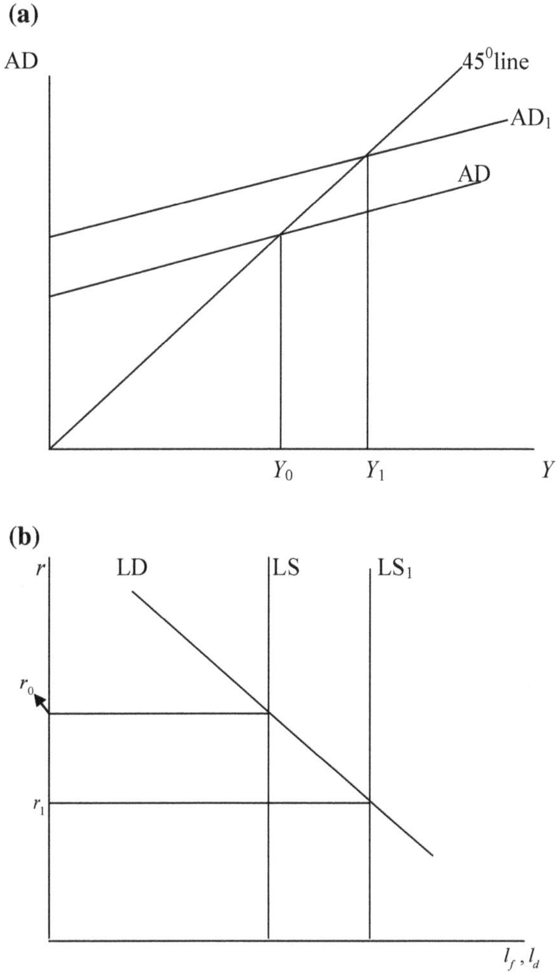

Fig. 2.2 Effect of an increase in G on Y and r

It is quite easy to explain (2.9) and (2.11). Focus on (2.11) first. The numerator of the expression on the RHS of (2.11) gives the total increase in the supply of new loans by the commercial banks at the initial equilibrium r following the increase in the supply of high-powered money by d(dH/P). This gives rise to excess supply of new loans at the initial equilibrium r of the same amount. r, therefore, has to fall to clear the loan market. Per unit decline in r, demand for loans increases by $-I'$. Hence, to raise demand for loans by $(1-\rho)\frac{dG}{\rho}$, r has to fall by $\frac{(1-\rho)\frac{dG}{\rho}}{-I'}$, in absolute value. This explains (2.11). Now consider (2.9). Following an increase in G by dG, aggregate planned supply of new loans of commercial banks increases by $(1-\rho)\frac{dG}{\rho}$, and this depresses r to raise investment demand by the same amount. Therefore, at the initial equilibrium Y, there emerges an excess demand of $dG + (1-\rho)\frac{dG}{\rho} = \frac{dG}{\rho}$. This is given by the numerator of the expression on the RHS of (2.9). Y will, therefore, have to increase to remove the excess demand. Per unit increase in Y, excess demand for goods and services falls by $(1 - c)$. Accordingly, excess demand for goods and services will fall by $\frac{dG}{\rho}$, when Y increases by $\frac{\frac{dG}{\rho}}{1-c}$. This explains (2.9).

Adjustment Process

Let us now describe how economic agents behave to bring about the changes in the equilibrium values of r and Y derived above. Following an increase in G by dG financed by borrowing from the central bank, the familiar multiplier process operates and raises GDP (Y) by $\frac{dG}{(1-c)}$. From this additional income of $\frac{dG}{(1-c)}$, people will save $(1 - c)\frac{dG}{(1-c)} = dG$, which they will deposit with the commercial banks, since, by assumption, people hold all their savings in the form of bank deposits. Out of these new deposits of dG, banks will plan to lend out $(1 - c)dG$ giving rise to an excess supply of loans of $(1 - \rho)dG$ at the initial equilibrium r. This will lower r by $\frac{(1-\rho)dG}{I'}$ so that investment, and therefore, demand for bank loans increases by $(1 - \rho)dG$. This is the end of the first round of expansion. In the first round, Y increases by $Y_1 = \frac{dG}{(1-c)}$, r falls by $dr_1 = \frac{(1-\rho)dG}{I'}$, saving, and bank deposit and money supply go up by $d(dS)_1 = d(dD)_1 = d(dm)_1 = dG$.

Now, there is an excess demand of $(1 - \rho)dG$ in the goods market due to the increase in investment demand in the first round. This will set into motion the second round of expansion. The multiplier process will begin to operate, and Y will increase by $dY_2 = \frac{(1-\rho)dG}{1-c}$. This will accrue as additional factor income to the people. The whole of this additional factor income will add to their disposable income. Out of this additional disposable income, people will save $(1 - c)\frac{(1-\rho)dG}{(1-c)} = (1 - \rho)dG$. They will deposit their saving in commercial banks. Out of these new deposits banks will plan to lend out $(1 - \rho)^2dG$ bringing about an excess supply of new credit. This will, as before, lower r by $\frac{(1-\rho)^2dG}{I'}$ so that investment demand, and therefore, demand for new loans from commercial banks increases by $(1 - \rho)^2dG$. This is the end of the second round. In the second round, changes in Y, r, S, D, and m are given by $dY_2 = \frac{(1-\rho)dG}{(1-c)}$, $dr_2 = \frac{(1-\rho)^2dG}{I'}$, and $d(dS)_2 = d(dD)_2 = d(dm)_2 = (1 - \rho)dG$. This is how expansion in Y, fall in r, and increases in S, D, and m will continue until the additional saving generated in each round eventually falls to zero. Thus, the total increase in Y, the total decline in r, and total increase in S, D, and m are given by

$$dY = \frac{dG}{(1-c)} + \frac{(1-\rho)dG}{(1-c)} + \frac{(1-\rho)^2dG}{(1-c)} + \cdots = \frac{dG}{\rho(1-c)} \quad (2.12)$$

$$dr = \frac{(1-\rho)dG}{I'} + \frac{(1-\rho)^2dG}{I'} + \cdots = \frac{(1-\rho)dG}{\rho I'} \quad (2.13)$$

$$ddS = ddD = ddm = dG + (1-\rho)dG + (1-\rho)^2dG + \cdots = \frac{dG}{\rho} \quad (2.14)$$

(2.12), (2.13), and (2.14) tally with (2.9), (2.11), and (2.10), respectively.

The model presented above clearly shows how the processes of generation of money, credit, spending, income, and saving are closely interwoven. More precisely, it shows how the creation of high-powered money and credit by the central bank leads to spending on goods and services. This expenditure in turn generates income. The saving made out of that income leads to the creation of more money and credit, which leads to another round of generation of spending, income, and saving, and this process goes on until the additional income that is generated in each round eventually falls to zero. We can summarize the finding of our above analysis in the form of the following proposition:

Proposition 2.1 *Our analysis of the impact of an increase in government expenditure financed with borrowing from the central bank clearly shows how the processes of generation of income, saving, credit, and expenditure are inextricably linked together. It also shows how the Keynesian government expenditure multiplier process and the money or the credit multiplier process in the present case operate together reinforcing each other.*

2.4 Monetary Policy

To examine the impact of monetary policy, we consider a cut in r_c by the central bank. To derive its impact on Y, we take total differential of (2.8) treating all exogenous variables other than r_c as fixed, and then, solve for Y. This gives

$$\mathrm{d}Y = \frac{\rho'(-\mathrm{d}r_c)Y}{\rho} \tag{2.15}$$

Again taking total differential of (2.5) treating all exogenous variables other than r_c as fixed, substituting (2.15) for $\mathrm{d}Y$, and then, solving for $\mathrm{d}r$, we get

$$\mathrm{d}r = \frac{(1-c)\frac{\rho'(-\mathrm{d}r_c)Y}{\rho}}{I'} \Rightarrow \mathrm{d}I = (1-c)\frac{\rho'(-\mathrm{d}r_c)Y}{\rho} \tag{2.16}$$

From (2.15), it follows that

$$ddS = ddm = ddD = (1-c)\frac{\rho'(-\mathrm{d}r_c)Y}{\rho} \tag{2.17}$$

We shall now explain (2.15), (2.16), and (2.17) describing the adjustment process.

Adjustment Process

As r_c is cut, the banks are able to extend new loans of $\rho'(-\mathrm{d}r_c)(1-c)Y$ out of their outstanding deposit of $(1-c)Y$. (Note that banks' outstanding deposits consist not only of the current saving $(1-c)Y$ but also the stock of past savings of the households. However, since the latter is given in the current period, we have ignored it for simplicity. It will not affect our results qualitatively). The excess supply in the loan market at the initial equilibrium r will drive down r until I goes up by

$\rho'(-\mathrm{d}r_c)(1-c)Y$. We denote this initial increase in I by $\mathrm{d}I_1 = \rho'(-\mathrm{d}r_c)(1-c)Y$ and the decline in r by $\mathrm{d}r_1 = \frac{\rho'(-\mathrm{d}r_c)(1-c)Y}{I'}$. This will raise Y in the first round by $\mathrm{d}Y_1 = \frac{\rho'(-\mathrm{d}r_c)(1-c)Y}{1-c} = \rho'(-\mathrm{d}r_c)Y$. As a result S, D, and m in the first round will increase by $d\mathrm{d}S_1 = d\mathrm{d}D_1 = d\mathrm{d}m_1 = \rho'(-\mathrm{d}r_c)(1-c)Y$. In consequence, bank credit and investment in the second round will go up by $\mathrm{d}I_2 = (1-\rho)\rho'(-\mathrm{d}r_c)(1-c)Y$, and interest rate will go down by $\mathrm{d}r_2 = \frac{(1-\rho)\rho'(-\mathrm{d}r_c)(1-c)Y}{I'} < 0$.

Because of the increase in investment in the second round, Y in the second round will increase by $\mathrm{d}Y_2 = \frac{(1-\rho)\rho'(-\mathrm{d}r_c)(1-c)Y}{1-c} = (1-\rho)\rho'(-\mathrm{d}r_c)Y$. Hence, S, D, and m in the second round will increase by $d\mathrm{d}S_2 = d\mathrm{d}D_2 = d\mathrm{d}m_2 = (1-c)(1-\rho)^2\rho'(-\mathrm{d}r_c)Y$. This will, as before, raise bank credit and investment in the third round by $\mathrm{d}I_3 = (1-c)(1-\rho)^2\rho'(-\mathrm{d}r_c)Y$.

As a result of this increase in investment demand in the third round, Y in the third round will go up by

$$\mathrm{d}Y_3 = \frac{(1-c)(1-\rho)^2\rho'(-\mathrm{d}r_c)Y}{1-c} = (1-\rho)^2\rho'(-\mathrm{d}r_c)Y.$$

Hence,

$$d\mathrm{d}S_3 = d\mathrm{d}D_3 = d\mathrm{d}m_3 = (1-c)(1-\rho)^2\rho'(-\mathrm{d}r_c)Y.$$

This process of expansion will continue until the additional saving generated in each successive round eventually falls to zero. Thus, the total increase in Y, S, D, and m and the total fall in r are given by

$$\begin{aligned}\mathrm{d}Y &= \rho'(-\mathrm{d}r_c)Y + (1-\rho)\rho'(-\mathrm{d}r_c)Y + (1-\rho)^2\rho'(-\mathrm{d}r_c)Y \\ &\quad + \cdots = \frac{\rho'(-\mathrm{d}r_c)Y}{\rho}\end{aligned} \tag{2.18}$$

$$\begin{aligned}d\mathrm{d}S = d\mathrm{d}D = d\mathrm{d}m &= (1-c)\rho'(-\mathrm{d}r_c)Y + (1-c)(1-\rho)\rho'(-\mathrm{d}r_c)Y \\ &\quad + (1-c)(1-\rho)^2\rho'(-\mathrm{d}r_c)Y + \cdots = \frac{(1-c)\rho'(-\mathrm{d}r_c)Y}{\rho}\end{aligned} \tag{2.19}$$

$$\begin{aligned}\mathrm{d}r &= \frac{(1-c)\rho'(-\mathrm{d}r_c)Y}{I'} + \frac{(1-c)(1-\rho)\rho'(-\mathrm{d}r_c)Y}{I'} \\ &\quad + \frac{(1-c)(1-\rho)^2\rho'(-\mathrm{d}r_c)Y}{I'} + \cdots = \frac{(1-c)\rho'(-\mathrm{d}r_c)Y}{I'\rho}\end{aligned} \tag{2.20}$$

Clearly, (2.18), (2.19), and (2.20) tally with (2.15), (2.16), and (2.17), respectively.

Thus, the model brings out clearly the interrelationship between income, saving, credit, and expenditure. We shall summarize the finding of our above discussion in the form of the following proposition:

Proposition 2.2 *Our analysis of a rate cut by the central bank shows how the credit multiplier process and the multiplier process in the real sector operate together* *highlighting the intimate interrelationship between the processes of generation of income, saving, money, credit, and expenditure.*

2.5 Irrelevance of the Money Market

The irrelevance of the money market comes out clearly from the equilibrium condition (2.8). Here, people want to hold all their saving in the form of bank deposits or money. Saving constitutes the only source of demand for new money (or additional money). From (2.8), we get $Y = \frac{G}{(1-c)\rho} = \frac{\frac{\mathrm{d}H}{P}}{(1-c)\rho} \Rightarrow (1-c)Y = \frac{G}{\rho} = \frac{\frac{\mathrm{d}H}{P}}{\rho}$. The LHS of the above equation gives the aggregate planned saving of the households. Since there are no taxes or undistributed corporate profit, Y also gives the aggregate disposable income of the households. Thus, the LHS of the above equation gives aggregate planned demand for new money in real terms. The RHS on the other hand gives aggregate supply of new money in real terms. It is, accordingly, clear that the equilibrium condition (2.8) also implies equality of demand for new money and supply of new money. As demand for money and supply of money were equal at the beginning of the period (since the whole of the initial supply of money was willingly held by the households as wealth), equality of demand for new money and supply of new money implies that of demand for money and supply of money. Thus, in our model, the money market need not be considered separately.

From the above, we get the following proposition:

Proposition 2.3 *In our model, equilibrium conditions of the goods and the credit market imply equality of demand for money and supply of money. Hence, one need not consider the money market separately.*

2.6 Mode of Financing and Autonomous Expenditure

One of the most important results of Keynesian theory is that the autonomous component of aggregate expenditure is a major determinant of GDP. We shall show here that whether an item of aggregate expenditure is truly autonomous or not depends crucially on how it is financed. To prove this, we incorporate an autonomous component in the investment function (2.4) to rewrite it as

$$I = \overline{I} + I(r) \tag{2.21}$$

(2.21) conforms to the Keynesian belief that the major part of the aggregate investment expenditure is autonomous, since investors' animal spirits drive investment in the main. However, if the entire expenditure is financed with new bank credit, $\overline{I}$ will cease to be a determinant of Y in the flexible interest rate regime. In equilibrium, the credit market will clear and the following condition should hold:

$$\overline{I} + I(r) = (1 - \rho)(1 - c)Y \tag{2.22}$$

Therefore, the goods market equilibrium condition will be given by

$$Y = cY + \overline{I} + I(r) + G = cY + (1 - \rho)(1 - c)Y + G \tag{2.23}$$

Hence, Y will be given by

$$Y = \frac{G}{1 - c - (1 - \rho)(1 - c)} \tag{2.24}$$

Thus, $\overline{I}$ ceases to be a determinant of Y.

$\overline{I}$ will play a role in the determination of Y if investors finance it by drawing down their bank deposits. In such a scenario, credit market equilibrium condition instead of being given by (2.22) will be given by

$$I(r) = (1 - \rho)(1 - c)Y - (1 - \rho)\overline{I} \tag{2.25}$$

Let us explain (2.25). As investors withdraw $\overline{I}$ amount of bank deposits from the banks, banks' planned supply of new loans falls by $(1 - \rho)\overline{I}$ from $(1 - c)(1 - \rho)Y$. This explains (2.25). Accordingly, the goods market equilibrium condition and the equilibrium Y are given, respectively, by

$$\begin{aligned} Y &= cY + \overline{I} + I(r) + G = cY + \overline{I} + (1 - \rho)(1 - c)Y - (1 - \rho)\overline{I} + G \\ &= cY + \rho\overline{I} + (1 - \rho)(1 - c)Y + G \end{aligned} \tag{2.26}$$

$$Y = \frac{\rho\overline{I} + G}{(1 - c)\rho} \tag{2.27}$$

Let us now explain (2.27). Investors finance $\overline{I}$ by drawing down their bank deposits. The fall in bank deposits by $\overline{I}$ reduces banks' supply of new loans by $(1 - \rho)\overline{I}$. This, in turn, lowers aggregate investment by $(1 - \rho)\overline{I}$. Thus, in the net, aggregate investment goes up by $\overline{I} - (1 - \rho)\overline{I} = \rho\overline{I}$. This sets off the multiplier process and generates production and income of $\frac{\rho\overline{I}}{(1-c)\rho}$ through the process described earlier. This will generate new saving, and therefore, new bank deposit of $(1 - c)\frac{\rho\overline{I}}{(1-c)\rho} = \overline{I}$. This restores bank deposits to their initial level. Similarly, if the government finances G with new loans from commercial banks or income tax, it will cease to be a determinant of Y. For G to be a determinant of Y, the government has to finance it either with new loans from the central bank or by drawing down its deposit with the central bank (work out this case yourself). We can summarize our discussion in the form of the following proposition:

Proposition 2.4 *Our model shows that, whether an item of autonomous expenditure will be a determinant of GDP in the flexible interest rate regime depends crucially* *upon how it is financed. If the spenders finance it by drawing down their bank deposits (wealth) or with new loans from the central bank, it will be a determinant of GDP. However, if the spenders finance it with new loans from the commercial banks, it will not play any role in the determination of GDP.*

2.7 Interest Rate Rigidity and the Behavior of the Economy

In reality, the banking sector is an oligopoly and the interest rates that the banks charge are rigid on account of oligopolistic interdependence among banks. If a bank unilaterally raises interest rates, it will lose its customers to its rivals and will, thereby, make losses. Similarly, if a bank unilaterally lowers interest rates, its rivals will lose customers. They will obviously not stay passive and cut their interest rates also. This will hurt all the banks. Hence, interest rates that the banks charge remain rigid. Banks fix their interest rates on the basis of cost and meet at the given interest rates all the demand for credit that they consider creditworthy. There are two sources of fund for the banks: deposits and loans from the central bank. The interest rate at which the central bank lends to the commercial banks is the policy rate of the central bank. We denote it by r_c. The RBI calls it the repo rate. While banks fix the deposit rate, r_c is given to them. They fix their lending rates by applying a markup to r_c and fix the deposit rates suitably below the lending rates to ensure a reasonable rate of profit. We do not distinguish between the deposit rate and lending rate at this stage and denote both by r and make it an increasing function of r_c. Thus, we have

$$r = r(r_c) \tag{2.28}$$

Normally, banks ration credit. They do not meet all the credit demand that comes forth at $r(r_c)$. They meet the credit demand of the quality borrowers (usually the large corporations) and ration small and medium producers [see in this connection Bernanke (1983), Bernanke et al. (1996, 1999) and Stiglitz and Weiss (1981), among others]. However, we shall first consider the case where there is no credit rationing.

2.7.1 *The Case of No Credit Rationing*

We assume for simplicity that only firms need loans to finance their investment and they finance their entire investment expenditure with new bank credit. Substituting (2.28) into (2.7), we rewrite the goods market equilibrium condition as

$$Y = cY + I(r(r_c), E) + G \tag{2.29}$$

There is a difference between (2.7) and (2.29) in the investment function. In (2.29), investment is a function not only of interest rate but also of investors' expectations regarding the future prospect of their businesses, which we denote by E. E is exogenously given. An increase in E indicates an improvement in their expectations. Hence, it gives a boost to investment.

We assume as before that government finances G by borrowing from the central bank.

The credit market equilibrium is given by

$$I(r(r_c), E) = (1-\rho)(1-c)Y + b \tag{2.30}$$

Let us explain (2.30). b in (2.30) denotes banks' borrowing from the central bank. It may be negative also. If the amount of new loans that the banks can extend using their deposits falls short of the amount of demand for new loans that comes forth at $r(r_c)$, banks borrow from the central bank, and b is positive. In the opposite case, the banks lend out their excess loanable fund to the central bank at the interest rate r_c. In that case b is negative. Thus, given our assumptions, there are two sources of generation of high-powered money in this model, namely G and b. Thus, we have

$$\frac{\mathrm{d}H}{P} = G + b \tag{2.31}$$

In this model, people do not hold currency. They may use it for making purchases. But they do not hold it, i.e., they do not use it for holding their saving. Therefore, the money supply in this model, i.e., the amount of money in the hands of the people is given by the stock of bank deposits only. Thus, the increase in money supply (denoted m) is given by

$$\mathrm{d}m = \mathrm{d}D = (1-c)Y \tag{2.32}$$

The specification of our model is now complete. It consists of four key equations, (2.29), (2.30), (2.31), and (2.32), in four endogenous variables Y, b, $\frac{\mathrm{d}H}{P}$, and $\mathrm{d}D$. We can solve them for the equilibrium values of these four variables. Let us explain the working of the model carrying out a few comparative static exercises.

An Improvement in the Expectations (Animal Spirits) of the Investors

We shall examine here how an autonomous increase in E affects the endogenous variables of our model. Taking total differential of (2.29) treating all variables other than Y and E as fixed, and then, solving for $\mathrm{d}Y$, we get

$$\mathrm{d}Y = \frac{I_E \mathrm{d}E}{(1-c)} \tag{2.33}$$

Again, taking total differential of (2.30) treating all variables other than E, Y, and b as fixed, substituting (2.33) into it, and then, solving for $\mathrm{d}b$, we get

$$\mathrm{d}b = \rho I_E \mathrm{d}E \tag{2.34}$$

Taking total differential of (2.31) and substituting (2.34) into it, we get

$$\mathrm{d}\left(\frac{\mathrm{d}H}{P}\right) = \rho I_E \mathrm{d}E \tag{2.35}$$

Taking total differential of (2.32) and substituting (2.33) into it, we get

$$\mathrm{d}(\mathrm{d}D) = \rho I_E \mathrm{d}E \tag{2.36}$$

Let us now explain (2.33), (2.34), (2.35), and (2.36). Following an increase in E by dE, aggregate investment rises by $I_E\mathrm{d}E$. Investors' demand for new bank credit rises by $I_E\mathrm{d}E$. Banks extend this additional loan by borrowing from the central bank. Hence, in the first round b increases by $\mathrm{d}b_1 = I_E\mathrm{d}E$. The increase in investment will set off the multiplier process and raise Y by $\frac{I_E\mathrm{d}E}{1-c}$. This increase in Y will raise saving and bank deposit by $(1-c)\frac{I_E\mathrm{d}E}{1-c} = I_E\mathrm{d}E$. This additional bank deposit of $I_E\mathrm{d}E$ will enable the banks to extend additional loan of $(1-\rho)I_E\mathrm{d}E$. The banks will extend this loan to the central bank. Hence, b will fall in the second round by $\mathrm{d}b_2 = -(1-\rho)I_E\mathrm{d}E$. Thus, in the net, b will increase by $\mathrm{d}b = I_E\mathrm{d}E - (1-\rho)I_E\mathrm{d}E = \rho I_E\mathrm{d}E$.

If we consider the asset-liability balance sheet of the central bank, the following changes occur in it. On the assets side, domestic credit goes up by $\rho I_E\mathrm{d}E$. On the liabilities side, banks' reserve goes up by $\rho I_E\mathrm{d}E$. Thus, the stock of high-powered money in the economy rises by $\rho I_E\mathrm{d}E$. From the text books of macroeconomics, we know that when there is no currency in circulation, money multiplier is $\frac{1}{\rho}$. Here also, the money multiplier is the same [see (2.36)]. Our model, therefore, shows that, even if people use currency to make purchases, the money multiplier is $\frac{1}{\rho}$, if people do not use currency to hold their savings.

An Increase in *G* Financed by Borrowing from the Central Bank

We shall examine here how Y, b, dD, and $\frac{\mathrm{d}H}{P}$ are affected following an increase in G financed by borrowing from the central bank. Taking total differential of (2.29) treating all variables other than Y and G as fixed, and then, solving for dY, we get

$$\mathrm{d}Y = \frac{\mathrm{d}G}{1-c} \tag{2.37}$$

Again, taking total differential of (2.30) treating all variables other than b and Y as fixed, substituting (2.37) into it, and then, solving for db, we get

$$\mathrm{d}b = (1-\rho)\mathrm{d}G \tag{2.38}$$

Taking total differential of (2.31) and substituting (2.38) into it, we get

$$\mathrm{d}\left(\frac{\mathrm{d}H}{P}\right) = \rho \mathrm{d}G \tag{2.39}$$

Finally, taking total differential of (2.32) and substituting (2.37) into it, we get

$$\mathrm{d}(\mathrm{d}D) = \mathrm{d}G \tag{2.40}$$

Let us now explain (2.37), (2.38), (2.39), and (2.40). Following an increase in G financed by borrowing from the central bank, the multiplier process sets into motion and Y increases by $\mathrm{d}Y = \frac{\mathrm{d}G}{1-c}$. This increase in Y raises saving and bank deposit by $(1-c)\mathrm{d}Y = (1-c)\frac{\mathrm{d}G}{1-c} = \mathrm{d}G$. Hence, banks can extend new loans of $(1-\rho)\mathrm{d}G$, which they have to lend to the central bank. Therefore, b falls by $-(1-\rho)\mathrm{d}G$. The following changes occur in the central bank's asset-liability balance sheet. On the asset side, net credit to government rises by $\mathrm{d}G$, while domestic credit falls by $-(1-\rho)\mathrm{d}G$. Therefore, in the net, total asset rises by $\rho\mathrm{d}G$. On the liabilities side, banks reserve increases by $\rho\mathrm{d}G$. Hence, the stock of high-powered money increases by $\rho\mathrm{d}G$. Clearly, here the money multiplier is $\frac{1}{\rho}$.

Monetary Policy in the Case of No Credit Rationing
We shall examine here how the conventional monetary policy of a cut in r_{c} affects the endogenous variables of the model. Taking total differential of (2.29) treating all variables other than Y and r_{c} as fixed, and then, solving for $\mathrm{d}Y$, we get

$$\mathrm{d}Y = \frac{I_r r_{\mathrm{c}} \mathrm{d}r_{\mathrm{c}}}{1-c} > 0 \quad \because \mathrm{d}r_{\mathrm{c}} < 0 \tag{2.41}$$

To derive the impact on b, we take total differential of (2.30) treating all variables other than Y, b, and r_{c} as fixed, substituting (2.41) into it, and then, solving for $\mathrm{d}b$, we get

$$\mathrm{d}b = \rho I_r r_{r_{\mathrm{c}}} \mathrm{d}r_{\mathrm{c}} > 0 \quad \because \mathrm{d}r_{\mathrm{c}} < 0 \tag{2.42}$$

Again, taking total differential of (2.31) and substituting (2.41) into it, we get

$$\mathrm{d}\left(\frac{\mathrm{d}H}{P}\right) = \rho I_r r_{r_{\mathrm{c}}} \mathrm{d}r_{\mathrm{c}} > 0 \tag{2.43}$$

Finally, taking total differential of (2.32) and substituting (2.41) into it, we get

$$d\mathrm{d}D = \rho I_r r_{r_{\mathrm{c}}} \mathrm{d}r_{\mathrm{c}} \tag{2.44}$$

One can explain (2.41), (2.42), (2.43), and (2.44) easily following the line spelled out in the earlier cases.

Currency Holding and Money Multiplier
We shall derive here the value of the money multiplier when people hold their saving in the form of not only bank deposits but also currency. We assume that people hold q fraction of their savings in the form of bank deposits and the rest in the form of currency. In this case, our model is given by (2.29), (2.31), and the following two equations:

$$I\big(r(r_{r_c}),E\big) = (1-\rho)q(1-c)Y + b \tag{2.45}$$

And

$$dm = \mathrm{d}D + \mathrm{d}cu = q\cdot(1-c)Y + (1-q)(1-c)Y \tag{2.46}$$

Equation (2.45) is self-explanatory. Let us explain (2.46). m denotes money supply, and dm denotes change in money supply. cu denotes currency holding of the people, and dcu denotes change in the currency holding of the people. To derive the value of the money multiplier in the present case, we shall carry out a comparative static exercise. Let us consider the impact that an exogenous increase in E will produce. Taking total differential of (2.29) treating all variables other than Y and E as fixed, and then, solving for dY, we get

$$\mathrm{d}Y = \frac{I_E\mathrm{d}E}{1-c} \tag{2.47}$$

To derive the value of db, we take total differential of (2.45) and substitute into it (2.47). This gives us

$$\mathrm{d}b = (1-(1-\rho)q)I_E\mathrm{d}E \tag{2.48}$$

Again, taking total differential of (2.30) and substituting into it (2.48), we get

$$\mathrm{d}\left(\frac{\mathrm{d}H}{P}\right) = (1-(1-\rho)q)I_E\mathrm{d}E \tag{2.49}$$

Finally, taking total differential of (2.46) and substituting into it (2.47), we get

$$\mathrm{d}(\mathrm{d}m) = I_E\mathrm{d}E \tag{2.50}$$

Let us explain the adjustment process. Following the autonomous increase in E, aggregate investment demand rises by $I_E\mathrm{d}E$ raising demand for new bank credit by the same amount. Banks meet this additional demand by borrowing from the central bank. Hence, b rises in the first round by $\mathrm{d}b_1 = I_E\mathrm{d}E$. The increase in aggregate investment sets off the multiplier process and raises Y by $\mathrm{d}Y = \frac{I_E\mathrm{d}E}{1-c}$. This raises saving by $(1-c)\cdot\frac{I_E\mathrm{d}E}{1-c} = I_E\mathrm{d}E$ of which $qI_E\mathrm{d}E$ is held in the form of bank deposits and the rest in the form of currency. Banks are, therefore, able to supply an additional $(1-\rho)qI_E\mathrm{d}E$ amount of credit, which they lend out to the central bank. Therefore, b in the second round falls by $\mathrm{d}b_2 = -(1-\rho)qI_E\mathrm{d}E$. Hence, the net increase in b is given by $\mathrm{d}b = (1-(1-\rho)q)I_E\mathrm{d}E$. In the central bank's asset-liability balance sheet, on the asset side domestic credit goes up by $(1-(1-\rho)q)I_E\mathrm{d}E$. On the liabilities side, banks' reserve and currency holding of the public increase by $\rho qI_E\mathrm{d}E$ and $(1-q)I_E\mathrm{d}E$, respectively. Therefore, the stock of high-powered money rises by $(1-(1-\rho)q)I_E\mathrm{d}E$, while money supply rises by

$I_E \mathrm{d}E$. Thus, the money multiplier is given by $\frac{1}{(1-(1-\rho)q)}$. Note that in the textbooks of macroeconomics, the money multiplier in the presence of both bank deposit and currency is given by $\frac{\lambda+1}{\lambda+\rho}$, where λ denotes the currency–deposit ratio, the ratio in which people hold currency and bank deposit. Therefore, in the context of our model $\lambda = \frac{1-q}{q}$. Putting it in $\frac{\lambda+1}{\lambda+\rho}$, we get

$$\frac{\lambda + 1}{\lambda + \rho} = \frac{1}{1 - (1 - \rho)q} \tag{2.51}$$

Thus, we get the standard money multiplier formula here. It is clear from our above discussion that people may use currency or bank deposits or both for carrying out their transactions. However, the money that people use for carrying out their transactions does not remain in their hands in equilibrium. Only the money that they use for holding their saving remains in their hands in equilibrium. The money multiplier gives the increase in money supply that takes place from the initial equilibrium to the new equilibrium per unit increase in the stock of high-powered money from the initial equilibrium to the new equilibrium. Thus, the money that people use to carry out their transactions is of no importance in the money multiplier formula. The standard macroeconomics textbooks, however, do not make any distinction between use of money for carrying out transactions and the use of money for holding saving. They fail to notice that in equilibrium, there is no transaction demand for money or holding of money for purposes of transactions. We can summarize our finding regarding the money multiplier in the form of the following proposition:

Proposition 2.5 *Our model derives the money multiplier formulae of the standard macroeconomics text books. It shows that the transaction demand for money has no role to play in the money multiplier formulae. This happens because there is no transaction demand for money in equilibrium, i.e., there is no holding of money for purposes of transactions in equilibrium. In equilibrium, people hold money only to hold their savings, and the money multiplier formulae give the increase in the stock of money which people hold to hold their saving from the initial equilibrium to the new one following a unit increase in the stock of high-powered money. The standard macroeconomics textbooks do not make this distinction. Moreover, we derive the money multiplier formulae in a general equilibrium setup where the multiplier in the real sector and the money multiplier work together reinforcing one another. More precisely, our model shows that one cannot work without the other, when even a part of aggregate expenditure is financed with commercial bank credit.*

2.7.2 *The Case of Credit Rationing*

In reality, interest rates of the banks are not only rigid, banks also ration credit. Usually, at the interest rates set by them, banks do not meet all the credit demand that comes forth. They meet all the credit demand of the quality borrowers (large corporations), but ration the small and medium producers [see in this connection Bernanke (1983), Benanke et al. (1996, 1999), among others]. Banks give to the small and medium producers only a fraction, say, β of the loanable fund that remains at their disposal after meeting the credit demand of the quality borrowers. The reason may be stated as follows. As banks increase β, supply of loans to the non-quality borrowers increases. This raises not only expected income of the banks but also the amount of risk taken by the banks. Depending upon their preference over risk and return, banks, a la Tobin (1958), decide on the optimum value of β. Distinguishing between investment functions of the quality and non-quality borrowers, we write the goods market equilibrium condition as

$$Y = cY + \overline{I}(r(r_c), \overline{E}) + I^n\big(r(r_c), E^n\big) + G \tag{2.52}$$

In (2.52), $\overline{I}(\cdot)$ and $I^n(\cdot)$ represent investment functions of quality borrowers and non-quality borrowers, respectively, while $\overline{E}$ and E^n denote expectations regarding future business prospects of the quality borrowers and non-quality borrowers, respectively. The financial sector is the same as that in the earlier case. The only difference is that here banks meet all the credit demands of the quality borrowers, but ration the non-quality borrowers. Supply of new commercial bank credit to non-quality borrowers denoted L^{ns} is given by

$$L^{ns} = \beta\big[(1-\rho)(1-c)Y - \overline{I}\big(r(r_c), \overline{E}\big)\big] \quad 0 < \beta < 1 \tag{2.53}$$

Since L^{ns} is less than $I^n(\cdot)$ by the assumption of credit rationing, aggregate investment is given by

$$\begin{aligned} I &= \overline{I}\big((r_c), \overline{E}\big) + \beta \cdot \big[(1-\rho)(1-c)Y - \overline{I}\big(r(r_c), \overline{E}\big)\big] \\ &= (1-\beta)\overline{I}\big(r(r_c), \overline{E}\big) + \beta \cdot (1-\rho)(1-c)Y \end{aligned} \tag{2.54}$$

Substituting (2.54) into (2.52), we rewrite it as

$$Y = cY + (1-\beta)\overline{I}\big(r(r_c), \overline{E}\big) + \beta \cdot (1-\rho)(1-c)Y + G \tag{2.55}$$

Note that in the present case banks' total reserve exceeds the minimum $\rho(1-c)Y$ by $(1-\beta)\big[(1-\rho)(1-c)Y - \overline{I}\big(r(r_c), \overline{E}\big)\big]$. Thus, banks' total reserve in the present case denoted R is given by

$$R = \rho(1-c)Y + (1-\beta)\big[(1-\rho)(1-c)Y - \overline{I}\big(r(r_c), \overline{E}\big)\big] \tag{2.56}$$

In this case also, we assume that G is financed with new loans from the central bank. Thus,

$$G = \frac{\mathrm{d}H}{P} \tag{2.57}$$

Here also, we assume that people hold all their savings in the form of bank deposits so that the change in money supply is given by

$$\mathrm{d}m = \mathrm{d}D = (1 - c)Y \tag{2.58}$$

The specification of our model is now complete. It is given by four key Eqs. (2.55), (2.56), (2.57), and (2.58) in four endogenous variables, namely Y, R, $\frac{\mathrm{d}H}{P}$, and dm. We shall now illustrate the working of the model carrying out a comparative static exercise.

An Improvement in the Expectations of the Quality Borrowers

We shall examine how an improvement in the expectations of the quality investors, which gets reflected in an autonomous increase in $\overline{E}$, affects the endogenous variables of the model. To derive the impact on Y, we take total differential of (2.55) treating all variables other than $\overline{E}$ and Y as fixed, and then, solve for dY. This gives the following:

$$\mathrm{d}Y = \frac{(1-\beta)\overline{I}_{\overline{E}}\mathrm{d}\overline{E}}{1 - c - \beta(1-\rho)(1-c)} = \frac{(1-\beta)\overline{I}_{\overline{E}}\mathrm{d}\overline{E}}{(1-c)[1-\beta(1-\rho)]} \tag{2.59}$$

To derive the impact on R, we take total differential of (2.56) treating all variables other than Y and $\overline{E}$ as fixed, substitute (2.59) into it, and then, solve for dR. This yields the following

$$\mathrm{d}R = (\rho + (1-\beta)(1-\rho))\frac{(1-\beta)\overline{I}_{\overline{E}}\mathrm{d}\overline{E}}{[1-\beta(1-\rho)]} - (1-\beta)\overline{I}_{\overline{E}}\mathrm{d}\overline{E} = 0 \tag{2.59i}$$

Again, taking total differential of (2.57), we get

$$\mathrm{d}\left(\frac{\mathrm{d}H}{P}\right) = 0 \tag{2.60}$$

Finally, taking total differential of (2.58) and substituting into it (2.59), we get

$$\mathrm{d}(\mathrm{d}m) = \mathrm{d}(\mathrm{d}D) = \frac{(1-\beta)\overline{I}_{\overline{E}}\mathrm{d}\overline{E}}{[1-\beta(1-\rho)]} \tag{2.61}$$

Let us now explain (2.58). Following an autonomous increase in $\overline{E}$ by d$\overline{E}$, aggregate planned investment demand of the quality investors goes up. They finance it by taking new loans from the commercial banks. The commercial banks meet this additional demand for credit by diverting their fund from the non-quality borrowers. As a result, aggregate investment demand at the initial equilibrium Y rises by $(1-\beta)\overline{I}_{\overline{E}}\overline{E}$. This lowers banks' reserve in the first round by $\mathrm{d}R_1 = -(1-\beta)\overline{I}_{\overline{E}}\overline{E}$. The increase in investment sets off the multiplier process, and Y increases in the first round by $\mathrm{d}Y_1 = \frac{(1-\beta)\overline{I}_{\overline{E}}\overline{E}}{1-c}$. This raises saving and bank deposits by $\mathrm{d}S_1 = \mathrm{d}(\mathrm{d}D)_1 = (1-\beta)\overline{I}_{\overline{E}}\mathrm{d}\overline{E}$. Banks, therefore, in the second round extend additional loan of $\beta(1-\rho)(1-\beta)\overline{I}_{\overline{E}}\mathrm{d}\overline{E}$ to non-quality borrowers raising their investment expenditure by the same amount. Banks' reserve in the second round, therefore, rises by $\mathrm{d}R_2 = (1-\beta)\overline{I}_{\overline{E}}\mathrm{d}\overline{E} - \beta(1-\rho)(1-\beta)\overline{I}_{\overline{E}}\mathrm{d}\overline{E}$. The increase in the investment expenditure sets off the multiplier process and Y in the second round increases by $\frac{\beta(1-\rho)(1-\beta)\overline{I}_{\overline{E}}\mathrm{d}\overline{E}}{1-c}$. This in turn raises saving, money supply, and bank deposit by $\mathrm{d}S_2 = \mathrm{d}(\mathrm{d}m)_2 = \mathrm{d}(\mathrm{d}D)_2 = \beta(1-\rho)(1-\beta)\overline{I}_{\overline{E}}\mathrm{d}\overline{E}$. The receipt of new deposits by banks starts the third round. Banks extend additional loan of $\beta(1-\rho)\mathrm{d}(\mathrm{d}D)_2 = [\beta(1-\rho)]^2(1-\beta)\overline{I}_{\overline{E}}\mathrm{d}\overline{E}$ raising non-quality borrowers' investment expenditure by the same amount. Banks' reserve in the third round, therefore, rises by $\mathrm{d}R_3 = \left[\beta(1-\rho)(1-\beta) - [\beta(1-\rho)]^2(1-\beta)\right]\overline{I}_{\overline{E}}\mathrm{d}\overline{E}$. The rise in investment expenditure sets off the multiplier process, and Y in the third round increases by $\mathrm{d}Y_3 = \frac{[\beta(1-\rho)]^2(1-\beta)\overline{I}_{\overline{E}}\mathrm{d}\overline{E}}{1-c}$. This process of cumulative expansion in Y will continue until the increase in bank deposit that takes place in each successive round eventually falls to zero. Thus, total increases in Y, R, $\mathrm{d}(\mathrm{d}D) = \mathrm{d}(\mathrm{d}m)$ are given by

$$\begin{aligned}\mathrm{d}Y &= \frac{(1-\beta)\overline{I}_{\overline{E}}\mathrm{d}\overline{E}}{1-c} + \frac{[\beta(1-\rho)](1-\beta)\overline{I}_{\overline{E}}\mathrm{d}\overline{E}}{1-c} + \frac{[\beta(1-\rho)]^2(1-\beta)\overline{I}_{\overline{E}}\mathrm{d}\overline{E}}{1-c} + \cdots \\ &= \frac{(1-\beta)\overline{I}_{\overline{E}}\mathrm{d}\overline{E}}{(1-c)(1-\beta(1-\rho))}\end{aligned} \tag{2.62}$$

$$\begin{aligned}\mathrm{d}R = &-(1-\beta)\overline{I}_{\overline{E}}\mathrm{d}\overline{E} + (1-\beta(1-\rho))\overline{I}_{\overline{E}}\mathrm{d}\overline{E} \\ &+ (1-\beta)\beta(1-\rho)(1-\beta(1-\rho))\overline{I}_{\overline{E}}\mathrm{d}\overline{E} \\ &+ (1-\beta)[\beta(1-\rho)]^2(1-\beta(1-\rho))\overline{I}_{\overline{E}}\mathrm{d}\overline{E} + \cdots = 0\end{aligned} \tag{2.63}$$

$$\begin{aligned}\mathrm{d}(\mathrm{d}D) = \mathrm{d}(\mathrm{d}m) &= (1-\beta)\overline{I}_{\overline{E}}\mathrm{d}\overline{E} + [\beta(1-\rho)](1-\beta)\overline{I}_{\overline{E}}\mathrm{d}\overline{E} \\ &+ [\beta(1-\rho)]^2(1-\beta)\overline{I}_{\overline{E}}\mathrm{d}\overline{E} + \cdots = \frac{(1-\beta)\overline{I}_{\overline{E}}\mathrm{d}\overline{E}}{(1-\beta(1-\rho))}\end{aligned} \tag{2.64}$$

From the above, it follows that the value of the multiplier operating on Y is much larger in the case of credit rationing.

Interest rate rigidity and credit rationing are normal features of the banking sector so much so that Stiglitz and Weiss (1981) sought to provide an ingenuous explanation of the phenomenon. The Keynesian precept that the level of autonomous spending in general and that of investment spending in particular are the most important determinants of GDP and that volatility of the growth rate of investment is the principal reason for trade cycles in a capitalist economy hold good most convincingly, as we show here, in the case where interest rates charged by banks are rigid. We shall show in the next section that this will hold even when we incorporate other financial assets such as bonds in our model. We present our finding in the following proposition:

Proposition 2.6 *In reality, interest rates charged by banks are rigid and banks supply as much credit as they deem fit at the fixed interest rates. Our analysis shows that the major Keynesian result that the level of autonomous spending in general and that of* *investment spending in particular are the major determinants of GDP hold good in the present case.*

We shall now extend our model by incorporating bonds.

2.7.3 Incorporation of Bonds

We shall now incorporate bonds in our model. We only consider risk-free bonds and risk-free deposits. To the savers, both are almost equivalent. There is no risk in either instrument if they are held to maturity. Savers will not sell off bonds prematurely except under two conditions, namely unforeseen exigency and speculation. The first factor is unlikely to be quantitatively significant. Moreover, to guard against the unforeseen contingencies, savers hold a fixed amount of saving in the form of chequable bank deposits or currency. We are concerned with the rest of the saving here. The second factor is unimportant too, as ordinary savers usually do not engage in speculation. It is extremely risky and ordinary savers are extremely risk-averse, and they do not have either the time or the skill to engage in speculation. They engage in speculation on a mass scale, when and only when giant global capitalists create bubbles in asset prices and catch the ordinary people through the media and the political parties into a mass speculative frenzy. However, here we do not consider such scenarios. To the banks also, risk-free bonds and risk-free loans are almost equivalent. Banks also cannot engage in speculation, given the rules and regulations governing their behavior. To the large corporation also, bonds and bank loans are almost equivalent. In the absence of speculation, therefore, interest rates on bank loans (denoted r) and bonds (denoted r_b) should be equal. If r exceeds r_b, banks will lose all their quality customers and savers will not buy bonds, as they will put all their saving in bank deposits (here we do not distinguish between deposit rate and lending rate for simplicity) leading to excess supply of bonds. Obviously, therefore, r_b will rise, and r and r_b will be equal in equilibrium. Similarly, if r_b is higher than r, large borrowers will not sell bonds to borrow, while lenders will prefer bonds to bank loans/deposits giving rise to excess demand for bonds. Hence, r_b will fall and become equal to r. We assume that r is rigid, as is the case in reality and denote it by $\bar{r}$ for simplicity. Thus, given our assumptions

$$r_b = \bar{r} \tag{2.65}$$

We also assume for simplicity that people do not directly buy bonds, but banks do. Given the interest rates (which are equal in equilibrium), banks invest α fraction of their deposits in bonds and the rest they lend out. Borrowers, therefore, get in equilibrium $\alpha \cdot (1-\rho)(1-c)Y$ amount of new loans by selling bonds. Thus, the value of new loans raised by selling new bonds, which we denote by B, is given by

$$B = \alpha \cdot (1-\rho)(1-c)Y \tag{2.66}$$

Assuming no credit rationing by banks, the equilibrium condition in the bank credit market is given by

$$\overline{I}(\bar{r}, E) - \alpha \cdot (1-\rho)(1-c)Y = (1-\alpha)(1-\rho)(1-c)Y + b \tag{2.67}$$

Here, given our assumptions,

$$\mathrm{d}D = \mathrm{d}m = (1-c)Y \tag{2.68}$$

The goods market equilibrium condition is, therefore, given by

$$Y = cY + I(\bar{r}, E) + G \tag{2.69}$$

Assuming G to be financed by borrowing from the central bank, the increase in the stock of high-powered money is given by

$$\frac{\mathrm{d}H}{P} = G + b \tag{2.70}$$

The specification of our model is complete. It consists of four key Eqs. (2.67), (2.68), (2.69) and (2.70) in four endogenous variables, namely, b, Y, dm, and $\frac{\mathrm{d}H}{P}$. Note that (2.67), (2.68), (2.69), and (2.70) are exactly the same as (2.30), (2.32), (2.29), and (2.31), respectively. The latter set of equations gives the equilibrium values of b, Y, dm, and $\frac{\mathrm{d}H}{P}$ in the case where bank deposits are the only instrument of saving and bank loans are the only kind of credit available, and there is no credit rationing. Thus, incorporation of bonds does not make any difference to the model.

Let us now consider the case of credit rationing. Here, we distinguish between quality borrowers and non-quality borrowers. In this case also, in equilibrium, (2.65) will hold good. Only the quality borrowers can borrow by issuing bonds, and banks meet all their credit demand. Therefore, the quality borrowers will get $\alpha \cdot (1-\rho)(1-c)Y$ amount of new credit by selling bonds, and they will meet the remaining part of their credit demand, $\overline{I}(\bar{r}, \overline{E}) - \alpha \cdot (1-\rho)(1-c)Y$, by securing new bank credit. Banks ration non-quality borrowers and supply them with new loans of $\beta\{(1-\alpha)(1-\rho)(1-c)Y - [I(\bar{r}, \overline{E}) - \alpha \cdot (1-\rho)(1-c)Y]\} = \beta \cdot [(1-\rho)(1-c)Y - \overline{I}(\bar{r}, \overline{E})]$. Therefore, aggregate investment, denoted I, is given by

$$I = (1-\beta)\overline{I}(\bar{r}, \overline{E}) + \beta \cdot (1-\rho)(1-c)Y \tag{2.71}$$

Using (2.71), we write the goods market equilibrium condition as

$$Y = cY + (1-\beta)\overline{I}(\bar{r}, \overline{E}) + \beta \cdot (1-\rho)(1-c)Y + G \tag{2.72}$$

G is financed by borrowing from the central bank so that

$$\frac{\mathrm{d}H}{P} = G \tag{2.73}$$

Finally,

$$\mathrm{d}m = \mathrm{d}D = (1 - c)Y \tag{2.74}$$

The model is now given by four key Eqs. (2.71), (2.72), (2.73), and (2.74). In this case of credit rationing also we find that (2.71), (2.72), (2.73), and (2.74) are the same as (2.54), (2.55), (2.57), and (2.58), respectively. The latter set of four equations gives the equilibrium value of I, Y, $\frac{\mathrm{d}H}{P}$, and dm in the case of credit rationing in the absence of bonds. Thus, incorporation of bonds does not make any difference. We summarize our finding in the form of the following proposition:

Proposition 2.7 *Incorporation of bonds leaves the equilibrium values of all the key endogenous variables such as aggregate investment, GDP, change in money supply, change in the stock of high-powered money unchanged in the cases of both no credit rationing and credit rationing.*

In what follows, therefore, it is not necessary to consider bonds or any financial asset other than bank deposits, or any financial institution other than banks.

2.8 The Model for an Open Economy

We shall now extend our model to the case of an open economy. We consider here a small open economy. For the present, we abstract from capital mobility or cross-border capital flows. We shall first focus on the fixed exchange rate regime:

2.8.1 The Fixed Exchange Rate Regime

The goods market equilibrium condition is given by

$$Y = cY + I(r, E) + G + X\left(\frac{P^{*}e}{P}, Y^{*}\right) - M\left(\frac{P^{*}e}{P}, Y\right) \tag{2.75}$$

In (2.75), $X \equiv$ exports, $M \equiv$ the value of imports **in terms of domestic goods**, $P^{*} \equiv$ the average price of foreign goods in foreign currency, $P \equiv$ the average price of domestic goods in domestic currency, $Y^{*} \equiv$ foreign GDP, and $e \equiv$ nominal exchange rate. As the economy is small, P^{*} and Y^{*} are given. P, as before, is taken to be fixed. We first focus on the fixed exchange rate regime. The exchange rate is pegged at $\bar{e}$. Incorporating this pegged value of e into (2.75), we have

$$Y = cY + I(r, E) + G + X\left(\frac{P^{*}\bar{e}}{P}, Y^{*}\right) - M\left(\frac{P^{*}\bar{e}}{P}, Y\right) \tag{2.76}$$

The central bank intervenes in the foreign exchange market to keep the exchange rate fixed at $\bar{e}$. $\left[X\left(\frac{P^{*}\bar{e}}{P}, Y^{*}\right) - M\left(\frac{P^{*}\bar{e}}{P}, Y\right)\right]\frac{P}{\bar{e}}$ gives the excess supply of foreign currency at the given exchange rate. The central bank buys up this excess supply with domestic currency at the price $\bar{e}$ creating high-powered money to keep e at $\bar{e}$. We further assume for the purpose of illustration that the government borrows from the central bank to finance the whole of its consumption expenditure. We assume that high-powered money is created only on account of government's borrowings from the central bank and central bank's intervention in the foreign exchange market to keep the exchange rate fixed. Thus, the increase in the stock of high-powered money in the period under consideration is given by

$$\mathrm{d}H = P\overline{G} + \bar{e}\left[X\left(\frac{P^{*}\bar{e}}{P}, Y^{*}\right) - M\left(\frac{P^{*}\bar{e}}{P}, Y\right)\right]\frac{P}{\bar{e}} \tag{2.77}$$

From (2.77), it follows that the stock of real balance created in the period under consideration is given by

$$\frac{\mathrm{d}H}{P} = \overline{G} + \left[X\left(\frac{P^{*}\bar{e}}{P}, Y^{*}\right) - M\left(\frac{P^{*}\bar{e}}{P}, Y\right)\right] \tag{2.78}$$

Again, as before, we assume that households do not take any loans, hold all their wealth in the form of bank deposits, and banks are the only source of loans to the firms. These are all simplifying assumptions. Given these assumptions, the increase in the stock of bank deposits or money supply is given by the following equation:

$$S = \mathrm{d}m = \mathrm{d}D = (1 - c)Y \tag{2.79}$$

We first focus on the flexible interest rate case. As before, in this case, the credit market equilibrium continues to be given by (2.5), which we reproduce below for convenience

$$I(r) = \left(1 - \rho(r_{c_{+}})\right)(1 - c)Y \tag{2.5}$$

The specification of our model is now complete. It contains four key Eqs. (2.76), (2.5), (2.78), and (2.79) in four unknowns Y, r, $\frac{\mathrm{d}H}{P}$, and $\mathrm{d}D$ or $\mathrm{d}m$. We can solve them as follows: We can solve (2.76) and (2.5) for the equilibrium values of Y and r. Putting the equilibrium value of Y into (2.78) and (2.79), we get the equilibrium values of $\frac{\mathrm{d}H}{P}$ and $\mathrm{d}m$. We shall now illustrate the working of the model using a comparative static exercise.

Fiscal policy: The Effect of an Increase in G by $\mathrm{d}G$ Financed by Borrowing from the Central Bank

Suppose the government raises G and finances it by borrowing from the central bank. How will it affect Y, r, $\frac{\mathrm{d}H}{P}$ and $\mathrm{d}D$ or $\mathrm{d}m$? We derive the results mathematically below:

Mathematical Derivation of the Results
To derive the results mathematically, we first substitute (2.5) into (2.76) to write it as

$$Y = cY + (1-c)(1-\rho)Y + G + X\left(\frac{P^*\bar{e}}{P}, Y^*\right) - M\left(\frac{P^*\bar{e}}{P}, Y\right) \quad (2.80)$$

It is clear from (2.80) that, as we have shown earlier, if the investment or any other component of autonomous spending gets financed by loans from commercial banks or some other such financial intermediaries or by selling bonds or stocks, it ceases to be a determinant of GDP in the flexible exchange rate regime.

Taking total differential of (2.80) treating all exogenous variables other than $\overline{G}$ as fixed, and solving for $\mathrm{d}Y$, we have

$$\mathrm{d}Y = \frac{\mathrm{d}\overline{G}}{\rho(1-c) + M_Y} \quad (2.81)$$

Again, taking total differential of (2.5), substituting for $\mathrm{d}Y$ its value given by (2.81), and then, solving for $\mathrm{d}r$, we get

$$\mathrm{d}r = \left[(1-\rho)(1-c)\frac{\mathrm{d}\overline{G}}{\rho(1-c) + M_Y}\right]\frac{1}{I'} \quad (2.82)$$

Again, from (2.78) and (2.81), we get

$$\mathrm{d}\left(\frac{\mathrm{d}H}{P}\right) = \mathrm{d}\overline{G} - M_Y\frac{\mathrm{d}\overline{G}}{\rho(1-c) + M_Y} = \frac{\rho(1-c)\mathrm{d}\overline{G}}{\rho(1-c) + M_Y} \quad (2.83)$$

Also note that, using (2.83), we get

$$\mathrm{d}(\mathrm{d}S) = \mathrm{d}(\mathrm{d}m) = \mathrm{d}(\mathrm{d}D) = \frac{(1-c)\mathrm{d}\overline{G}}{\rho(1-c) + M_Y} = \frac{\mathrm{d}\left(\frac{\mathrm{d}H}{P}\right)}{\rho} \quad (2.84)$$

We shall now explain below how these changes come about. Following the increase in $\overline{G}$ by $\mathrm{d}\overline{G}$, Y through the multiplier process increases by $\mathrm{d}Y = \frac{\mathrm{d}\overline{G}}{1-(c-M_Y)}$. From this additional income, people save $(1-c)\frac{\mathrm{d}\overline{G}}{1-(c-M_Y)}$ and they hold this in the form of bank deposits. Banks receive an additional deposit of $(1-c)\frac{\mathrm{d}\overline{G}}{1-(c-M_Y)}$. Accordingly, their reserves and, therefore, the stock of high-powered money increases by $(1-c)\frac{\mathrm{d}\overline{G}}{1-(c-M_Y)}$. Let us explain this point a little more. When the government borrows from the central bank $\mathrm{d}\overline{G}$ amount, the stock of high-powered money in the economy rises by the same amount. But following the increase in Y by $\frac{\mathrm{d}\overline{G}}{1-(c-M_Y)}$, import demand rises by $M_Y \cdot \frac{\mathrm{d}\overline{G}}{1-(c-M_Y)}$ generating an excess demand for foreign currency (in terms of domestic goods) by the same amount. The central bank has to buy up $M_Y \cdot \frac{d\overline{G}}{1-(c-M_Y)}$ amount of domestic currency (in terms of domestic goods) with foreign currency. Thus, at the end of the multiplier process, the stock of high-powered money (in terms of domestic goods) in the domestic economy rises by $d\overline{G} - M_Y \cdot \frac{d\overline{G}}{1-(c-M_Y)} = (1-c)\frac{d\overline{G}}{1-(c-M_Y)}$. Banks get this, as we have already explained, in the form of additional deposits and reserve. Let us make this point clearer. As Y increases by $dY_1 = \frac{d\overline{G}}{1-(c-M_Y)}$, people's saving increases by $(1-c)\frac{d\overline{G}}{1-(c-M_Y)}$. Besides this, they also have in their hands $M_Y \cdot \frac{d\overline{G}}{1-(c-M_Y)}$ part of their income, which they do not spend on domestic goods. Note that $(1-c)\frac{d\overline{G}}{1-(c-M_Y)} + M_Y \cdot \left[\frac{d\overline{G}}{1-(c-M_Y)}\right] = d\overline{G}$. However, they will not deposit $M_Y \cdot \left[\frac{d\overline{G}}{1-(c-M_Y)}\right]$ amount of income with the banks. They will sell it to the central bank for foreign currency. So, the banks will get an additional deposit of $(1-c)\frac{d\overline{G}}{1-(c-M_Y)}$. In the central bank's balance sheet, the following changes will occur. On the asset side, central bank's credit to the government will increase by $d\overline{G}$, and its stock of foreign exchange will go down by $M_Y \cdot \left[\frac{d\overline{G}}{1-(c-M_Y)}\right]$ so that, in the net, central bank's total asset increases by $d\overline{G} - M_Y.\left[\frac{d\overline{G}}{1-(c-M_Y)}\right] = (1-c)\frac{d\overline{G}}{1-(c-M_Y)}$. On the liabilities side, banks' reserve rises by $(1-c)\frac{d\overline{G}}{1-(c-M_Y)}$.

Banks will not want to keep this whole of this additional reserve idle. They will plan to extend an additional credit of $(1-\rho)(1-c)\frac{d\overline{G}}{1-(c-M_Y)}$.$r$ will, therefore, fall by $\left\{(1-\rho)(1-c)\frac{d\overline{G}}{1-(c-M_Y)}\right\}/I'$ to raise investment by the amount of the additional supply of bank credit. This will bring about the second round of expansion in Y. At the end of the first round, increases in Y, $\frac{dH}{P}$, dS, dD, dm and dl_f (which denotes new credit supplied by the commercial banks) and the decline in r are given, respectively, by

$$dY_1 = \frac{d\overline{G}}{1-(c-M_Y)}, \; d\left(\frac{dH}{P}\right)_1 = dS_1 = d(dD)_1 = d(dm)_1$$

$$= (1-\rho)(1-c)\frac{d\overline{G}}{1-(c-M_Y)},$$

$$d(dl_f)_1 = dl_1 = (1-\rho)(1-c)\frac{d\overline{G}}{1-(c-M_Y)}$$

and

$$dr_1 = \left[(1-\rho)(1-c)\frac{d\overline{G}}{\rho(1-c)+M_Y}\right]/I'$$

In the second round, the increase in investment by $(1-\rho)(1-c)\frac{d\overline{G}}{\rho(1-c)+M_Y}$ will lead through the multiplier process to an increase in Y by $(1-\rho)(1-c)\frac{d\overline{G}}{[1-(c-M_Y)]^2} \equiv$

dY_2. Out of this additional income of $\mathrm{d}Y_2$, people will save $(1-c)\mathrm{d}Y_2$ and will not spend $M_Y\mathrm{d}Y_2$ on domestic goods. Note that $(1-c)\mathrm{d}Y_2 + M_Y\mathrm{d}Y_2 = (1-\rho)(1-c)\mathrm{d}Y_1$, which is the amount of new credit extended by the commercial banks at the end of the first round. However, the banks will not get back the whole of this credit as new deposit. People will deposit $(1-c)\mathrm{d}Y_2$ with the banks and sell $M_Y\mathrm{d}Y_2$ to the central bank. In the balance sheet of the central bank, following changes will occur. On the asset side, central banks' stock of foreign exchange will fall by $M_Y\mathrm{d}Y_2$ and on the liabilities side, banks' reserve will go down by the same amount. In the second round, therefore, the stock of high-powered money will decline by $\mathrm{d}\left(\frac{\mathrm{d}H}{P}\right)_2 = -M_Y\mathrm{d}Y_2$. In the second round, aggregate saving increases by $\mathrm{d}S_2 = (1-\rho)(1-c)^2\frac{\mathrm{d}\overline{G}}{[1-(c-M_Y)]^2}$, which the households will hold in the form of bank deposits. Banks will receive additional deposits of $(\mathrm{d}D)_2 = \mathrm{d}(\mathrm{d}m)_2 = (1-\rho)(1-c)^2\frac{\mathrm{d}\overline{G}}{[1-(c-M_Y)]^2}$, which will induce them to extend additional credit of $(\mathrm{d}l_f)_2 = \mathrm{d}(\mathrm{d}m)_2 = (1-\rho)^2(1-c)^2\frac{\mathrm{d}\overline{G}}{[1-(c-M_Y)]^2}$. This will increase investment by the same amount through the decline in r by $\left\{(1-\rho)^2(1-c)^2\frac{\mathrm{d}\overline{G}}{[1-(c-M_Y)]^2}\right\}/I'$. Thus, another round of expansion will begin. This process will go on until the amount of additional investment generated falls to zero. When that happens, the economy achieves a new equilibrium. Thus, the total increases in $\mathrm{d}Y$, $\mathrm{d}\left(\frac{\mathrm{d}H}{P}\right)$, $\mathrm{d}S = \mathrm{d}(\mathrm{d}D) = \mathrm{d}(\mathrm{d}m)$ and $\mathrm{d}l_f$ and the decline in r are given, respectively, by

$$\begin{aligned}\mathrm{d}Y &= \frac{\mathrm{d}\overline{G}}{1-(c-M_Y)} + \frac{\mathrm{d}\overline{G}}{[1-(c-M_Y)]^2} + (1-\rho)^2(1-c)^2\frac{\mathrm{d}\overline{G}}{[1-(c-M_Y)]^3} + \cdots \\ &= \frac{\mathrm{d}\overline{G}}{\rho(1-c)+M_Y}\end{aligned} \tag{2.85}$$

$$\begin{aligned}\mathrm{d}\left(\frac{dH}{P}\right) &= \mathrm{d}\overline{G} - M_Y\frac{\mathrm{d}\overline{G}}{1-(c-M_Y)} - M_Y\cdot(1-\rho)(1-c)\frac{\mathrm{d}G}{[1-(c-M_Y]^2} \\ &\quad - M_Y\cdot(1-\rho)^2(1-c)^2\frac{\mathrm{d}\overline{G}}{[1-(c-M_Y)]^3} + \cdots = \frac{\rho(1-c)\mathrm{d}\overline{G}}{\rho(1-c)+M_Y}\end{aligned} \tag{2.86}$$

$$\begin{aligned}\mathrm{d}(\mathrm{d}l_f) &= (1-\rho)(1-c)\frac{\mathrm{d}\overline{G}}{1-(c-M_Y)} + (1-\rho)^2(1-c)^2\frac{\mathrm{d}\overline{G}}{[1-(c-M_Y)]^3} \\ &\quad + \cdots = \frac{(1-\rho)(1-c)\mathrm{d}\overline{G}}{\rho(1-c)+M_Y}\end{aligned} \tag{2.87}$$

$$\begin{aligned}\mathrm{d}S &= \mathrm{d}(\mathrm{d}D) = \mathrm{d}(\mathrm{d}m) = (1-c)\mathrm{d}Y_1 + (1-c)\mathrm{d}Y_2 + (1-c)\mathrm{d}Y_3 + \cdots \\ &= (1-c)\mathrm{d}Y = (1-c)\frac{\mathrm{d}\overline{G}}{\rho(1-c)+M_Y}\end{aligned} \tag{2.88}$$

Using (2.86), we can write (2.88) as follows:

$$\mathrm{d}S = \mathrm{d}(\mathrm{d}D) = \mathrm{d}(\mathrm{d}m) = \frac{\frac{\mathrm{d}H}{P}}{\rho} \tag{2.89}$$

$$\begin{aligned}\mathrm{d}r &= (1-\rho)(1-c)\frac{\mathrm{d}\overline{G}}{[1-(c-M_Y)]}\cdot\frac{1}{I'} \\ &\quad + (1-\rho)^2(1-c)^2\frac{\mathrm{d}\overline{G}}{[1-(c-M_Y)]^3}\cdot\frac{1}{I'}+\cdots \\ &= \frac{(1-\rho)(1-c)\mathrm{d}\overline{G}}{\rho(1-c)+M_Y}\cdot\frac{1}{I'}\end{aligned} \tag{2.90}$$

Clearly, (2.85), (2.86), (2.89), and (2.90) tally with the values of $\mathrm{d}Y$, $\mathrm{d}\left(\frac{\mathrm{d}H}{P}\right)$, $\mathrm{d}(\mathrm{d}m)$ and $\mathrm{d}r$ derived mathematically earlier and given by (2.81), (2.83), (2.84), and (2.82), respectively.

Irrelevance of the Money Market
In our model, the saving constitutes a demand for money, which is always equal to the supply of deposits or supply of money. Hence, the money market is irrelevant here.

We now sum up the finding of our discussion in the form of the following proposition:

Proposition 2.8 *In the case of an open economy with fixed exchange rate regime, autonomous spending ceases to be a determinant of GDP if it is financed with new loans taken from financial institutions in the flexible interest rate regime. In this case also, processes of generation of income, saving, credit, money, and spending are inextricably linked together and the standard money multiplier formulae hold.*

Interest Rate Rigidity in the Fixed Exchange Rate Regime
We shall now incorporate interest rate rigidity in our model. Incorporating (2.28) into (2.76), we rewrite it as

$$Y = cY + I(r(r_c), E) + G + X\left(\frac{P^*\bar{e}}{P}, Y^*\right) - M\left(\frac{P^*\bar{e}}{P}, Y\right) \tag{2.91}$$

Here, we focus on the case of no credit rationing. The credit market equilibrium condition is, therefore, given by (2.30), which we reproduce below for convenience

$$I(r(r_c), E) = (1-\rho)(1-c)Y + b \tag{2.30}$$

Besides G, b is another source of creation of high-powered money. Incorporating it, we rewrite (2.78) as

$$\frac{\mathrm{d}H}{P} = G + X\left(\frac{P^*\bar{e}}{P}, Y^*\right) - M\left(\frac{P^*\bar{e}}{P}, Y\right) + b \tag{2.92}$$

Finally, (2.79), as before, continues to give the values of S, dD, and dm. The specification of the model is now complete. It consists of four key Eqs. (2.91), (2.30), (2.92), and (2.79) in four endogenous variables, namely Y, b, $\frac{\mathrm{d}H}{P}$, dm (or dD or S). We shall now examine how an exogenous increase in E affects the endogenous variables of our model.

An Exogenous Improvement in the Expectations of the Investors

To derive the impact on Y, we take total differential of (2.91) treating all variables other than Y and E as fixed, and then, solve for dY. This gives the following

$$\mathrm{d}Y = \frac{I_E \mathrm{d}E}{1-(c-M_Y)} \tag{2.93}$$

We, then, take total differential of (2.30) treating all variables other than Y, b, and E as fixed, substitute (2.93) into it, and then, solving for db, we get

$$\mathrm{d}b = I_E \mathrm{d}E\left[1-(1-\rho)(1-c)\frac{1}{1-(c-M_Y)}\right] \tag{2.94}$$

Again, taking total differential of (2.92) treating all variables other than Y and b as fixed, substituting (2.93) and (2.94) into it, and then, solving for $\mathrm{d}\left(\frac{\mathrm{d}H}{P}\right)$, we get

$$\begin{aligned}\mathrm{d}\left(\frac{\mathrm{d}H}{P}\right) &= I_E \mathrm{d}E\left[1-(1-\rho)(1-c)\frac{1}{1-(c-M_Y)} - M_Y\frac{1}{1-(c-M_Y)}\right]\\ &= \rho(1-c)\frac{I_E \mathrm{d}E}{1-(c-M_Y)} = \rho(1-c)\mathrm{d}Y \end{aligned} \tag{2.95}$$

Finally, taking total differential of (2.79) treating all variables other than dm (or dD or S) and Y as fixed, substituting (2.93) into it, and then, solving for d(dm), we get

$$\mathrm{d}(\mathrm{d}m) = \mathrm{d}S = \mathrm{d}(\mathrm{d}D) = (1-c)\mathrm{d}Y = (1-c)\frac{I_E \mathrm{d}E}{1-(c-M_Y)} \tag{2.96}$$

From (2.95) and (2.96), we find that

$$\mathrm{d}(\mathrm{d}m) = \frac{1}{\rho}\mathrm{d}\left(\frac{\mathrm{d}H}{P}\right) \tag{2.97}$$

Thus, the standard money multiplier formula holds in this case. Let us explain the adjustment process. Following an improvement in the expectations of the investors for exogenous reasons, investment, and, therefore, demand for new bank loans rises by $I_E \mathrm{d}E$. The banks meet this additional loan demand by borrowing from the central bank raising b and the stock of high-powered money by $I_E \mathrm{d}E$. The multiplier process sets into motion and Y rises by $\frac{I_E \mathrm{d}E}{1-(c-M_Y)}$. People save $(1-c)$ fraction of this additional income so that $\mathrm{d}(\mathrm{d}m) = \mathrm{d}S = \mathrm{d}(\mathrm{d}D) = (1-c)\frac{I_E \mathrm{d}E}{1-(c-M_Y)}$. Out of this additional deposit, banks lend out $(1-\rho)(1-c)\frac{I_E \mathrm{d}E}{1-(c-M_Y)}$ to the central bank. Hence, central bank's domestic credit, which rose initially by $I_E \mathrm{d}E$, now falls by $(1-\rho)(1-c)\frac{I_E \mathrm{d}E}{1-(c-M_Y)}$. Again, out of the additional income of $\frac{I_E \mathrm{d}E}{1-(c-M_Y)}$, people spend $M_Y\frac{I_E \mathrm{d}E}{1-(c-M_Y)}$ on import. For this reason, they sell $P \cdot M_Y \cdot \frac{I_E \mathrm{d}E}{1-(c-M_Y)}$ amount of domestic currency to secure $\frac{P}{e} \cdot M_Y \cdot \frac{I_E \mathrm{d}E}{1-(c-M_Y)}$ amount of foreign currency. The central banks' foreign exchange reserve, therefore, goes down by $M_Y \cdot \frac{I_E \mathrm{d}E}{1-(c-M_Y)}$ in terms of domestic goods. Hence, in the net, asset of the central bank rises by $I_E \mathrm{d}E-(1-\rho)(1-c)\frac{I_E \mathrm{d}E}{1-(c-M_Y)}-M_Y \cdot \frac{I_E \mathrm{d}E}{1-(c-M_Y)}=\rho(1-c)\frac{I_E \mathrm{d}E}{1-(c-M_Y)}$. On the liabilities side of the central bank's asset-liability balance sheet, banks' reserve goes up by $\rho(1-c)\frac{I_E \mathrm{d}E}{1-(c-M_Y)}$. Therefore, the stock of high-powered money rises by the same amount. This completes the adjustment process. The above discussion suggests the following proposition:

Proposition 2.9 *In case of an open economy with fixed exchange rate, animal spirits of the investors emerge as the major determinant of GDP when interest rates are rigid. The standard money multiplier formulae also hold.*

2.8.2 The Flexible Exchange Rate Regime

We now focus on the flexible exchange rate regime. The goods market equilibrium in this case is given by

$$Y = cY + I(r, E) + \overline{G} + X\left(\frac{P^*\bar{e}}{P}, Y^*\right) - M\left(\frac{P^*\bar{e}}{P}, Y\right) \tag{2.98}$$

Note that here $\overline{G}$ is financed entirely with loans from the central bank and it is the only reason for the creation of high-powered money. Hence,

$$\overline{G} = \frac{\mathrm{d}H}{P} \tag{2.99}$$

The financial sector is the same as before. Hence, (2.79) holds. We reproduce it below

$$S = \mathrm{d}D = \mathrm{d}m = (1-c)Y \tag{2.79}$$

We first focus on the flexible interest rate case. Accordingly, the credit market equilibrium condition is given by (2.5), which we reproduce below for convenience:

$$I(r, E) = (1-\rho(r_c))(1-c)Y \tag{2.5}$$

Finally, the balance of payments (BOP) is in equilibrium, and therefore, the foreign currency market is in equilibrium, when the following condition is satisfied:

$$X\left(\frac{P^*e}{P}, Y^*\right) - M\left(\frac{P^*e}{P}, Y\right) = 0 \tag{2.100}$$

The specification of the model is now complete. The key equations of the model are (2.98), (2.99), (2.5), (2.79), and (2.100). They contain five endogenous variables: Y, $\frac{\mathrm{d}H}{P}$, $\mathrm{d}m$ (or S or $\mathrm{d}D$), and e. We can, therefore, solve them for the equilibrium values of the five endogenous variables. We solve them as follows: Substituting (2.100) and (2.5) into (2.98), we get

$$Y = cY + (1 - \rho(r_c))(1 - c)Y + \overline{G} \tag{2.101}$$

We can solve (2.101) for Y. It is clear from (2.101) that if investment expenditure or any other component of autonomous expenditure is financed by borrowing from the commercial banks or any other such financial intermediary, they will, as we have seen in the previous cases, cease to be determinants of GDP in the flexible interest rate regime. Putting the equilibrium value of Y into (2.5), we get the equilibrium value of r. Again, putting the equilibrium value of Y into (2.79) and (2.100), we get the equilibrium values of $\mathrm{d}m$ and e, respectively.

We shall explain the working of the model by carrying out a comparative static exercise.

Fiscal Policy

Suppose $\overline{G}$ increases by $\mathrm{d}\overline{G}$, which the government finances by borrowing from the central bank. To derive how it will affect Y, we take total differential of (2.101) treating all exogenous variables other than $\overline{G}$ as fixed, and then, solve for $\mathrm{d}Y$. This yields

$$\mathrm{d}Y = \frac{\mathrm{d}\overline{G}}{\rho(1-c)} = \frac{\mathrm{d}\left(\frac{\mathrm{d}H}{P}\right)}{\rho(1-c)} \tag{2.102}$$

Again, taking total differential of (2.5) treating all exogenous variables as fixed, substituting for $\mathrm{d}Y$ its value given by (2.102), and then, solving for $\mathrm{d}r$, we get

$$\mathrm{d}r = \frac{(1-\rho)\frac{\mathrm{d}\overline{G}}{\rho}}{I'} = \frac{(1-\rho)\frac{\mathrm{d}\left(\frac{\mathrm{d}H}{P}\right)}{\rho}}{I'} \tag{2.103}$$

Again, taking total differential of (2.100) treating all exogenous variables as fixed, substituting for $\mathrm{d}Y$ its value given by (2.102), and then, solving for $\mathrm{d}e$, we get

$$\mathrm{d}e = \frac{M_Y}{(X_p - M_p)\frac{P^*}{P}} \cdot \frac{\mathrm{d}\overline{G}}{\rho(1-c)};\ p \equiv \frac{P^*e}{P} \tag{2.104}$$

Taking total differential of (2.79), substituting (2.102) into it, and then, solving, we get

$$\mathrm{d}S = \mathrm{d}(\mathrm{d}D) = \mathrm{d}(\mathrm{d}m) = \frac{\mathrm{d}\overline{G}}{\rho} = \frac{\mathrm{d}(\frac{\mathrm{d}H}{P})}{\rho} \tag{2.105}$$

Adjustment Process

We shall now explain how these changes come about. As the government spends $\mathrm{d}\overline{G}$ on goods and services, producers face an excess demand of $\mathrm{d}\overline{G}$. They raise production by the same amount. Owners of factors of production get this $\mathrm{d}\overline{G}$ amount of factor income. Out of this, they spend $(c - M_Y)\mathrm{d}\overline{G}$ on domestic goods and try to use $M_Y\mathrm{d}\overline{G}$ to buy foreign currency to spend on foreign consumption goods. This gives rise to an excess demand for foreign currency of $\frac{P}{e}M_Y\mathrm{d}\overline{G}$ at the initial equilibrium exchange rate. So, e will rise so that $\frac{P}{e}(X - M)$, which declined by $\frac{P}{e}M_Y\mathrm{d}\overline{G}$, rises by $\frac{P}{e}M_Y\mathrm{d}\overline{G}$ restoring equilibrium in the foreign currency market. Per unit increase in e, $\frac{P}{e}(X - M)$ increases by $\frac{P}{-e^2}(X - M) + \frac{P}{e}(X_p - M_p)\frac{P*}{P} = \frac{P}{e}(X_p - M_p)\frac{P*}{P}$ since $X - M = 0$. Therefore, $\frac{P}{e}(X - M)$ will increase by $\frac{P}{e}M_Y\mathrm{d}\overline{G}$, when e rises by $\frac{\frac{P}{e}M_Y\mathrm{d}\overline{G}}{\frac{P}{e}(X_p-M_p)\frac{P*}{P}} = \frac{M_Y\mathrm{d}\overline{G}}{(X_p-M_p)\frac{P*}{P}}$. Let us now examine by how much demand for domestic goods given by $C + I + \overline{G} + (X - M)$ increases following the increase in Y (or aggregate factor income) by $\mathrm{d}\overline{G}$. C rises by $c\mathrm{d}\overline{G}$, while all other components of aggregate demand including $(X - M)$ remains unaffected, since the increase in e described above restores $X - M$ to its initial equilibrium value . Hence, aggregate demand for domestic goods will increase by $c\mathrm{d}\overline{G}$. This multiplier process will go on, and finally, Y will increase by $\frac{\mathrm{d}\overline{G}}{1-c}$. Out of this additional factor income of $\frac{\mathrm{d}\overline{G}}{1-c}$, people will save $(1 - c)\frac{\mathrm{d}\overline{G}}{1-c} = \mathrm{d}\overline{G}$. As people save only in the form of bank deposits, they will deposit their saving of $\mathrm{d}\overline{G}$ with the banks. The banks will, of course, not hold the whole of this additional bank deposits in the form of reserve. They will want to lend out $(1 - \rho)\mathrm{d}\overline{G}$ giving rise to excess supply of bank credit. So, r will fall by $\frac{(1-\rho)\mathrm{d}\overline{G}}{I'}$ so that investment demand goes up by $(1 - \rho)\mathrm{d}\overline{G}$. This is the end of Round 1. At the end of Round 1, therefore, $\mathrm{d}Y_1 = \frac{\mathrm{d}\overline{G}}{1-c}$, $\mathrm{d}S_1 = \mathrm{d}(\mathrm{d}D)_1 = \mathrm{d}(\mathrm{d}m)_1 = \mathrm{d}\overline{G}$, $\mathrm{d}(\frac{\mathrm{d}H}{P})_1 = \mathrm{d}\overline{G}$, $\mathrm{d}I_1 = (1 - \rho)\mathrm{d}\overline{G}$, $\mathrm{d}r_1 = \frac{(1-\rho)\mathrm{d}\overline{G}}{I'}$, and $\mathrm{d}e_1 = \frac{M_Y\mathrm{d}Y_1}{(X_p-M_p)\frac{P*}{P}}$.

The increase in investment demand will again set off the multiplier process, which will raise Y further by $\mathrm{d}Y_2 = \frac{(1-\rho)\mathrm{d}\overline{G}}{1-c}$ and raise e by $\mathrm{d}e_2 = \frac{M_Y\mathrm{d}Y_2}{(X_p-M_p)\frac{P*}{P}}$. The increase in Y will again raise saving by $\mathrm{d}S_2 = \mathrm{d}(\mathrm{d}D)_2 = \mathrm{d}(\mathrm{d}m)_2 = (1 - \rho)\mathrm{d}\overline{G}$, which the savers will again deposit with the banks. The banks, in turn, will lend out again $(1 - \rho)^2\mathrm{d}\overline{G}$ raising I and Y by $\mathrm{d}I_2 = (1 - \rho)^2\mathrm{d}G$ and $\mathrm{d}Y_3 = \frac{(1-\rho)^2\mathrm{d}\overline{G}}{1-c}$, respectively. This process of expansion will go on until the additional saving generated falls to zero. Thus, the total increase in Y, total increases in S, $\mathrm{d}D$, and $\mathrm{d}M$ and total decrease in r, and total increase in e are given by

$$\mathrm{d}Y = \frac{\mathrm{d}\overline{G}}{1-c} + \frac{(1-\rho)\mathrm{d}\overline{G}}{1-c} + \frac{(1-\rho)^2\mathrm{d}\overline{G}}{1-c} + \cdots = \frac{\mathrm{d}\overline{G}}{1-c} \tag{2.106}$$

$$\mathrm{d}S = \mathrm{d}(\mathrm{d}D) = \mathrm{d}(\mathrm{d}m) = \mathrm{d}\overline{G} + (1-\rho)\mathrm{d}\overline{G} + (1-\rho)^2\mathrm{d}\overline{G}$$

$$+\cdots=\frac{\mathrm{d}\left(\frac{\mathrm{d}H}{P}\right)}{\rho} \tag{2.107}$$

$$\mathrm{d}r=\frac{(1-\rho)\mathrm{d}\overline{G}}{I'}+\frac{(1-\rho)^2\mathrm{d}\overline{G}}{I'}+\cdots=\frac{(1-\rho)\mathrm{d}\overline{G}}{\rho I'} \tag{2.108}$$

$$\begin{aligned}\mathrm{d}e=&\frac{\mathrm{d}\overline{G}}{1-c}\frac{M_Y}{\left(X_p-M_p\right)\frac{P*}{P}}+\frac{(1-\rho)\mathrm{d}\overline{G}}{1-c}\frac{M_Y}{\left(X_p-M_p\right)\frac{P*}{P}}\\&+\frac{(1-\rho)^2\mathrm{d}\overline{G}}{1-c}\frac{M_Y}{\left(X_p-M_p\right)\frac{P*}{P}}+\cdots=\frac{\mathrm{d}\overline{G}}{\rho(1-c)}\frac{M_Y}{\left(X_p-M_p\right)\frac{P*}{P}}\end{aligned} \tag{2.109}$$

It is clear that (2.106), (2.107), (2.108), and (2.109) tally with (2.102), (2.105), (2.103), and (2.104), respectively. The adjustment process described above brings out clearly the close interaction between the processes of generation of income saving, credit, and expenditure.

Monetary Policy

We shall examine here how expansionary monetary policy, which consists in a cut in the central bank's policy rate r_c, affects Y, r, and e. To derive its impact on Y, we take total differential of (2.98) treating all exogenous variables other than r_c as fixed, and then, solve for dY. This yields

$$\mathrm{d}Y=\frac{\rho'(-\mathrm{d}r_c)(1-c)Y}{(1-c)\rho}=\frac{\rho'(-\mathrm{d}r_c)Y}{\rho}>0 \tag{2.110}$$

Again, taking total differential of (2.5) treating all exogenous variables other than r_c as fixed, substituting the value of dY given by (2.110), and then, solving for dr, we get

$$\mathrm{d}r=\frac{(1-c)\rho'(-\mathrm{d}r_c)Y}{\rho I'}<0 \tag{2.111}$$

Again, taking total differential of (2.100), substituting for dY its value given by (2.110), and then, solving for de, we get

$$\mathrm{d}e=\frac{M_Y}{(X_p-M_p)\frac{P*}{P}}\frac{\rho'(-\mathrm{d}r_c)Y}{\rho}>0 \tag{2.112}$$

The adjustment process is very similar to the one of the fiscal policy delineated above. We sum up our findings in the flexible exchange rate and flexible interest rate regimes in the form of the following proposition:

Proposition 2.10 *The model shows that in the flexible exchange rate and flexible interest rate regimes, just as in all other cases considered here, processes of generation of income, saving, credit, money, and expenditure are inextricably linked together. Autonomous components of aggregate expenditure also cease to be deter-*

minants of GDP if they are financed with new loans from the commercial banks or any other financial intermediary or institution.

We shall now focus on the case where the interest rate is rigid instead of being flexible.

Interest Rate Rigidity in the Flexible Exchange Rate Regime

We shall now incorporate interest rate rigidity and focus on the case, where there is no credit rationing. Here, as in reality, banks set the interest rate on the basis of r_c. Substituting (2.28) into (2.98), we rewrite it as follows:

$$Y = cY + I(r(r_c), E) + \overline{G} + X\left(\frac{P^*e}{P}, Y^*\right) - M\left(\frac{P^*e}{P}, Y\right) \tag{2.113}$$

Here, as before, $\overline{G}$ is financed with borrowing from the central bank. When interest rate is rigid, banks may or may not ration credit. We first focus on the no credit rationing case. The financial sector is the same as in the earlier cases. Hence, the commercial banks in this case of no credit rationing may have to borrow from the central bank to meet the demand for new bank credit that comes forth at $r(r_c)$. Hence, (2.30) gives the credit market equilibrium in this case. Besides $\overline{G}$, b constitutes another source of high-powered money. Thus, the change in the stock of high-powered money is given in the present case by (2.31). The change in money supply, as before, is given by (2.79). The BOP equilibrium condition, as before, is given by (2.100). Our model now consists of five key Eqs. (2.113), (2.30), (2.31), (2.79), and (2.100) in five endogenous variables Y, b, $\frac{\mathrm{d}H}{P}$, and $\mathrm{d}m$. We solve the equations for the equilibrium values of the five endogenous variables as follows. Substituting (2.100) into (2.113), we rewrite it as

$$Y = cY + I(r(r_c), E) + \overline{G} \tag{2.114}$$

Solving (2.114), we get the equilibrium value of Y. Putting it into (2.30) and (2.79), we get the equilibrium values of b and $\mathrm{d}m$ (or S or $\mathrm{d}D$). Putting the equilibrium value of b in (2.31), we get the equilibrium value of $\frac{\mathrm{d}H}{P}$. Finally, putting the equilibrium value of Y in (2.100), we solve it for the equilibrium value of e. We shall now explain the working of the model carrying out a comparative static exercise.

An Improvement in the Expectations of the Investors for Exogenous Reasons

We shall examine here how an exogenous increase in E affects the endogenous variables. To derive the impact on Y, we shall take total differential of (2.114) treating all variables other than Y and e as fixed, and then, solve for $\mathrm{d}Y$. This yields the following:

$$\mathrm{d}Y = \frac{I_E \mathrm{d}E}{1 - c} \tag{2.115}$$

Taking total differential of (2.30), substituting (2.115) into it, and then, solving for $\mathrm{d}b$, we get

$$db = \rho I_E dE \tag{2.116}$$

Taking total differential of (2.31), substituting (2.116) into it, we get

$$d\left(\frac{dH}{P}\right) = \rho I_E dE \tag{2.117}$$

Again, taking total differential of (2.79) and substituting (2.115) into it, we get

$$dS = d(dD) = d(dm) = I_E dE \tag{2.118}$$

From (2.117) and (2.118), it is clear that the standard money multiplier formula holds in this case. Finally, taking total differential of (2.100), substituting (2.115) into it, and then, solving for *de*, we get

$$de = \frac{1}{(X_p - M_p)\frac{P^*}{P}}\left[M_Y\left(\frac{I_E dE}{1-c}\right)\right] \tag{2.119}$$

Let us now explain the adjustment process. Following the autonomous increase in investment demand by $I_E dE$, demand for new bank credit also rises by the same amount. The commercial banks borrow this amount from the central bank and meet their additional credit demand. Hence, b goes up by $I_E dE$. The increase in investment demand raises Y by $I_E dE$. The increase in Y raises aggregate demand for goods and services by $cI_E dE$ and demand for imported goods by $M_Y I_E dE$. People, therefore, try to sell $PM_Y I_E dE$ amount of domestic currency to secure $\frac{P}{e} M_Y I_E dE$ amount of foreign currency giving rise to that much of excess demand for foreign currency. There will, thus, take place an increase in e to change the excess demand for foreign currency by $-\frac{P}{e} M_Y I_E dE$ to zero. The amount of excess demand for foreign currency is given by $\frac{P}{e}\left[M\left(\frac{P^* e}{P}\right) - X\left(\frac{P^* e}{P}\right)\right]$. It changes by $-\frac{P}{e^2}(M - X) + \frac{P}{e}(M_p - X_p)\frac{P^*}{P} = \frac{P}{e}(M_p - X_p)\frac{P^*}{P} < 0$ (since $X - M = 0$ in equilibrium) per unit increase in e. Accordingly, e rises by $\frac{-M_Y I_E dE}{(M_p - X_P)\frac{P^*}{P}}$. Following a ceteris paribus increase in the exchange rate by *de*, net export rises by $(X_p - M_p)\frac{P^*}{P} de$. Hence, with the rise in e by $\frac{-M_Y I_E dE}{(M_p - X_P)\frac{P^*}{P}}$, net export increases by $(X_p - M_p)\frac{P^*}{P}\frac{-M_Y I_E dE}{(M_p - X_P)\frac{P^*}{P}} = M_Y I_E dE$. Thus, with the rise in Y by $I_E dE$, net export dropped by $M_Y I_E dE$. However, the increase in e that followed raised net export by the same amount. Hence, the increase in Y by $I_E dE$ creates an additional demand for domestic goods by $cI_E dE$. People also save in the first round $(1-c)I_E dE$, which they deposit with the banks. Out of this new deposit, banks hold as reserve $\rho(1-c)I_E dE$ and lend out the rest, $(1-\rho)(1-c)I_E dE$, to the central bank. This is the end of Round 1. In the first round, therefore, increases in Y, b, d, and e are given by $dY_1 = I_E dE, db_1 = [1 - (1-\rho)(1-c)]I^E dE$, $dS_1 = d(dD)_1 = d(dm)_1 = (1-c)I^E dE$, and $de_1 = \frac{-M_Y I_E dE}{(M_p - X_P)\frac{P^*}{P}}$. In the second round, as we have already pointed out, the increase in Y by $I^E dE$ in the first round raises aggregate demand for domestic goods given by $[C + I + G + X - M]$ by $cI^E \mathrm{d}E$, since the adjustment in *e* that takes place following the first round increase in *Y* restores net export to its initial equilibrium value. In the second round, therefore, *Y* goes up by $\mathrm{d}Y_2 = cI_E\mathrm{d}E$. This raises import demand and, thereby, lowers net export by $M_Y cI_E\mathrm{d}E$. Therefore, *e* in the second round rises to raise net export by $M_Y cI_E\mathrm{d}E$ so that net export gets restored to its initial equilibrium value. Hence, *e* in the second round rises by $\frac{-M_Y I_E \mathrm{d}E}{(M_p - X_P)\frac{P^*}{P}}$. Out of the additional income of $cI_E\mathrm{d}E$, people save $(1-c)cI_E\mathrm{d}E$ so that $\mathrm{d}S_2 = \mathrm{d}(\mathrm{d}D)_2 = \mathrm{d}(\mathrm{d}m)_2 = (1-c)cI_E\mathrm{d}E$. Out of this new deposit, banks hold as reserve $\rho(1-c)cI_E\mathrm{d}E$ and lend out the rest to the central bank so that $\mathrm{d}b_2 = -(1-\rho)(1-c)cI_E\mathrm{d}E$. The additional income of $cI_E\mathrm{d}E$ in the second round raises aggregate demand for domestic goods given by $[C + I + G + X - M]$ by $c^2 I_E\mathrm{d}E$ since the adjustment in *e* that takes place following the second round increase in *Y* restores net export to its initial equilibrium value. In the third round, therefore, *Y* goes up by $\mathrm{d}Y_3 = c^2 I_E\mathrm{d}E$. Accordingly, as before, $\mathrm{d}e_3 = \frac{-M_Y c^2 I_E \mathrm{d}E}{(M_p - X_P)\frac{P^*}{P}}$, $\mathrm{d}S_3 = \mathrm{d}(\mathrm{d}D)_3 = \mathrm{d}(\mathrm{d}m)_3 = (1-c)c^2 I_E\mathrm{d}E$, and $\mathrm{d}b_3 = -(1-\rho)(1-c)c^2 I_E\mathrm{d}E$. This process of expansion will continue until the additional demand for domestic goods and services that is created in each successive round eventually falls to zero. Thus, the total changes in *Y*, *S*, d*m*, and d*b* that take place at the end of the multiplier process is given by

$$\mathrm{d}Y = I_E\mathrm{d}E + cI_E\mathrm{d}E + c^2 I_E\mathrm{d}E + \cdots = \frac{I_E\mathrm{d}E}{1-c} \tag{2.120}$$

$$\begin{aligned}\mathrm{d}(\mathrm{d}m) = \mathrm{d}S = \mathrm{d}(\mathrm{d}D) &= (1-c)I_E\mathrm{d}E + (1-c)cI_E\mathrm{d}E + (1-c)c^2\mathrm{I}_E\mathrm{d}E \\ &+ \cdots = I_E\mathrm{d}E\end{aligned} \tag{2.121}$$

$$\begin{aligned}\mathrm{d}b = I_E\mathrm{d}E &- (1-\rho)(1-c)I_E\mathrm{d}E - (1-\rho)(1-c)cI_E\mathrm{d}E \\ &- (1-\rho)(1-c)c^2 I_E\mathrm{d}E - \cdots = I_E\mathrm{d}E - (1-\rho)I_E\mathrm{d}E = \rho I_E\mathrm{d}E\end{aligned} \tag{2.122}$$

It is clear that (2.120), (2.121), and (2.122) tally with (2.115), (2.118), and (2.116), respectively. Let us now figure out by how much the stock of high-powered money has gone up. Focus on the asset-liability balance sheet of the central bank. On the asset side, as it is clear from (2.122), domestic credit of the central bank rises by $\rho I_E\mathrm{d}E$. On the liabilities side, banks' reserve, as follows from (2.121), increases by $\rho I_E\mathrm{d}E$. Thus, the stock of high-powered money in the economy goes up by $\rho I_E\mathrm{d}E$. Comparing it to (2.121), we find that we get the standard money multiplier formula. The above discussion yields the following proposition:

Proposition 2.11 *In the flexible exchange rate regime also, animal spirits of the investors emerge as a major determinant of GDP when interest rate, as happens normally in reality, is rigid. In the present case of flexible exchange rate and rigid interest rate regime also, our model shows that processes of generation of income, saving, money, credit, and expenditure are inextricable linked together and the standard money multiplier formulae hold.*

2.9 Conclusion: Evaluation of the Model

This simple model redresses all the problems mentioned in the introduction regarding the deficiencies of the characterization of the financial sector in the IS-LM. The model brings out clearly the interrelationships that exist among the processes that generate income, saving, new credit, new money, and expenditure. It shows that the multiplier process that occurs in the real sector and the money or credit multiplier process that occurs in the financial sector take place simultaneously reinforcing each other. It brings to the fore the process through which the financial institutions mobilize savings and use them to extend credit.

This model also shows that equilibrium in the goods market and the credit market implies equality of demand for money and supply of money. Hence, there is no need to consider the money market.

Unlike the IS-LM model, which cannot handle the situation where interest rates are rigid, this model can handle the situation where the interest rates are flexible as well as the one where interest rates are fixed. We have shown that, when interest rates are flexible, whether the autonomous component of aggregate expenditure will be a determinant of GDP or not depends crucially on how it is financed. It will be a determinant of GDP if the spenders finance it by drawing down their financial assets. It will cease to be a determinant of GDP if it is financed with new credit. However, when interest rates are rigid, as is usually the case in reality, autonomous spending, and therefore, animal spirits of investors emerge as major determinants of GDP.

Here, we have kept P unchanged. We can easily drop this assumption and explicitly consider the process that determines P. We shall do this later.

References

Bernanke, B. S. (1983). Non-monetary effects of the financial crisis in the propagation of the great depression. *American Economic Review, 73*(3), 257–276.

Bernanke, B. S., & Blinder, A. S. (1988). Credit, money and aggregate demand. *The American Economic Review, 78*(2), 435–439.

Bernanke, B. S., Gertler, M., & Gilchrist, S. (1996). The financial accelerator and the flight to quality. *The Review of Economics and Statistics, 78*(1), 1–15.

Bernanke, B. S., Gertler, M., & Gilchrist, S. (1999). The financial accelerator in a quantitative business cycle framework, Chapter 21. In *Handbook of macroeconomics* (Vol. 1, Part C, pp. 1341–1393).

Blanchard, O. (1981). Output, the stock market and interest rates. *The American Economic Review, 71*(1), 132–143.

Blinder, A. S. (1987). Credit rationing and effective supply failures. *The Economic Journal, 97*(386), 327–352.

Rakshit, M. (1993). Money, credit and monetary policy. In T. Majumdar (Ed.), *Nature, man and the environment*. Delhi: Oxford University Press.

Romer, D. (2000). Keynesian macroeconomics without the LM curve. *Journal of Economic Perspectives, 14*(2), 149–169. Spring.

Romer, D. (2013). *Short-run fluctuations*. Berkeley (mimeo): University of California.

Stiglitz, J. E., & Weiss, A. (1981). Credit rationing in markets with imperfect information. *The American Economic Review, 71*(3), 393–410.

Tobin, J. (1958). Liquidity preference as behaviour towards risk. *The Review of Economic Studies, 25*(2), 65–86.

Chapter 3
An Alternative to the IS-LM Model: Extension to the Case of Perfect Capital Mobility

Abstract In this chapter, we extend the model developed in the previous chapter to consider cross-border capital flows. Here, however, we shall only focus on the case of perfect capital mobility. The model will seek to capture the behavior of a small open economy in both the fixed and flexible exchange rate regimes under conditions of perfect capital mobility.

3.1 Introduction

In this chapter, we shall extend the model developed in Chap. 2 to incorporate perfect capital mobility. We incorporate capital mobility in the following way for simplicity. As before, here also domestic households hold all their savings in the form of bank deposits with the domestic commercial banks. So, here domestic households do not allocate their savings between deposits of domestic banks and those of foreign banks. Similarly, domestic government seeks loans only from the domestic central bank. Domestic firms, however, can secure loans from domestic commercial banks as well as from the world credit market at the interest rate prevailing in the world credit market. Domestic commercial banks can lend not only to domestic firms but also in the world credit market at interest rates prevailing in the world credit market. Both the domestic commercial banks and domestic firms are assumed to be risk-neutral. Since the domestic economy is assumed to be small, the world interest rate in foreign currency is given to the domestic economic agents. As there is perfect capital mobility, borrowing from the domestic commercial banks and the world market is equivalent to domestic borrowers if the interest rates in domestic currency on the two types of loans are equal. Again, lending to domestic firms and to the world market is equivalent to the domestic commercial banks if the interest rates in domestic currency on the two types of loans are equal. For simplicity, we have ignored for the present households' allocation of savings between domestic and foreign assets. We are now in a position to develop a model to determine domestic NDP, interest rate, and exchange rate. We first focus on the flexible exchange rate regime, where the central bank does not intervene in the foreign exchange market to keep the exchange rate under control.

C. Ghosh and A. N. Ghosh, *Keynesian Macroeconomics Beyond the IS-LM Model*, https://doi.org/10.1007/978-981-13-7888-1_3

3.2 The Model (The Flexible Exchange Rate Regime)

The world interest rate is denoted by r^*. Domestic firms can borrow as much as they want from the world credit market at r^*. Domestic commercial banks can also lend as much as they want at r^*. In keeping with the assumption of the Mundell–Fleming model (Fleming 1962; Mundell 1963), we assume that the expected rate of depreciation of domestic currency is zero. Hence, to domestic firms and domestic commercial banks, interest rate on borrowing from and lending to the world credit market in domestic currency is also r^* (see Appendix 1). Interest rate in domestic currency on loans from domestic commercial banks and interest rate in domestic currency on deposits of domestic commercial banks is r. Here, for simplicity, we do not distinguish between deposit rate and lending rate of domestic commercial banks. Thus, in equilibrium, we shall have

$$r = r^* \tag{3.1}$$

If r exceeds r^*, domestic firms will want to borrow only from the world credit market, while domestic commercial banks will want to lend only to domestic firms bringing about an excess supply in the domestic bank credit market. Hence, r will go on falling until it becomes equal to r^*. Similarly, if r is less than r^*, domestic firms will want to borrow only from the domestic commercial banks, but the latter will want to lend only in the world market. Thus, there will emerge an excess demand for domestic bank credit. It will be corrected only when r rises and becomes equal to r^*.

The goods market equilibrium condition, as before, is given by

$$Y = cY + I(r) + \overline{G} + X\left(\frac{P^*e}{P}; Y^*\right) - M\left(\frac{P^*e}{P}, Y\right) \tag{3.2}$$

Substituting (3.1) into (3.2), we rewrite it as

$$Y = cY + I(r^*) + \overline{G} + X\left(\frac{P^*e}{P}; Y^*\right) - M\left(\frac{P^*e}{P}; Y\right) \tag{3.3}$$

We assume for simplicity that the whole of $\overline{G}$ is financed with new loans from the central bank. We also assume that, this is the only way high-powered money is created in the economy. Accordingly, the increase in the stock of high-powered money in real terms in the period under consideration, denoted by $\frac{\mathrm{d}H}{P}$, is given by

$$\frac{\mathrm{d}H}{P} = \overline{G} \tag{3.4}$$

The planned supply of new loans by the commercial banks is given by

$$l = \left(1 - \rho\left(r_{c_+}\right)\right)(1 - c)Y \tag{3.5}$$

where l denotes the supply of new loans by the commercial banks, and ρ denotes reserve–deposit ratio, which we regard as an increasing function of r_c. It denotes the policy rate of the central bank, i.e., the interest rate at which the central bank lends to the commercial banks. We get (3.5) under the assumption that the domestic households hold all their saving in the form of domestic bank deposits and foreigners do not invest their savings in domestic banks so that the only source of deposits of the domestic banks is the domestic households. We make this assumption for the present for simplicity.

The entire investment is financed with loans. However, domestic investors can borrow from foreigners and domestic banks can also lend to foreigners. Hence, the domestic credit market is in equilibrium when

$$(1 - \rho(r_c))(1 - c)Y = I(r) - K \tag{3.6}$$

where K denotes net inflow of capital from abroad. To explain (3.6), we first substitute (3.1) into it to get

$$(1 - \rho(r_c))(1 - c)Y = I(r^*) - K \tag{3.7}$$

Equation (3.7) may be explained as follows. If $I(r^*)$ exceeds the supply of loans given by the LHS of (3.7), the firms will meet their excess demand for loans by securing loans from the world credit market. In this case, there will take place an inflow of capital to the domestic economy by the amount $I(r^*) - (1 - \rho)(1 - c)Y$ and, therefore, $K = I(r^*) - (1 - \rho)(1 - c)Y > 0$. Again, if $(1 - \rho)(1 - c)Y > I(r^*)$, there is excess supply of loans and the banks will lend this excess supply of loans to the world market. There will thus take place outflow of capital and the value of K will be given by $K = I(r^*) - (1 - \rho)(1 - c)Y < 0$.

Finally, the balance of payments (BOP) will be in equilibrium, when

$$X\left(\frac{P^*e}{P}; Y^*\right) - M\left(\frac{P^*e}{P}, Y\right) + K = 0 \tag{3.8}$$

The specification of our model is complete. It consists of three key Eqs. (3.3), (3.7), and (3.8) in three unknowns Y, e, and K. We can solve the three equations for their equilibrium values as follows:

Substituting (3.7) and (3.8) into (3.3), we rewrite it as

$$Y = cY + (1 - \rho(r_c))(1 - c)Y + \overline{G} \tag{3.9}$$

We can solve (3.9) for the equilibrium value of Y. Putting this equilibrium value of Y in (3.7), we get the equilibrium value of K. Putting these equilibrium values of Y and K in (3.8), we get the equilibrium value of e.

We shall now explain the working of the model carrying out a few comparative static exercises.

3.2.1 *Fiscal Policy: An Increase in Government Consumption Financed with Borrowing from the Central Bank*

Let us examine the impact of an increase in $\overline{G}$ financed by borrowing from the central bank. Taking total differential of (3.9) treating all exogenous variables other than $\overline{G}$ as fixed and, then, solving for dY, we get

$$\mathrm{d}Y = \frac{\mathrm{d}\overline{G}}{\rho}\left(\frac{1}{1-c}\right) = \frac{\mathrm{d}\left(\frac{\mathrm{d}H}{P}\right)}{\rho}\left(\frac{1}{1-c}\right) \quad \text{(see 3.4)} \tag{3.10}$$

Here, as we have already mentioned, the only source of deposits of the domestic banks is domestic saving, which is made only by the domestic households. Thus,

$$S = \mathrm{d}(\mathrm{d}D) = \mathrm{d}(\mathrm{d}m) = (1-c)\mathrm{d}Y = \frac{\mathrm{d}\left(\frac{\mathrm{d}H}{P}\right)}{\rho} \tag{3.11}$$

From (3.11), it is clear that we get the standard money multiplier formula in this case also.

Again, taking total differential of (3.7) treating all exogenous variables as fixed, substituting for dY its value given by (3.11) and, then, solving for dK, we get

$$\mathrm{d}K = -(1-\rho(r_c))\frac{\mathrm{d}\overline{G}}{\rho} = -(1-\rho(r_c))\frac{\mathrm{d}\left(\frac{\mathrm{d}H}{P}\right)}{\rho} \tag{3.12}$$

Again, taking total differential of (3.8), substituting for dY and dK their values given by (3.10) and (3.12), respectively, and solving for de, we get

$$\mathrm{d}e = \left[\frac{M_Y + (1-c)(1-\rho)}{(X_p - M_p)\frac{P^*}{P}}\right]\frac{\mathrm{d}\overline{G}}{\rho}\left(\frac{1}{1-c}\right) = \left[\frac{M_Y + (1-c)(1-\rho)}{(X_p - M_p)\frac{P^*}{P}}\right]\frac{\mathrm{d}\left(\frac{\mathrm{d}H}{P}\right)}{\rho}\left(\frac{1}{1-c}\right) \tag{3.13}$$

Adjustment Process

The adjustment process may be explained as follows. The government borrows d$\overline{G}$ from the central bank and spends it on purchasing goods and services. The multiplier process operates and Y goes up by $\frac{\mathrm{d}\overline{G}}{1-c}$. Note that, all through the multiplier process, e rises to keep net export, which declines on account of the increase in Y, unchanged so that the BOP remains in equilibrium. Out of this additional income of $\frac{\mathrm{d}\overline{G}}{1-c}$, people save $(1-c)\frac{\mathrm{d}\overline{G}}{1-c} = \mathrm{d}\overline{G}$. They will put it in domestic banks (henceforth referred to as banks only) as deposit. Clearly, the banks will not want to hold these deposits in the form of reserve. They will plan to lend out $(1-\rho)\mathrm{d}\overline{G}$ giving rise to excess supply of loans at the interest rate r^*. The banks will, therefore, plan to lend it out at r^* in the world credit market. For this, they will try to sell $P(1-\rho)\mathrm{d}\overline{G}$ amount of domestic currency for foreign currency giving rise to excess demand for foreign currency of $\frac{P}{e}(1-\rho)\mathrm{d}\overline{G}$ in the foreign currency market at the prevailing exchange rate. The net supply of foreign currency is given by $\left[X\left(\frac{P^*e}{P}, Y^*\right) - M\left(\frac{P^*e}{P}, Y\right) + K\right]\frac{P}{e}$. The exchange rate will rise to equilibrate the foreign currency market. Per unit increase in e, net supply of foreign currency increases by $\left\{\left(X_p - M_p\right)\frac{P^*}{P}\right\}\frac{P}{e}$, since $(X - M) = 0$. Therefore, to raise net supply of foreign currency by $\frac{P}{e}(1-\rho)\mathrm{d}\overline{G}$, and, thereby, equilibrate the foreign currency market, e has to increase by $\frac{\frac{P}{e}(1-\rho)\mathrm{d}\overline{G}}{\left\{(X_p-M_p)\frac{P^*}{P}\right\}\frac{P}{e}} = \frac{(1-\rho)\mathrm{d}\overline{G}}{\left\{(X_p-M_p)\frac{P^*}{P}\right\}}$. This will raise net export by $(1-\rho)\mathrm{d}\overline{G}$, since per unit increase in e, net export increases by $\left\{\left(X_p - M_p\right)\frac{P^*}{P}\right\}$. Banks are, therefore, able to invest $(1-\rho)\mathrm{d}\overline{G}$ in foreign financial assets. Hence, K falls by $-(1-\rho)\mathrm{d}\overline{G}$. Note that, initially, as Y increased by $\frac{\mathrm{d}\overline{G}}{1-c}$ raising import by $M_Y \cdot \frac{\mathrm{d}\overline{G}}{1-c}$, e went up by $\frac{M_Y}{\left\{(X_p-M_p)\frac{P^*}{P}\right\}} \cdot \left(\frac{\mathrm{d}\overline{G}}{1-c}\right)$ to keep BOP in equilibrium. Thus, in the first round, the increases in Y, S, and $\mathrm{d}D$, the fall in K and the rise in e are given, respectively, by $\mathrm{d}Y_1 = \frac{\mathrm{d}\overline{G}}{1-c} = \frac{\mathrm{d}\left(\frac{\mathrm{d}H}{P}\right)}{1-c}$, $\mathrm{d}S_1 = \mathrm{d}(\mathrm{d}D)_1 = \mathrm{d}(\mathrm{d}m)_1 = \mathrm{d}\overline{G}$, and $\mathrm{d}e_1 = \frac{M_Y\left(\frac{\mathrm{d}\overline{G}}{1-c}\right)+(1-\rho)\mathrm{d}\overline{G}}{\left\{(X_p-M_p)\frac{P^*}{P}\right\}}$.

The increase in net export by $(1-\rho)\mathrm{d}\overline{G}$ in the first round will again create an excess demand for domestic goods of $(1-\rho)\mathrm{d}\overline{G}$ setting off another round of multiplier process. Y in this second round will increase by $\mathrm{d}Y_2 = \frac{(1-\rho)\mathrm{d}\overline{G}}{1-c}$. All through this multiplier process e will rise to keep net export at its initial equilibrium level, and at the end of the process, total increase in e will be $\frac{M_Y \mathrm{d}Y_2}{\left\{(X_p-M_p)\frac{P^*}{P}\right\}}$ Out of this additional income of $\mathrm{d}Y_2 = \frac{(1-\rho)\mathrm{d}\overline{G}}{1-c}$, people will save and deposit with the banks $\mathrm{d}S_2 = \mathrm{d}(\mathrm{d}D)_2 = \mathrm{d}(\mathrm{d}m)_2 = (1-\rho)\mathrm{d}\overline{G}$. Since domestic demand for bank credit at r^* is already exhausted, out of these new deposits, banks will try to lend out $(1-\rho)^2\mathrm{d}\overline{G}$ to the foreigners raising e and net export by $\frac{(1-\rho)^2\mathrm{d}\overline{G}}{\left\{(X_p-M_p)\frac{P^*}{P}\right\}}$ and $(1-\rho)^2\mathrm{d}\overline{G}$, respectively. Thus, the banks will be able to lend out to foreigners $(1-\rho)^2\mathrm{d}\overline{G}$. Hence, K in the second round will go down by $\mathrm{d}K_2 = -(1-\rho)^2\mathrm{d}\overline{G}$. The total increase in e in the second round is $\mathrm{d}e_2 = \frac{M_Y\mathrm{d}Y_2+(1-\rho)^2\mathrm{d}\overline{G}}{\left\{(X_p-M_p)\frac{P^*}{P}\right\}}$.

The increase in net export by $(1-\rho)^2\mathrm{d}\overline{G}$ in the second round will again raise Y by $\mathrm{d}Y_3 = \frac{(1-\rho)^2\mathrm{d}\overline{G}}{1-c}$. This process will continue until the additional saving created in each round eventually falls to zero. Thus, the total changes in Y, S, $\mathrm{d}D$, K, and e are given, respectively, by

$$\mathrm{d}Y = \frac{\mathrm{d}\overline{G}}{1-c} + (1-\rho)\frac{\mathrm{d}\overline{G}}{1-c} + (1-\rho)^2\frac{\mathrm{d}\overline{G}}{1-c} + \cdots = \frac{\mathrm{d}\overline{G}}{\rho(1-c)} \tag{3.14}$$

$$\mathrm{d}S = \mathrm{d}(\mathrm{d}D) = \mathrm{d}(\mathrm{d}m) = \mathrm{d}\overline{G} + (1-\rho)\mathrm{d}\overline{G} + (1-\rho)^2\mathrm{d}\overline{G} + \cdots = \frac{\mathrm{d}\overline{G}}{\rho} = \frac{\mathrm{d}\left(\frac{\mathrm{d}H}{P}\right)}{\rho} \tag{3.15}$$

$$\mathrm{d}K = -(1-\rho)\mathrm{d}\overline{G} - (1-\rho)^2\mathrm{d}\overline{G} - \cdots = -\frac{(1-\rho)\mathrm{d}\overline{G}}{\rho} \tag{3.16}$$

$$\mathrm{d}e = \frac{M_Y \mathrm{d}Y_1 + (1-\rho)\mathrm{d}\overline{G}}{\left\{(X_p - M_p)\frac{P*}{P}\right\}} \cdot + \frac{M_Y \mathrm{d}Y_2 + (1-\rho)^2 \mathrm{d}\overline{G}}{\left\{(X_p - M_p)\frac{P*}{P}\right\}} + \cdots$$
$$= \frac{M_Y \mathrm{d}Y + \frac{(1-\rho)\mathrm{d}G}{\rho}}{\left\{(X_p - M_p)\frac{P*}{P}\right\}} = \frac{M_Y \frac{\mathrm{d}G}{\rho(1-c)} + \frac{(1-\rho)\mathrm{d}G}{\rho}}{\left\{(X_p - M_p)\frac{P*}{P}\right\}} \tag{3.17}$$

We find that (3.14), (3.15), (3.16), and (3.17) tally with (3.10), (3.11), (3.12), and (3.13), respectively. This explains the working of the model. This adjustment process shows very clearly how processes of generation of income, saving, credit, and expenditure are inextricably interrelated. The model is completely transparent as regards how the real sector and financial sector interact with one another.

3.2.2 *Monetary Policy*

We shall examine here the effect of an expansionary monetary policy, which consists in a cut in the central bank's policy rate r_c. We shall derive the results mathematically. Taking total differential of (3.9) treating all exogenous variables other than r_c as fixed, and, then solving for dY, we get

$$\mathrm{d}Y = \frac{\rho'(-\mathrm{d}r_c)Y}{\rho} > 0 \tag{3.18}$$

From (3.9), we get

$$Y = \frac{\overline{G}}{\rho(1-c)} = \frac{\frac{\mathrm{d}H}{P}}{\rho(1-c)} \tag{3.19}$$

Using (3.19), we get

$$\mathrm{d}S = \mathrm{d}(\mathrm{d}D) = \mathrm{d}(\mathrm{d}m) = (1-c)\frac{\rho'(-\mathrm{d}r_c)Y}{\rho} = \frac{\rho'(-\mathrm{d}r_c)\frac{\overline{G}}{\rho}}{\rho} = \frac{\rho'(-\mathrm{d}r_c)\frac{\left(\frac{\mathrm{d}H}{P}\right)}{\rho}}{\rho} \tag{3.20}$$

Again, taking total differential of (3.7) treating all exogenous variables other than r_c as fixed, we get

$$\mathrm{d}K = -\frac{\rho'(-\mathrm{d}r_c)(1-c)Y}{\rho} < 0 \tag{3.21}$$

Finally, taking total differential of (3.8) treating all exogenous variables as fixed, substituting (3.18) and (3.21) into it, and, then, solving for de, we get

$$de = \left(\frac{1}{[X_p - M_p]\frac{P*}{P}}\right)\left[\frac{M_Y \rho'(-\mathrm{d}r_c)Y}{\rho} + \frac{\rho'(-\mathrm{d}r_c)(1-c)Y}{\rho}\right] > 0 \tag{3.22}$$

The adjustment process of this case is very similar to that of the previous case of fiscal policy. We can summarize the findings of our above discussion in the form of the following proposition:

Proposition 3.1 *In the case of a small open economy with perfect capital mobility and flexible exchange rate also, as our model shows, the processes of generation of income, saving, credit, money, and expenditure are inextricably linked with one another. Since in this case, domestic interest rate has to be perfectly flexible, autonomous spending, when it is financed with new credit, ceases to be a determinant of GDP. Both the fiscal policy and monetary policy are effective here.*

3.3 Perfect Capital Mobility with Fixed Exchange Rate

Let us now focus on the case of perfect capital mobility, with a fixed exchange rate. In the fixed exchange rate regime, the central bank intervenes in the foreign exchange market to keep the exchange rate fixed at a target rate, say, $\bar{e}$. If there emerges an excess supply of foreign currency at $\bar{e}$, the central bank has to buy up this excess supply of foreign currency at $\bar{e}$ with domestic currency so that e does not fall from $\bar{e}$. This clearly brings about an increase in the supply of high-powered money. Similarly, if there emerges an excess demand for foreign currency at $\bar{e}$, the central bank has to meet this excess demand for foreign currency by selling foreign currency from its stock in exchange for domestic currency so that e does not rise above $\bar{e}$. In this case, obviously, the stock of high-powered money goes down. The amount of excess supply of foreign currency at $\bar{e}$ is given by $\left[X\left(\frac{P^*\bar{e}}{P}; Y^*\right) - M\left(\frac{P^*\bar{e}}{P}, Y\right) + K\right]\frac{P}{\bar{e}}$, which may be positive or negative. When it is negative, it represents excess demand. The change in the stock of high-powered money is, therefore, given by

$$\mathrm{d}H = \frac{P}{\bar{e}}\left[X\left(\frac{P^*\bar{e}}{P}; Y^*\right) - M\left(\frac{P^*\bar{e}}{P}, Y\right) + K\right]\cdot \bar{e} + P\overline{G} \tag{3.23}$$

We write (3.23) as

$$\frac{\mathrm{d}H}{P} = \left[X\left(\frac{P^*\bar{e}}{P}; Y^*\right) - M\left(\frac{P^*\bar{e}}{P}, Y\right) + K\right] + \overline{G} \tag{3.24}$$

In the present regime, therefore, besides r being equal to r^* because of perfect capital mobility, e is also equal to $\bar{e}$ on account of the fixed exchange rate policy of the central bank.

In the flexible exchange rate case considered earlier, $\frac{dH}{P} = \overline{G}$. In the present case, however, $\frac{dH}{P}$ is given by (3.24). The credit market equilibrium condition continues to be given by (3.7).

Again, substituting $\bar{e}$ into (3.3), we write the goods market equilibrium condition for the present regime as

$$Y = C(Y) + I(r^*) + \overline{G} + X\left(\frac{P^*\bar{e}}{P}; Y^*\right) - M\left(\frac{P^*\bar{e}}{P}, Y\right) \tag{3.25}$$

As before, people hold their savings as bank deposits so that the increase in money supply or bank deposits is given by

$$S = dD = dm = (1 - c)Y \tag{3.26}$$

The specification of our model is now complete. It consists of four key Eqs. (3.24), (3.7), (3.25), and (3.26) in four unknowns Y, K, dm (or dD or S), and $\frac{dH}{P}$. We can, therefore, solve these four equations for the equilibrium values of the four endogenous variables. We solve (3.25) for the equilibrium value of Y. Putting this equilibrium value of Y in (3.7) and (3.26), we can solve them for the equilibrium values of K and dm, respectively. Finally, putting these equilibrium values of Y and K in (3.24), we get the value of $\frac{dH}{P}$. We shall now explain the working of the model carrying out a few comparative static exercises.

3.3.1 *Fiscal Policy: An Increase in Government Expenditure Financed by Borrowing from the Central Bank*

Here, we shall examine how an increase in $\overline{G}$ by d$\overline{G}$ financed by borrowing from the central bank affects Y, $\frac{dH}{P}$, dm, and K. We derive the results mathematically below:

Mathematical Derivation of the Results

We shall now derive the results mathematically. Taking total differential of (3.25) treating all exogenous variables other than $\overline{G}$ as fixed, and, then, solving for dY, we get

$$dY = \frac{d\overline{G}}{1 - (c - M_Y)} \tag{3.27}$$

Taking total differential of (3.7) treating all exogenous variables as fixed, substituting for dY its value given by (3.27), and then solving for dK, we get

$$dK = -(1 - \rho)\frac{(1 - c)}{1 - (c - M_Y)}d\overline{G} \tag{3.28}$$

Finally, taking total differential of (3.24), substituting (3.26) and (3.27) into it, and then solving for $\mathrm{d}\left(\frac{\mathrm{d}H}{P}\right)$, we get

$$\begin{aligned}\mathrm{d}\left(\frac{\mathrm{d}H}{P}\right) &= \mathrm{d}\overline{G} - [M_Y + (1-\rho)(1-c)]\frac{\mathrm{d}\overline{G}}{1-(c-M_Y)} \\ &= \rho(1-c)\frac{\mathrm{d}\overline{G}}{1-(c-M_Y)} \qquad (3.29)\end{aligned}$$

Again, taking total differential of (3.26), substituting (3.27) into it, and then solving, we get

$$\mathrm{d}S = \mathrm{d}(\mathrm{d}D) = \mathrm{d}(\mathrm{d}m) = (1-c)\frac{\mathrm{d}\overline{G}}{1-(c-M_Y)} \qquad (3.30)$$

From (3.29) and (3.30), it is clear that the standard money multiplier formula holds good.

We shall now explain how these changes come about.

The Adjustment Process

Following an increase in $\overline{G}$ by $\mathrm{d}\overline{G}$ financed by borrowing from the central bank, the multiplier process begins to work and Y goes up by $\frac{\mathrm{d}\overline{G}}{1-(c-M_Y)}$. This raises import demand by $M_Y \cdot \left(\frac{\mathrm{d}\overline{G}}{1-(c-M_Y)}\right)$. Out of their additional income of $\frac{\mathrm{d}\overline{G}}{1-(c-M_Y)}$, people try to sell $M_Y \cdot \left(\frac{\mathrm{d}\overline{G}}{1-(c-M_Y)}\right)P$ amount of domestic currency to secure foreign currency. The central bank has to buy this domestic currency in exchange for $M_Y \cdot \left(\frac{\mathrm{d}\overline{G}}{1-(c-M_Y)}\right)\frac{P}{\bar{e}}$ amount of foreign currency to keep e at $\bar{e}$. Hence, $\left(\frac{\mathrm{d}H}{P}\right)$ will go down by $M_Y\left(\frac{\mathrm{d}\overline{G}}{1-(c-M_Y)}\right)$. Out of their additional income, people will save $(1-c)\frac{\mathrm{d}\overline{G}}{1-(c-M_Y)}$ and deposit it with the commercial banks so that bank deposits and money supply go up by the same amount. The banks will, therefore, plan to supply an additional loan of $(1-\rho)(1-c)\frac{\mathrm{d}\overline{G}}{1-(c-M_Y)}$. Since domestic demand for bank credit is already exhausted, they will plan to invest this in foreign assets. They will, therefore, try to sell $P(1-\rho)(1-c)\frac{\mathrm{d}\overline{G}}{1-(c-M_Y)}$ amount of domestic currency for foreign currency. The central bank will have to buy up this much of domestic currency in exchange for $\frac{P}{e}(1-\rho)(1-c)\frac{\mathrm{d}\overline{G}}{1-(c-M_Y)}$ amount of foreign currency to keep e at $\bar{e}$. Thus, $\left(\frac{\mathrm{d}H}{P}\right)$ and K will fall by $(1-\rho)(1-c)\frac{\mathrm{d}\overline{G}}{1-(c-M_Y)}$. The adjustment process will end here. Thus, at the end of the adjustment process we find that

$$\mathrm{d}Y = \frac{\mathrm{d}\overline{G}}{1-(c-M_Y)} \qquad (3.31)$$

$$\mathrm{d}K = -(1-\rho)(1-c)\frac{\mathrm{d}G}{1-(c-M_Y)} \qquad (3.32)$$

$$dS = d(dD) = d(dm) = (1-c)\frac{d\overline{G}}{1-(c-M_Y)} \tag{3.33}$$

and

$$d\left(\frac{dH}{P}\right) = d\overline{G} - (M_Y + (1-\rho)(1-c))\left(\frac{d\overline{G}}{1-(c-M_Y)}\right) \tag{3.34}$$

Clearly, (3.31), (3.32), (3.33), and (3.34) tally with (3.27), (3.28), (3.30), and (3.29), respectively.

3.3.2 Monetary Policy

We shall examine here how expansionary monetary policy, which consists in a cut in the central bank's policy rate r_c, affects the endogenous variables of the model. We shall derive the results mathematically. Taking total differential of (3.25) treating all exogenous variables other than r_c as fixed, we get

$$dY = 0 \tag{3.35}$$

Again, taking total differential of (3.7) treating all exogenous variables other than r_c as fixed, substituting (3.35) into it, and then solving for dK, we get

$$dK = -\rho'(-dr_c)(1-c)Y \tag{3.36}$$

Again, taking total differential of (3.24) treating all exogenous variables other than r_c as fixed, substituting (3.35) and (3.36) into it, and then solving for $d\left(\frac{dH}{P}\right)$, we get

$$d\left(\frac{dH}{P}\right) = -\rho'(-dr_c)(1-c)Y \tag{3.37}$$

From (3.35), it is clear that expansionary monetary policy does not produce any impact on output and employment. The result is quite easy to explain. Following a cut in r_c, commercial banks will be able to extend $\rho'(-dr_c)(1-c)Y$ amount of more loans. Since at $r = r^*$, domestic demand for bank credit is already exhausted, they will lend it out to foreigners. To do that, they will sell off $\left[P\rho'(-dr_c)(1-c)Y\right]$ amount of domestic currency to the central bank to secure $\frac{P}{e}\rho'(-dr_c)(1-c)Y$ amount of foreign currency. Therefore, K and $\left(\frac{dH}{P}\right)$ will fall by $\rho'(-dr_c)(1-c)Y$. Since the additional loan is extended to foreigners, it will produce no impact on Y. Since in this case domestic interest rate is determined by the world interest rate, the monetary policy of reducing the policy rate of the central bank fails to produce any impact on

r and, therefore, leaves Y unaffected. We summarize our discussion in the form of the following proposition.

Proposition 3.2 *In the case of a small open economy with fixed exchange rate and perfect capital mobility, our model shows clearly how the processes of generation of income, saving, credit, money, and expenditure are inextricably linked together. It also shows that, while fiscal policy is effective here, monetary policy of a rate cut is completely ineffective.*

3.4 Conclusion

Here, we have extended the model developed in the previous chapter to incorporate cross-border capital flows. However, we have focused only on the situation of perfect capital mobility. The present model is, therefore, an alternative to the Mundell–Fleming model. We consider this model better than the Mundell–Fleming model as it explicitly considers the operations of the financial intermediaries and financing of all the different kinds of expenditure. It brings out clearly the linkages binding intimately the processes of generation of income, saving, credit, money, and expenditure.

Appendix 1[1]

Comparison Between r *and r**

One cannot compare r and r^*, since the former is given in terms of domestic currency, while the latter is specified in foreign currency. Let us explain it with an example. Suppose domestic interest rate is 20%. It implies that $r = (1/5)$, i.e., if you invest, assuming the domestic country to be India, in domestic bank deposits Re. 1, you will get after one year (1/5)th of a rupee as interest and you can buy Indian bank deposits only with Indian rupee. Similarly, if the foreign country is the USA, say, you can buy US bank deposits only with US dollar and if $r^* = (1/20)$, \$1 worth of US bank deposit will fetch \$1.05 after 1 year in principal and interest. Hence, to make a comparison between rate of return on domestic bank deposits and foreign bank deposits, we have to derive rate of return on foreign bank deposits in terms of domestic currency for domestic wealth holders. Then, it will be comparable to r. (Alternatively, we can derive the rate of return on domestic bank deposits in terms of foreign currency and compare it to r^*. This is of interest to the foreign wealth holders.)

[1]This appendix draws from portions of Chap. 4 of the authors' previously published book 'Indian Economy: A Macro-theoretic Analysis' published by PHI Learning Private Limited in 2016 (ISBN-978-81-203-5244-5).

We shall first derive the rate of return on foreign bank deposits in terms of domestic currency. For this purpose, we consider a domestic agent who seeks to keep Rs. A in foreign bank deposit. For that, he has to first purchase foreign currency. He spends Rs. A to buy Rs. (A/e_0) amount of foreign currency, where e_0 is the exchange rate of the current period, which we shall refer to as period 0. To simplify notations, we shall denote Rs. A by only A. In the next period, period 1, (A/e_0) amount of foreign currency will yield $(A/e_0)(1+r^*)$ amount of foreign currency in principal and interest, and this equals $(A/e_0)(1+r^*)e_1$ in domestic currency, since e_1 denotes the exchange rate in period 1. Thus, the additional income in domestic currency the investor makes in period 1 from an investment of A in period 0 is $(A/e_0)(1+r^*)e_1 - A$. Therefore, the additional income in domestic currency per unit of domestic currency invested in the foreign bank deposits, i.e., the return on the foreign bank deposits in domestic currency is $[(A/e_0)(1+r^*)e_1 - A]/A = r^*\left(\frac{e_1}{e_0}\right) + \left(\frac{e_1}{e_0} - 1\right) = r^*\left(\frac{e_1}{e_0}\right) + \varepsilon$, where $\varepsilon \equiv \frac{e_1 - e_0}{e_0}$. Note that, while r and r^* are not comparable, r and $r^*\left(\frac{e_1}{e_0}\right) + \varepsilon$ are comparable, since they give, respectively, additional incomes earned in period 1 in domestic currency per unit of domestic currency invested in domestic and foreign bank deposits, respectively, in period 0. ε gives the proportional rate of increase in the exchange rate. We commonly refer to it as the rate of appreciation of foreign currency or the rate of depreciation of domestic currency.

We now consider the case of foreign wealth holders and derive the rates of return on the two kinds of bank deposits in foreign currency. The rate of return on foreign bank deposits in foreign currency is r^*. Let us now derive the rate of return on domestic bank deposits in foreign currency. Suppose a foreign wealth holder in period 0 spends (A/e_0) amount of foreign currency to buy A amount of domestic currency and invests it in domestic bank deposits. This investment will yield $A(1+r)$ in principal and interest in domestic currency in the next period, period 1. In foreign currency, this equals $A(1+r)/e_1$ in period 1. Therefore, the additional income the foreign wealth holder gets in foreign currency in period 1 from his investment is $A(1+r)/e_1 - (A/e_0)$. Thus, the additional income that domestic bank deposits yield in period 1 in foreign currency per unit of foreign currency invested in domestic bank deposits is given by

$$\frac{\frac{A(1+r)}{e_1} - \frac{A}{e_0}}{\frac{A}{e_0}} = \frac{e_0}{e_1}(1+r) - 1 = \frac{e_0}{e_1}r - \varepsilon.$$

Thus, the foreign wealth holder will compare r^* and $r\frac{e_0}{e_1} - \varepsilon$ while deciding on how to allocate his given wealth between domestic bank deposits and foreign bank deposits.

If we make time continuous, we shall get simpler expressions for $r^*\left(\frac{e_1}{e_0}\right) + \varepsilon$ and $r\frac{e_0}{e_1} - \varepsilon$. We explain it below. Suppose a domestic wealth holder invests A amount of foreign currency at time t in foreign bank deposits. For that, he has to buy A amount of foreign currency with $Z_t = Ae_t$ amount of domestic currency at time t. Differentiating Z_t with respect to t, we get

$$\frac{dZ_t}{dt} = e_t \frac{dA}{dt} + A \frac{de_t}{dt} \tag{3.a.1}$$

The above expression gives the increase in Z_t at the next point of time on account of its being invested in foreign bank deposits. The first term gives the increase in the invested amount at the next point of time, given the exchange rate. This increase is obviously due to interest payment. Clearly,

$$\frac{dA}{dt} = r^* A \tag{3.a.2}$$

The second term in (3.a.1) gives the increase in the invested amount due to an increase in the exchange rate. Obviously, an increase in the exchange rate will increase the amount of income from foreign bank deposits in domestic currency. Putting (3.a.2) into (3.a.1), we get

$$\frac{dZ_t}{dt} = e_t r^* A + A \frac{de_t}{dt} \tag{3.a.3}$$

The above expression gives the income in domestic currency from an investment of Z_t amount of domestic currency in foreign bank deposits at the time t. Therefore, income in domestic currency from foreign bank deposits per unit of domestic currency invested in foreign bank deposits is given by

$$\frac{\frac{dZ_t}{dt}}{Z_t} = \frac{e_t r^* A + A \frac{de_t}{dt}}{Ae_t} = r^* + \frac{\frac{de_t}{dt}}{e_t} = r^* + \varepsilon \tag{3.a.4}$$

In (3.a.4), ε gives the proportional rate of increase in e_t. Now, r and $r^* + \varepsilon$ are comparable. They give income in domestic currency per unit of domestic currency invested in domestic and foreign bank deposits, respectively. However, at the time of making investment, domestic wealth holders do not know the value of (de/dt) and, therefore, that of ε. They have to take the decision on the basis of the expected value of ε, which we denote by ε^E. Thus, domestic wealth holders compare r and $r^* + \varepsilon^E$.

We now consider the foreign wealth holders. To invest A amount in domestic currency at time t, they have to spend $\widetilde{Z}_t = (A/e_t)$ amount of foreign currency at time t to buy A amount of domestic currency. To derive the amount by which $\widetilde{Z}_t = (A/e_t)$ increases at the next point of time on account of its being invested in domestic bank deposits, we have to differentiate it with respect to t. This gives us

$$\frac{d\widetilde{Z}_t}{dt} = \frac{1}{e_t}\frac{dA}{dt} - A\frac{1}{e_t^2}\frac{de_t}{dt} \tag{3.a.5}$$

We find from (3.a.5) that there are two reasons why the amount of foreign currency invested in domestic bank deposits changes from the point of time t to the next instant. First, the amount by which the amount of domestic currency invested in domestic bank deposits changes, with the exchange rate remaining unchanged (given by the first term in (3.a.5)). Second, the change in the invested amount that takes place on account of the change in the exchange rate (which is given by the second term in (3.a.5)). Let us focus on the first term of (3.a.5). The amount of domestic currency invested in domestic bank deposits increases from the point of time t to the next instant on account of interest payment. Thus, $(\mathrm{d}A/\mathrm{d}t) = Ar$, which yields $\frac{1}{e_t}Ar$ in foreign currency at the initial exchange rate. Again, the amount of foreign currency invested in domestic bank deposits declines if the exchange rate increases from the point of time t to the next instant, since domestic bank deposits yield principal and interest in domestic currency. This change is given by the second term in (3.a.5). Thus, we rewrite (3.a.5) as

$$\frac{\mathrm{d}\widetilde{Z}_t}{\mathrm{d}t} = \frac{1}{e_t}Ar - A\frac{1}{e_t^2}\frac{\mathrm{d}e_t}{\mathrm{d}t} \tag{3.a.6}$$

If we divide (3.a.6) by $\widetilde{Z}_t = (A/e_t)$, we shall get the amount of income yielded by domestic bank deposits in foreign currency per unit of foreign currency invested in domestic bank deposits. This is given by

$$\frac{\frac{\mathrm{d}\widetilde{Z}_t}{\mathrm{d}t}}{\widetilde{Z}_t} = r - \varepsilon \tag{3.a.7}$$

Thus, foreign investors compare r^* and $r - \varepsilon$, since they give the incomes yielded in foreign currency per unit of foreign currency invested in foreign and domestic bank deposits, respectively. However, at the time t, ε is not known. Hence, foreign wealth holders, while deciding on how to allocate a given amount of wealth between domestic and foreign bonds, have to do so on the basis of the expected value of ε, which we denote by ε^E. Thus, foreign investors at the time t compare r^* and $r - \varepsilon^E$.

The discussion made above yields the following: Both the domestic investors and foreign investors have to make their choices on the basis of ε^E. However, we do not know how individuals form their expectations regarding ε. Exchange rate is volatile to the extreme. There are a large number of factors that drive the movements in e. It is almost impossible to predict how these factors are going to change over time. Hence, it may be reasonable to assume that it is exogenously given. This is what this model does. For simplicity, it also assumes that $\varepsilon^E = 0$. For this reason, r and r^* give, respectively, the rates of return on domestic and foreign bank deposits in both domestic and foreign currency.

References

Fleming, J. M. (1962). Domestic financial policies under fixed and floating exchange rates. *IMF Staff Papers, 9*, 369–379.

Mundell, R. A. (1963). Capital mobility and stabilization policy under fixed and flexible exchange rates. *Canadian Journal of Economic and Political Science, 29*(4), 475–485.

Chapter 4
An Alternative to the IS-LM Model: Extension to the Case of Imperfect Capital Mobility

Abstract The objective of this chapter is to extend the model developed in Chap. 2 to the case of a small open economy, with imperfect capital mobility across borders. We consider both the fixed and flexible exchange rate regimes. The endeavor is worthwhile in light of our argument developed here to show that imperfect capital mobility is the general case, while perfect capital mobility is a special one.

4.1 Introduction

The objective of this chapter is to extend the model developed in Chap. 2 to the case of imperfect capital mobility across borders. The endeavor is important for the following reason. We shall argue in the next section that in general capital is imperfectly mobile across countries. Hence, it is imperative that we extend the model developed in Chap. 2 to capture the case of imperfect capital mobility.

4.2 Imperfect Capital Mobility: The General Case[1]

We shall argue here that imperfect capital mobility is the general case, while perfect capital mobility is a special one. A prima facie evidence in support of this proposition is the following. If capital were perfectly mobile across countries, central banks in small open economies like India would have had no control over domestic interest rates. However, central banks in almost all the countries in the world including India seek to and successfully regulate domestic interest rates. Let us now explain why imperfect capital mobility is the general case. We explained it in great detail in Chap. 4 of our previous work Ghosh and Ghosh (2016). We present a part of this argument in brief below. An individual in a small open economy can invest either in domestic assets or in foreign assets. Let us assume for simplicity that domestic assets consist

[1]Section 4.2 of this chapter drawn from portions of Chap. 4 of the authors' previous book 'Indian Economy: A Macro-theoretic Analysis' published by PHI Learning Private Limited in 2016 (ISBN—978-81-203-5244-5).

C. Ghosh and A. N. Ghosh, *Keynesian Macroeconomics Beyond the IS-LM Model*, https://doi.org/10.1007/978-981-13-7888-1_4

of domestic bonds, while foreign assets consist of foreign bonds. Even if both types of bonds give the same return and are completely default risk-free, the two types of bonds are not perfect substitutes to domestic agents because foreign bonds are risky since they involve exchange rate risk. If foreign bonds yield higher expected return, a domestic agent can increase his expected income from his wealth by allocating a larger part of his wealth to foreign bonds. But this will not only increase expected income from his portfolio but also increase risk. Depending upon his preference over risk and return, he will decide how much of his wealth to be held in foreign bonds. Let us illustrate this point with an example developed on the line of Tobin (1958).

Considers a domestic economic agent with a given amount of wealth, $\overline{W}$, which he can hold in the form of either domestic bond or foreign bond. The return on domestic bonds is r. The comparable return on foreign bond, as we have explained in the appendix of the previous chapter, is $r^* + \varepsilon$, where ε denotes expected rate of depreciation of domestic currency. However, the individual does not have just one expected rate of depreciation of domestic currency, but a subjective probability distribution over many possible values of the expected rate of depreciation of domestic currency. Under these circumstances, as we shall presently show, the choice between domestic and foreign bonds even for an individual wealth holder is unlikely to be an all-or-nothing one. Even when r and r^* are different, individuals instead of putting all their wealth in the form of the bond that yields higher return/expected return will allocate their wealth between both types of bonds. We shall now establish this point. Consider a domestic wealth holder. Suppose he has a given amount of wealth in domestic currency, which we denote by $\overline{W}$. He has to decide how he will allocate his given amount of wealth between domestic bonds and foreign bonds. Here, we consider only risk-free (i.e., default risk-free) domestic and foreign bonds. Domestic bonds are safe to him. But foreign bonds, though default risk-free, are risky to domestic investors as they involve exchange rate risk. Thus, to a domestic investor, the return on domestic bonds denoted by r is fully certain. Expected return on risk-free foreign bonds to a domestic investor in terms of domestic currency, as we have already explained in the appendix in the previous chapter, is $r^* + \varepsilon^E$, where ε^E is the expected rate of depreciation of domestic currency. The wealth holder has a subjective probability distribution defined over all values of ε^E. For the domestic wealth holder under consideration, the mean of his probability distribution is defined as the mathematical expectation of ε^E, $E(\varepsilon^E)$. We shall denote $E(\varepsilon^E)$ by μ. Again, the standard deviation of his probability distribution is given by $\sqrt{E(\varepsilon^E - \mu)^2}$. We denote this standard deviation by σ. We denote the fraction of the given wealth that the domestic investor invests in foreign bonds by A_2. Accordingly, he invests $(1 - A_2)$ fraction of his given wealth in domestic bonds. Every unit of domestic currency invested in domestic bonds yields after one instant/period an additional income of r in domestic currency. Hence, $(1 - A_2)\overline{W}$ amount of domestic currency invested in domestic bonds will yield an additional income of $(1 - A_2)\overline{W}r$ in the next instant/period in domestic currency. Similarly, every unit of domestic currency invested in foreign bonds yields in the next instant/period $r^* + \varepsilon$ in domestic currency. Hence, $A_2\overline{W}$ amount of domestic currency invested in foreign bonds will yield an additional income of $A_2\overline{W}(r^* + \varepsilon)$ in the next instant/period in domestic currency. Thus, the income that a domestic investor earns from his portfolio containing $A_2\overline{W}$ amount of wealth invested in foreign bonds and $(1 - A_2)\overline{W}$ amount of wealth invested in domestic bonds is given by

$$\widetilde{R} = \left[(1 - A_2)r + A_2\left(r^* + \varepsilon\right)\right]\overline{W} \tag{4.1}$$

At the time of making the choice regarding A_2, the value of ε is not known. He has to make his choice on the basis of his expected values of ε, ε^E, over which he has a subjective probability distribution. Thus, while making the choice regarding A_2, the individual has to take into reckoning, after substituting ε^E for ε in the expression of $\widetilde{R}$, the mathematical expectation of $\widetilde{R}$, $E\left(\widetilde{R}\right)$, which we shall denote by R. It gives the domestic wealth holder's expected mean income from his portfolio. Thus

$$\begin{aligned} R \equiv E\left(\widetilde{R}\right) &= \left[(1 - A_2)r + A_2\left(r^* + E\left(\varepsilon^E\right)\right)\right]\overline{W} \\ &= \left[(1 - A_2)r + A_2 r^* + A_2\mu\right]\overline{W}; \quad E\left(\varepsilon^E\right) \equiv \mu \end{aligned} \tag{4.2}$$

The risk involved in the portfolio is measured, as standard, by the standard deviation of $\widetilde{R}$. It is given by

$$\rho \equiv \sqrt{E\left(\widetilde{R} - R\right)^2} = \sqrt{E\left[\overline{W}\left(A_2\varepsilon^E - A_2\mu\right)\right]^2} = A_2\overline{W}\sigma \quad \sigma \equiv \sqrt{E\left(\varepsilon^E - \mu\right)^2} \tag{4.3}$$

From (4.2) and (4.3), it follows that corresponding to any given A_2, there is a unique value of R and ρ. By choosing different values of A_2, the domestic investor can choose different combinations of R and ρ, given r, r^* and the mean and standard deviation of his subjective probability distribution over ε^E. All the different combinations of R and ρ that the domestic investor can choose from by varying A_2 may be derived as follows. Solving (4.3) for A_2, we get

$$A_2 = \frac{\rho}{\sigma}\frac{1}{\overline{W}} \tag{4.4}$$

Substituting (4.4) into (4.2), we get

$$R = \overline{W}r + \frac{\rho}{\sigma}\left(r^* + \mu - r\right) \tag{4.5}$$

Equation (4.5) gives all the combinations of R and ρ the domestic investor can assume by varying $A_2 \in [0, 1]$. Equation (4.5) is referred to as the budget line of the domestic investor. The budget line is a straight line. In Fig. 4.1, in the upper panel, the straight line AA represents the budget line. Note that, the maximum value of ρ, as follows from (4.3), is $\sigma\overline{W}$, since the maximum value that A_2 can assume is 1. As the budget line is a straight line, it is defined by its vertical intercept and slope. The

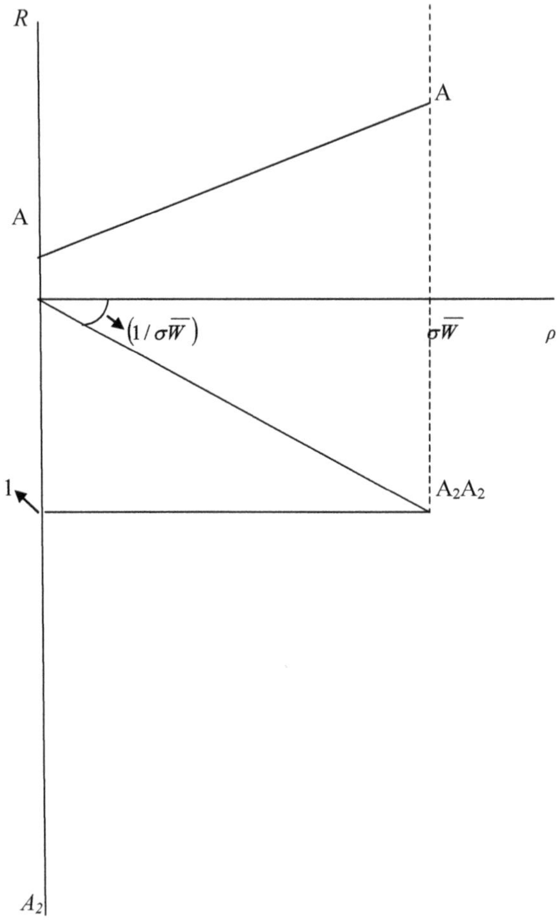

Fig. 4.1 Budget line of the domestic investor

vertical intercept of the budget line is $r\overline{W}$, and its slope is $\frac{1}{\sigma}(r^* + \mu - r)$. Let us now explain them. The vertical incept gives the value of R, when $\rho = 0$. If the domestic investor does not want to assume any risk, i.e., if he wants to set $\rho = 0$, he has to make A_2, as follows from (4.3), zero. This means that the domestic investor has to invest all his wealth in domestic bonds. So, income from his portfolio in domestic currency in the next instant/period is $r\overline{W}$, i.e., $R = r\overline{W}$. This explains the vertical intercept of the budget line.

Let us now explain the slope of the budget line. Starting from a (ρ, R) on the budget line, the slope of the budget line gives the amount of increase in R that satisfies (4.5) following a unit increase in ρ from the given (ρ, R). Let us explain. Take any (ρ, R) on the budget line. If the domestic investor wants to raise ρ by one unit, he has to raise A_2 by $\frac{1}{\sigma \overline{W}}$—see (4.3). One additional unit of domestic currency invested in foreign bonds yields in the next instant/period an additional mean expected income of $(r^* + \mu)$. Hence, $\frac{1}{\sigma \overline{W}}.\overline{W} = \frac{1}{\sigma}$ additional amount of domestic currency invested in foreign bonds yields an additional expected mean income of $\frac{1}{\sigma}(r^* + \mu)$. As A_2 rises by $\frac{1}{\sigma \overline{W}}$, the amount of domestic currency invested in domestic bonds falls by $\frac{1}{\sigma \overline{W}}\overline{W} = \frac{1}{\sigma}$. Hence, additional income from domestic bonds falls by $(1/\sigma)r$. Therefore, when ρ rises by unity, the expected mean income from the portfolio rises by $(1/\sigma)(r^* + \mu) - (1/\sigma)r = (1/\sigma)(r^* + \mu - r)$. This explains the slope of the budget line. We shall henceforth refer to this slope as the actual marginal rate of compensation for risk-taking. It gives us the amount by which R of the individual's portfolio will increase if he takes one unit more risk, i.e., if he raises ρ by 1 unit.

In the lower panel of Fig. 4.1, we measure positive values of A_2 on the vertical axis in the downward direction. In the lower panel, the line A_2A_2 represents (4.4). It gives the value of A_2, as given by (4.4), corresponding to every different value of ρ.

From Fig. 4.1, it is clear that the domestic agent can increase expected income from his wealth by raising A_2, when $r^* + \mu > r$. But, this will also raise the amount of risk he assumes. Depending upon his tastes and preference over risk and return, he will decide which (ρ, R) to choose. We have to therefore incorporate the individual's tastes and preferences to show how he chooses a specific value of A_2.

4.2.1 *Risk Aversion and Preference Ordering*

Let us now focus on the individual's preference ordering or his utility function defined over the set of all possible combinations of R and ρ. This preference ordering is represented by a set of indifference curves. For risk-averse individuals, these indifference curves are positively sloped. Let us explain. Given the portfolio risk, ρ, an increase in R makes every individual better-off. However, if an individual is risk-averse, an increase in ρ, given R, makes him worse-off. Therefore, starting from a (ρ, R) on a given indifference curve of a risk-averse individual, an increase in ρ, with R remaining unchanged, will lower his utility level. If the risk-averse individual is to be kept on the initial indifference curve with this higher value of ρ, R has to be raised commensurately. This makes indifference curves of risk-averse individuals positively sloped in the (ρ, R) plane. Corresponding to any given ρ, value of R is higher on a higher indifference curve. Hence, a higher indifference curve represents a higher level of utility.

4.2.2 *Risk Aversion and Choice*

We consider it sensible to assume that most of the individuals are risk-averse. We shall, therefore, consider a domestic economic agent who is risk-averse. His indifference curves, as we have already pointed out, are positively sloped. His budget line as given by (4.6) may be positively sloped or negatively sloped. We shall first focus on his choice when his budget line is negatively sloped, i.e., when $r^* + \mu - r < 0$. In such a situation, he will invest all his wealth in domestic bonds. The reason is quite obvious. If he invests all his wealth in domestic bonds, i.e., if he sets A_2 equal to 0, he does not take any risk, with $\rho = 0$ and $R = \overline{W}r$—see (4.3) and (4.2). If he raises A_2 and, thereby, ρ, R will decline making him worse-off. Therefore, he will choose to invest all his wealth in domestic bonds.

Now, we focus on a domestic agent for whom $r^* + \mu$ exceeds r so that his budget line is positively sloped. We further assume that his indifference curves are not only positively sloped but also strictly convex downward. This means that the slope of such an indifference curve rises as ρ increases along the given indifference curve. These indifference curves are represented by I_0 and I_1 in Fig. 4.2. The slope of an indifference curve at a given (ρ, R) on the indifference curve gives us the amount of increase in R that is required to keep the domestic agent on the same indifference curve as before following a unit increase in ρ from the given (ρ, R) on the given indifference curve. We shall refer to the slope of an indifference curve as the required marginal rate of compensation for risk-taking. Along a strictly convex downward indifference curve, the required marginal rate of compensation for risk-taking rises with an increase in ρ along the indifference curve. The domestic agent will choose from the budget line given by (4.2) and represented by the line AA in Fig. 4.2, the point on the highest indifference curve. The chosen point is labeled '*a*' in Fig. 4.2. Why does the domestic agent choose '*a*' from the budget line? Let us explain that. At '*a*', an indifference curve is tangent to the budget line. Therefore, at '*a*', the slope of the budget line equals that of the indifference curve. In other words, at '*a*', the actual marginal rate of compensation for risk-taking equals the required marginal rate of compensation for risk-taking. Consider any point to the left of '*a*' on the budget line. The indifference curve that passes through the point intersects the budget line from above. At such a point, therefore, the slope of the indifference curve passing through the point is less than that of the budget line; i.e., the required marginal rate of compensation for risk-taking is less than the actual marginal rate of compensation for risk-taking. This means that, if from the given point the domestic agent raises ρ by unity, the increase in R that will take place will be larger than the increase in R that is required to keep him on the same indifference curve. Hence, from the given point by taking one unit more risk, he will be able to move over to a higher indifference curve. Similarly, explain why the domestic agent will not choose a point to the right of '*a*' on his budget line.

In the lower panel of Fig. 4.2, just as in the lower panel of Fig. 4.1, the line A_2A_2 representing (4.4) gives the value of A_2 corresponding to every given value of ρ. The value of A_2 corresponding to the chosen point '*a*' is denoted by A_{20}. This has the following implication. Note that μ may be positive or negative and its value may be small or large. Thus, even if $r^* + \mu > r$, r may be substantially higher than r^* and even at $r > r^*$, the value of A_2 chosen by the domestic agent may be substantially greater than zero as long as $r < r^* + \mu$. This means that, even when $r > r^*$, a risk-averse individual may not want to hold the whole of his wealth in the form of

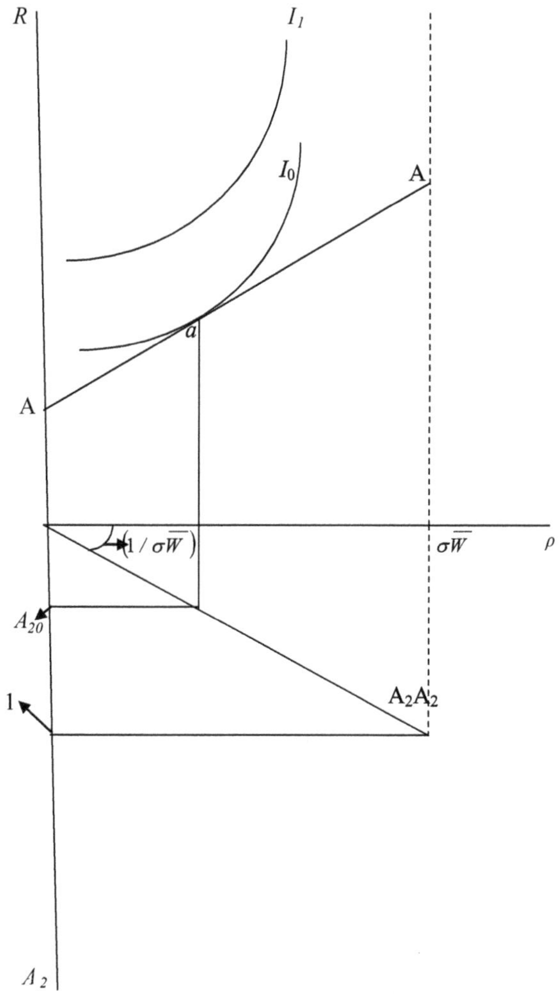

Fig. 4.2 Choice of the portfolio by the domestic investor

domestic bonds. He may want to hold just a fraction of his wealth in the form of domestic bonds.

From the above, it follows that, over a wide range of values of r, given r^*, domestic economic agents instead of preferring one kind of bonds to another, will want to allocate their wealth between the two kinds of bonds. At any such r, those who are holding more foreign bonds than what they want to (i.e., those for whom actual A_2 is greater the optimum A_2) will desire to switch from foreign bonds to domestic bonds and those who are holding less foreign bonds than what they want to (i.e., those for whom the actual A_2 is less than the optimum A_2) will want to switch from domestic bonds to foreign bonds. Thus, corresponding to any given r, with r^* fixed at a given level, the net inflow of capital, K, is finite. In fact, at any such r, individuals whose actual A_2 is greater than their optimum A_2 will want to buy a finite amount of domestic bonds by selling foreign bonds. Again, those individuals whose actual A_2 is less than the optimum A_2 will offer to sell a finite amount of domestic bonds for purchasing foreign bonds. Therefore, even at a $r > r^*$, demand for purchase of domestic bonds may be less than the amount of domestic bonds on offer for sale putting an upward pressure on r. Given everything else, the higher the r relative to r^*, one can easily show, the smaller is likely to be the value of the optimum A_2, since risk-taking becomes less rewarding as indicated by a smaller value of $r^* + \mu - r$. Hence, the higher the r relative to r^*, the optimum A_2 is likely to be smaller relative to the actual A_2 for the domestic people. Hence, demand for purchase of domestic bonds by selling foreign bonds is likely to increase, while the amount of domestic bonds offered for sale for purchasing foreign bonds is likely to fall and K is likely to increase. From the above discussion, it follows that, given expectations (captured by the subjective probability distributions over the possible values of ε^E defined by the values of μ and σ), we may write K as

$$K = K\left(\underset{+}{r - r^*}\right) \tag{4.6}$$

This is the case of imperfect capital mobility. Here, even at a $r > r^*$, there may be excess supply of domestic bonds (matched by an excess demand for foreign bonds) putting upward pressure on r. Here, unlike what happens in the perfect mobility case, the domestic bond market may be in equilibrium with $r > r^*$ or $r < r^*$. The finding of the above discussion may be summarized in the form of the following proposition:

Proposition 4.1 *When expected return on foreign bonds is higher than that on domestic bonds, risk-averse domestic individuals by raising the fraction of their wealth invested in foreign bonds can increase the expected income from their portfolio. However, this increase in expected income will be accompanied by an increase in risk. Depending upon their tastes and preferences over risk and return, risk-averse individuals will choose the optimum fraction of their wealth to be invested in foreign bonds. We have found that for a wide range of values of* r*, given* r^**, people will choose to diversify their wealth between domestic bonds and foreign bonds; it does not matter whether* $r > r^*$ *or* $r < r^*$*. This gives rise to imperfect capital mobility as the general case.*

We shall now develop models to capture the behavior of a small open economy with imperfect capital mobility. We shall first focus on the flexible exchange rate regime. In this case, the central bank does not intervene in the foreign exchange market to regulate the exchange rate.

4.3 A Small Open Economy with Imperfect Capital Mobility and Flexible Exchange Rate Regime

We consider here a small open economy with imperfect capital mobility and a flexible exchange rate system. In such an economy, the goods market equilibrium condition, as before, is given by

$$Y = C(Y) + I(r) + \overline{G} + X\left(\frac{P^*e}{P}; Y^*\right) - M\left(\frac{P^*e}{P}; Y\right) \tag{4.7}$$

Under imperfect capital mobility, r may differ from r^* and the former is determined in the domestic loan market. As before, we assume that the entire government consumption expenditure is financed by borrowing from the domestic central bank. Central bank's loans to the government constitute the only source of high-powered money in the economy. Thus,

$$\frac{\mathrm{d}H}{P} = \overline{G} \tag{4.8}$$

Again, given the assumption that domestic firms do not save and domestic households save in the form of domestic bank deposits only, total planned supply of new loans by the domestic commercial banks, denoted l_b, is given by (for reasons we have already explained in previous chapters)

$$l_b = (1 - \rho(r_c))(Y - C(Y)) \tag{4.9}$$

In (4.9), ρ denotes the CRR (in the previous section, ρ denoted portfolio risk, but, henceforth, it will denote CRR). We have made it an increasing function of r_c, where r_c denotes the policy rate of the central bank: It is the rate at which the central bank lends to the commercial banks.

Let us now focus on capital flows across borders. We consider here a small open economy. Since the economy is small, domestic economic agents can borrow from and lend to the world credit market as much as they want at the interest rate prevailing in the world credit market, which is denoted by r^*. This implies that domestic savers can hold their saving in the form of either domestic bank deposits or loans in the world market or both. Similarly, domestic commercial banks can secure deposits from domestic households as well as from foreigners. They can also lend either to domestic firms or in the world credit market or both. Domestic firms can also borrow from either domestic commercial banks or the world credit market or both. However, for simplicity, we shall make the following assumptions. Domestic savers hold their saving in the form of domestic bank deposits only. Domestic commercial banks lend to both domestic firms and in the world credit market, even though they receive their deposits from domestic savers only. Domestic borrowers (consisting of domestic firms other than banks and domestic households) borrow from both domestic commercial banks and the world credit market. Under imperfect capital mobility, K is an increasing function of the interest rate differential, given domestic agents' expectations regarding the future course of the exchange rate. Let us explain this point a little more. Domestic commercial banks can lend to domestic borrowers, or they can lend to foreigners at the given interest rate r^*. Lending to foreigners, however, involves exchange rate risk. Hence, given r and r^* and their expectations, domestic commercial banks, in accordance with the model developed in the previous section, will plan to allocate their total lending between domestic borrowers and foreigners. The higher the r relative to r^*, the larger is the domestic commercial banks' planned supply of loans to domestic borrowers and the less is their planned supply of loans to foreigners. The latter constitutes planned outflow of capital. Similarly, domestic borrowers can borrow from either domestic commercial banks at the interest rate r or foreigners at the given interest rate r^*. However, borrowing from foreigners involves exchange rate risk. We can easily modify the model developed in the previous section to the case of borrowers and apply this model to domestic borrowers. This modified model, as one can easily deduce, suggests that they will plan to allocate their total loan demand between domestic and foreign sources on the basis of the given values of r and r^*, given their expectations. Borrowing from foreigners means capital inflow. The higher the r relative to r^*, the less will be their planned demand from domestic sources, and hence, the larger will be their planned demand from foreign sources; i.e., the larger will be capital inflow on account of domestic borrowers' decisions. Thus, given the expectations of domestic commercial banks and domestic borrowers, the higher the r relative to r^*, the larger will be the net inflow of loans or capital. The aggregate net supply of new loans to domestic borrowers is, therefore, given by total planned supply of loans by domestic commercial banks, $(1 - \rho(r_c))(Y - C(Y))$, minus the planned outflow of capital (i.e., the planned supply of new loans to foreigners by domestic commercial banks) plus the planned inflow of capital (i.e., the amount of new loans the domestic borrowers plan to secure from abroad). Accordingly, the total supply of new loans to domestic firms, denoted l, is given by

$$l = (1 - \rho(r_c))(Y - C(Y)) + K\left(r - r^*\right) + \overline{K} \tag{4.10}$$

In (4.10), the net inflow of capital given by $K(r - r^*) + \overline{K}$ includes the autonomous component $\overline{K}$. It captures that part of the net inflow of capital which is determined by people's expectations regarding the future course of the exchange rate. Since we do not know how these expectations are formed, it is best to regard the part of capital inflow that is due to people's expectations regarding the future course of the exchange rate as exogenously given. Demand for new loans, denoted l^d, comes from the domestic borrowers who finance their entire investment expenditure with loans. Domestic borrowers do not require loans for any other purposes. We first focus on the case where the banking sector is perfectly competitive and interest rates are perfectly flexible.

4.3.1 Perfectly Flexible Interest Rate Case

In this case, domestic loan market will be in equilibrium when

$$(1-\rho(r_c))(Y-C(Y))+K\big(r-r^*\big)+\overline{K}=I(r) \tag{4.11}$$

Since the exchange rate is perfectly flexible here, the foreign currency market will be in equilibrium, when the excess supply of foreign currency given by $\big[X\big(\frac{P^*e}{P};Y^*\big)-M\big(\frac{P^*e}{P};Y\big)+K(r-r^*)+\overline{K}\big]\frac{P}{e}$ is zero, i.e., when the following condition is satisfied:

$$\left[\left\{X\left(\frac{P^*e}{P};Y^*\right)-M\left(\frac{P^*e}{P};Y\right)\right\}+K\big(r-r^*\big)+\overline{K}\right]\frac{P}{e}=0$$
$$\Rightarrow\left[X\left(\frac{P^*e}{P};Y^*\right)-M\left(\frac{P^*e}{P},Y\right)\right]+K\big(r-r^*\big)+\overline{K}=0 \tag{4.12}$$

The specification of our model is now complete. It consists of three key Eqs. (4.7), (4.11), and (4.12) in three endogenous variables: Y, r and e. We may solve them as follows. Substituting (4.11) and (4.12) into (4.7), we may rewrite it as

$$Y=C(Y)+(1-\rho(r_c))(Y-C(Y))+\overline{G} \tag{4.13}$$

We can solve (4.13) for the equilibrium value of Y. The solution is shown diagrammatically in Fig. 4.3a, where the AD schedule gives the value of aggregate demand for domestic goods, given by the RHS of (4.13), corresponding to different values of Y. The equilibrium value of Y corresponds to the point of intersection of the AD schedule and the 45° line. The equilibrium Y is labeled Y_0. Putting the equilibrium value of Y in (4.11), we get the equilibrium value of r. The solution is shown in Fig. 4.3b, where ls(Y_0) schedule represents the LHS of (4.11), with Y fixed at its equilibrium value Y_0. It gives the value of net aggregate supply of new loans to domestic borrowers corresponding to different values of r, when Y is fixed at its equilibrium value. The ld schedule represents the RHS of (4.11) and gives the value of demand for new loans of domestic borrowers at different values of r. The equilibrium value of r, labeled r_0, corresponds to the point of intersection of the ld and ls schedules. Putting the equilibrium values of Y and r in (4.12), we can solve it for the equilibrium value of e. The solution is shown in Fig. 4.3c, where $TK(Y_0, r_0)$ schedule plots the value of the LHS of (4.12) against e, when Y and r are fixed at their equilibrium values Y_0 and r_0, respectively. The equilibrium value of e corresponds to the point of intersection of the $TK(Y_0, r_0)$ schedule and the horizontal axis. It is labeled e_0.

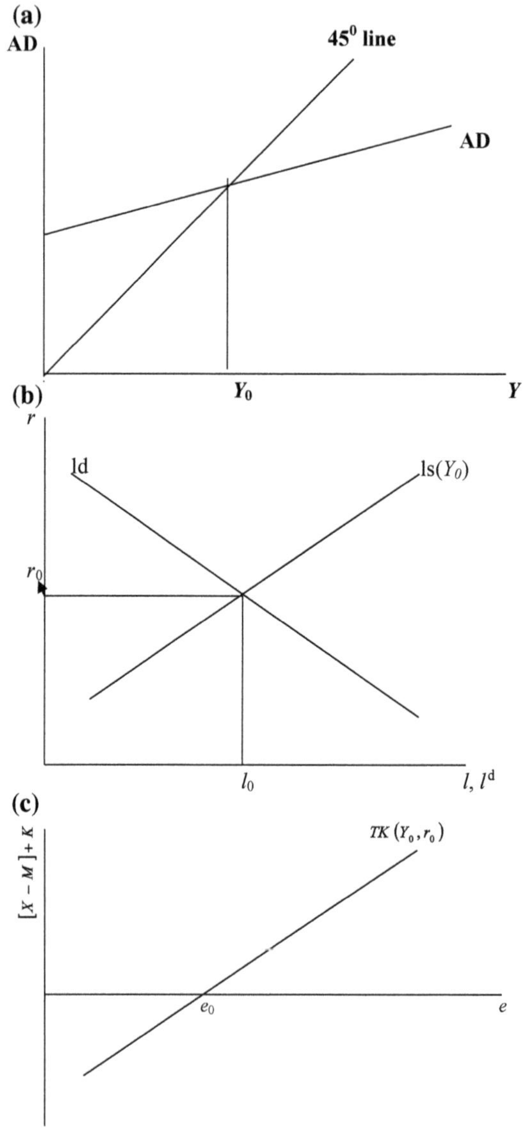

Fig. 4.3 Determination of Y, r, and e in the flexible exchange rate regime under imperfect capital mobility

Fiscal Policy: An Increase in Government Consumption Financed by Borrowing from the Central Bank

We shall now examine how an increase in $\overline{G}$ financed by borrowing from the central bank affects Y, r, and e. Let us do it diagrammatically first. We shall do it using Fig. 4.4a–c, where the initial equilibrium values of Y, r, and e are labeled Y_0, r_0 and e_0, respectively. Following an increase in $\overline{G}$ by $\mathrm{d}\overline{G}$, as is clear from the RHS of (4.13), aggregate demand at every Y rises by $\mathrm{d}\overline{G}$. Hence, the AD schedule in Fig. 4.4a shifts upward by $\mathrm{d}\overline{G}$ raising the equilibrium Y to Y_1. The new AD schedule is labeled AD_1. The ls schedule representing the LHS of (4.11) in Fig. 4.4b now corresponds to a larger Y, Y_1. Hence, the $\mathrm{ls}(Y_1)$ schedule will be to the right of $\mathrm{ls}(Y_0)$ schedule. The ld schedule, as given by the RHS of (4.11), will remain unaffected. Hence, r in the new equilibrium will be less. It is labeled r_1.

It follows from the LHS of (4.12) that the value of $(X - M) + K$ corresponding to every e will fall following an increase in Y and a decline in r. Therefore, $TK(Y_1, r_1)$ schedule will lie below $TK(Y_0, r_0)$ schedule in Fig. 4.4c. Hence, e will be higher in the new equilibrium. The new equilibrium value of e is labeled e_1 in Fig. 4.4c.

Mathematical Derivation of the Results

We shall now derive these results mathematically. Taking total differential of (4.13) treating all exogenous variables other than $\overline{G}$ as fixed, we get

$$\mathrm{d}Y = \frac{\mathrm{d}\overline{G}}{\rho(r_c)(1 - C')} \tag{4.14}$$

It is quite easy to explain (4.14). Following an increase in $\overline{G}$ by $\mathrm{d}\overline{G}$, there emerges an excess demand of $\mathrm{d}\overline{G}$ at the initial equilibrium (Y, r, e). This is given by the numerator of the expression on the RHS of (4.14). To meet this excess demand, producers raise Y. Per unit increase in Y, aggregate demand remaining unchanged, excess demand falls by 1 unit. However, aggregate demand does not remain unchanged. The unit increase in Y, ceteris paribus, raises aggregate demand by C'. However, the whole of this C' does not represent additional demand for domestic goods alone. A part of it given by M_Y represents demand for imported goods. This increased demand for import creates BOP deficit. As a result, e will rise, raise net export by M_Y, and, thereby, restore BOP equilibrium [see (4.12)]. Hence, a unit increase in Y raises aggregate demand for domestic goods (given by $C + I + G + X - M$) by C', when e adjusts to keep the BOP in equilibrium. Out of the additional unit of Y, people will make new saving of $\left(1 - C'\right)$, which they will put in the banks as deposit. Out of this new deposit, banks will plan to lend out $(1 - \rho)\left(1 - C'\right)$ bringing about an excess supply of loan at the initial equilibrium r. r will, therefore, begin to fall to clear the loan market. As r falls, I rises and K falls. The loan market comes to equilibrium when the fall in r is such that the sum of the increase in I and the absolute value

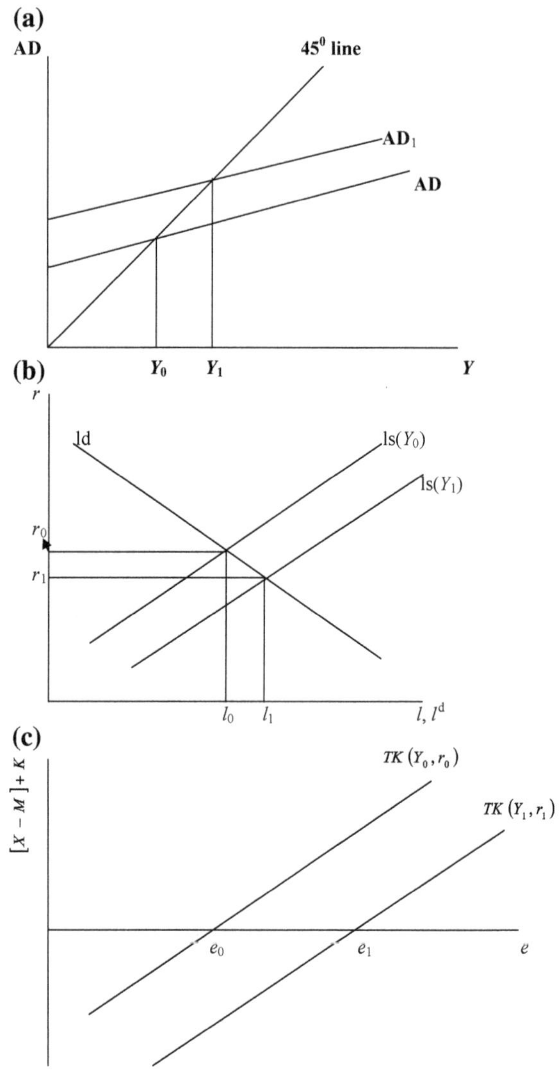

Fig. 4.4 Effect of an increase in $\overline{G}$ on Y, r, and e in the flexible exchange rate regime under imperfect capital mobility

of the fall in K equals $(1 - \rho)(1 - C')$ [see (4.11)]. However, the fall in K creates BOP deficit pushing up the exchange rate. e will rise and restore BOP equilibrium by raising net export by an amount equal to the absolute value of fall in K. Thus, as r and e adjust and equilibrate the loan market and the foreign exchange market, net export and I together increase by $(1 - \rho)(1 - C')$. Thus, per unit increase in Y aggregate demand for domestic goods increases by $C' + (1 - \rho)(1 - C')$, as e and r adjust to keep the BOP and the loan market in equilibrium. Therefore, per unit increase in Y, excess demand for Y falls by $1 - C' - (1 - \rho)(1 - C') = \rho(1 - C')$, when e and r adjust along with the unit increase in Y to keep the BOP and the loan market in equilibrium. This is given by the denominator. Hence, the expression on the RHS of (4.14) gives the increase in the equilibrium value of Y.

Again, taking total differential of (4.11), substituting for $\mathrm{d}Y$ its value given by (4.14) and solving for $\mathrm{d}r$, we get

$$\mathrm{d}r = -\frac{(1-\rho(r_c))\frac{\mathrm{d}\overline{G}}{\rho(r_c)}}{-I' + K_{\tilde{r}}} \quad \tilde{r} \equiv r - r^* \tag{4.15}$$

It is quite easy to explain (4.15). As Y increases from the initial equilibrium to the new equilibrium by $\frac{\mathrm{d}\overline{G}}{\rho(r_c)(1-C')}$, people's saving goes up by $\left(1-C'\right).\frac{\mathrm{d}\overline{G}}{\rho(r_c)(1-C')} = \frac{\mathrm{d}\overline{G}}{\rho(r_c)}$ giving rise to an excess supply of loan of $(1-\rho(r_c))\frac{\mathrm{d}\overline{G}}{\rho(r_c)}$ at the initial equilibrium r. The numerator of the expression on the RHS of (4.15) measures this. r will, therefore, have to fall to equilibrate the loan market. From (4.11), it is clear that, per unit fall in r, with Y fixed at its new equilibrium value, excess supply of loan given by $[(1-\rho(r_c))(Y - C(Y)) + K(r - r^*) - I(r)]$ falls by $\left(-I' + K_{\tilde{r}}\right)$ (in absolute value). This is given by the denominator. Therefore, the change in the value of r from the initial equilibrium to the new equilibrium is given by the expression on the RHS of (4.15).

Again, taking total differential of (4.12) treating all exogenous variables as fixed, substituting for $\mathrm{d}Y$ and $\mathrm{d}r$ their values given by (4.14) and (4.15), respectively, and, then, solving for $\mathrm{d}e$, we get

$$\mathrm{d}e = \frac{M_Y\frac{\mathrm{d}\overline{G}}{\rho(1-C')} + K_{\tilde{r}}\frac{\frac{\mathrm{d}\overline{G}(1-\rho)}{\rho}}{-I'+K_{\tilde{r}}}}{\left(X_p - M_p\right)\frac{P^*}{P}} > 0 \tag{4.16}$$

It is quite easy to explain (4.16). From the initial equilibrium to the new one, Y has risen by $\frac{\mathrm{d}\overline{G}}{\rho(1-C')}$ raising import by $M_Y\frac{\mathrm{d}\overline{G}}{\rho(1-C')}$. Again, r has fallen by $-\frac{\frac{\mathrm{d}\overline{G}(1-\rho)}{\rho}}{-I'+K_{\tilde{r}}}$ lowering K by $-K_{\tilde{r}}\left(\frac{\frac{\mathrm{d}\overline{G}(1-\rho)}{\rho}}{-I'+K_{\tilde{r}}}\right)$. The above-mentioned changes create a BOP deficit of $M_Y\frac{\mathrm{d}\overline{G}}{\rho(1-C')} + K_{\tilde{r}}\frac{\frac{\mathrm{d}\overline{G}(1-\rho)}{\rho}}{-I'+K_{\tilde{r}}}$ at the initial equilibrium e. So, with Y and r fixed at their new equilibrium values, e has to rise to restore BOP equilibrium. Per unit increase in e, $[(X - M) + K]$, with Y and r fixed at their new equilibrium values, rises by $\left(X_p - M_p\right)\frac{P^*}{P}$, where $\left(p \equiv \frac{P^*e}{P}\right)$, since $(X - M) = 0$ at the initial equilibrium e. Hence, $[(X - M) + K]$ will rise by $M_Y\frac{\mathrm{d}\overline{G}}{\rho(1-C')} + K_{\tilde{r}}\frac{\frac{\mathrm{d}\overline{G}(1-\rho)}{\rho}}{-I'+K_{\tilde{r}}}$, when e increases by $\frac{M_Y\frac{\mathrm{d}\overline{G}}{\rho(1-C')} + K_{\tilde{r}}\frac{\frac{\mathrm{d}\overline{G}(1-\rho)}{\rho}}{-I'+K_{\tilde{r}}}}{\left(X_p - M_p\right)\frac{P^*}{P}}$. This explains (4.16).

Adjustment Process

We shall now describe the adjustment process; i.e., we shall now explain how different economic agents behave following the increase in $\overline{G}$ by $\mathrm{d}\overline{G}$ to bring about the changes in Y, r and e derived above. Following an increase in $\overline{G}$ by $\mathrm{d}\overline{G}$, Y goes up by $\mathrm{d}\overline{G}$. Out of this additional income of $\mathrm{d}\overline{G}$, people spend $\left(C' - M_Y\right)\mathrm{d}\overline{G}$ on domestic goods.

They also spend $PM_Y\mathrm{d}\overline{G}$ in the foreign currency market to buy foreign currency to purchase foreign consumption goods. Hence, excess demand emerges in the foreign currency market raising e. e will rise until $(X - M)$ rises by $M_Y\mathrm{d}\overline{G}$ and restores BOP equilibrium. To raise $(X - M)$ by $M_Y\mathrm{d}\overline{G}$, e will have to rise by $\frac{M_Y\mathrm{d}\overline{G}}{(X_p - M_p)\frac{P^*}{P}}$. Therefore, the additional income of $\mathrm{d}\overline{G}$ creates an additional demand for domestic goods (given by $C+I+G+X-M$) of $\left(C' - M_Y\right)\mathrm{d}\overline{G} + M_Y\mathrm{d}\overline{G} = C'\mathrm{d}\overline{G}$. This will raise Y by $C'\mathrm{d}\overline{G}$. This increase in Y will create an additional consumption demand for domestic goods of $\left(C' - M_Y\right)C'\mathrm{d}\overline{G}$ and raise import demand by $M_Y C'\mathrm{d}\overline{G}$. The latter will induce an increase in e by $\frac{M_Y C'\mathrm{d}\overline{G}}{(X_p - M_p)\frac{P^*}{P}}$ so that $(X - M)$ rises by $M_Y C'\mathrm{d}\overline{G}$ and restores BOP equilibrium. Thus, demand for domestic goods will increase by $\left(C' - M_Y\right)C'\mathrm{d}\overline{G} + C'M_Y\mathrm{d}\overline{G} = C'^2\mathrm{d}\overline{G}$. This is how the multiplier process will operate and raise Y at the end of the process by $\frac{\mathrm{d}\overline{G}}{1-C'}$ and e by $\frac{\mathrm{d}\overline{G}}{(1-C')}\cdot\frac{M_Y}{(X_p - M_p)\frac{P^*}{P}}$. This is the end of the first round of change. Thus, the changes in Y and e in the first round, denoted by $\mathrm{d}Y_1$ and $\mathrm{d}e_1$, respectively, are given by

$$\mathrm{d}Y_1 = \frac{\mathrm{d}\overline{G}}{(1 - C')} \text{ and } \mathrm{d}e_1 = \frac{\mathrm{d}\overline{G}}{(1 - C')}\cdot\frac{M_Y}{\left(X_p - M_p\right)\frac{P^*}{P}}.$$

Out of the additional income of $\frac{\mathrm{d}\overline{G}}{1-C'}$ generated in the first round, people will save $\frac{\mathrm{d}\overline{G}}{(1-C')}\left(1 - C'\right) = \mathrm{d}\overline{G}$. They will deposit this amount in domestic commercial banks, which in turn will extend out of these new deposits new loans of $(1 - \rho)\mathrm{d}\overline{G}$ creating an excess supply in the domestic loan market. r will, therefore, fall to clear the loan market. Per unit fall in r, demand for new loans of domestic borrowers rises by $-I'$, while net supply of new loans from abroad falls by $K_{\tilde{r}}$. Hence, per unit fall in r, excess supply of new loans to domestic borrowers falls by $-I' + K_{\tilde{r}}$. Therefore, r will fall by $\frac{(1-\rho)\mathrm{d}\overline{G}}{-I'+K_{\tilde{r}}}$ in absolute value and reduce excess supply of new loans by $(1 - \rho)\mathrm{d}\overline{G}$ to zero and, thereby, restore equilibrium in the domestic loan market. This fall in r will raise I by $\frac{(1-\rho)\mathrm{d}\overline{G}}{-I'+K_{\tilde{r}}}\left(-I'\right)$. It will also lower K by $K_{\tilde{r}}\frac{(1-\rho)\mathrm{d}\overline{G}}{-I'+K_{\tilde{r}}}$ creating BOP deficit. e will, therefore, rise by $\left[K_{\tilde{r}}\frac{(1-\rho)\mathrm{d}\overline{G}}{-I'+K_{\tilde{r}}}\right]\left[\frac{1}{(X_p - M_p)\frac{P^*}{P}}\right]$ to raise $(X - M)$ by $K_{\tilde{r}}\frac{(1-\rho)\mathrm{d}\overline{G}}{-I'+K_{\tilde{r}}}$. Thus, aggregate planned investment and net export increase by $\frac{(1-\rho)\mathrm{d}\overline{G}}{-I'+K_{\tilde{r}}}\left(-I'\right) + K_{\tilde{r}}\frac{(1-\rho)\mathrm{d}\overline{G}}{-I'+K_{\tilde{r}}} = (1 - \rho)\mathrm{d}\overline{G}$. This, just as in the first round, sets into motion the multiplier process and Y at the end of the multiplier process goes up by $\frac{(1-\rho)\mathrm{d}\overline{G}}{1-C'}$ in the second round. Along with this increase in Y, as before, e will increase by $\frac{(1-\rho)\mathrm{d}\overline{G}}{1-C'}\left[\frac{M_Y}{(X_p - M_p)\frac{P^*}{P}}\right]$. This is the end of the second round of change. Thus, in the second round, Y, r, and e change by

$$\mathrm{d}Y_2 = \frac{(1 - \rho)\mathrm{d}\overline{G}}{1 - C'}$$

$$dr_2 = -\frac{(1-\rho)d\overline{G}}{-I' + K_{\tilde{r}}}$$

and

$$de_2 = \left[K_{\tilde{r}} \frac{(1-\rho)d\bar{G}}{-I' + K_{\tilde{r}}} \right] \left[\frac{1}{(X_p - M_p)\frac{P^*}{P}} \right] + \left[\frac{(1-\rho)d\bar{G}}{1-C'} \right] \left[\frac{M_Y}{(X_p - M_p)\frac{P^*}{P}} \right]$$
$$= (\bar{\theta} + \theta)(1-\rho)d\bar{G},$$

where

$$\theta \equiv \left[\frac{K_{\tilde{r}}}{-I' + K_{\tilde{r}}} \right] \left[\frac{1}{(X_p - M_p)\frac{P^*}{P}} \right] \text{ and } \bar{\theta} \equiv \left[\frac{M_Y}{(1-C')} \right] \left[\frac{1}{(X_p - M_p)\frac{P^*}{P}} \right]$$

The increase in Y in the second round, as before, will create an additional saving of $(1-C')\frac{(1-\rho)d\bar{G}}{1-C'} = (1-\rho)d\bar{G}$, which the households will deposit with the domestic commercial banks. The banks will plan to extend out of these new deposits new loans of $(1-\rho)^2 d\bar{G}$, which, as before, will lower r by $\frac{(1-\rho)^2 d\bar{G}}{-I'+K_{\tilde{r}}}$. This, in turn, will raise I by $\frac{(1-\rho)^2 d\bar{G}}{-I'+K_{\tilde{r}}}(-I')$ and lower K by $\frac{(1-\rho)^2 d\bar{G}}{-I'+K_{\tilde{r}}} K_{\tilde{r}}$. The fall in K will create BOP deficit. This will raise e by $\left[K_{\tilde{r}} \frac{(1-\rho)^2 d\bar{G}}{-I'+K_{\tilde{r}}} \right] \left[\frac{1}{(X_p - M_p)\frac{P^*}{P}} \right]$ so that $(X - M)$ rises by $K_{\tilde{r}} \frac{(1-\rho)^2 d\bar{G}}{-I'+K_{\tilde{r}}}$. Aggregate planned investment and net export together will, therefore, go up by $\frac{(1-\rho)^2 d\bar{G}}{-I'+K_{\tilde{r}}}(-I') + K_{\tilde{r}} \frac{(1-\rho)^2 d\bar{G}}{-I'+K_{\tilde{r}}} = (1-\rho)^2 d\bar{G}$. This will at the end of the multiplier process raise Y by $\frac{(1-\rho)^2 d\bar{G}}{1-C'}$. This increase in Y will be accompanied by an increase in e by $\left[(1-\rho)^2 d\bar{G} \right] \left[\frac{M_Y}{(X_p - M_p)\frac{P^*}{P}} \right]$. This is the end of the third round of change. In the third round, the changes in Y, r, and e, denoted by dY_3, dr_3, and de_3, respectively, are given by

$$dY_3 = \frac{(1-\rho)^2 d\bar{G}}{1-C'}, \, dr_3 = -\frac{(1-\rho)^2 d\bar{G}}{-I' + K_{\tilde{r}}} \text{ and } de_3 = (\theta + \bar{\theta})(1-\rho)^2 d\bar{G}$$

This process of expansion will continue until the additional demand that is created in each round eventually falls to zero. The total increase in Y and e and the total fall in r brought about by the increase in $\overline{G}$ by $d\overline{G}$ are, therefore, given by

$$dY = \frac{d\overline{G}}{1-C'} + \frac{(1-\rho)d\overline{G}}{1-C'} + \frac{(1-\rho)^2 d\overline{G}}{1-C'} + \cdots = \frac{d\overline{G}}{\rho(1-C')} \quad (4.17)$$

$$dr = -\frac{(1-\rho)d\overline{G}}{-I' + K_{\tilde{r}}} - \frac{(1-\rho)^2 d\overline{G}}{-I' + K_{\tilde{r}}} - \frac{(1-\rho)^3 d\overline{G}}{-I' + K_{\tilde{r}}} - \cdots = -\frac{\frac{(1-\rho)}{\rho} d\overline{G}}{-I' + K_{\tilde{r}}} \quad (4.18)$$

$$de = \bar{\theta} d\overline{G} + (\theta + \bar{\theta})(1-\rho)d\overline{G} + (\theta + \bar{\theta})(1-\rho)^2 d\overline{G} + \cdots$$

$$= \bar{\theta}\frac{d\overline{G}}{\rho} + \theta\frac{(1-\rho)d\overline{G}}{\rho} \tag{4.19}$$

From (4.17), it follows that the total increases in saving, stock of bank deposit, and money supply (denoted S, D, and m, respectively) are given by

$$dS = d(dD) = d(dm) = d\overline{G} + (1-\rho)d\overline{G} + (1-\rho)^2 d\overline{G} + \ldots = \frac{d\overline{G}}{\rho} \tag{4.20}$$

Equation (4.20) shows that the standard money multiplier formula holds in this case, since $d\overline{G} = \frac{dH}{P}$.

It is clear that (4.17), (4.18), and (4.19) tally with (4.14), (4.15), and (4.16), respectively.

Monetary Policy

Here, we shall examine how an expansionary monetary policy consisting in a cut in r_c affects r, Y, and e in our model. We derive the results mathematically. First, note that, solving (4.13), we get

$$S = dD = dm = \frac{\overline{G}}{\rho} = \frac{\frac{dH}{P}}{\rho} \tag{4.21}$$

Taking total differential of (4.13) treating all exogenous variables other than r_c as fixed, substituting (4.21) into it, and, then, solving for dY, we get

$$dY = \frac{\rho' \cdot (Y - C(Y))(-dr_c)}{\rho(1-C')} = \frac{\rho' \cdot \left(\frac{\bar{G}}{\rho}\right)(-dr_c)}{\rho(1-C')} > 0 \text{ using (4.13)} \tag{4.22}$$

Taking total differential of (4.11) treating all exogenous variables other than r_c as fixed, and solving for dr, we get

$$dr = -\frac{\left(\frac{\rho'}{\rho}\right)\left(\frac{\overline{G}}{\rho}\right)(-dr_c)}{-I' + K_{\tilde{r}}} < 0 \tag{4.23}$$

Again, taking total differential of (4.12) treating all exogenous variables as fixed, substituting for dY and dr their values given by (4.22) and (4.23), respectively, and, finally, solving for de, we get

$$de = \frac{M_y\frac{\rho'\left(\frac{\overline{G}}{\rho}\right)(-dr_c)}{\rho(1-C')} + K_{\tilde{r}}\frac{\rho'\left(\frac{\overline{G}}{\rho}\right)(-dr_c)}{-\rho(-I'+K_{\tilde{r}})}}{\left(X_p - M_p\right)\frac{P*}{P}} \tag{4.24}$$

From the above, it follows that monetary policy is effective in influencing output and employment in the flexible interest rate case in the flexible exchange rate regime, with imperfect capital mobility. The intuition is quite simple. Following a cut in r_c, the commercial banks lower their reserve–deposit ratio. This raises supply of commercial bank loans in the market by $\rho'\left(\frac{\overline{G}}{\rho}\right)$, assuming $\frac{\overline{G}}{\rho} = \frac{\frac{dH}{P}}{\rho}$ to be the total stock of bank deposit. This will raise, through adjustments in r and e, investment and net export by the same amount as the increase in loan supply setting into motion the multiplier process. The detailed adjustment process is very similar to that in the case of fiscal policy.

Irrelevance of the Money Market

From (4.13), we get (4.21).

The LHS of (4.21) gives households' saving, which constitutes demand for additional money, while the RHS gives the supply of additional money. Thus, when the equilibrium conditions of the model are satisfied, demand for money and supply of money become equal automatically. We sum up the findings of our above discussion in the form of the following proposition:

Proposition 4.2 *We consider here a small open economy with flexible exchange rate, imperfect capital mobility, and flexible interest rate. In this kind of an economy, private autonomous spending, just as in the earlier cases, ceases to be a determinant of GDP. In this case also, the model brings out clearly the fact that processes of generation of income, saving, credit, money, and spending are inextricably linked together. Here also the equality between demand for money and supply of money is irrelevant in defining equilibrium and both fiscal and monetary policies are effective.*

We shall now focus on the case where interest rate is rigid.

4.3.2 *Interest Rate Rigidity*

We assume here that the banking sector is an oligopoly and oligopolistic interdependence among banks makes the interest rates rigid. Banks set their interest rate by applying a markup to r_c so that r is an increasing function of r_c. Thus, we have

$$r = r\left(\underset{+}{r_c}\right) \tag{4.25}$$

Incorporating exogenously given investors' expectations regarding the future prospect of their businesses denoted E in the investment function and (4.25) into (4.7), we rewrite it as

$$Y = C(Y) + I(r(r_c), E) + \overline{G} + X\left(\frac{P^*e}{P}; Y^*\right) - M\left(\frac{P^*e}{P}; Y\right) \tag{4.26}$$

As before, government finances its consumption expenditure by borrowing from the central bank. Hence, (4.7) holds good in this case also. Regarding the credit market, all the assumptions made in the earlier case hold in the present case also. Thus, domestic households deposit all their saving $[Y - C(Y)]$ with the commercial banks. The commercial banks on the basis of $(r^*, r(r_c))$ decide on the allocation of their new credit supply $(1-\rho)(Y - C(Y))$ between domestic and foreign borrowers. Domestic investors, who are the only domestic borrowers of the domestic commercial banks, also decide on the allocation of their total borrowing between domestic and foreign lenders on the basis of $(r^*, r(r_c))$. Therefore, total supply of new credit to domestic investors is given by $l(r(r_c)) = (1-\rho)(Y - C(Y)) + K(r(r_c) - r^*) + \overline{K}$. However, $l(r(r_c))$ may not match with domestic investors' demand for new credit given by $I(r(r_c))$. We assume that commercial banks, in case of excess demand, meet it by borrowing from the central bank. In case of excess supply, they park it with the central bank. Denoting commercial banks' borrowing from the central bank by b, which may be positive or negative, we write the credit market equilibrium condition as follows:

$$(1-\rho)(Y - C(Y)) + K\big(r(r_c) - r^*\big) + \overline{K} + b = I(r(r_c)) \tag{4.27}$$

Incorporating (4.25) into (4.12), we write the BOP equilibrium condition as

$$\left[X\left(\frac{P^*e}{P}; Y^*\right) - M\left(\frac{P^*e}{P}, Y\right)\right] + K\big(r(r_c) - r^*\big) + \overline{K} = 0 \tag{4.28}$$

The specification of our model is now complete. It consists of three key Eqs. (4.26), (4.27), and (4.28) in three endogenous variables Y, b, and e. We solve them as follows. Substituting (4.12) into (4.26), we rewrite it as

$$Y = C(Y) + I(r(r_c), E) + \overline{G} - K\big(r(r_c) - r^*\big) - \overline{K} \tag{4.29}$$

We can solve (4.29) for Y. Putting the equilibrium value of Y in (4.27), we get the equilibrium value of b. Again, putting the equilibrium value of Y in (4.28), we get the equilibrium value of e. We shall now carry out a comparative static exercise to illustrate the working of the model.

An Improvement in Investors' Expectations for Exogenous Reasons

We shall examine here how an increase in E for exogenous reasons affects the endogenous variables of the model. To derive the impact on Y, we take total differential of (4.29) treating all variables other than Y and E as fixed and, then, solve for $\mathrm{d}Y$. This gives

$$\mathrm{d}Y = \frac{I_E \mathrm{d}E}{1 - C'} \tag{4.30}$$

Again, taking total differential of (4.27) treating all variables other than Y and b as fixed, substituting (4.30) into it, and, then, solving for $\mathrm{d}b$, we get

$$\mathrm{d}b = -(1-\rho)I_E\mathrm{d}E \tag{4.31}$$

Finally, taking total differential of (4.28) treating all variables other than e and Y as fixed, substituting (4.30) into it, and, then, solving for de, we get

$$\mathrm{d}e = \frac{M_Y\frac{I_E\mathrm{d}E}{1-C'}}{\left(X_p - M_p\right)\frac{P^*}{P}} \tag{4.32}$$

Let us explain the adjustment process. Following an autonomous improvement in the expectations (the animal spirits) of the investors, aggregate planned investment demand and, therefore, demand for new bank credit goes up by $I_E\mathrm{d}E$. Commercial banks meet this additional demand by borrowing from the central bank so that b initially rises by $I_E\mathrm{d}E$. The increase in planned aggregate investment demand sets off the multiplier process raising Y by $\frac{I_E\mathrm{d}E}{1-C'}$. Let us explain. Per unit increase in Y, demand for domestic goods, with e remaining unchanged at its initial equilibrium value, rises by $\left(C' - M_Y\right)$. However, the M_Y amount of increase in import demand that a unit increase in Y gives rise to, creates BOP deficit and e rises by $\frac{M_Y}{(X_p-M_p)\frac{P^*}{P}}$ raising net export by M_Y so that net export rises to its initial equilibrium value. Thus, the total increase in demand for domestic goods per unit increase in Y is given by $\left(C' - M_Y\right) + M_Y = C'$. Thus, following the increase in aggregate investment demand by $I_E\mathrm{d}E$, producers in the first round raise Y by $I_E\mathrm{d}E$. This increase in Y raises aggregate planned consumption demand by $C'I_E\mathrm{d}E$ and lower net export by $M_YI_E\mathrm{d}E$. However, e will rise by $\frac{M_YI_E\mathrm{d}E}{(X_p-M_p)\frac{P^*}{P}}$ to restore net export to its initial equilibrium value. Hence, aggregate demand for domestic goods will rise by $C'I_E\mathrm{d}E$ inducing producers to raise Y by the same amount in the second round. In the second round, e, as we have just shown, rises by $\frac{M_YC'I_E\mathrm{d}E}{(X_p-M_p)\frac{P^*}{P}}$. Similarly, in the third round, Y and e will go up by $C'^2I_E\mathrm{d}E$ and $\frac{M_YC'^2I_E\mathrm{d}E}{(X_p-M_p)\frac{P^*}{P}}$, respectively. This process of expansion will continue until the increase in demand that takes place in each successive round eventually falls to zero. Thus, the total increase in Y and e are given by

$$\mathrm{d}Y = I_E\mathrm{d}E + C'I_E\mathrm{d}E + C'^2I_E\mathrm{d}E + \ldots = \frac{I_E\mathrm{d}E}{1-C'} \tag{4.33}$$

and

$$\mathrm{d}e = \frac{M_YI_E\mathrm{d}E}{\left(X_p - M_p\right)\frac{P^*}{P}} + \frac{M_YC'I_E\mathrm{d}E}{\left(X_p - M_p\right)\frac{P^*}{P}} + \frac{M_YC'^2I_E\mathrm{d}E}{\left(X_p - M_p\right)\frac{P^*}{P}} + \ldots = \frac{M_Y\frac{I_E\mathrm{d}E}{1-C'}}{\left(X_p - M_p\right)\frac{P^*}{P}} \tag{4.34}$$

It is clear that (4.30) and (4.32) tally with (4.33) and (4.34), respectively. Out of the additional income of $\frac{I_E\mathrm{d}E}{1-C'}$, people make an additional saving of $I_E\mathrm{d}E$, which they deposit with the commercial banks. Out of this additional deposit, commercial banks lend out $(1-\rho)I_E\mathrm{d}E$ to the central bank. Therefore, the net increase in b is given by $I_E\mathrm{d}E - (1-\rho)I_E\mathrm{d}E = \rho I_E\mathrm{d}E$. Thus, while the stock of high-powered money rises by $\rho I_E\mathrm{d}E$, money supply increases by $I_E\mathrm{d}E$ giving us the standard money multiplier formula. This explains the results. The following proposition sums up the findings of our discussion here:

Proposition 4.3 *In the case of a small open economy, with flexible exchange rate and imperfect capital mobility, animal spirits of investors emerge as a major determinant of GDP if interest rates charged by banks, as is the case in reality, are rigid. In this case also, our model shows that the processes of generation of income, saving, credit, money, and spending are inextricably linked with one another and the standard money multiplier formula holds.*

4.4 A Small Open Economy with Imperfect Capital Mobility and Fixed Exchange Rate

We shall examine here how a small open economy with imperfect capital mobility behaves in a fixed exchange rate regime. In a fixed exchange rate regime, the central bank seeks to keep e at a target level to be denoted by $\bar{e}$. In this case, the goods market equilibrium condition is given by

$$Y = C(Y) + I(r) + \overline{G} + X\left(\frac{P^*\bar{e}}{P}; Y^*\right) - M\left(\frac{P^*\bar{e}}{P}; Y\right) \tag{4.35}$$

The central bank intervenes in the foreign currency market to keep the exchange rate at $\bar{e}$. If there emerges excess supply of foreign currency at $\bar{e}$, the central bank has to buy up this excess supply at $\bar{e}$ with domestic currency so that the stock of high-powered money increases by the value of the excess supply of foreign currency in terms of domestic currency valued at $\bar{e}$. Again, if there emerges excess demand for foreign currency at $\bar{e}$, the central bank has to meet this excess demand for foreign currency by selling foreign currency at $\bar{e}$ in exchange for domestic currency. Clearly, in this case, the stock of high-powered money goes down by the value of the excess demand for foreign currency in terms of domestic currency valued at $\bar{e}$. Therefore, given the assumption that the entire government consumption expenditure is financed by borrowing from the central bank, the increase in the stock of high-powered money in the given period in the economy is given by the following equation:

$$\frac{\mathrm{d}H}{P} = \overline{G} + \left[X\left(\frac{P^*\bar{e}}{P}; Y^*\right) - M\left(\frac{P^*\bar{e}}{P}, Y\right) + K\left(r - r^*\right) + \overline{K}\right] \tag{4.36}$$

The assumption underlying (4.36) is that the stock of high-powered money in the domestic economy changes only for two reasons, namely government's borrowing from the central bank to finance its consumption expenditure and central bank's intervention in the foreign currency market to keep the exchange rate at the target level. Let us explain (4.36). Note that $\frac{P}{\bar{e}}\left[X\left(\frac{P^*\bar{e}}{P}; Y^*\right) - M\left(\frac{P^*\bar{e}}{P}, Y\right) + K(r - r^*) + \overline{K}\right]$ gives the excess supply of foreign currency at $\bar{e}$, which may be positive or negative. If it is negative, it represents excess demand. The domestic central bank has to buy up this excess supply of foreign currency with $\bar{e}.\frac{P}{\bar{e}}\left[X\left(\frac{P^*\bar{e}}{P}; Y^*\right) - M\left(\frac{P^*\bar{e}}{P}, Y\right) + K(r - r^*) + \overline{K}\right]$ amount of domestic currency raising the stock of high-powered money by $P\left[X\left(\frac{P^*\bar{e}}{P}; Y^*\right) - M\left(\frac{P^*\bar{e}}{P}, Y\right) + K(r - r^*) + \overline{K}\right]$ and that of real balance by $\left[X\left(\frac{P^*\bar{e}}{P}; Y^*\right) - M\left(\frac{P^*\bar{e}}{P}, Y\right) + K(r - r^*) + \overline{K}\right]$. This explains (4.36).

Since economic agents hold their savings only in the form of domestic commercial bank deposits and as we have considered no other source of domestic commercial bank deposits, total planned supply of new loans by domestic commercial banks is given by $(1 - \rho(r_c))(Y - C(Y))$. As explained above in the context of the flexible exchange rate regime, total net supply of new loans to domestic borrowers from abroad is given by $\overline{K} + K(r - r^*)$. To recall, $\overline{K} + K(r - r^*)$ is made up of the total amount of new loans secured by domestic borrowers from abroad net of the total amount of new loans extended by domestic commercial banks to foreigners. Therefore, as before, total supply of new loans to domestic borrowers denoted l is given by

$$l = \left(1 - \rho\left(\underset{+}{r_c}\right)\right)(Y - C(Y)) + \overline{K} + K\left(r - r^*\right) \quad (4.37)$$

Demand for loans comes only from domestic investors, who finance their entire investment demand with new loans. Thus, demand for new loans of domestic borrowers denoted by l^d is given by

$$l^d = I(r) \quad (4.38)$$

We shall first focus on the case where interest rate is flexible.

4.4.1 Flexible Interest Rate Case

Domestic loan market is in equilibrium when

$$\left(1 - \rho\left(\underset{+}{r_c}\right)\right)(Y - C(Y)) + \left(K\left(r - r^*\right) + \overline{K}\right) = I(r) \quad (4.39)$$

The specification of our model is complete. It consists of three key equations, (4.35), (4.36), and (4.39) in three endogenous variables, Y, r and $\frac{dH}{P}$. We solve them as follows. We solve (4.35) and (4.39) for the equilibrium values of Y and r. The solution is shown in Fig. 4.5 where equilibrium values of Y and r, labeled Y_0 and r_0, correspond to the point of intersection of the IS and LL curves representing (4.35) and (4.39), respectively. IS is steeper than LL for reasons of stability. Substituting

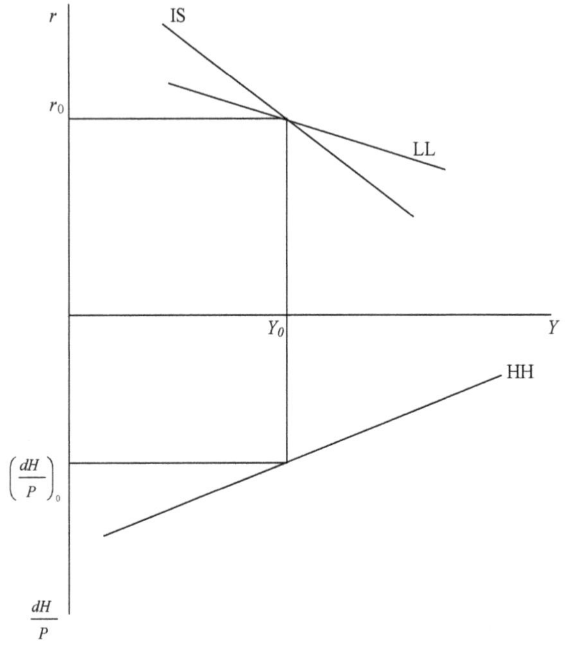

Fig. 4.5 Determination of Y, r, and $\frac{\mathrm{d}H}{P}$ in the fixed exchange rate regime under imperfect capital mobility

the equilibrium values of Y and r in (4.36), we get the equilibrium value of $\frac{\mathrm{d}H}{P}$. We can show the equilibrium value of $\frac{\mathrm{d}H}{P}$ in a diagram as follows. Solving (4.39), we get the equilibrium value of r as a function of Y, given r_{c} and other parameters of (4.39). Thus,

$$r = r\left(\underset{-}{Y}; \underset{+}{r_{\mathrm{c}}}, \underset{-}{\overline{K}}\right) \tag{4.40}$$

Signs of partial derivatives of (4.40) can be easily derived from (4.39). Substituting (4.40) into (4.36), we rewrite it as

$$\frac{\mathrm{d}H}{P} = \overline{G} + \left[X\left(\frac{P^*\bar{e}}{P}; Y^*\right) - M\left(\frac{P^*\bar{e}}{P}, Y\right) + K\left(r\left(\underset{-}{Y}; \underset{+}{r_{\mathrm{c}}}, \underset{-}{\overline{K}}\right) - r^*\right) + \overline{K}\right] \tag{4.41}$$

We measure positive values of $\frac{\mathrm{d}H}{P}$ in the downward direction on the vertical axis in the lower panel of Fig. 4.5, where HH represents (4.41). Its slope is negative. Hence, we have drawn it as negatively sloped. The equilibrium value of $\frac{\mathrm{d}H}{P}$ corresponds to the equilibrium value of Y on the HH line. The equilibrium value of $\frac{\mathrm{d}H}{P}$ is labeled $\left(\frac{\mathrm{d}H}{P}\right)_0$.

Fiscal Policy: An Increase in $\overline{G}$ Financed by Borrowing from the Central Bank

We shall here examine how an increase in $\overline{G}$ financed by borrowing from the central bank affects the endogenous variables of the model. We shall first do it diagrammatically using Fig. 4.6, where the initial equilibrium values of Y and r, which correspond to the point of intersection of IS and LL schedules representing (4.35) and (4.39), respectively, are labeled Y_0 and r_0. The initial equilibrium value of $\frac{\mathrm{d}H}{P}$, which corresponds to Y_0 on the HH schedule representing (4.41) in the lower panel, is labeled $\left(\frac{\mathrm{d}H}{P}\right)_0$. Following an increase in $\overline{G}$ by $\mathrm{d}\overline{G}$, the IS shifts to the right by $\frac{\mathrm{d}\overline{G}}{1-C'+M_Y}$. The new IS is labeled IS_1 in Fig. 4.5. The LL schedule, as follows from (4.39), remains unaffected. Hence, Y goes up and r falls. The new equilibrium values of Y and r are labeled Y_1 and r_1, respectively. Let us now focus on the HH schedule representing (4.41). An increase in $\overline{G}$ by $\mathrm{d}\overline{G}$ financed by borrowing from the central bank directly raises $\frac{\mathrm{d}H}{P}$ by $\mathrm{d}\overline{G}$ corresponding to any given Y. Hence, HH schedule shifts southward by $\mathrm{d}\overline{G}$. Hence, as follows from Fig. 4.6, the direction of change in $\frac{\mathrm{d}H}{P}$ is ambiguous.

Mathematical Derivation of the Result

Substituting (4.39) into (4.35) and, then, using (4.36), we rewrite (4.35) as

$$Y = C(Y) + (1-\rho)(Y - C(Y)) + \frac{\mathrm{d}H}{P} \tag{4.42}$$

Taking total differential of (4.42) treating all exogenous variables other than $\left(\frac{\mathrm{d}H}{P}\right)$ as fixed and solving for $\mathrm{d}Y$, we get

$$\mathrm{d}Y = \frac{\mathrm{d}\left(\frac{\mathrm{d}H}{P}\right)}{\rho(1-C')} \tag{4.43}$$

Denoting the amount of new bank deposits by $\mathrm{d}D$, we get

$$\mathrm{d}D = \mathrm{d}m = (Y - C(Y)) \tag{4.44}$$

Taking total differential of (4.44), substituting (4.43) for $\mathrm{d}Y$, and, then, solving for $\mathrm{d}(\mathrm{d}D)$, we get

$$\mathrm{d}(\mathrm{d}D) = \frac{\mathrm{d}\left(\frac{\mathrm{d}H}{P}\right)}{\rho} = \mathrm{d}m \tag{4.45}$$

From (4.45), it is clear that the standard money multiplier formula holds in this case too.

Taking total differential of (4.39) treating all variables other than Y and r as fixed and, then, solving for $\frac{\mathrm{d}r}{\mathrm{d}Y} \equiv r_y$, we get

$$\frac{\mathrm{d}r}{\mathrm{d}Y} \equiv r_y = -\frac{(1-\rho)\left(1-C'\right)}{K_{\tilde{r}} - I'} < 0 \tag{4.46}$$

Note that r_y gives the value of the slope of the LL schedule in Figs. 4.5 and 4.6. It measures the amount of fall in r that is required to keep the credit market in equilibrium following a unit increase in Y from any given (Y, r) satisfying (4.39).

Taking total differential of (4.36) treating all variables other than $\overline{G}$, Y and r as fixed, substituting (4.46) into it, and, then solving for $\mathrm{d}\left(\frac{\mathrm{d}H}{P}\right)$, we get

$$\mathrm{d}\left(\frac{\mathrm{d}H}{P}\right) = \mathrm{d}\overline{G} - M_Y\mathrm{d}Y + K_{\tilde{r}}r_y\mathrm{d}Y \tag{4.47}$$

Substituting (4.47) into (4.43) and, then, solving for dY, we get

$$\mathrm{d}Y = \frac{\mathrm{d}\overline{G}}{\rho(1 - C') + M_Y + K_{\tilde{r}}\left(-r_y\right)} > 0 \tag{4.48}$$

Substituting (4.48) into (4.47) and solving for $\mathrm{d}\left(\frac{\mathrm{d}H}{P}\right)$, we get

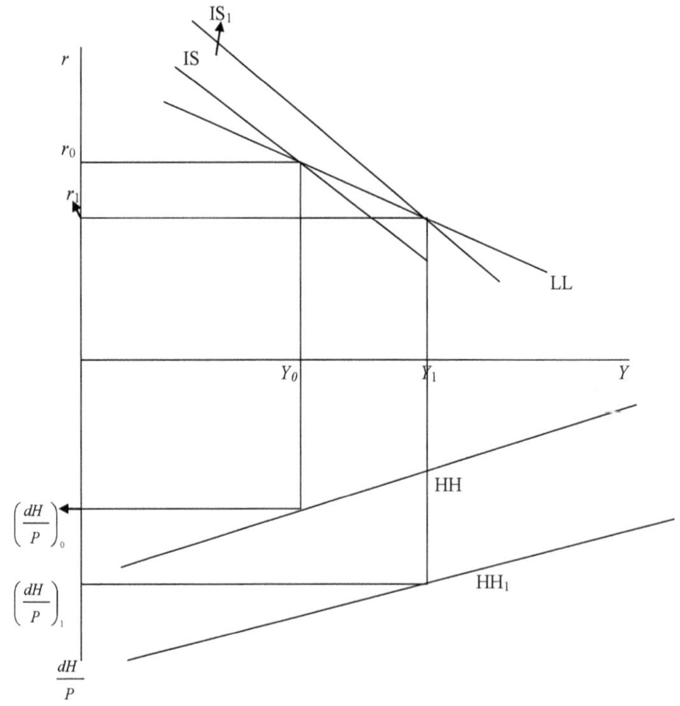

Fig. 4.6 Effect of an increase in $\overline{G}$ on Y, r, and $\frac{\mathrm{d}H}{P}$ in the fixed exchange rate regime under imperfect capital mobility

$$\mathrm{d}\left(\frac{\mathrm{d}H}{P}\right) = \frac{\rho(1 - C')\mathrm{d}\overline{G}}{\rho(1 - C') + M_Y + K_{\bar{r}}(-r_y)} > 0 \tag{4.49}$$

Again, taking total differential of (4.39), substituting (4.48) into it, and, then, solving for dr, we get

$$\mathrm{d}r = r_y.\frac{\mathrm{d}\overline{G}}{\rho(1 - C') + M_Y + K_{\bar{r}}\phi} < 0 \tag{4.50}$$

We shall now explain (4.48), (4.49), and (4.50) by describing the adjustment process. As government raises its expenditure by $\mathrm{d}\overline{G}$ by borrowing from the central bank, producers respond to it by raising Y by $\mathrm{d}\overline{G}$. This is the end of the first round of changes. Denoting the changes Y, $\left(\frac{\mathrm{d}H}{P}\right)$ and r that take place in the ith round by $\mathrm{d}Y_i$, $\mathrm{d}\left(\frac{\mathrm{d}H}{P}\right)_i$ and $\mathrm{d}r_i$ respectively, we get $\mathrm{d}Y_1 = \mathrm{d}\overline{G}, \mathrm{d}\left(\frac{\mathrm{d}H}{P}\right)_1 = \mathrm{d}\overline{G}$ and $\mathrm{d}r_1 = 0$. The increase in Y by $\mathrm{d}\overline{G}$ will raise consumption expenditure on domestic goods by $(C' - M_Y)\mathrm{d}\overline{G}$. People will also make an additional saving of $(1 - C')\mathrm{d}\overline{G}$, which they will deposit in banks. The banks will, therefore, raise their planned supply of loans by $(1 - \rho)(1 - C')\mathrm{d}\overline{G}$ creating excess supply of loans at the initial equilibrium r. r will fall by $r_y \cdot \mathrm{d}\overline{G}$ to clear the loan market. K will, as a result, fall by $K_{\bar{r}} r_y \cdot \mathrm{d}\overline{G}$. Hence, supply of new loans to the investors in the new loan market equilibrium will rise by $(1 - \rho)(1 - C')\mathrm{d}\overline{G} - K_{\bar{r}}(-r_y) \cdot \mathrm{d}\overline{G}$ raising investment by the same amount. Y in the second round will, therefore, increase by $(C' - M_Y)\mathrm{d}\overline{G} + (1 - \rho)(1 - C')\mathrm{d}\overline{G} - K_{\bar{r}}(-r_y) \cdot \mathrm{d}\overline{G}$. As people spend $M_Y\mathrm{d}\overline{G}$ amount of their additional income on imported goods, they first seek to purchase foreign currency with $PM_Y\mathrm{d}\overline{G}$ amount of domestic currency. The central bank has to meet this demand to keep e at $\bar{e}$. Hence, $\left(\frac{\mathrm{d}H}{P}\right)$ falls by $-M_Y\mathrm{d}\overline{G}$. Again, the fall in K by $K_{\bar{r}} r_y \cdot \mathrm{d}\overline{G}$ creates an excess demand for foreign currency of $\frac{P}{\bar{e}}\left(K_{\bar{r}}(-r_y) \cdot \mathrm{d}\overline{G}\right)$ at $\bar{e}$. The central bank has to meet this excess demand by buying up $P\left(K_{\bar{r}}(-r_y) \cdot \mathrm{d}\overline{G}\right)$ amount of domestic currency with $\frac{P}{\bar{e}}\left(K_{\bar{r}}(-r_y) \cdot \mathrm{d}\overline{G}\right)$ amount of foreign currency. So, $\left(\frac{\mathrm{d}H}{P}\right)$ will fall again by $-\left(K_{\bar{r}}(-r_y) \cdot \mathrm{d}\overline{G}\right)$. Thus, in the second round, changes in Y, $\left(\frac{\mathrm{d}H}{P}\right)$, and r are given by $\mathrm{d}Y_2 = \left[(C' - M_Y) + (1 - \rho)(1 - C') - K_{\bar{r}}(-r_y).\right]\mathrm{d}\overline{G}$, $\mathrm{d}r_2 = r_y \cdot \mathrm{d}\overline{G}$ and $\mathrm{d}\left(\frac{\mathrm{d}H}{P}\right)_2 = -\left[M_Y + K_{\bar{r}}(-r_y)\right]\mathrm{d}\overline{G}$.

Similarly, one can easily show that in the third round, $\mathrm{d}Y_3 = \left[(C' - M_Y) + (1 - \rho)(1 - C') - K_{\bar{r}}(-r_y)\right]\mathrm{d}Y_2$, $\mathrm{d}r_3 = r_y \cdot \mathrm{d}Y_2$ and $\mathrm{d}\left(\frac{\mathrm{d}H}{P}\right)_3 = -\left[M_Y + K_{\bar{r}}(-r_y)\right]\mathrm{d}Y_2$.

This process of expansion will continue until the additional demand for Y that is created in each round eventually falls to zero. When that happens, the new equilibrium is reached. Therefore, the total changes in Y, $\left(\frac{\mathrm{d}H}{P}\right)$ and r are given by

$$\begin{aligned}\mathrm{d}Y = \mathrm{d}\bar{G} &+ \left[(C' - M_Y) + (1 - \rho)(1 - C') - K_{\bar{r}}(-r_y)\right]\mathrm{d}\bar{G} \\ &+ \left[(C' - M_Y) + (1 - \rho)(1 - C') - K_{\bar{r}}(-r_y)\right]^2\mathrm{d}\bar{G} + \cdots\end{aligned}$$

$$= \frac{\mathrm{d}\bar{G}}{\rho(1-C') + M_Y + K_{\tilde{r}}(-r_y)} \tag{4.51}$$

$$\mathrm{d}\left(\frac{\mathrm{d}H}{P}\right) = \mathrm{d}\bar{G} - \left[M_Y + K_{\tilde{r}}(-r_y)\right][\mathrm{d}Y_1 + \mathrm{d}Y_2 + \ldots]$$

$$= \mathrm{d}\bar{G} - \left[M_Y + K_{\tilde{r}}(-r_y).\right]\mathrm{d}Y$$

$$= \frac{\rho(1-C')}{\rho(1-C') + M_Y + K_{\tilde{r}}(-r_y)} \tag{4.52}$$

$$\mathrm{d}r_3 = r_y \cdot [\mathrm{d}Y_1 + \mathrm{d}Y_2 + \ldots] = r_y \cdot \frac{\mathrm{d}\overline{G}}{\rho(1-C') + M_Y + K_{\tilde{r}}\phi} \tag{4.53}$$

It is clear that (4.51), (4.52), and (4.53) tally with (4.48), (4.49), and (4.50), respectively.

Monetary Policy

We shall examine here the impact of expansionary monetary policy, which consists in the central bank lowering its policy rate r_c. We shall derive the impact mathematically. First, focus on (4.42). From (4.42), we get

$$Y - C(Y) = \frac{\frac{\mathrm{d}H}{P}}{\rho} \tag{4.54}$$

Now, taking total differential of (4.42) treating all exogenous variables other than r_c as fixed, substituting (4.54) into it, and, then, solving for dY, we get

$$\mathrm{d}Y = \frac{1}{\rho(1-C')}\rho'\frac{\frac{\mathrm{d}H}{P}}{\rho}(-\mathrm{d}r_c) + \left[\frac{1}{\rho(1-C')}\right]\mathrm{d}\left(\frac{\mathrm{d}H}{P}\right) \tag{4.55}$$

We shall now derive the value of $\mathrm{d}\left(\frac{\mathrm{d}H}{P}\right)$. Taking total differential of (4.36) treating all exogenous variables as fixed, we get

$$\mathrm{d}\left(\frac{\mathrm{d}H}{P}\right) = -M_Y\mathrm{d}Y + K_{\tilde{r}}\mathrm{d}r \tag{4.56}$$

To derive the value of dr, we take total differential of (4.39) treating all exogenous variables other than r_c as fixed, substitute (4.54) into it and, then, solve for dr. This gives

$$\mathrm{d}r = r_y\mathrm{d}Y + \frac{\frac{\rho'\frac{\mathrm{d}H}{P}}{\rho}(-\mathrm{d}r_c)}{-[K_{\tilde{r}} - I']} \quad \text{[see (4.46)]} \tag{4.57}$$

Substituting (4.57) into (4.56), we get

$$\mathrm{d}\left(\frac{\mathrm{d}H}{P}\right) = -\left[M_Y + K_{\tilde{r}}\left(-r_y\right)\right]\mathrm{d}Y - K_{\tilde{r}}\frac{\frac{\rho'\frac{\mathrm{d}H}{P}}{\rho}(-\mathrm{d}r_{\mathrm{c}})}{[K_{\tilde{r}} - I']} \tag{4.58}$$

Substituting (4.58) into (4.55) and, then, solving for d*Y*, we get

$$\mathrm{d}Y = \frac{1}{\rho(1 - C') + M_Y + K_{\tilde{r}}\left(-r_y\right)}\left[1 - \frac{K_{\tilde{r}}}{K_{\tilde{r}} - I'}\right]\rho'\frac{\frac{\mathrm{d}H}{P}}{\rho}(-\mathrm{d}r_{\mathrm{c}}) \tag{4.59}$$

Let us now explain the adjustment process. From (4.44) and (4.54), we find that the total amount of new commercial bank deposit, denoted by d*D*, is given by

$$\mathrm{d}D = Y - C(Y) = \frac{\frac{\mathrm{d}H}{P}}{\rho} \tag{4.60}$$

We assume, for simplicity, that d*D* is the total outstanding deposit of the bank. The cut in r_{c} reduces ρ and, thereby, raises supply of new loans of commercial banks by $\rho'\frac{\frac{\mathrm{d}H}{P}}{\rho}(-\mathrm{d}r_{\mathrm{c}})$ creating an excess supply of new loans at the initial equilibrium (Y, r). Hence, *r* will fall by $-\frac{\rho'\frac{\frac{\mathrm{d}H}{P}}{\rho}(-\mathrm{d}r_{\mathrm{c}})}{K_{\tilde{r}}-I'}$ to equilibrate the loan market. In this new loan market equilibrium at the initial equilibrium *Y*, supply of new loans to domestic investors and, therefore, investment will go up by $\left[1 - \frac{K_{\tilde{r}}}{K_{\tilde{r}}-I'}\right]\rho'\frac{\frac{\mathrm{d}H}{P}}{\rho}(-\mathrm{d}r_{\mathrm{c}})$ (see (4.39). There will, thus, emerge an excess demand for *Y* at the initial equilibrium *Y* and *Y* will go up by $\left[1 - \frac{K_{\tilde{r}}}{K_{\tilde{r}}-I'}\right]\rho'\frac{\frac{\mathrm{d}H}{P}}{\rho}(-\mathrm{d}r_{\mathrm{c}})$ in the first round. The rest of the adjustment process is similar to that in the case of fiscal policy.

Irrelevance of the Money Market

We have already pointed out that (4.44) and (4.54) yield the following:

Demand for money (for holding saving) $Y - C(Y) = \mathrm{d}D = \frac{\frac{\mathrm{d}H}{P}}{\rho} = \mathrm{d}m$. The major finding of the above discussion may be summed up in the form of the following proposition:

Proposition 4.4 *In the case of a small open economy with flexible exchange rate and flexible interest rate, autonomous spending ceases to be a determinant of GDP if it is financed with new credit. Here also the processes of generation of income, saving, credit, money, and spending are inextricably linked together. The standard money multiplier formula holds and the equality of demand for money and supply of money is irrelevant for defining equilibrium, as it is implied by the equilibrium conditions of the goods market and the credit market.*

We shall now focus on the case where interest rate is rigid.

4.4.2 The Case of Interest Rate Rigidity

Here, we consider the case where the banking sector is an oligopoly. Commercial banks set the interest rate by applying a markup to r_c so that (4.25) gives the value of r. When interest rates are rigid, we may have two possible cases: In one, the banks ration credit, and in the other, they do not ration credit. We shall focus on the second case here. Incorporating (4.25) into (4.35) and investors' expectations regarding future prospects of their businesses denoted E in the investment function, we rewrite it as follows:

$$Y = C(Y) + I(r(r_c), E) + \overline{G} + X\left(\frac{P^*\bar{e}}{P}; Y^*\right) - M\left(\frac{P^*\bar{e}}{P}; Y\right) \tag{4.61}$$

Let us now focus on the credit market equilibrium condition of the flexible interest rate case (4.39). The LHS of (4.39) gives the supply of new credit to domestic borrowers, and the RHS gives the demand for new credit of domestic borrowers. When interest rate is fixed at $r(r_c)$, there is no guarantee that the LHS and RHS of (4.39) will be equal. If the supply of new credit exceeds demand for new credit, commercial banks in the rigid interest rate regime lend out the excess supply to the central bank. Similarly, in the event of excess demand, commercial banks meet the excess demand by borrowing from the central bank. Denoting commercial banks' borrowing from the central bank by b, which may be positive or negative, and incorporating $r(r_c)$ into (4.39), we write the credit market equilibrium condition in the rigid interest rate regime as follows:

$$(1 - \rho(r_c))(Y - C(Y)) + \left(K\left(r(r_c) - r^*\right) + \overline{K}\right) + b = I(r(r_c), E) \tag{4.62}$$

Note that, b is a source of high-powered money in the economy. Substituting (4.25) into (4.36) and incorporating b into it, we rewrite it as follows:

$$\frac{\mathrm{d}H}{P} = \overline{G} + \left[X\left(\frac{P^*\bar{e}}{P}; Y^*\right) - M\left(\frac{P^*\bar{e}}{P}, Y\right) + K\left(r(r_c) - r^*\right) + \overline{K}\right] + b \tag{4.63}$$

The specification of our model is now complete. It consists of three key equations, (4.61), (4.62), and (4.63), in three endogenous variables Y, b, and $\frac{\mathrm{d}H}{P}$. We can, therefore, solve them for the equilibrium values of the endogenous variables. We can solve (4.61) for Y. Putting the equilibrium value of Y in (4.62), we get the equilibrium value of b. Again, putting the equilibrium values of Y and b in (4.63), we get the equilibrium value of $\frac{\mathrm{d}H}{P}$. We shall now explain the working of the model by carrying out a comparative static exercise.

An Improvement in the Expectations of the Investors

We shall examine here how an increase in E affects the endogenous variables. Taking total differential of (4.61) treating all variables other than Y and E as fixed and, then, solving for $\mathrm{d}Y$, we get

$$\mathrm{d}Y = \frac{I^E \mathrm{d}E}{1 - (C' - M_Y)} \tag{4.64}$$

Taking total differential of (4.62) treating all variables other than Y and b as fixed, substituting (4.64) into it, and, then, solving for $\mathrm{d}b$, we get

$$\mathrm{d}b = I^E \mathrm{d}E - (1 - \rho)(1 - C')\frac{I^E \mathrm{d}E}{1 - (C' - M_Y)} = \left[\frac{\rho(1 - C') + M_Y}{1 - (C' - M_Y)}\right] I^E \mathrm{d}E \tag{4.65}$$

Finally, taking total differential of (4.63) treating all variables other than $\frac{\mathrm{d}H}{P}$, Y and b as fixed, substituting (4.64) and (4.65) into it, and, then, solving for $\mathrm{d}\left(\frac{\mathrm{d}H}{P}\right)$, we get

$$\mathrm{d}\left(\frac{\mathrm{d}H}{P}\right) = -M_Y \frac{I^E \mathrm{d}E}{1 - (C' - M_Y)} + \left[\frac{\rho(1 - C') + M_Y}{1 - (C' - M_Y)}\right] I^E \mathrm{d}E \tag{4.66}$$

Let us now explain the adjustment process. Following an improvement in the expectations or the animal spirits of the investors, aggregate planned investment demand goes up by $I^E \mathrm{d}E$ creating an excess demand for credit. Domestic commercial banks meet this excess demand for credit by borrowing from the central bank so that b in the first round rises by $I^E \mathrm{d}E$. The increase in the aggregate planned investment demand sets off the multiplier process, and Y goes up by $\mathrm{d}Y = \frac{I^E \mathrm{d}E}{1-(C'-M_Y)}$. Out of this additional income, people save $(1 - C') \cdot \left[\frac{I^E \mathrm{d}E}{1-(C'-M_Y)}\right]$. People deposit this amount with the commercial banks. The commercial banks, in turn, lend out $(1 - \rho)(1 - C')\frac{I^E \mathrm{d}E}{1-(C'-M_Y)}$ to the central bank so that b goes down by the same amount. Thus, in the net, b rises by $I^E \mathrm{d}E - (1 - \rho)(1 - C')\left[\frac{I^E \mathrm{d}E}{1-(C'-M_Y)}\right] = \frac{\rho(1-C')+M_Y}{1-(C'-M_Y)} I^E \mathrm{d}E$. With the increase in Y, people's import demand rises by $M_Y \cdot \left[\frac{I^E \mathrm{d}E}{1-(C'-M_Y)}\right]$. They will plan to sell $P \cdot M_Y \cdot \left[\frac{I^E \mathrm{d}E}{1-(C'-M_Y)}\right]$ amount of domestic currency to secure foreign currency. The central bank has to buy up this much of domestic currency with $\bar{e} \cdot P \cdot M_Y \cdot \left[\frac{I^E \mathrm{d}E}{1-(C'-M_Y)}\right]$ amount of foreign currency. Therefore, the stock of high-powered money for this reason will go down by $P \cdot M_Y \cdot \left[\frac{I^E \mathrm{d}E}{1-(C'-M_Y)}\right]$. Let us now focus on the asset-liability balance sheet of the central bank. On the asset side, central bank's stock of foreign exchange reserve in terms of domestic goods falls by $-M_Y \cdot \left[\frac{I^E \mathrm{d}E}{1-(C'-M_Y)}\right]$ and domestic credit in terms of domestic goods rises by $\frac{\rho(1-C')+M_Y}{1-(C'-M_Y)} I^E \mathrm{d}E$. Therefore, net increase in the central bank's sock of assets is given by $\rho(1 - C')\left[\frac{I^E \mathrm{d}E}{1-(C'-M_Y)}\right]$. On the liabilities side, commercial bank's reserve increases by $\rho(1 - C')\left[\frac{I^E \mathrm{d}E}{1-(C'-M_Y)}\right]$. Thus, the stock of high-powered money in terms of domestic hoods goes up by the same amount. The stock of bank deposit and, therefore, the stock of money supply increase by $\left(1 - C'\right)\left[\frac{I^{E}\mathrm{d}E}{1-(C'-M_{Y})}\right]$. Hence, the standard money multiplier formula holds. This explains the adjustment process. The major findings of the above discussion may be summarized in the form of the following proposition:

Proposition 4.5 *In case of a small open economy with fixed exchange rate, autonomous spending emerges as the major determinant of GDP when interest rates charged by commercial banks are rigid. In this case also, processes of generation of income, saving, credit, money, and spending are inextricably interlinked. Money market is completely irrelevant in defining equilibrium and the standard money multiplier formulae hold.*

4.5 Conclusion

The model presented here resolves almost all the problems of the IS-LM model for an open economy, with imperfect capital mobility. The model is spelt out in terms of flows only. There is a full-fledged financial sector, with the central bank and the commercial banks. Financing of every kind of expenditure is explicitly considered here. It brings out clearly the close connection between the generation of income, saving, credit, and expenditure. Interest rate is determined, as it should be, in the credit market. Equilibrium conditions of the model also ensure equality of demand for money and supply of money. This model considers only the banks: the central bank and the commercial banks. We have already shown in Chap. 2 that incorporation of other assets and institutions does not affect the results qualitatively.

References

Ghosh, C., & Ghosh, A. (2016). *Indian economy: A macro-theoretic analysis*. Delhi, India: PHI Learning Private Limited.

Tobin, J. (1958). Liquidity preference as behaviour towards risk. *The Review of Economic Studies, 25*(2), 65–86.

Part II
Capitalism at Work: India, Greece and the USA

Chapter 5
Democracy, Dependence, and Neo-Imperialism: The Case of India

Abstract This chapter seeks to present a hypothesis as regards how and why India got itself caught in an external debt trap and delivered itself helplessly in the control of the foreign investors/global capitalists in 1991. It also shows how the New Economic Policy (NEP) that the IMF thrust on India in 1991 constitutes a strategy to deepen manifold India's dependence on global capitalists and to bring about extreme inequality creating a small island of unbelievable opulence in the midst of abysmal poverty, destitution and hunger. It also suggests that political reform driven by mass awareness that gives the political parties the opportunity of truly representing and working for the masses is the only solution to the crisis India at the present is subject to.

5.1 Introduction

In a democracy, political parties are privately funded, and as we have argued in Chap. 7, giant capitalists fund and run these political parties and, thereby, usurp state power. If we look at history, we find that the giant capitalists in Western Europe and the USA using their control over state powers invaded and colonized the rest of the world to expand their business empire by establishing monopoly rights of business in their colonies. By the beginning of World War I, the process of colonization was complete. However, at that time, the giant capitalists were a divided lot. They were divided on the basis of nationalities. Hence, they fought two world wars with one another to gain a larger share of the colonies. However, these two world wars were extremely damaging and weakened them considerably. The weakening of the Russian Empire of the Tsars led to the birth of the first socialist state in the world, Soviet Union, which posed an enormous threat to capitalism. After the conclusion of World War II, another powerful socialist state was born in China. Socialism began to emerge as an alternative to capitalism. Obviously, the giant capitalists in all the major capitalist countries felt threatened. Socialism emerged as the single most important adversary of the giant capitalists, and they devised all kinds of strategies to demolish it ushering in the era of Cold War, which they eventually won destroying Soviet Union. During the period of the Cold War, the giant capitalists of the major capitalist

C. Ghosh and A. N. Ghosh, *Keynesian Macroeconomics Beyond the IS-LM Model*, https://doi.org/10.1007/978-981-13-7888-1_5

countries joined hands and became a united force, which found its manifestation in the formation of NATO. They realized that they will not be able to counter socialist states without being united. The joint stock companies allowed them to invest in one another's companies so that their business interests became the same. Thus, there are strong reasons to believe that the giant capitalists the world over jointly own today's large global companies. The giant capitalists of the major capitalist countries now run their global business empire together through the multinational companies.

Following the devastation wrought by World War II in the major capitalist countries and the rise of socialist powers, the capitalist powers had to garner all their resources to reconstruct their countries and to combat socialism. Global capitalists no longer considered it profitable to spend any resources to keep the colonies under their occupation quashing the strong and rising nationalist movements. They granted them independence. However, in our view, they devised several strategies to keep them under their control. We shall illustrate our hypothesis with the example of India. The British Government in India followed the divide-and-rule policy, funded and promoted communal parties and, finally, before granting independence divided the country on communal lines into India and Pakistan [for supportive data and discussions, see, for example, Dutt (1970), Khan Durrani (1944) and Stewart (1951)]. Both the countries embraced democracy. The newly independent countries were too weak to survive without the assistance of either the Soviet Union or the global capitalists of the major capitalist powers led by the USA. While India sided with the Soviet Union, Pakistan allied with the USA. Thus, global capitalists through their hold over Pakistan could keep India under constant pressure.

India adopted Soviet model of planned economic development and sought to develop India into a socialist state. The Indian version of this strategy of planned economic development is called the Nehru–Mahalanobis strategy. India followed Nehru–Mahalanobis strategy until July 1991. Under this strategy, planners imposed stringent restrictions on all kinds of economic activities such as production, investment, consumption, export, import, cross-border capital flows. Through these restrictions, planners determined the allocation of resources; i.e., the planners decided which commodities are to be produced and in what quantities. The objective of the planners was to achieve self-reliance and to provide the masses with the necessities of life at affordable prices. With this end in view, planners utilized whatever resources India could amass to set up basic and heavy industries, to invest on a large scale in irrigation, flood control facilities and agricultural R&D to develop agriculture, to invest substantially in education and health care to provide the masses with these services at negligible costs and, finally, to develop a public distribution system to provide the masses with food and other necessities of life at affordable prices. Restrictions were imposed on all kinds of economic activities to prevent leakage of scarce productive resources into the production of non-essential items of consumption and investment. These restrictions were necessary to maximize the production of those goods, which were necessary to achieve the plan objectives of self-reliance and providing the masses with the basic necessities of life along with health care and education at negligible or low prices. To stop leakage of society's savings into non-essential uses, Government of India nationalized all major financial institutions and set up a nationwide financial network. The objective was to mobilize the savings of the masses by providing them with safe avenues of saving and utilize the savings to meet the investment and production targets specified in the plan. Thus, India adopted a strategy that focused on achieving self-reliance and providing the masses with food, clothing, shelter, education and health care on an adequate scale. India pursued this extremely desirable and humane strategy of development for forty years and succeeded in setting up a universal health care and education system and a broad-based industrial sector capable of producing most of the industrial goods India needed. It brought about Green Revolution in agriculture, which increased India's land productivity manifold and developed a sound financial sector that provided the masses with completely safe and remunerative avenues of holding their savings, and met all the essential credit needs of the society specified in the plans. It also set up a distribution system that provided the masses with food, clothing and shelter at affordable prices. Despite its successes and commendable qualities, India had to give it up in 1991, the year in which Soviet Union officially ceased to exist. Why did India fail to continue with the strategy? In our view, the global capitalists forced it to abandon its socialist strategy. In what follows, we shall seek to establish our hypothesis.

During Nehru–Mahalanobis era, India was heavily dependent on imported capital and intermediate goods. India did not have the technology to set up the heavy and basic industries. It had to import the technology in the form of capital goods. However, inexplicably, it did not make any effort to imbibe the imported technology and build on it. During this era, the sources of instability were all on the supply side. Adverse natural factors led to poor performance of the agricultural sector giving rise to food deficit necessitating food imports. This reduced other kinds of essential imports slowing down the rates of capital formation and growth. Similarly, external shocks such as a slowdown in the global economy or an increase in the prices of essential imported goods caused a recession by cutting down India's import capacity. Obviously, conventional fiscal and monetary policies were of no use in tackling these problems. The instability stemmed from the underdevelopment of India, which made it dependent on foreign countries. The solution lay in developing its own technology and infrastructure to eliminate its vulnerability to natural calamities and dependence on imported inputs. However, under Nehru–Mahalanobis strategy, no effort was made to gain technological independence and, hence, India's dependence on imported capital goods and intermediate inputs persisted. Even though Soviet Union from its very birth sought to develop its own knowledge and technological base with all its might and succeeded with aplomb, India never sought to emulate Soviet Union in this respect. How can one explain this puzzle? In our view, the only plausible explanation is the following. Though Soviet Union was a superpower, its financial might was much less than that of all the major capitalist powers taken together. Soviet Union was not in a position to provide India with all the external assistance that India needed either to implement its strategy or to keep its borders safe from the global capitalists, who always tried to invade India through Pakistan. In our view, the global capitalists offered India peace, but in exchange India had to desist from engaging in developing its own knowledge and technology base and had to buy global capitalists' technology with the soft loans they offered. India could have chosen less import-intensive and eminently more sensible and sustainable agriculture and cottage industry-based development strategy fortified with intensive R&D effort. Such a strategy would have been much more suitable for India, given its own endowment of productive resources. However, in that area also, in our view, global capitalists' threat of invasion of India through her neighbor forced India's hands.

The scenario that unfolded in the eighties in India constitutes another puzzle. Until the end of the seventies, India desisted from external commercial borrowing. It sought to secure only foreign aid. Even when the oil shocks occurred in the seventies, India did not seek external commercial loans to tide over the crisis. However, in the eighties India suddenly woke up to the necessity of modernizing its industries after three decades of import-substituting industrialization, substantially relaxed its import restrictions and started importing heavily much in excess of its export earning and other current account receipts giving rise to large and growing current account deficits. India financed it by borrowing heavily from the international credit market and NRIs at high interest rates. It should have been obvious to the policy makers that the external borrowing was unsustainable and fruitless. Modernization of industries was never possible with imported technology. By the time, India would complete modernization of its industries; a new set of superior technology would come up in the major capitalist countries. Modernization required acquisition of the capacity to produce state-of-the-art technology indigenously, which India never tried to achieve. Modernization was never possible with imported technology. External commercial borrowing was also clearly unsustainable. India produced with imported technology, which was never state of the art. Hence, its export potential was extremely limited. Without the state-of-the-art indigenous technology, there was no hope for any improvement in its export potential. Under these circumstances, external commercial borrowing to finance large current account deficit was unsustainable for India. Despite this, India went on borrowing heavily from foreign commercial sources all through the eighties and its external debt service charges went on increasing rapidly as a percentage of its current external receipts. Finally, when the Gulf War broke out and oil price increased steeply in 1990 bringing about a sharp increase in India's already large current account deficit, global capitalists and the NRIs decided to stop lending to India. This forced India to seek the assistance of IMF to meet its current account deficit. IMF complied with the request. However, in exchange, it made India give up its socialist strategy of planned economic development and thrust on India its own development program called The New Economic Policy (NEP). Thus, The Golden Era of India's post-Independence period came to an end, and India finally officially lost its policy-making autonomy. We can explain this extremely puzzling suicidal external borrowing spree on the part of India in the eighties only in the following way. In the 1980s, the separatist Khalistan movement aided by the some of the Sikhs living in the USA and Europe turned extremely violent [see in this connection Pruthi (2004) and Van Dyke (2009)]. Clearly, the Khalistan movement was a manifestation of the Cold War. Despite the support of Soviet Union, Government of India could not keep the movement under control. Extremely nervous Indian leaders in power, to save their own lives and the country, perhaps sought the help of the global capitalists for a resolution of the crisis. The global capitalists perhaps promised help, but in exchange the Indian leaders in power had to abide by their dictates and had to take resort to large-scale external borrowing. This is the only way we can explain the extremely irrational external borrowing spree on the part of India in the eighties.

The objective of NEP is to usher in and facilitate the expansion of capitalism in India, and thereby, it seeks to deepen India's dependence on foreign assistance, funds, or loans manifold instead of doing the opposite. The NEP consists in removing all restrictions of the Nehru–Mahalanobis era (which is also referred to as the pre-reform period) on economic activities of economic agents such as consumption, investment, production, import, and export. The NEP has, therefore, made the economic agents free to import as much as they want for purposes of consumption, investment, production, and export. The NEP also seeks to remove all restrictions on cross-border capital flows. This means that it seeks to make the foreigners free to invest as much as they want in Indian assets (comprising of loans to Indians, bonds, stocks, bank deposits, land, forests, mines, etc.) or set up production facilities in India and also make the Indians free to purchase as much foreign assets as they want or set up production facilities in foreign countries. India is gradually lifting these restrictions. Even though there still exist considerable restrictions on Indians purchasing foreign assets, restrictions on foreigners investing in Indian assets have been removed to a significant extent. Removal of all these restrictions mentioned above has the following onerous implications for India. First, in the Nehru–Mahalanobis era, planners imposed stringent restrictions on economic activities of individual economic agents to make sure that allocation and utilization of society's productive resources conformed to the pattern envisaged by the planners. Removal of these restrictions amounts to leaving the allocation and utilization of productive resources to market forces. This implies that under NEP, people with market power, i.e., the rich, will bag most of the country's resources leaving very little for the poor. Like all the major capitalist countries, India is also characterized by a high degree of inequality. According to Oxfam India (2018), 1% of Indians own 76% of India's wealth. This estimate has been made on the basis of the officially declared assets. If undeclared assets were taken into account, the inequality in the distribution of wealth would have been much greater. The inequality in the distribution of wealth reflects the inequality in the distribution of income. Therefore, if the allocation of resources is left to market forces, about 80% of the country's resources will get utilized to cater to the needs of only 1% of Indians leaving only about 20% of the resources to meet the needs of the remaining 99% of the people. Since 1% of the richest Indians are extremely rich, they will want to partake of the finest consumption items available worldwide. As India is technologically backward, most of the finest consumption items have to be sourced from foreign countries. Hence, import demand for luxury consumption goods will swell enormously under NEP. Most of the investment will also be made to cater to the needs of the richest 1% of Indians. Thus, they will be geared for the production of high-end goods and services and the technology for producing these goods has to be imported from abroad. Hence, import demand for foreign capital goods will swell. Moreover, the imported technology has a high degree of automation. Hence, the kind of investments that will be made will lead to jobless growth.

The enormous swelling of demand for luxury foreign consumption and capital goods will get materialized only on account of relaxation of restrictions on the inflow of foreign capital and the bounty of the global capitalists. Let us explain. Since India has an extremely low export potential, without external borrowing or other forms of inflow of foreign capital, the increase in import demand will only raise exchange rate making imports costly discouraging imports. The increase in the exchange rate will continue until import demand becomes equal to export, which is small. Thus, the enormous increase in import demand the NEP gives rise to will get materialized in actual increase in imports if and only if global capitalists lend to Indian importers or invest generously in other Indian assets. Thus, the NEP creates an enormous opportunity for the global capitalists to catch India in a perpetual external debt trap and the global capitalists, as we shall demonstrate shortly, did just that.

Stringent restrictions on the size of the fiscal deficit (which stands for government's borrowing) as a proportion of GDP are an integral part of the New Economic Policy. Ceilings imposed on fiscal deficit as a proportion of GDP restrict government's command over GDP. Fixing direct tax rates at minimum possible levels is another important feature of NEP. The scope for raising indirect tax rates is also extremely limited, as it raises prices, and thereby, adversely affects demand through its distribution effects and its impact on trade balance. As a result, NEP has severely reduced government's command over resources. Consequently, the government has to rely on the private sector to produce most of the goods the society needs. To elaborate, the drastic reduction of government's command over resources under NEP has substantially impaired government's ability to invest in irrigation, flood control, agricultural R&D, etc., to improve the performance of agriculture, which is directly and indirectly the source of livelihood of most of the poor people in India. Thus, NEP has gravely threatened India's food security and has put the lives and livelihood of most of the Indians at jeopardy. It has significantly eroded government's ability to invest in education and health care to provide the common people with these services at low costs. It has also substantially reduced government's capacity to run a public distribution system to provide the poor masses with the basic necessities of life at affordable prices. Spending on old age care or unemployment allowance is a far cry. The NEP is, therefore, pro-rich and anti-poor. NEP has left hardly any scope for the government to develop an indigenous technological base or an indigenous knowledge base. By reducing government's command over resources to the minimum possible level, the NEP has deepened India's dependence on foreign technology and, therefore, on foreign intermediate and capital goods and delivered India hopelessly under the control of the global capitalists. One may also note in this regard that the private sector in India is too weak financially to compete with the global companies, and hence, they do not consider it profitable to develop technologies of their own. In what follows, we shall develop a suitable model to show how NEP has helped the global capitalists to catch India in a perpetual debt trap robbing it of all its policy-making autonomy.

5.2 The Model

We develop a simple Keynesian model here, where aggregate output is demand-determined. The goods market equilibrium condition is, therefore, given by

$$
\begin{aligned}
Y = {} & C\left(Y\frac{1}{1+\tau}(1-t)\right) + I\left(\underset{-}{r}, \underset{-}{e}\right) + G \\
& + \mathrm{NX}\left(\underset{+}{\frac{P^{*}e}{P(1+\tau)}}, C\left(Y\frac{1}{1+\tau}(1-t)\right), I(r,e); \underset{+}{Y^{*}}, \underset{+}{\phi}, \underset{-}{\gamma}\right)
\end{aligned}
\tag{5.1}
$$

In (5.1), $Y \equiv$ NDP, $\tau \equiv$ indirect tax rate, $P \equiv$ domestic price received by the producers, $t \equiv$ income tax rate on income, $P^{*} \equiv$ foreign price level in foreign currency, $e \equiv$ nominal exchange rate, $Y^{*} \equiv$ foreign GDP, $\phi \equiv$ a parameter that indicates global capitalists' attitude toward India and $\gamma \equiv$ degree of inequality in the distribution of income. An increase in ϕ implies an improvement in global capitalists' attitude toward India. Hence, export and, therefore, net export denoted NX are an increasing function of ϕ. In (5.1), consumption is made a function of aggregate real disposable income. Let us explain. Aggregate factor income of the people is given by PY, since P is the price received by the producers. They pay $P\tau$ as indirect tax to the government per unit of Y. Hence, the price they charge the buyers is $P(1+\tau)$. Thus, aggregate gross real factor income of the people is given by $\frac{PY}{P(1+\tau)} = \frac{Y}{(1+\tau)}$. Hence, aggregate real disposable income is given by $\frac{Y}{(1+\tau)}(1-t)$. Investment is made a decreasing function of the interest rate r as well as that of e. The reason why we have made I a decreasing function of e is the following: In India, there are strong reasons to believe that it is a decreasing function of e, as well. In case of India, an important determinant of the cost of investment is the exchange rate as a large part of investment demand represents demand for imported capital goods. So, an increase in e raises the cost of investment and, hence, given expectations, reduces investment demand for Y. Production in India is highly import-intensive. An increase in e, therefore, generates a strong cost-push. The corporate sector in India, which derives its income principally from the domestic economy in domestic currency, has large stocks of foreign debt. An increase in e raises debt service charges on external loans in domestic currency substantially. All these adverse supply shocks demoralize the investors and dampen investment demand. Data on exchange rates, growth rates and capital formation given in Tables 5.2 and 5.1 show that in all the years of recession (2011–12 to 2013–14) exchange rate increased substantially indicating a strong inverse relationship between the exchange rate, rate of capital formation, and growth rate in India [for details, one may go through Ghosh and Ghosh (2016)]. For all these reasons, we think that investment is highly sensitive to exchange rate in India. Hence, we have incorporated e as a determinant of investment and made it a decreasing function of e.

Net export, as standard, is made an increasing function of the real exchange rate. Moreover, consumption and investment are highly import-intensive. Hence, we have incorporated them in the net export function. Their increase represents a rise in

Table 5.1 Growth rate of GDP, net FDI, foreign portfolio investment, government consumption, and gross fiscal deficit (GFD)

Year	Growth rate of GDP at factor cost (at constant prices base 2004–05)	Net FDI (US $ million)	Net portfolio investment (US $ million)	Total (US $ million)	Government consumption (in Rs bn)	GFD[a] (% of GDP)	Rate of GDCF[b]	Rate of NDCF
2000–01	5.3	3270	2590	5860	3247.27	5.65	24.6	16.7
2001–02	5.5	4734	1952	6686	3323.69	6.19	24.6	16.5
2002–03	5.0	3157	944	4101	3317.53	5.91	25.4	17.3
2003–04	8.1	2388	11,377	13,765	3409.62	5.48	27.3	19.5
2004–05	7.0	3712	9291	13,003	3545.18	3.88	32.8	25.5
2005–06	9.5	3033	12,492	15,525	3860.07	3.96	34.9	27.8
2006–07	9.6	7693	6947	14,640	4005.79	3.38	36.2	29.2
2007–08	9.6	15,891	27,434	43,325	4389.19	2.54	39.0	32.2
2008–09	6.7	22,343	−14,032	8311	4845.59	5.99	35.6	27.9
2009–10	8.4	17,965	32,396	50,361	5517.02	6.48	38.4	30.9
2010–11	8.4	11,305	30,292	41,597	5843.52	5.87	39.8	32.5
2011–12	6.5	22,006	17,171	39,177	6345.59	5.89	38.8	31.1
2012–13	4.5	19,819	26,891	46,710	6620.33	5.06	38.9	30.9
2013–14	4.7	21,564	4822	26,386	6873.89	4.85		

Source RBI
[a]Gross fiscal deficit, [b]Gross domestic capital formation

import demand. Hence, net export falls. Net export is also an increasing function of Y^*. Since India is a small open economy, it has to regard $Y^*$and P^* as given. We, therefore, take their values as given exogenously. We have made net export a decreasing function of γ for the following reasons. As we have already mentioned, there is a very high degree of income inequality in India. The richest 1% of Indians have in their command perhaps about 80% of India's aggregate income. Hence, firms produce and invest mainly to cater to the needs of these richest 1% of people in India. These rich people consume high-quality goods and producers have to produce them with the finest imported technology. As a result, both production and investment in India are highly import-intensive. Clearly, an increase in γ raises import intensities of both consumption and investment. For simplicity, we have captured this by making net export a decreasing function of γ. Of course, an increase in γ may lower C. However, for simplicity, we have ignored this as this omission will not affect our results qualitatively.

Let us now focus on the external sector. Besides exports and imports of produced goods and services, there also occur cross-border capital flows. Since net inflow of capital depends on the plans and programs of the global capitalists in the main in India, we take it as exogenously given and denote its exogenously given value by $\overline{K}$. Thus, we write the BOP equilibrium condition as

$$\mathrm{NX}\left(\underset{+}{\frac{P^*e}{P(1+\tau)}}, C\left(Y\frac{1}{1+\tau}(1-t)\right), I(r,e); \underset{+}{Y^*}, \underset{+}{\phi}, \underset{-}{\gamma}\right) + \overline{K} = 0 \tag{5.2}$$

Producers set P on the basis of cost. The determinants of cost are W and P^*e. G may be an important determinant of cost. A reduction in G may lead to deterioration in law and order and administrative services, deteriorating conditions of road and other infrastructure, slower functioning of judiciary, etc. All of these will lead to a substantial increase in cost of production. We assume W to be given in the short run. We, therefore, write P as an increasing function of e and G. We do not show W and P^* as determinants of P explicitly, as it is not necessary for our purpose. Thus, we have

$$P = P\left(\underset{+}{e}, \underset{-}{G}\right) \tag{5.3}$$

Substituting (5.3) into (5.2), we write it as

$$\mathrm{NX}\left(\frac{P^*e}{P(e,G)(1+\tau)}, C\left(Y\underset{+}{\frac{1}{(1+\tau)}}(1-t)\right), I(r,e); \underset{+}{Y^*}, \underset{+}{\phi}\right) + \overline{K} = 0 \tag{5.4}$$

Let us now compute the aggregate real indirect tax revenue collected by the government. We denote it by $\widetilde{T}$. Clearly,

$$\widetilde{T} = \frac{P\tau Y}{P(1+\tau)} = \frac{\tau}{(1+\tau)}Y \equiv vY \tag{5.5}$$

NEP imposes stringent restrictions on government's fiscal deficit, which means government's borrowing. We assume for simplicity and without any loss of generality that the government seeks to achieve a target of zero borrowing so that government's budget constraint is given by

$$G = vY + tY \tag{5.6}$$

We shall now describe the financial sector. We assume that the financial sector consists only of banks. The banking sector is oligopolistic. Oligopolistic interdependence makes the interest rate rigid. Banks set the interest rate on basis of, among others, the policy rate of the central bank denoted r_c. The central bank lends as much as the banks want at r_c. Thus, we have

$$r = r(r_c) \tag{5.7}$$

We assume that there is no credit rationing. Banks at the given interest rate meet all the credit demand that comes forth. Substituting (5.6) and (5.7) into (5.4) and using (5.5), we rewrite (5.4) as

$$\mathrm{NX}\left(\frac{P^*e}{P(e,(v+t)Y)}(1-v), C(Y(1-v)(1-t)), I(r(r_c), e); Y^*, \phi\right) + \overline{K} = 0 \tag{5.8}$$

Note that in (5.8), following a ceteris paribus increase in e, both P^*e and P go up. Since production in India is highly import-intensive, the increase in P is likely to be substantial. Hence, increase in the real exchange rate will be quite small. For simplicity, we shall assume $\frac{P^*e}{P}$, which we denote by p, to be independent of e and a function only of $(v+\tau)Y$. We, therefore, rewrite (5.8) as follows:

$$\mathrm{NX}\left(p\left(\underset{+}{(v+t)Y}\right)(1-v), C(Y(1-v)(1-t)), I(r(r_c), e); Y^*, \phi, \gamma\right) + \overline{K} = 0 \tag{5.9}$$

We can solve (5.9) for e as a function of, among others, $Y, t, v, Y^*, \phi, \gamma$ and $\overline{K}$. Thus, we get

$$e = e\left(\underset{-}{Y}, \underset{-}{t}, \underset{+}{v}, \underset{-}{Y^*}, \underset{-}{\phi}, \underset{+}{\gamma}, \underset{-}{\overline{K}}\right) \tag{5.10}$$

We can explain the partial derivatives of (5.10) using Fig. 5.1, where the equilibrium value of e corresponds to the point of intersection of the NX + K schedule representing the LHS of (5.9) and the horizontal axis. The NX + K schedule is upward sloping for the following reason. Following an increase in e, investment falls. This lowers import and, thereby, raises net export. Let us now examine how a ceteris paribus increase in Y is likely to affect the equilibrium value of e. Following a ceteris paribus given increase in Y, consumption demand will go up bringing about an increase in demand for imported consumption goods. Note that, given the very high degree of income inequality in India, most of the additional income will accrue to a small section of extremely rich people. Hence, most of the increase in consumption demand will represent additional demand for imported consumption goods bringing about a BOP deficit. The increase in Y will also produce an opposite effect. It will raise government revenue and expenditure and, thereby, will lower cost of production and P. The fall in P will raise net export. Since close substitutes of Indian goods are available everywhere, a fall in P is likely to substantially improve export performance and lower import, and, thereby, raise net export. We shall assume the latter effect to be stronger than the former, as it is more likely to be true. Even if we assume the opposite, our results will not be affected qualitatively. Therefore, given our assumption, following a ceteris paribus increase in Y, the NX + K schedule shifts upward in Fig. 5.1 bringing about an decrease in the equilibrium value of e. We shall explain the signs of the other partial derivatives later. Let us derive the value of e_Y. Taking total differential of (5.9) treating all variables other than Y and e to be fixed and solving for $\frac{\mathrm{d}e}{\mathrm{d}Y}$, we get

$$e_Y\left(\equiv\frac{\mathrm{d}e}{\mathrm{d}Y}\right)=\frac{\left[(-\mathrm{NX}_c)C'(1-v)(1-t)\right]-\left[\mathrm{NX}_{\overline{p}}(1-v)p'(v+t)\right]}{(-\mathrm{NX}_I)(-I_e)}<0;\quad \overline{p}\equiv p(1-v) \tag{5.11}$$

Consider the expression on the RHS of (5.11). Focus on the numerator. We assume, as explained above, that the first term in the numerator is smaller than the second term.

Substituting (5.9) and (5.10) into (5.1), we rewrite it as follows:

$$Y=C((1-t)(1-v)Y)+I\big(r(r_c),e\big(Y,t,v,Y^*,\phi,\overline{K}\big)\big)+(t+v)Y-\overline{K} \tag{5.12}$$

The specification of our model is now complete. It contains two key Eqs. (5.12) and (5.10). We can solve (5.12) for the equilibrium value of Y. Putting it in (5.10), we get the equilibrium value of e. We are now in a position to carry out the comparative static exercises.

5.3 Global Capitalists' Two Instruments for Controlling Indian Economy: $\overline{K}$ and ϕ

We shall examine here how an increase in $\overline{K}$ and ϕ affects the economy. Let us focus on $\overline{K}$ first. Taking total differential of (5.12) treating all variables other than Y and $\overline{K}$ as fixed and, then solving for $\mathrm{d}Y$, we get

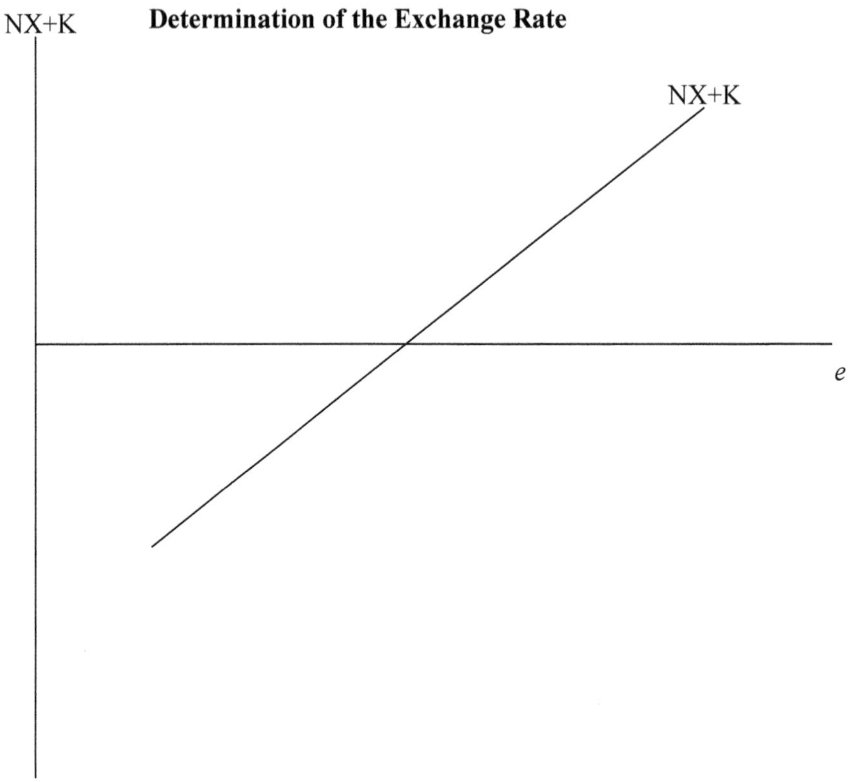

Fig. 5.1 Determination of the exchange rate

$$dY = \frac{(I_e e_K - 1)d\overline{K}}{1 - [C'(1-v)(1-t) + (t+v) + I_e e_Y]} \tag{5.13}$$

We shall now derive the value of $I_e e_K$. Taking total differential of (5.9) treating all variables other than e and $\overline{K}$ as fixed and, then solving for $\frac{de}{d\overline{K}}$. we get

$$e_K\left(\equiv \frac{de}{d\overline{K}}\right) = \frac{1}{(-NX_I)I_e} \tag{5.14}$$

Therefore,

$$I_e e_K = \frac{1}{(-NX_I)} > 1 \quad \text{since} \quad 0 < -NX_I < 1 \tag{5.15}$$

Note that $-NX_I$ measures the import intensity of investment (i.e., the amount of imported goods required per unit of investment). It is less than unity.

Substituting (5.15) into (5.13), we get

$$\mathrm{d}Y = \frac{\left(\frac{1}{(-\mathrm{NX}_I)} - 1\right)\mathrm{d}\overline{K}}{1 - [C'(1-v)(1-t) + (v+t) + I_e e_Y]} > 0 \tag{5.16}$$

Let us now explain the expression on the RHS of (5.16). Following a given increase in $\overline{K}$ by $\mathrm{d}\overline{K}$, there emerges excess supply of foreign currency at the initial equilibrium (e, Y) of $\mathrm{d}\overline{K}$. e begins to fall to clear the foreign currency market. To clear the foreign currency market, e has to fall by such an amount that the net export goes down by $\mathrm{d}\overline{K}$ making (NX+K) zero again. As we have already mentioned, the impact of a fall in e on the real exchange rate is insignificant. It clears the foreign currency market mainly through its impact on investment. Investment rises and, since it is highly import-intensive, raises import and, thereby, lowers net export. As per unit increase in I net export falls by $(-\mathrm{NX}_I)$, I has to rise by $\frac{\mathrm{d}\overline{K}}{-\mathrm{NX}_I}$ to lower net export by $\mathrm{d}\overline{K}$ and, thereby, restore BOP equilibrium. At the initial equilibrium Y *(and the new lower e and NX, which we shall henceforth refer to as the initial equilibrium values of e and NX, respectively)*, therefore, there emerges an excess demand for goods and services of $\left(\frac{1}{-\mathrm{NX}_I} - 1\right)\mathrm{d}\overline{K}$, which is the numerator of the expression on the RHS of (5.16). This sets off a multiplier process. Since economy's marginal propensity to consume out of Y (personal and public combined) is $C'(1-t)(1-v) + (v+t)$, Y in the first round will go up by $\mathrm{d}Y_1 = \frac{\left(\frac{1}{-\mathrm{NX}_I} - 1\right)\mathrm{d}\overline{K}}{1-[C'(1-t)(1-v)+(t+v)]}$. The increase in consumption demand that this increase in Y gives rise to will be partly spent on imported goods. Hence, at the initial equilibrium e, import demand will rise. On the other hand, the increase in Y in the first round raises government's tax revenue. This enables the government to raise its expenditure. This will increase the quantity of government's services reducing cost. This, in turn, will lower the price level. Since close substitutes of Indian goods are available everywhere, the fall in the domestic price will substantially increase net export at the initial equilibrium e. In the net, given our assumption, net export will rise at the initial equilibrium e lowering e. e will fall by $e_Y \mathrm{d}Y_1$ and restore net export to its initial equilibrium value. However, the fall in e will raise I by $I_e e_Y \mathrm{d}Y_1$ creating an excess demand of the same value. The multiplier process will operate again, and Y will increase in the second round by $\mathrm{d}Y_2 = \frac{I_e e_Y \mathrm{d}Y_1}{1-C'(1-t)(1-v)}$. Obviously, the process will not stop here. The increase in Y in the second round will again raise net export and lower e by $e_Y \mathrm{d}Y_2$ and, thereby, raise investment by $I_e e_Y \mathrm{d}Y_2$ setting off another multiplier process. Hence, in the third round, Y will go up by $\mathrm{d}Y_3 = \frac{I_e e_Y \mathrm{d}Y_2}{1-C'(1-t)(1-v)} = \left[\frac{I_e e_Y}{1-C'(1-t)(1-v)}\right]^2 \mathrm{d}Y_1$. This process of expansion will continue until the excess demand that is created in each successive round eventually falls to zero. Thus, the total increase in Y is given by

$$\begin{aligned}\mathrm{d}Y &= \mathrm{d}Y_1 + \frac{I_e e_Y}{1 - C'(1-t)(1-v)}\mathrm{d}Y_1 + \left[\frac{I_e e_Y}{1 - C'(1-t)(1-v)}\right]^2 \mathrm{d}Y_1 + \dots \\ &= \frac{1 - C'(1-t)(1-v)}{1 - C'(1-t)(1-v) - I_e e_Y}\mathrm{d}Y_1 = \frac{\left(\frac{1}{-\mathrm{NX}_I} - 1\right)\mathrm{d}\overline{K}}{1 - C'(1-t)(1-v) - I_e e_Y}\end{aligned} \tag{5.17}$$

It is clear that (5.17) tallies with (5.16). Thus, the global capitalists can create booms and recessions in Indian economy through their control over $\overline{K}$. In fact, from the data given in Table 5.1, we find that during 2003–04 to 2010–11, with the exception of the year 2008–09, India experienced unprecedented high rates of growth of GDP. The growth rate more than doubled from 2002–03 to 2003–04 and this very remarkable jump in India's growth rate can only be explained in terms of a substantial increase in net inflow of capital (foreign investment). From 2002–03 to 2003–04, foreign investment more than trebled (see Table 5.1). All through the boom period, India received very large foreign investment. In fact, the dip in the growth rate in 2008–09 was also accompanied by a sharp fall in foreign investment (see Table 5.1) Thus, there is prima facie evidence that the global capitalists created the boom in India during 2003–04 to 2010–11 by raising their investment in Indian assets very substantially. During the boom period mentioned above, India's average annual growth rate of GDP was around 8.5%. However, India went into a recession since 2011–12, when growth rate slumped to 6.5%. The growth rate dropped further in 2012–13 and 2013–14 when growth rates of GDP were 4.5 and 4.7%, respectively (see Table 5.1). In both 2012–13 and 2013–14, the deep recession was on account of large drops in global capitalists' investment in India (see Table 5.1). Let us first focus on the experiences in 2012–13. In February 2012, Government of India announced general anti-avoidance rule in the budget and also undertook retrospective amendment to income tax law pertaining to indirect transfer of Indian assets. Both these measures aimed at restricting the scope for tax evasion on the part of foreign investors. This angered the global capitalists. The global credit rating agencies downgraded India's credit rating and threatened to downgrade it further to junk status in April 2012. There took place a large fall in the foreign investment. Exchange rate soared. This made both the domestic investors and the government extremely nervous. The growth rate plummeted to a low level in the first quarter of 2012–13. Hastily, to reassure the foreign investors, the GoI announced postponement of the implementation of the two measures mentioned above, removed the then Finance Minister, Pranab Mukherjee, who tabled the budget and announced the anti-foreign investor measures and brought in his place P. C. Chidambaram. The GoI also allowed foreign investment in retail and promised further relaxation of restrictions on foreign investment on that line in the future. The GoI also brought about a steep hike in the administered price of diesel and cooking gas. These hikes were so harsh on the common people that the then Prime Minister of India had to address the nation to defend these measures. In the speech delivered on September 21, 2012, PM said 'We are at a point where we can reverse the slowdown in our growth. We need a revival in investor confidence domestically and globally. The decisions we have taken recently are necessary for this purpose. Let us begin with the rise in diesel prices and the cap on LPG cylinders.......If we had not acted, it would have meant a higher fiscal deficit. If unchecked this would lead to a ......loss in confidence in our country. The last time we faced this problem was in 1991. Nobody was willing to lend us even small amounts of money then.......I know what happened in 1991 and I would be failing in my duty as Prime Minister of this great country if I did not take strong preventive action.' Thus, the large fall in foreign investment and the nervousness it created together with, as we shall show later, the drastic cut in diesel subsidy were responsible for the deepening of recession in 2012–13. The deep recession in 2013–14 was also the handiwork of the global capitalists. They spread the rumor that the Fed was going to hike its policy rate. This created a basis for expecting higher return from investments in US assets. As if using this rumor as an excuse, foreign investors cut down their investment in India substantially (see Table 5.1). Exchange rate increased sharply. In fact, between May and September 2013, exchange rate increased by 17% (see Table 5.2). As a result, investment and growth rate declined sharply perpetuating the recession. From the above, it is clear that in the post-reform period, India is completely under the control of the global capitalists. They create recessions and booms in India at will by changing their investment levels in Indian assets.

The Effect of an Increase in ϕ

We shall now examine how an increase in ϕ for exogenous reasons affects India's growth rate. Taking total differential of (5.12) treating all variables other than Y and ϕ as fixed and, then, solving for dY, we get

$$\mathrm{d}Y = \frac{I_e e_\phi \mathrm{d}\phi}{1 - [C'(1-v)(1-t) + (v+t) + I_e e_Y]} \tag{5.18}$$

Let us now derive the value of e_ϕ. Taking total differential of (5.9) treating all variables other than e and ϕ as fixed and, then, solving for $\frac{\mathrm{d}e}{\mathrm{d}\phi}(\equiv e_\phi)$, we get

$$e_\phi = \frac{\mathrm{NX}_\phi}{-\mathrm{NX}_I I_e} \tag{5.19}$$

Substituting (5.19) into (5.18), we get

$$\mathrm{d}Y = \frac{\frac{\mathrm{NX}_\phi \mathrm{d}\phi}{-\mathrm{NX}_I}}{1 - C'(1-t)(1-v) - I_e e_Y} > 0 \tag{5.20}$$

Let us explain the expression on the RHS of (5.20). Following an increase in ϕ by dϕ, net export rises by $\mathrm{NX}_\phi \mathrm{d}\phi$ at the initial equilibrium (Y, e) creating BOP surplus. So, e will fall until net export falls to its initial equilibrium value. The fall in e will lower net export mainly by raising investment. Net export will fall to its initial equilibrium value, when the decline in e raises investment by $\frac{\mathrm{NX}_\phi \mathrm{d}\phi}{-\mathrm{NX}_I}$, which is the numerator. This sets off a multiplier process, and Y goes up substantially by the expression on the RHS of (5.20). The multiplier process is similar to the one in the previous case.

The global capitalists, therefore, can control India's growth rate through their control over India's exports. In fact, the unprecedented boom that India experienced during 2003–04 to 2010–11 came to an end since 2011–12. In 2011–12, the growth rate slumped to 6.5% from 8.5%. This large decline in the growth rate was due to a decline in the growth rate of export for exogenous reasons.

Table 5.2 Exchange rate of the Indian rupee vis-a-vis the US dollar (monthly average)

Year/month	US $ average	Year/month	US $ average	Year/month	US $ average	Year/month	US $ average
2008		Oct	46.7211	Jul	44.4174	Apr	54.4971
Jan	39.3737	Nov	46.5673	Aug	45.2788	May	55.1156
Feb	39.7326	Dec	46.6288	Sep	47.6320	Jun	58.5059
Mar	40.3561	2010		Oct	49.2579	Jul	60.0412
Apr	40.0224	Jan	45.9598	Nov	50.8564	Aug	64.5517
May	42.1250	Feb	46.3279	Dec	52.6769	Sep	64.3885
June	42.8202	Mar	45.4965	2012		Oct	61.7563
Jul	42.8380	Apr	44.4995	Jan	51.3992	Nov	62.7221
Aug	42.9374	May	45.8115	Feb	49.1671	Dec	61.7793
Sep	45.5635	June	46.5670	Mar	50.3213	2014	
Oct	48.6555	Jul	46.8373	Apr	51.8029	Jan	62.1708
Nov	48.9994	Aug	46.5679	May	54.4735	Feb	62.3136
Dec	48.6345	Sep	46.0616	June	56.0302	Mar	61.0021
2009		Oct	46.7211	Jul	55.4948	Apr	60.3813
Jan	48.8338	Nov	46.5673	Aug	48.3350	May	59.3255
Feb	49.2611	Dec	46.6288	Sep	54.3353	June	59.7143
Mar	51.2287	2011		Oct	52.8917	Jul	60.0263
Apr	50.0619	Jan	45.3934	Nov	54.6845	Aug	60.9923
May	48.5330	Feb	45.4358	Dec	54.6439		
June	47.7714	Mar	44.9914	2013			
Jul	48.4783	Apr	44.3700	Jan	54.3084		
Aug	48.3350	May	44.9045	Feb	53.7265		
Sep	48.4389	June	44.8536	Mar	54.5754		

Source RBI

Proposition 5.1 *The global capitalists can create large booms and recessions in India at their will by raising or lowering their investments in India and/or by purchasing more or less of India's produced goods and services. Available evidences lend prima facie support to the proposition that the unprecedented boom in India during 2003–04 to 2010–11 was on account of remarkable increases in foreign investment in India and the recession in 2011–12 was due to a large fall in the growth rate of India's exports. The perpetuation and deepening of recession in 2012–13 and 2013–14 were also on account of large falls in the level of foreign investment.*

We cannot extend our analysis beyond 2013–14 because comparable data on growth rates are not available for the subsequent financial years.

5.4 Low Income Tax Rates: A Clever Ploy to Keep India Dependent

Despite extreme inequality in the distribution of income and wealth in India as reported by Oxfam India (2018), income tax rate is capped at 30% (see Table 5.3). From the data released by Oxfam India (2018), one can safely conclude that more than 80% of India's wealth and income is in the hands of just 1% of Indians. Even then, India's income tax structure given by the data shown in Table 5.3 reveals an extremely unjust and unwise scenario. Individuals earning an annual income of Rs. 250,000 or less are taxed at the rate of 0%. Individuals' annual income in excess of Rs. 250,000 up to Rs. 500,000 is taxed at the rate of 5%. The tax rate applicable to individuals' annual income in excess of Rs. 500,000 and not exceeding Rs. 1,000,000 is 20%, a 15% increase. However, individuals' income above Rs. 1,000,000 is taxed at the rate 30%. Instead of raising income tax rates steeply for every additional Rs. 500,000 of income, Government of India (GoI) has kept income tax rates unchanged for income levels in excess of Rs. 1,000,000; it does not matter by how much the income level exceeds Rs. 1,000,000. In what follows, we shall examine the implications of GoI's bounty toward the rich.

Taking total differential of (5.12) treating all variables other than Y and t as fixed and, then solving for $\mathrm{d}Y$, we get

$$\mathrm{d}Y = \frac{(I_e e_t + Y)\mathrm{d}t}{1 - [C'(1-v)(1-t) + (v+t) + I_e e_Y]} \tag{5.21}$$

We shall now derive the value of e_t. Taking total differential of (5.9) treating all variables other than e and t as fixed and, then, solving for $\frac{\mathrm{d}e}{\mathrm{d}t}$, we get

$$e_t \left(\equiv \frac{\mathrm{d}e}{\mathrm{d}t} \right) = \frac{-\left[\mathrm{NX}_p p_G + (-\mathrm{NX}_C)C'(1-v)\right]}{-\mathrm{NX}_I(-I_e)} < 0 \tag{5.22}$$

Substituting (5.22) into (5.21), we get

Table 5.3 Income tax slabs for individuals and Hindu undivided family of less than 60 years of age for the financial year 2018–19

Income tax slab	Tax rate	Health and education cess
Income up to Rs. 250,000	No tax	
Income from Rs. 250,000 to Rs. 500,000	5%	4% of total tax
Income from Rs. 500,000 to Rs. 100,000	20%	4% of total tax
Income more than Rs. 100,000	30%	4% of total tax

Surcharge: 10% of total income tax for income from Rs. 50 lakh to Rs. 1 crore
Surcharge: 15% of total income tax for income more than Rs. 1 crore
Source Income Tax Department, Government of India

$$\mathrm{d}Y = \frac{\left[\frac{\mathrm{NX}_p p_G Y + (-\mathrm{NX}_C)C'(1-v)Y}{-\mathrm{NX}_I} + Y\right]\mathrm{d}t}{1 - [C'(1-v)(1-t) + (v+t) + I_e e_Y]} < 0 \quad \because \mathrm{d}t < 0 \tag{5.23}$$

Let us now explain the expression on the RHS of (5.23). Following a reduction in the tax rate by $\mathrm{d}t$, government's tax revenue at the initial equilibrium (Y, e) falls by $Y\mathrm{d}t$ reducing government expenditure by the same amount. The decline in government consumption expenditure raises P and thereby lowers net export by $\mathrm{NX}_p p_G Y\mathrm{d}t$. Again, the fall in income tax collection raises consumption expenditure by $-C'(1-v)Y\mathrm{d}t$, which, in turn, by raising demand for imported consumption goods reduces net export by $(-\mathrm{NX}_C)C'(1-v)Y\mathrm{d}t$. Thus, at the initial equilibrium (Y, e), net export falls by $(-\mathrm{NX}_C)C'(1-v)Y\mathrm{d}t + \mathrm{NX}_p p_G Y\mathrm{d}t$ creating a BOP deficit. Hence, e will rise to raise net export to its initial equilibrium value. It will do so mainly by lowering investment, and it will fall by a multiple of the increase in net export. It will fall by $\frac{(-\mathrm{NX}_C)C'(1-v)Y\mathrm{d}t + \mathrm{NX}_p p_G Y\mathrm{d}t}{-\mathrm{NX}_I}$. Government's consumption expenditure has also fallen by $Y\mathrm{d}t$. Thus, there emerges a large excess supply at the initial equilibrium Y given by the absolute value of the numerator of the expression on the RHS of (5.23). Hence, there will take place a cumulative contraction in Y through a multiplier process, which we have described in the previous cases.

From the above, it follows that NEP by fixing income tax rates applicable to the rich, who have in their command about eighty percent of India's aggregate income and wealth, at minimum possible levels has reduced India's potential growth rate, the growth rate that India can sustain without depending upon the assistance of the global capitalists, to a very low level. India, therefore, has to depend upon the bounties of the global capitalists even to maintain a moderately high growth rate.

The above discussion yields the following proposition:

Proposition 5.2 *A cut in income tax rate in a country like India will bring about a substantial fall in the growth rate. The NEP, by fixing the income tax rate on the rich* *at the minimum possible level, has reduced its potential growth rate, defined as the growth rate that India can sustain without depending on the global capitalists, to a very low level. Therefore, to sustain even moderately high growth rates, India has to depend upon the bounties of the global capitalists.*

5.5 Dependence of GoI on Indirect Taxes Under NEP: Deepening of Dependence on Global Capitalists

Since under NEP the GoI has fixed income tax rates on the rich at the lowest possible level, it has to rely on indirect taxes as its main source of revenue. It has also undertaken in recent years sweeping reforms in the area of indirect taxes and has introduced in 2018 a single indirect tax called the goods and services tax (GST) replacing almost all other indirect taxes. GST has been designed in such a manner that all the producers/sellers come under its purview it does not matter how small they are (see Banerjee and Prasad 2017). Data recorded in Table 5.4 show that now the major part of tax revenue comes from indirect taxes, even though indirect taxes are highly unjust and regressive. In what follows, we shall examine how a hike in the indirect tax rate is likely to affect India's growth rate.

Taking total differential of (5.12) treating all variables other than Y and v as fixed and, then, solving for $\mathrm{d}Y$, we get

$$\mathrm{d}Y = \frac{\left[\left\{1 - C'(1-t)\right\}Y - (-I_e)e_v\right]\mathrm{d}v}{1 - [C'(1-v)(1-t) + (v+t) + I_e e_Y]} \quad (5.24)$$

We shall now derive the value of e_v. Taking total differential of (5.9) treating all variables other than e and v as fixed and, then, solving for $e_v \left(\equiv \frac{\mathrm{d}e}{\mathrm{d}v}\right)$, we get

$$e_v = \frac{\mathrm{NX}_p p - \left[\mathrm{NX}_p(p_G(1-v)Y) + (-\mathrm{NX}_C)C'(1-t)Y\right]}{-\mathrm{NX}_I(-I_e)} > 0 \quad (5.25)$$

Let us focus on the sign of (5.25). Focus on the expression on the RHS of (5.25). Consider the numerator. Following a unit increase in v, domestic price rises. Since close substitutes of Indian goods are available everywhere, it will bring about a substantial fall in net export. The absolute value of the fall in net export is given by

Table 5.4 Percentages of direct and indirect taxes in total tax revenue

	2009–10	2013–14	14–15	15–16	16–17	17–18
Direct tax	60.78	56.32	56.16	51.13	49.66	49.41
Indirect tax	39.22	43.68	43.84	48.87	50.34	50.59

Source RBI

the term $NX_p p$. The unit increase in v will also tend to raise net export in two ways. First, it will lower consumption demand and, thereby, reduce demand for imported consumption goods. Hence, net export will go up by $(-NX_C)C'(1-t)Y$. Second, it will raise government's tax revenue and expenditure by Y and, thereby lower domestic price level for reasons we have already explained earlier. This will raise net export by $NX_p(p_G(1-v)Y)$. The sum of these two increases in net export is given by the term within third brackets in the numerator. However, the fall in net export on account of the increase in the domestic price level that the hike in the indirect tax rate directly gives rise to is highly likely to dominate by far the rise in net export on account of the two factors mentioned above. This contraction in net export is given by the first term in the numerator. The first term is likely to be much larger than the second term for the following reasons. First, the direct decrease in $p(1-v)$ due to a unit increase in v is highly likely to be much larger than the rise in $p(1-v)$ on account of the increase in G that the unit increase in v brings about. Second, since close substitutes of all the goods India produces are available everywhere, even a slight increase in the domestic price level relative to the foreign price is likely to bring about a very large fall in net export. For these reasons, a hike in the indirect tax rate is likely to reduce net export substantially at the initial equilibrium (Y, e). e will rise to restore net export to its initial equilibrium value. The numerator of the expression on the RHS of (5.25) gives increase in net export that is required to restore it to its initial equilibrium value. An increase in e will raise net export mainly by lowering I. The denominator of the expression on the RHS of (5.25) gives the amount of increase in net export that a unit increase in e brings about.

The rise in e by e_v will lower I by $I_e e_v$, whose value is given by

$$I_e e_v = \frac{NX_p p - \left[NX_p(p_G(1-v)Y) + (-NX_C)C'(1-t)Y\right]}{NX_I} < 0 \tag{5.26}$$

We are now in a position to explain (5.24). Focus on the expression on the RHS. Consider the numerator. Following an increase in v by dv, government's revenue and consumption expenditure at the initial equilibrium (Y, e) increases by Ydv and personal consumption expenditure falls by $C'(1-t)Ydv$. In the net, therefore, public and personal consumption expenditure together increases by $\left(1-C'(1-t)\right)Ydv$. As we have just discussed above, at the initial equilibrium (Y, e), net export goes down substantially raising e and, thereby, lowering I by $I_e e_v dv$, whose value is given by (5.26). The fall in I is likely to be much larger than the rise in consumption demand. Thus, there is likely to emerge a large excess supply at the initial equilibrium Y. The absolute value of the numerator of the expression on the RHS of (5.24) gives the amount of this excess supply. This will set off a multiplier process, and there will take place a cumulative contraction in Y through the multiplier process described earlier.

From the above, it follows that following a hike in the indirect tax rate, it is highly likely that there will take place a large contraction in Y. We get prima facie evidence in support of this conjecture from India's experiences in 2012–13. In February 2012, as we have mentioned already, Government of India announced general anti-avoidance rule in the budget and also undertook retrospective amendment to income tax law pertaining to indirect transfer of Indian assets. Both these measures aimed at restricting the scope for tax evasion on the part of foreign investors. This angered the global capitalists. International credit rating agencies downgraded India's credit rating, and there took place a large fall in the net capital inflow. Exchange rate soared. This made both the investors and the government extremely nervous. The growth rate plummeted to a low level in the first quarter of 2012–13. GoI hastily announced postponement of the implementation of both the measures. GoI, as we have already mentioned, also hiked the administered prices of diesel, cooking gas, and kerosene to appease the foreign investors. These steps made the global capitalists happy and net capital inflow again surged back to desired levels. Despite that, India's growth rate did not pick up. In fact, it slumped further in the third and fourth quarters. We attribute this to the steep hike in the administered price of diesel, which amounts to a drastic reduction in diesel subsidy or a hike in the net indirect tax rate (indirect tax rate net of the rate of subsidy). The fall in the growth rates in the third and fourth quarters supports our conjecture that a hike in the net indirect tax rate brings about a fall in the growth rate. The above discussion yields the following proposition:

Proposition 5.3 *Following a hike in the indirect tax rate in a country like India, there is a strong likelihood that the exchange rate will soar and the growth rate will decline substantially. Events that unfolded in India in 2012–13 lend prima facie support to this claim.*

As NEP keeps income taxes on the rich at the minimum possible level, government has to rely on indirect taxes as the major source of tax revenue. However, hikes in indirect tax rates create inflation, BOP difficulties, and cause a decline in the growth rate. The tax scenario described above subjects the Government to severe budget crunch. Since India does not have any independent knowledge or technological base, India's investment and production are highly import-intensive. As a result, domestic investors feel confident only when supply of foreign exchange becomes plentiful through large-scale investments by the global capitalists. This scenario makes India completely dependent on the bounties of the global capitalists for sustaining even modest growth rates.

5.6 Deregulation of Investment, Jobless Growth and Widening Inequality Under NEP

Under NEP, India is withdrawing all kinds of restrictions on investment. This has the following implication. Under capitalism, capitalists and workers have conflicting interests. Capitalists have to keep workers under control for uninterrupted production and profit making. To keep the workers under control and to increase the share of profit in total income, the capitalists have to weaken the bargaining strength of the workers. To do that, they have to reduce their dependence on workers and create unemployment. As a result, capitalists continuously invest on a large scale in

R&D to bring about labor-saving technological changes. With the deregulation of investment under NEP, both the foreign and domestic investors have imported more and more capital-intensive and labor-saving technologies in India giving rise to the phenomenon of jobless growth. The organized sector in India, i.e., the modern sector comprising of large firms that are subject to Company Laws, has grown phenomenally under NEP at an average annual rate of more than 6% per year without creating any employment (see Table 5.5). From the data of Table 5.6, we find that the share of the organized sector has grown in GDP under NEP. This means that the value added of the organized sector has grown at a faster rate than GDP under NEP. The phenomenon of jobless growth in the organized sector in India has significantly weakened the bargaining strength of workers, and as a result, there has also taken place a secular and sharp decline in the share of wages in the value added of organized manufacturing sector (see Table 5.7).

In the Nehru–Mahalanobis era, the government reserved a number of sectors for small producers such as textiles, retail, agricultural trade. Moreover, the government granted the small producers and farmers a large number of fiscal concessions and provided them with loans on an adequate scale at subsidized rates. Since basic and heavy industries were naturally highly capital intensive, the government sought to encourage the growth of small producers in other areas to generate employment and to reduce inequality. The NEP is gradually withdrawing these protections, concessions and subsidies given to the small producers and agriculture. Since large firms enjoy economies of scale and have access to cheap institutional credit and nationwide media services on the required scale, they have much greater competitive strength vis-a-vis their smaller counterparts. Hence, with the withdrawal of concessions to

Table 5.5 Employment in the organized sector (in million)

Year	Growth rate of GDP at constant (2004–05) prices	Number of workers employed
1994–95	6.4	27.53
2000–01	5.3	27.79
2001–02	5.5	27.20
2003–04	8.1	26.45
2004–05	7.0	26.46
2005–06	9.5	26.96
2006–07	9.6	27.24
2007–08	9.6	27.55
2008–09	6.7	28.18
2009–10	8.4	29.00
2010–11	8.4	29
2011–12	5.3	29.65

Source RBI

Table 5.6 Contributions of the organized sector and the unorganized sector to the value added of major sectors of production and NDP

	1993–94		2003–04		2010–2011	
Industry	Organized	Unorganized	Organized	Unorganized	Organized	Unorganized
Agriculture, forestry, and fishing	3.5	96.5	4.1	95.9	5.8	94.2
Mining, manufacturing	64.2	35.8	60.5	39.5	64.5	35.5
Electricity, construction, and services	47.1	58.9	53.1	46.9	42.2	51.8
NDP	36.8	63.2	43.3	56.7	45.1	54.9

Source CSO (2005), National Accounts Statistics (2005), Government of India and National Accounts Statistics (2012), Government of India

the small producers, NEP has helped the organized sector to increase their market share at the expense of the small producers.

During Nehru–Mahalanobis era, the government administered all interest rates including interest rates on all saving instruments such as bank fixed deposits, small saving schemes. The interest rates on the saving instruments were quite high, and savers got the assurance of a guaranteed remunerative return on their savings. Interest rates have come down very substantially under NEP. Since workers are net lenders and capitalists are net borrowers, the decline in interest rates has brought about a large redistribution of income from the workers to the capitalists.

All the factors mentioned above have raised income inequality considerably. In what follows, we shall examine how the widening of inequality, which we capture in our model through a rise in γ, is likely to affect India's growth performance.

To derive the impact of a ceteris paribus increase in γ, we take total differential of (5.12) treating all variables other than Y and γ as fixed and, then, solve for $\mathrm{d}Y$. This gives

$$\mathrm{d}Y = \frac{I_e e_\gamma \mathrm{d}\gamma}{1 - [C'(1-t)(1-v) + I_e e_Y + (t+v)]} < 0 \tag{5.27}$$

Let us derive the value of $I_e e_\gamma \mathrm{d}\gamma$. Taking total differential of (5.9) treating all variables other than e and γ as fixed and, then, solving for $\frac{\mathrm{d}e}{\mathrm{d}\gamma}$ and multiplying it by I_e, we get

$$I_e e_\gamma = \frac{-\mathrm{NX}_\gamma}{\mathrm{NX}_I} < 0 \tag{5.28}$$

Table 5.7 Share of wage in the net value added of the organized manufacturing sector

Year	Wage/NVA	E/NVA
1990–91	25.60837619	39.962135
1991–92	24.77360615	38.24844028
1992–93	23.62322467	38.68204933
1993–94	19.89892122	32.3853645
1994–95	20.29125577	32.5677205
1995–96	20.06521796	32.36510722
1996–97	16.87517837	29.48901451
1997–98	17.89320363	31.46523061
1998–99	17.06744177	30.67889995
1999–2000	16.97329792	30.8718755
2000–2001	19.26644502	35.3141847
2001–2002	19.01443998	35.38379755
2002–2003	17.22701817	32.00533666
2003–04	15.01709971	28.74386123
2004–05	12.94119363	24.78039248
2005–06	12.07694285	23.73090671
2006–07	11.19244953	22.42742604
2007–08	10.59613904	21.89461019
2008–09	11.32545249	24.52627358
2009–10	11.64315067	24.82748124
2010–11	12.1556146	26.01504869
2011–12 (R)	13.08202487	28.13385202
2012–13	13.01676982	27.94267692

Source Annual Survey of Industries, Ministry of Statistics and Program Implementation
Whcre *W* Wages to workers, *E* Total emoluments, and *NVA* Net value added

Substituting (5.28) into (5.27), we rewrite it as

$$dY = \frac{-\frac{-\mathrm{NX}_\gamma}{-\mathrm{NX}_I}d\gamma}{1 - [C'(1-t)(1-v) + I_e e_Y + (t+v)]} < 0 \tag{5.29}$$

Let us now explain the expression on the RHS of (5.29). Following an exogenous increase in γ by $d\gamma$, import demand goes up lowering net export by $\mathrm{NX}_\gamma d\gamma$ at the initial equilibrium (Y, e). e rises to raise net export by $-\mathrm{NX}_\gamma d\gamma$ to restore net export to its initial equilibrium value. The increase in e raises net export mainly by lowering I. Hence, the rise in e lowers investment by $\frac{-\mathrm{NX}_\gamma d\gamma}{-\mathrm{NX}_I}$, which is a multiple of the increase in net export since import intensity of investment given by $-\mathrm{NX}_I$ is less than unity.

Thus, at the initial equilibrium Y, there emerges a large excess supply of $\frac{-\mathrm{NX}_{\gamma}\mathrm{d}\gamma}{-\mathrm{NX}_{I}}$ in the goods market setting off a cumulative process of contraction. Y will fall by a multiple of the initial large excess supply through the multiplier process described in the case of the other comparative static exercises. The above discussion yields the following proposition:

Proposition 5.4 *Under NEP, the Government of India has relaxed the restrictions on investment considerably leading to labor-saving technological changes occurring at a fierce pace giving rise to the phenomenon of jobless growth in the organized sector in India. Under NEP, GoI has allowed to a great extent the large firms to enter the sectors reserved for small producers during the Nehru–Mahalanobis era. GoI under NEP has also substantially withdrawn the fiscal concessions and subsidies on credit given to the small producers during the Nehru–Mahalanobis era eroding substantially their competitive strength. It has also under NEP substantially reduced interest rates on the saving instruments. All these measures have significantly raised income and wealth inequality raising substantially import intensities of consumption and investment. This brings about a cumulative contraction in the growth rate deepening India's dependence on global capitalists' investments in our assets even to sustain a moderate growth rate.*

5.7 Communalism, Territorial Disputes with Neighboring Countries and Dependence

The British Government followed the infamous divide-and-rule policy to rule their colonies. It weakens the ruled and obfuscates who the actual exploiter is. In case of India, the British Government promoted and funded communal parties, created tremendous communal tension and finally divided the country into India and Pakistan before granting Independence [see in this connection (Sunderland (1928), Dutt (1970), Khan Durrani (1944), Stewart (1951) et al.]. Even though India declared itself a secular state and allied with Soviet Union, Pakistan became a predominantly Muslim state and sided with the capitalist powers led by the USA. The global capitalists kept India under pressure through Pakistan and had the two countries caught in an arms race. Communal forces in India, considerably powerful, fomented communal tension in India and made the territorial disputes and arms race more fierce. Obviously, the arms race costs both these very poor countries, where most of the people are ill fed and half clad, very dear. Instead of devoting all their efforts and resources for meeting the basic needs of the people and achieving self-reliance through intensive R&D, they have to fritter away their resources in the arms race. This deepens their underdevelopment and dependence on the bounties of the global capitalists. We shall seek to establish this claim below.

We assume that a fraction α of G is spent on defense. Since countries like India and Pakistan are technologically backward and dependent, arms race takes the form of import of modern arms, and hence, a sizable part of the defense budget is spent on import of arms. Since only $(1-\alpha)G = (1-\alpha)(v+t)Y$ is spent on the production of non-defense essential services, p becomes a function of only $(1-\alpha)G = (1-\alpha)(v+t)Y$. Incorporating all these changes in (5.9), (5.10), and (5.12), we write them as follows:

$$\mathrm{NX}\Big(p\Big((1-\alpha)(v+t)Y\Big)(1-v), C(Y(1-v)(1-t)), I(r(r_c), e); \\ Y^*, \varphi, \gamma, \alpha\underset{-}{(v+t)Y}\Big) + \bar{K} = 0 \tag{5.30}$$

$$e = e\Big(\underset{-}{Y}, \underset{-}{t}, \underset{+}{v}, \underset{-}{Y^*}, \underset{-}{\phi}, \underset{+}{\gamma}, \underset{+}{\alpha}, \underset{-}{\overline{K}}\Big) \tag{5.31}$$

and

$$Y = C((1-t)(1-v)Y) + I\big(r(r_c), e\big(Y, t, v, Y^*, \phi, \alpha, \overline{K}\big)\big) + (t+v)Y - \overline{K} \tag{5.32}$$

Escalation of the arms race means an increase in α. We can derive the impact of a ceteris paribus increase in α on Y by taking total differential of (5.32) treating all variables other than Y and α as fixed and, then, solving for dY. This gives us the following value of dY:

$$\mathrm{d}Y = -\frac{-I_e e_\alpha \mathrm{d}\alpha}{1-[C'(1-t)(1-v) + I_e e_Y + (t+v)]} < 0 \tag{5.33}$$

Let us derive the value of $I_e e_\alpha \mathrm{d}\alpha$. Taking total differential of (5.30) treating all variables other than e and α as fixed and, then, solving for $I_e e_\alpha \mathrm{d}\alpha$, we get

$$I_e e_\alpha \mathrm{d}\alpha = -\frac{\big[\mathrm{NX}_p p'(v+t)Y(1-v) + \big(-\mathrm{NX}_{\mathrm{gd}}\big)(v+t)Y\big]\mathrm{d}\alpha}{-\mathrm{NX}_I} < 0 \tag{5.34}$$

Let us now explain (5.34) and (5.33). Let us start with the expression on the RHS of (5.34). Following an increase in α, net export falls very substantially for two reasons. First, import of armaments increases by $\big(-\mathrm{NX}_{\mathrm{gd}}\big)(v+t)Y$, where $\mathrm{NX}_{\mathrm{gd}}$ denotes partial derivative of net export function with respect to government's defense spending. Second, given government's budget constraint, there takes place a fall in government's spending on the production of non-defense essential services raising domestic price level. This brings about a substantial fall in net export whose absolute value is given by the term $\mathrm{NX}_p p'(v+t)Y(1-v)$. Thus, at the initial equilibrium (Y, e), there takes place a large fall in net export. e, therefore, rises to raise net export by the amount given by the numerator of the expression on the RHS of (5.34) to restore net export to its initial equilibrium value. The rise in e lowers net export mainly by lowering investment. To raise net export by the required amount at the initial equilibrium Y, e has to rise by such an amount that I decreases by a multiple of the required increase in net export, since $-NX_I < 1$. The fall in I at the initial equilibrium Y is given by the expression on the RHS of (5.34). This will create an excess supply in the goods market at the initial equilibrium Y setting off a cumulative contraction in Y through the multiplier process described earlier. Thus, the arms race helps the cause of the global capitalists. It lowers the growth rate substantially and, thereby, enormously deepens India's dependence on the global capitalists for sustaining even a modest rate of growth.

We can summarize our discussion in the form of the following proposition:

Proposition 5.5 *Global capitalists followed divide-and-rule policy, and divided India into India and Pakistan on communal lines. Through their control over political parties and communal forces, they keep India's border disputes with neighboring countries alive and get India engaged in an arms race with the neighbors. This substantially lowers India's growth potential and enormously deepens India's dependence on the global capitalists for sustaining even a modest growth rate.*

5.8 Stabilization Policy Under NEP: The Preeminence of Ineffective Monetary Policy

Under NEP, monetary policy has emerged as the major instrument of stabilization. The RBI seeks to regulate the interest rates to keep the economy stable. In times of recession, it adopts measures to lower interest rates to counter it. In periods of inflation, it seeks to raise interest rates to reduce it. Workers are net lenders, while capitalists are net borrowers. A reduction in interest rate benefits the capitalists at the expense of the workers. A recession gives the central bank an excuse to adopt all kinds of measures to lower interest rate to the minimum possible level hurting the workers substantially. Following the fall in the interest rate, workers' savings become available to the giant capitalists at the minimum possible interest rates. However, interest rates faced by the small and medium enterprises instead of falling rise sharply in times of recession eroding severely their competitive strength despite the fall in the risk-free interest rate to the minimum possible level. This happens on account of a steep rise in the risk premium on loans given to small and medium borrowers in times of recession (see Mishkin (2009) in this context). Therefore, recessions give the large corporations opportunities to compete their smaller counterparts out and increase their market share. Recessions, therefore, help the giant capitalists monopolize production and distribution in an economy and secure workers' savings at minimum possible cost. The following facts about the major capitalist powers, namely the USA, Europe and Japan, are noteworthy. Japan is in recession since 1992, and Bank of Japan cut its policy rate to zero as soon as the recession started in 1992 and at the present has lowered it further and made it negative. Interest rates in Japan since 1992 are at the minimum possible level. However, despite this very drastic cut in interest rates, Japan is still in recession, with its annual growth rates far below what it achieved in the pre-recession period. Thus, monetary policy of rate cut failed completely in

Japan. It failed in Europe and USA also. We shall substantiate this claim with data in case of the USA. Data given in Tables 5.8 and 5.9 strongly suggest that conventional monetary policy of rate cut cannot make any contribution to growth. Let us elaborate. During 1994–2000, average growth rate of real GDP in the USA was quite high (4.04%), but so were both nominal and real short-term and long-term interest rates. This implies that high interest rates do not discourage growth. They do not make the investors depressed. Following the slump in the growth rate in 2001, interest rates were reduced immediately. However, during the seven-year period 2001–2007, the average growth rate was only 2.5%, which was substantially below what the US economy achieved in the previous seven-year period despite much higher nominal and real interest rates. The reduction in interest rates of course led to the swelling of the house price bubble, which deepened the recession into a full-fledged crisis. During 2008–2014, the average growth rate was only 0.8% even though interest rates were cut drastically in 2009. Thus, investors did not feel enthusiastic in the six years that elapsed following the cut in interest rates. This clearly shows that conventional monetary policy is completely ineffective in restoring investor confidence. It only hurts the savers and facilitates the formation of bubbles without doing any real good to the economy.

We shall argue here that the RBI cannot counter recession through its monetary policy. Instead of regarding interest rate as an instrument for stabilization, the government should regard it as return on saving. The workers, who constitute the poorer section of people, live on their saving in their old age, when they become infirm. The government should make sure that the interest rates on savings are sufficiently remunerative so that the workers' loss in income in their old age is fully compensated for. The interest rate on loans given to producers of essential goods should be kept low through subsidies, and the government should finance the subsidies by taxing the income of the rich and also by fixing high interest rates on loans given for production and investment in the non-essential sector. In what follows, we shall modify the model developed above to show that in a country like India, the conventional monetary policy of rate cut to counter recession is likely to intensify recession instead of removing it.

5.8.1 The Model

Modifying (5.1), we rewrite it as

$$Y = C((1-t)Y) + I(r, e) + G + \mathrm{NX}\left(\frac{P^{*}e}{P}, C((1-t)Y), I(r(r_{c}), e)\right) - q\left(\underset{-}{r}\right)\cdot\{(1-t)Y - C((1-t)Y)\} \tag{5.35}$$

Table 5.8 Consumer price inflation and interest rates in the USA

Year	CPI	r^b	R^c	Y^d
1994	2.6	7.15	8.35	4.0
1995	2.8	8.83	7.95	2.7
1996	3.0	8.27	7.8	3.8
1997	2.3	8.44	7.6	4.5
1998	1.6	8.35	6.94	4.5
1999	2.2	8.00	7.43	4.7
2000	3.4	9.23	8.06	4.1
2001	2.8	6.91	6.97	1.0
2002	1.6	4.67	6.54	1.8
2003	2.3	4.12	5.82	2.8
2004	2.7	4.34	5.84	3.8
2005	3.4	6.19	5.86	3.3
2006	3.2	7.96	6.41	2.7
2007	2.8	8.05	6.34	1.8
2008	3.8	5.09	5.04	−0.3
2009	−0.4	3.25	4.69	−2.8
2010	1.6	3.25	4.46	2.5
2011	3.2	3.25	3.66	1.6
2012	2.9	3.25	3.98	2.2
2013		3.25	0.31	1.5

[b]Average majority prime rate charged by banks on short-term loans to business, [c]Contract rate on 30-year fixed rate conventional home mortgage commitments, [d]Percentage increase in real GDP from the previous year

Source HPI has been computed from the house price index published by Freddie Mac

Data of CPI and percentage change in real GDP are taken from US Bureau of Economic Analysis

Data on interest rates have been taken from the Board of Governors of the Federal Reserve System

Table 5.9 Average growth rate of real GDP and average interest rates

Year	Average growth rate[a]	Average prime lending rates of banks	Average interest rates on 30-year mortgage contracts
1994–2000	4.04	8.32	7.73
2001–2007	2.5	6.03	6.25
2008–2013	0.8	4.27	4.64

[a]Simple arithmetic mean of the year-on-year growth rates of GDP

Source Computed from the data given in Table 5.4

Table 5.10 Consumer price inflation, deposit rate, and real interest rate on savings

FY	CPI (IW)[a]	CPI (AL)[b]	Deposit rate (%) 1 year	Real rate of interest (%)	
				IW	AL
2009–10	18.32	13.25	6	−6.32	−7.25
2010–11	10.03	10.10	8.25	−7.78	−7.85
2011–12	8.41	8.21	9.25	0.84	7.04
2012–13	10.43	10.00	8.75	−7.68	−7.25
2013–14	18.38	17.62	8.75	−3.63	−8.87
2014–15 (Apr–Jul)	6.95	8.05	8.75	1.8	0.7

[a]*CPI(IW)* Consumer price inflation for industrial workers, [b]*CPI(AL)* Consumer price inflation for agricultural labor
Source RBI

Let us now explain the difference between (5.35) and (5.1). In (5.35), we assume that τ, and therefore, v are zero. There is another difference. This is in the net export function. We assume here that people hold q fraction of their saving in the form of gold, gems, jewelry, etc., which are all imported. We make q a decreasing function of r. Let us explain. People hold their saving in the form of not only domestic financial assets but also physical assets such as precious metals, gems jewelry. The lower the r, the less is the incentive to hold savings in the form of domestic financial assets (bank deposits in our model) relative to other assets, and hence, the higher is the value of q. In fact, as we find from Table 5.10, real interest rate has been negative in India in most of the recent years. This acted as a great disincentive for holding savings in the form of domestic financial assets. The recession started in India from 2011 to 2012. This made the savers apprehensive of large cuts in r_c by RBI to bring about a substantial fall in interest rate. This apprehension was bolstered by the fact that in the USA immediately after the onset of the Great Recession in 2008, Fed cut its policy rate (the Fed rate) to zero and adopted all kinds of measures to lower interest rate to the minimum possible level. European Central Bank (ECB) also behaved in the same way, when recession struck European countries in 2008 [see Blinder and Zandi (2010) and Mishkin (2009, 2011) in this context]. Hence, savers in India reduced the fraction of their saving held in the form of domestic financial assets drastically since 2011–12 (see Table 5.11). This, in our view, is the only plausible explanation of this phenomenon. Thus, q_r is likely to be quite large in India. Since $q\left(\underset{-}{r}\right)[(1-t)Y - C((1-t)Y)]$ represents demand for imported goods for holding a part of the saving, we write the net export function in (5.35) as

$$\mathrm{NX}\left(\frac{P^*e}{P}, C((1-t)Y - C((1-t)Y)), I(r,e)\right) - q\left(\underset{-}{r}\right)[(1-t)Y - C((1-t)Y)].$$

Since τ and, therefore, v are zero, the value of G instead of being given by (5.6) is given by

Table 5.11 Percentage of financial savings in the total savings of the households

Financial year	Financial savings (% of total savings) in the household sector
2009–10	47.51
2010–11	48.98
2011–12	30.77
2012–13	38.42

Source RBI, Table 5.10, sector-wise domestic savings

$$G = tY \tag{5.36}$$

The financial sector is the same as before. The interest rate is given by (5.7). At the given interest rate, as before, commercial banks meet all the credit demand of the economic agents so that the expenditure plans of all the economic agents are fulfilled.

Let us now consider the external sector. Using (5.7) to substitute $r(r_c)$ for r, we write the BOP equilibrium condition in our modified model as

$$\mathrm{NX}\left(\frac{P^*e}{P}, C((1-t)Y), I(r(r_c), e)\right) - q\left(\underset{-}{r(r_c)}\right) \cdot \{(1-t)Y - C((1-t)Y)\} = 0 \tag{5.37}$$

In (5.37), we have ignored cross-border capital flows for simplicity and without any loss of generality.

P is set on the basis of cost. Two most important determinants of cost in India are the wage rate and e. As we pointed out earlier, it also depends upon G (see 5.3). The money wage rate is rigid in the short run. For simplicity, we also disregard G as a determinant of P and make P an increasing function of only e. Thus, we write

$$P = P\left(\underset{+}{e}\right) \tag{5.38}$$

The real exchange rate is given by

$$p = \frac{P^*e}{P} \tag{5.39}$$

Substituting (5.38) into (5.39), we get

$$p = \frac{P^*e}{P(e)} = \overline{p} \tag{5.40}$$

Let us explain (5.40). Following an increase in e, P increases substantially, since India's production is highly import-intensive. Hence, following a ceteris paribus increase in e, p is likely to change by a small amount. We, therefore, regard p as fixed at $\overline{p}$ for simplicity.

Substituting (5.40) into (5.37), we rewrite it as follows:

$$\mathrm{NX}(\overline{p}, C((1-t)Y), I(r(r_{\mathrm{c}}), e)) - q\left(\underset{-}{r(r_{\mathrm{c}})}\right) \cdot \{(1-t)Y - C((1-t)Y)\} = 0 \tag{5.41}$$

Substituting (5.36), (5.7), and (5.41) into (5.31), we rewrite it as

$$Y = C((1-t)Y) + I(r(r_{\mathrm{c}}), e) + tY = 0 \tag{5.42}$$

The specification of our model is now complete. It consists of two key equations, (5.41) and (5.42), in two endogenous variables Y and e. We solve them as follows: We solve (5.41) for e as a function of Y and r_{c}, among others. Thus, we have

$$e = e\left(\underset{+}{Y}, \underset{-}{r_{\mathrm{c}}}\right) \tag{5.43}$$

Let us now derive and explain the signs of the partial derivatives of (5.43). Taking total differential of (5.41) treating all variables other than Y and e as fixed and, then, solving for $e_Y \left(\equiv \frac{\mathrm{d}e}{\mathrm{d}Y}\right)$, we get

$$e_Y = \frac{-\mathrm{NX}_C C'(1-t) + q \cdot \left(1 - C'\right)(1-t)}{\mathrm{NX}_I I_e} > 0 \tag{5.44}$$

Let us explain the expression on the RHS of (5.44). Following a ceteris paribus increase in Y, net export falls for two reasons. First, consumption demand goes up raising demand for imported consumption goods. Second, the amount of saving held in the form of imported goods rises. Hence, at the initial equilibrium e, there emerges BOP deficit and e rises to raise net export by the amount given by the numerator. The denominator gives the increase in net export per unit increase in e. Therefore, the expression on the RHS of (5.44) gives the value of e_Y. Value of $I_e e_Y$ is given by

$$I_e e_Y = \frac{-\mathrm{NX}_C C'(1-t) + q \cdot \left(1 - C'\right)(1-t)}{\mathrm{NX}_I} < 0 \tag{5.45}$$

Again, taking total differential of (5.41) treating all variables other than e and r_{c} as fixed and, then, solving for $e_{r_{\mathrm{c}}} \left(\equiv \frac{\mathrm{d}e}{\mathrm{d}r_{\mathrm{c}}}\right)$, we get

$$e_{r_{\mathrm{c}}} = -\frac{[\mathrm{NX}_I I_r - q_r S] \cdot r_{r_{\mathrm{c}}}}{\mathrm{NX}_I I_e} < 0; \quad S \equiv (1-t)Y - C((1-t)Y) \tag{5.46}$$

Let us explain the expression on the RHS of (5.46). Following a ceteris paribus increase in r_{c}, r rises. This raises net export for two reasons. First, investment falls lowering import. Second, the part of saving held in the form of imported goods falls. The total value of the increase in net export is given by the expression within the third brackets in the numerator. At the initial equilibrium e, there emerges BOP surplus. e, therefore, falls to reduce net export by the amount given by the numerator. The denominator gives the absolute value of the fall in net export per unit decrease in e. Thus, the expression on the RHS of (5.46) gives the fall in e that takes place at the initial equilibrium Y per unit increase in r_c, when r_c is raised by a small amount dr_c. Therefore, following a cut in r_c by dr_c, e goes up by

$$e_{r_c} dr_c = \frac{[NX_I I_r - q_r S] \cdot r_{r_c}}{NX_I I_e}(-dr_c) > 0 \quad \because dr_c < 0 \tag{5.47}$$

Therefore, following a cut in r_c by dr_c, investment at the initial equilibrium Y falls by the amount given by

$$\begin{aligned} I_e e_{r_c} dr_c &= \frac{-[-NX_I I_r + q_r S] \cdot r_{r_c}}{NX_I}(-dr_c) \\ &= I_r r_c(-dr_c) + \frac{q_r S r_c(-dr_c)}{-NX_I} < 0 \quad \because dr_c < 0 \end{aligned} \tag{5.48}$$

Let us explain (5.48). Following a cut in r_c by $-dr_c$, I rises by $-I_r r_{r_c}(-dr_c)$ and saving held in the form of imported goods rises by $-q_r S r_{r_c}(-dr_c)$. Both of these lower net export by $[-NX_I(-I_r) + (-q_r)S] \cdot r_{r_c}(-dr_c)$ in absolute quantity at the initial equilibrium (Y, e). Therefore, e will rise to restore net export to its initial equilibrium value. e will do this, for reasons we have already explained, mainly by lowering investment. Per unit rise in e net export rises by $NX_I I_e$. Hence, the rise in e will lower investment by the amount given by (5.48).

Substituting (5.43) into (5.42), we rewrite it as follows:

$$Y = C((1-t)Y) + I(r(r_c), e(Y, r_c)) + tY = 0 \tag{5.49}$$

We can solve (5.49) for the equilibrium value of Y. To derive the impact of a cut in r_c on Y, we take total differential of (5.49) treating all variables other than Y and r_c as fixed, and, then, solve for dY. This gives the following:

$$dY = \frac{(-I_r) r_{r_c}(-dr_c) + (-I_e) e_{r_c}(-dr_c)}{1 - [C'(1-t) - (-I_e) e_Y]} \tag{5.50}$$

Substituting (5.48) into (5.50), we rewrite it as

$$dY = -\frac{\frac{-q_r S r_{r_c}(-dr_c)}{-NX_I}}{1 - [C'(1-t) + t - (-I_e) e_Y]} < 0 \tag{5.51}$$

We shall now explain the expression on the RHS of (5.51). The numerator is negative. The denominator is positive by assumption. One can easily show that the assumption is necessary and sufficient for stability. Let us now explain (5.51). Following a cut in r_c by dr_c, r falls raising I. This increase in I is unlikely to be significant since in times of recession firms operate with large-scale excess capacity. The increase in I at the initial equilibrium (Y, e) will raise import demand creating a BOP deficit. e as a result will rise to restore net export to its initial equilibrium value. It will do so mainly by lowering I. Thus, the rise in e will restore I almost to its initial equilibrium value. Thus, the cut in r_c fails to produce any positive impact on I. However, the fall in r induced by the cut in r_c produces another effect. It makes it profitable for people to divert their savings from bank deposits to imported goods. This also creates BOP deficit at the initial equilibrium (Y, e). This raises e, and the rise in e removes the BOP deficit mainly by lowering I. Thus, excess supply emerges at the initial equilibrium Y. The numerator (denoted N) gives the amount of this excess supply. Producers will respond to it by lowering Y in the first round by $dY_1 = N$. The fall in Y will reduce people's income and government's tax receipts, and, hence, personal and public consumption will go down by $\left[C'(1-t)+t\right]dY_1 = \left[C'(1-t)+t\right]N$. However, the fall in Y will lower e and, thereby, raise investment demand by $I_e e_Y N$. Hence, the net fall in demand is $\left[C'(1-t)+t-(-I_e)e_Y\right]N$. We assume it to be positive. Hence, Y in the second round will go down by $dY_2 = \left[C'(1-t)+t-(-I_e)e_Y\right]N$. Similarly, Y in the third round will fall by

$$dY_3 = \left[C'(1-t)+t-(-I_e)e_Y\right]dY_2 = \left[C'(1-t)+t-(-I_e)e_Y\right]^2 N.$$

This process of cumulative contraction will continue until the amount of fall in demand that takes place in each successive round eventually falls to zero. For this to happen, $\left[C'(1-t)+t-(-I_e)e_Y\right]$ has to be less than unity. We assume this to be the case. Thus, the total decrease in Y is given by

$$\begin{aligned} dY &= N + \left[C'(1-t)+t-(-I_e)e_Y\right]N + \left[C'(1-t)+t-(-I_e)e_Y\right]^2 N + \ldots \\ &= \frac{N}{1-[C'(1-t)+t-(-I_e)e_Y]} \end{aligned} \tag{5.52}$$

(5.52) gives the absolute value of fall in Y. The actual change in Y is

$$dY = -\frac{N}{1-[C'(1-t)+t-(-I_e)e_Y]} \tag{5.53}$$

This explains (5.51). The above discussion yields the following proposition:

Proposition 5.6 *If in a country like India, the central bank takes measures to reduce interest rates in times of recession to counter it, it will be counterproductive. It will unleash forces that will bring about a cumulative contraction in GDP instead of the other way round.*

As we have pointed out above (see Proposition 5.2), the only way of tackling recession, BOP difficulties, and inflation in a country like India is to raise income tax rates applicable to the incomes of the rich. This program is also eminently just.

5.9 Conclusion

India followed the Nehru–Mahalanobis strategy of development, which was fashioned after the Soviet model of planned economic development. The objective of the strategy was to achieve self-reliance and to provide the masses with the basic necessities of life such as food, clothing, shelter, and to create a universal health care and education system giving the masses unlimited free access to these essential services. The key to achieving self-reliance lay in expending intensive efforts at developing indigenous basis of knowledge and technology that would produce the kind of technology and strategy that would eliminate India's dependence on imported products, technology, and knowledge. However, surprisingly, India never made such an effort. India also chose a basic and heavy industry-based development strategy, which was so highly import-intensive that it was not possible for India to implement it without assistance not only from the Soviet Union but also from the major capitalist powers, which were obviously averse to India's socialist program and wanted to disrupt it at the first opportunity. Both of these lacunae are extremely puzzling. How does one explain this puzzle? In our view, the only explanation of the puzzle is the following: The global capitalists through Pakistan and the communal forces in India kept the territorial disputes alive and threatened escalation of the disputes into full-fledged wars causing grave disruption of the development process. To appease the global capitalists, in our view, India had to desist from investing in developing an independent knowledge and R&D sector and chose a strategy that made India dependent on the bounties of the global capitalists. From the beginning of the eighties, India began to borrow from the foreigners heavily at high interest rates knowing fully well that, given India's extremely low export capacity, it would get India caught in a perpetual external debt trap and deliver it fully under the control of the global capitalists/lenders. How can one explain this suicidal borrowing spree on the part of India? The only plausible explanation is perhaps the following: Relentless and continuous engagement with the global capitalists in the Cold War made Soviet Union weak in the eighties so much so that the separatist Khalistan movement broke out at the heart of India. Indian leaders in power took fright and to save themselves and the country surrendered to the global capitalists, who, keen on regaining full control over India, asked the Indian leaders to start borrowing heavily from them. As a result, India's external debt service charges started rising rapidly and precipitously as a proportion of India's external current receipts forcing India eventually to a position where India had to seek IMF's assistance to avoid defaulting on its external debt service obligations. Thus, the foreign investors or the global capitalists won India back and started building India on capitalist lines removing all the vestiges of socialism.

IMF has thrust on India New Economic Policy (NEP). The objective of NEP is to establish capitalism in India and facilitate its expansion. Instead of trying to make India self-reliant, as we have shown above, it constitutes a strategy that deepens manifold India's dependence on the bounties of global capitalists so that their control over India becomes absolute. NEP has removed all kinds of control imposed during the Mahalanobis era over consumption, production, import, etc., so that instead of planners market forces determine the allocation and utilization of resources. India is an extremely unequal country. Available evidences suggest that only one percent of Indians have in their command about 80% of India's GDP and wealth. In such a scenario, if allocation of resources is left to market forces, 80% of the country's resources will be utilized to cater to the needs of 1% of Indians, while the remaining 99% of Indians will have to make do with the rest. Capitalism sets one class of people, the capitalists, against another, the workers. Their interests conflict, and they struggle with one another to grab a larger share of aggregate production. Capitalists seek to achieve greater bargaining strength by continuously bringing about labor-displacing technological changes creating a large pool of unemployed labor. NEP has removed controls over investment and imports and cross-border capital flows. Global capitalists have also invested on a large scale in Indian assets making supplies of foreign exchange plentiful. This has induced domestic investors to import labor-displacing technologies on a large scale so much so that the organized sector in India in the post-reform period has grown phenomenally without creating any additional employment. During Nehru–Mahalanobis era, many sectors were reserved exclusively for small and medium producers. Arrangements were made so that they get institutional credit at subsidized rates. They also enjoyed a large number of tax and other fiscal concessions. Planners encouraged growth of these producers to generate employment and also to foster equality. NEP seeks to withdraw all these facilities to erode the competitive strength of the small and medium producers. This facilitates the expansion of the organized sector at the expense of the unorganized sector destroying jobs and fostering inequality. NEP also imposes stringent restrictions on government's borrowing and fixes income tax rates at the lowest possible level. The scope for hiking indirect tax rates is extremely limited since such measures raise domestic price level and, thereby, generate strong recessionary forces through their adverse effect on income distribution and BOP. For all these reasons, NEP has severely reduced government's ability to invest in agriculture, health, education, and public distribution system. It threatens India's food security and severely undermines common people's access to food, health care, and education. Thus, NEP not only delivers India hopelessly under the control of the global capitalists but also fosters extreme inequality and creates a tiny island of unbelievable opulence in the midst of abysmal poverty, unemployment, ill health, and hunger.

What is the way out? The way out of this extremely unjust dependent capitalism may be the following: First, the masses have to be made aware of the current state of affairs and the reason for their plight. The masses have to get united and stand up for their rights. They have to wrest the political parties from the giant capitalists global and local. To do this, they have to pressurize the government to make all kinds of private funding of political parties illegal. The government should create infrastructure so that all political parties get equal opportunities for airing their views. In such a scenario, political parties will get an opportunity to truly work for the masses. To make India truly independent, all the surplus income of the rich should be taxed away to minimize import and the resources released should be utilized to develop the mass consumption good and the knowledge sector so that technologies and strategies can be developed to eliminate India's dependence on imports.

References

Banerjee, S., & Prasad, S. (2017, September 23). Small businesses in the GST regime. *Economic and Political Weekly, LII*(38).

Blinder, A. S., & Zandi, M. (2010). *How the great recession was brought to an end*. Available at www.dismal.com/mark-zandi/documents/End'of-Great-Recession.pdf.

Dutt, R. P. (1970). *India Today*, 2nd ed. Calcutta: Manisha.

Ghosh, C., & Ghosh, A. (2016). *Indian Economy: A macro-theoretic analysis*. Delhi: PHI Learning Private Limited.

Khan Durrani, F. K. (1944). *The meaning of Pakistan*. Lahore: S. H. Muhemmad Ashraf.

Mishkin, F. S. (2009). Is monetary policy effective during financial crises. *American Economic Review, 99*(2), 573–577.

Mishkin, F. S. (2011, Winter). Over the cliff: From the subprime to the global financial crisis. *Journal of Economic Perspectives, 25*(1), 49–70.

Oxfam India (2018). India Inequality Report 2018. https://www.oxfamindia.org/sites/.../himanhshu_inequality_inequality_report_2018.pdf.

Pruthi, R. (2004). *Sikhism and Indian civilization*. India: Discovery Publishing House.

Stewart, N. (1951, Winter). British policy in Indian history. *Science & Society, 15*(1), 49–55.

Sunderland, J. T. (1928). *India in bondage: Her right to freedom*. Calcutta: R. Chatterjee.

Van Dyke, V. (2009, November/December). The Khalistan movement in Punjab, India and the post-militancy era: Structural change and new political compulsions. *Asian Survey, 49*(6), 975–997.

Chapter 6
Macroeconomics of Non-performing Assets of Banks in India

Abstract Following the adoption of the New Economic Policy (NEP) by India in July 1991, Government of India (GoI) has started viewing banks as commercially organized profit-driven financial institutions whose viability depends upon their ability to make profit. Like all capitalist economies, India is also subject to trade cycles and onset of a recession leads to a drop in banks' profit levels and an increase in their stock of non-performing assets. This prompts the government/central bank to take such measures as asking banks to tighten lending norms, raise capital adequacy ratio, etc. This chapter, on the basis of the models presented in Part I of the book, develops a simple baseline model to examine the implications of this kind of policies. It shows that the policies noted above deepens recession, increases inequality, and exacerbates the problem of non-performing assets and low profit. It also shows that, instead of taking the banks and the defaulting firms to task for a factor that is completely beyond their control, the best way of tackling this problem is to adopt appropriate stabilization programs to counter the recession.

6.1 Introduction

Non-performing assets of public sector banks have begun to rise since 2011–12 (see Table 6.1). Both Government of India and RBI have taken alarm and have adopted a number of measures to arrest the growth of non-performing assets. The government is planning to infuse new capital into the banks to maintain capital adequacy ratio. Some of the public sector banks have been put under the category that requires 'Prompt Corrective Action' (PCA). All the banks in general and the public sector banks in particular have been put on high alert. Most alarmingly, the GOI has proposed to introduce the Financial Regulation and Deposit Insurance (FRDI) Bill, which empowers the government to forfeit the deposits of the depositors to rescue banks that have become insolvent. Clearly, these measures tend to destroy people's faith in banks. They will be disinclined to hold their savings with the banks bringing about a collapse of the banking system and, thereby, that of the economy as a whole. We shall examine the implications of all these measures in this and the next chapter.

C. Ghosh and A. N. Ghosh, *Keynesian Macroeconomics Beyond the IS-LM Model*, https://doi.org/10.1007/978-981-13-7888-1_6

One should note that, to adopt appropriate measures, one has to identify the reasons for the increase in the stock of non-performing assets. From the data of growth rate and non-performing assets, it is clear that the non-performing assets as a percentage of total advances started rising since the onset of recession in 2011–12 (see Tables 6.1 and 6.2). The period from 2003–04 to 2010–11 was one of unprecedented boom during which GDP grew at an average annual rate of around 8.5%. The growth rate dropped to 6.5% in 2011–12 and further to 4.5 and 4.8%, respectively, in 2012–13 and 2013–14. Even going by the new data derived using new methodology and a new base year 2011–12, which have substantially raised the growth rates of 2012–13 and 2013–14, the average annual growth rate during 2012–13 to 2015–16 is around 6.5%. If we had applied the same methodology and the base year to estimate the growth rates of the boom period (2003–04 to 2010–11), the annual growth rates of the boom period would have been much higher than what we have shown in Table 6.1 making the average annual growth rate during the boom period much higher than 8.5%. During the boom period spanning eight years, investors' morale was high. Driven by

Table 6.1 Non-performing asset in absolute terms and as percentage of total advances in four bank groups

Year	GNPA (in billion rupees)				GNPA (as % of total advances)			
	Scheduled	Public	Private	Foreign	Scheduled	Public	Private	Foreign
2015	6119.47	5399.56	561.86	158.05	7.5	9.3	2.8	4.2
2014	3233.35	2784.68	341.06	107.61	4.3	5.0	2.1	3.2
2013	2633.72	2272.64	245.42	115.65	3.8	4.4	1.8	3.9
2012	1935.09	1644.61	210.71	79.77	3.2	3.6	1.8	3.1
2011	1423.26	1172.62	187.68	62.97	3.1	3.3	2.2	2.8
2010	979.00	746.00	145.00	50.00	2.5	2.4	2.7	2.5
2009	846.98	599.26	140.17	71.33	2.4	2.2	2.9	4.3
2008	683.28	449.57	138.54	64.44	2.3	2.0	3.1	3.8
2007	563.09	404.52	104.40	28.59	2.3	2.2	2.5	1.8
2006	504.86	389.68	62.87	22.63	2.5	2.7	1.9	1.8
2005	510.97	413.58	40.52	19.28	3.3	3.6	1.7	1.9
2004	593.73	483.99	45.82	21.92	5.2	5.5	3.6	2.8
2003	648.12	515.37	59.83	28.94	7.2	7.8	5.0	4.6
2002	687.17	540.90	72.32	28.45	8.8	9.4	7.6	5.3
2001	708.61	564.73	68.11	27.26	10.4	11.1	8.9	5.4
2000	637.41	546.72	16.17	31.06	11.4	12.4	5.1	6.8
1999	604.08	530.33	9.46	26.14	12.7	14.0	4.1	7.0
1998	587.22	517.10	8.71	23.57	14.7	15.9	6.2	7.6
1997	508.15	456.53	3.92	19.76	14.4	16.0	3.5	6.4
1996	473.00	435.77	2.17	11.81	15.7	17.8	2.6	4.3

Source Database on Indian Economy, India

Table 6.2 Annual growth rate of GDP at constant prices

Year	Growth rate of GDP at factor prices (base year 2004–05)	Growth rate of GVA at basic prices (base year 2011–12 new series)
1990–91	5.3	
1991–92	1.4	
1992–93	5.4	
1993–94	5.7	
1994–95	6.4	
1995–96	7.3	
1996–97	8.0	
1997–98	4.3	
1998–99	6.7	
1999–00	8.0	
2000–01	4.1	
2001–02	5.4	
2002–03	3.9	
2003–04	8.0	
2004–05	7.1	
2005–06	9.5	
2006–07	9.6	
2007–08	9.3	
2008–09	6.7	
2009–10	8.6	
2010–11	8.9	
2011–12	6.7	
2012–13	4.5	5.4
2013–14	4.8	6.1
2014–15		7.2
2015–16		7.9
2016–17		6.6

Source RBI

their enthusiasm to invest, advances grew at a high rate. However, the expectation of a high growth of demand that drove investment during the boom period turned awry since 2011–12. Large expensive capacities created during the boom period turned idle saddling the investors' with large losses. Investors' morale went for a toss. This led to two changes: Default rate rose sharply raising the growth rate of non-performing assets, while growth rate of advances fell. These two factors together brought about an increase in the stock of non-performing assets as a fraction of total advances. Obviously, neither the investors nor the banks are at a fault as capitalist economies are subject to trade cycles and both upswings and downturns are unpredictable. The best way of tackling recessions and the attendant problem of non-performing assets is to undertake appropriate expansionary stabilization policies to put the economy on an upswing, provide debt relief to ailing firms until the economy revives, and provide adequate capital to the banks to fully compensate for their losses until the economy begins to boom again and the firms begin to make profit and start paying back the loans along with the interest [in fact, some of these policies were adopted by the US Government and Fed to rescue the banks and the economy following the financial meltdown in the USA since 2007 (see Mishkin 2011; Blinder and Zandi 2010a, b)]. If instead of adopting intelligent, well-informed counter-recessionary policies, the government takes the banks to task, it will have the confidence of banks', savers' and investors' badly shaken, credit disbursement will dip sharply and the economy will slip into a deep recession. In this and the next chapter, we shall illustrate these points. More precisely, the objective of this chapter is the following: It examines the efficacy of tighter lending norms that the government and the central bank impose on banks following an increase in their stock of non-performing assets.

6.2 A Baseline Model for Examining Banking Sector Reforms

We first develop a simple baseline model to examine the implications of the recent banking sector reforms in India. We consider a small open economy divided into two sectors: a real sector and a financial sector. We focus on the real sector first.

Real Sector

In the real sector, aggregate output or GDP is demand-determined. The equilibrium condition of the real sector is given by

$$Y = cY + I(r) + G + X\left(\frac{P^{*}e}{P}; Y^{*}\right) - \frac{P^{*}e}{P}M\left(\frac{P^{*}e}{P}, Y\right) \tag{6.1}$$

We assume that government expenditure is financed by borrowing from the central bank so that

$$G = \frac{\mathrm{d}H}{P} \tag{6.2}$$

In (6.2), dH denotes increase in the stock of high-powered money. For the time being, we ignore cross-border capital flows and consider the flexible exchange rate regime. The BOP equilibrium condition is, therefore, given by

$$X\left(\frac{P^{*}e}{P}, Y^{*}\right) - \frac{P^{*}e}{P}M\left(\frac{P^{*}e}{P}, Y\right) = 0 \tag{6.3}$$

Financial Sector

We assume for simplicity that the only kind of financial institutions that exist in the financial sector are banks. Banks raise their funds by inviting deposits and also by selling equities. Banks sell new equities in the market at a fixed price. At the fixed price, either they are able to sell as many equities as they want or they face demand constraint. We consider both the cases here. We postulate for simplicity that only banks issue equities. We ignore here the secondary market in equities. However, we assume for simplicity that the buyers of the equity can sell their equities back to the issuer banks at the price at which they bought them. These assumptions simplify our analysis without scuttling the generality of the results.

We assume that savers hold their saving (denoted S) in the form of equity, bank deposits, and currency. They hold q and q_1 fractions of their saving in the form of equity and currency, respectively, and the rest in the form of bank deposits. We also assume here that banks do not hold any excess reserve and they sell equities only to meet the capital adequacy requirement. Given these assumptions, the amount of new equities the banks want to sell is given by

$$E^s = \frac{1}{\theta}L^S = \frac{1}{\theta}(1-\rho)\mathrm{d}D \tag{6.4}$$

In (6.4), $E^S \equiv$ planned supply of new equity by the banks, $L^S \equiv$ planned supply of new bank loans, $\frac{1}{\theta} \equiv$ capital adequacy ratio, $\rho \equiv$ CRR, and $\mathrm{d}D \equiv$ new deposit received by the banks.

Demand for new equities comes from the savers who hold q fraction of their saving in the form of new equities. Thus,

$$E^d = q \cdot (1-c)Y \tag{6.5}$$

New deposits received by the banks are given by

$$\mathrm{d}D = (1-q-q_1)(1-c)Y \tag{6.6}$$

Substituting (6.6) into (6.4), we get

$$E^s = \frac{1}{\theta}(1-\rho)(1-q-q_1)(1-c)Y \tag{6.7}$$

There are clearly two possibilities, $E^s > E^d$, $E^s \leq E^d$. In the first case, banks are rationed in the equity market. Hence, their planned supply of new loan will be given by

$$L^s = \theta E^d = \theta q(1-c)Y \tag{6.8}$$

In this case,

$$\frac{1}{\theta}(1-\rho)(1-q-q_1)(1-c)Y > q(1-c)Y \Rightarrow (1-\rho)(1-q-q_1)(1-c)Y > \theta q(1-c)Y \quad (6.9)$$

From the above it follows that in this case, banks supply less new credit than what they would have done in the absence of the capital adequacy norm.

Let us now focus on the second case. In this case, banks are able to sell as much equity as they want to, but savers are unable to buy as much equity as they want to. We assume for simplicity that they hold in the form of bank deposits the part of the saving that they plan to hold in equity but cannot. In this case, therefore, planned q and actual q differ. Clearly, the value of actual q is such that it equates E^s and E^d. Denoting the actual q by $\overline{q}$, we get

$$\frac{1}{\theta}(1-\rho)(1-\overline{q}-q_1)(1-c)Y = \overline{q}(1-c)Y \Rightarrow \frac{1}{\theta}(1-\rho)(1-\overline{q}-q_1) = \overline{q} \quad (6.10)$$

We can solve (6.10) for $\overline{q}$. The solution is given by

$$\overline{q} = \frac{(1-\rho)(1-q_1)}{\theta + (1-\rho)} \quad (6.11)$$

The solution of (6.10) is shown in Fig. 6.1, where the 45° line and the SS schedule give the values of the RHS and the LHS of (6.10), respectively, corresponding to different values of $\overline{q}$. The SS schedule is negatively sloped. Since θ is greater than unity, the absolute value of the slope of the SS schedule is less than unity. The equilibrium value of $\overline{q}$ corresponds to the point of intersection of the two schedules. We now explain using the diagram how the equilibrium value of $\overline{q}$ is arrived at. Note that, in this case, the planned q exceeds the equilibrium value of $\overline{q}$. For the sake of illustration, we take the value of planned q to be q_0 in the diagram. At $q = q_0$, banks receive new deposits of $(1-q_o-q_1)(1-c)Y$ corresponding to any given Y and plan to supply new loan of $(1-\rho)(1-q_0-q_1)(1-c)Y$. To do that, they will have to sell new equity worth $\frac{1}{\theta}(1-\rho)(1-q_0-q_1)(1-c)Y$, which is less than the demand for new equity given by $q_0(1-c)Y$. The savers who are unable to secure new equities will, therefore, start transferring their saving from equity to bank deposit reducing their q. Hence, supply of new loan and, therefore, that of new equity will start rising and demand for new equity will start falling. This process will continue until q falls to the equilibrium value of $\overline{q}$. In what follows, we shall assume $\overline{q}$ to be always equal to its equilibrium value, which is given by (6.11).

Since in the present case banks are able to sell as much new equity as they plan to, their planned supply of new loans is not constrained by the capital adequacy ratio. Hence, their supply of new loans is given by

$$L^s = \theta E^s = (1-\rho)(1-\overline{q}-q_1)(1-c)Y \quad (6.12)$$

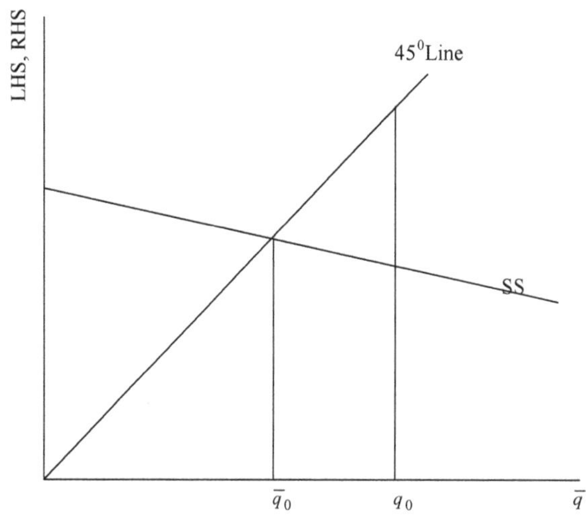

Fig. 6.1 Determination of the equilibrium value of $\overline{q}$

In consonance with reality, we also assume that the banking sector is oligopolistic and the interest rate charged by banks on loans is rigid and depends only upon the repo rate. Denoting the lending rate of banks and the repo rate by r and r_p respectively, we have

$$r = r\left(\underset{+}{r_p}\right) \tag{6.13}$$

Demand for loans comes from the investors, who finance their entire investment with bank loans. In this connection, we divide aggregate investment into two parts. One part of investment is undertaken by the quality borrowers (large corporate houses with substantial financial and business standing) whom banks never ration, and the other part is undertaken by those investors whom banks ration (see Bernanke et al. (1996) in this connection). We denote the former by I_0 and the latter by I_1 and write the investment function as

$$I = I_0\left(r\left(r_p\right), \varepsilon_0\right) + I_1\left(r\left(r_p\right), \varepsilon_1\right) \tag{6.14}$$

In (6.14), ε_0 and ε_1 denote expectations of the two types of borrowers. We assume here that at the given interest rate, non-quality investors are rationed in the credit market and investment of the non-quality borrowers is determined by the supply of new loans to them.

We now discuss banks' behavior. Banks ration credit. They give loans only to those whom they consider creditworthy. Normally, they cannot disburse as much credit as they want to. Let us elaborate. Keeping deposits idle over and above the part, which the banks consider optimal to be held in the form of cash, is not profitable for banks. However, the dilemma of the banks stems from the fact that extension of loans to non-quality borrowers raises not only banks' expected income but also the amount of risk the banks assume. Thus, by raising the fraction of its loanable funds given out as loan to non-quality borrowers, banks raise both their expected income and risk. Therefore, on the basis of banks' preferences over risk and expected income, banks choose what fraction of their loanable funds to be given out as loans to non-quality borrowers. It is, thus, clear that (6.8) and (6.12) give potential supplies of bank loans. The actual planned supplies of bank loans are only parts of those. To get actual planned supplies of bank loans, we have to modify the loan supply functions, Eqs. (6.8) and (6.12), as follows:

Equation (6.8), which gives the potential loan supply equation in the case where banks are rationed in the equity market (henceforth referred to as Case 1), is modified to get actual planned supply of bank loans, denoted by $L_1^{s'}$, as follows:

$$L_1^{s'} = I_0(r(r_p), \varepsilon_0) + \beta \cdot \left[(\theta q(1-c)Y - I_0(r(r_p), \varepsilon_0)\right] \quad 0 < \beta \leq 1 \tag{6.15}$$

Similarly, in the case where banks are not rationed in the equity market (henceforth referred to as Case 2), Eq. (6.12) is modified as follows:

$$L_2^{s'} = I_0(r(r_p), \varepsilon_0) + \beta \cdot \left[(1-\rho)(1-\overline{q}-q_1)(1-c)Y - I_0(r(r_p), \varepsilon_0)\right] \quad 0 < \beta \leq 1 \tag{6.16}$$

In (6.15) and (6.16), β denotes the fraction of the banks' potential supply of new loans net of the loans given to the quality borrowers that banks consider optimal to disburse to their non-quality borrowers. From the above, it follows that aggregate investment is determined by the quality investors' investment demand and the actual planned supply of new bank credit to non-quality investors. Hence, investments in Case 1 and Case 2 are given by (6.17) and (6.18), respectively.

$$I = I_0(r(r_p), \varepsilon_0) + \beta \cdot \left(\theta q(1-c)Y - I_0(r(r_p), \varepsilon_0)\right) \tag{6.17}$$

$$I = I_0(r(r_p), \varepsilon_0) + \beta \cdot \left[(1-\rho)(1-\overline{q}-q_1)(1-c)Y - I_0(r(r_p), \varepsilon_0)\right] \tag{6.18}$$

We first focus on the second case where capital adequacy norm does not act as a constraint, i.e., banks are able to sell as much equity as they want to in the equity market.

The Case Where Capital Adequacy Ratio Does Not Act as a Constraint on Loan Supply

Substituting (6.2), (6.3), and (6.18) into (6.1), we rewrite it as

$$Y = c \cdot Y + I_0(r(r_p), \varepsilon_0) + \beta \cdot \left[(1-\rho)(1-\overline{q}-q_1)(1-c)Y - I_0(r(r_p), \varepsilon_0)\right] + \frac{\mathrm{d}H}{P} \tag{6.19}$$

The model is now given by two key Eqs. (6.3) and (6.19) in two endogenous variables: Y and e. We can solve (6.19) for the equilibrium value of Y. Putting this equilibrium value of Y into (6.3), we can solve it for the equilibrium value of e.

We now carry out a comparative static exercise to explain the working of the model. Suppose the government raises its expenditure by $\mathrm{d}G$ and finances it by borrowing from the central bank so that $\mathrm{d}G = \mathrm{d}(\frac{\mathrm{d}H}{P})$. Taking total differential of (6.19) and solving for $\mathrm{d}Y$, we get

$$\mathrm{d}Y = \frac{\mathrm{d}(\frac{\mathrm{d}H}{P})}{1 - [c + \beta \cdot (1-\rho)(1-\overline{q}-q_1)(1-c)]} \tag{6.20}$$

Again, taking total differential of (6.3), using the fact that $X = pM$, where $p \equiv \frac{P^*e}{P}$, holds in the initial equilibrium, we get

$$\begin{aligned} \mathrm{d}e &= \frac{pM_Y}{\frac{P^*}{P}M(\eta_X + \eta_M - 1)}\mathrm{d}Y \\ &= \left(\frac{pM_Y}{\frac{P^*}{P}M(\eta_X + \eta_M - 1)}\right) \cdot \left(\frac{\mathrm{d}(\frac{\mathrm{d}H}{P})}{1 - [c + \beta \cdot (1-\rho)(1-\overline{q}-q_1)(1-c)]}\right) \end{aligned} \tag{6.21}$$

In (6.21), $\eta_X \equiv \frac{p}{X}\frac{\partial X}{\partial p} \equiv$ price elasticity of export and $\eta_M \equiv -\frac{p}{M}\frac{\partial M}{\partial p} \equiv$ price elasticity of import. Moreover, we assume Marshall–Lerner condition to hold so that $\eta_X + \eta_M > 1$.

Again, from (6.6) we get

$$\mathrm{d}(\mathrm{d}D) = (1-\overline{q}-q_1)(1-c)\frac{P\mathrm{d}(\frac{\mathrm{d}H}{P})}{1 - [c + \beta \cdot (1-\rho)(1-\overline{q}-q_1)(1-c)]} \tag{6.22}$$

Note that if $\overline{q} = q_1 = 0$ and $\beta = 1$, i.e., if savers hold their entire saving in the form of only bank deposits and there is no credit rationing, we get our standard money supply formula:

$$\mathrm{d}(\mathrm{d}D) = \frac{1}{\rho}P\mathrm{d}\left(\frac{\mathrm{d}H}{P}\right) \tag{6.23}$$

Equation (6.23) gives us the usual money supply formula. Again, when $q_1 > 0$, but $\overline{q} = 0$ and $\beta = 1$, i.e., if the savers hold their saving only in the form of bank deposits and currency, we get

$$\begin{aligned} \mathrm{d}(\mathrm{d}D) + \mathrm{d}CU = \mathrm{d}M^s &= \frac{P\mathrm{d}(\frac{\mathrm{d}H}{P})}{1-(1-\rho)(1-q_1)} \\ &= \frac{\frac{1}{1-q_1}}{\frac{q_1}{1-q_1}+\rho}P\mathrm{d}\left(\frac{\mathrm{d}H}{P}\right) = \frac{1+\lambda}{\rho+\lambda}P\mathrm{d}\left(\frac{\mathrm{d}H}{P}\right) \quad \lambda \equiv \frac{q_1}{1-q_1} \end{aligned} \tag{6.24}$$

In (6.24), $dCU \equiv$ saving held in currency, $M^s \equiv$ money supply, and $\lambda \equiv$ the ratio in which people hold their saving in currency and deposit. Thus, (6.24) also gives the standard money supply formula.

Let us now explain the adjustment process. Following an increase in G by $\mathrm{d}G$ financed by borrowing from the central bank, the multiplier process operates and Y increases by $\frac{\mathrm{d}G}{1-c}$. During the multiplier process, transactions may be carried out with currency or bank deposits or both. Let us explain the multiplier process a little. Per unit increase in Y, demand for domestic goods rises by $c - pM_y$. However, the increase in import demand raises the exchange rate by $\frac{pM_y}{b}$, where $b \equiv \frac{P^*}{P}M(\eta_x + \eta_m - 1)$ so that net export goes up by pM_y restoring BOP equilibrium. Therefore, in the net, demand for domestic goods rises by c per unit increase in Y. Therefore, to remove the excess demand of $\mathrm{d}G$, Y has to increase by $\frac{\mathrm{d}G}{1-c}$. Out of this additional income, people will save $(1-c) \cdot \frac{\mathrm{d}G}{1-c} = \mathrm{d}G$, which they will allocate over bank deposit, equities, and currency. Out of this additional saving, banks will receive new deposits of $(1 - \overline{q} - q_1) \cdot \mathrm{d}G \cdot P$ and people will hold additional currency of $q_1 \cdot P \cdot \mathrm{d}G$. Out of these new deposits, banks will be able to extend new loans in real terms of $\beta \cdot (1 - \overline{q} - q_1) \cdot \mathrm{d}G$ which will raise planned investment by the same amount. At this point, the first round of transactions is complete. The first round increases in $Y, e, S, \mathrm{d}D, CU, L^{s'}$ and I are denoted by $\mathrm{d}Y_1, \mathrm{d}e_1, \mathrm{d}S_1, \mathrm{d}(\mathrm{d}D)_1, \mathrm{d}CU_1, \mathrm{d}L_1$ and $\mathrm{d}I_1$, respectively, and they are given by

$$\begin{aligned}
&\mathrm{d}Y_1 = \frac{dG}{1-c}, \mathrm{d}e_1 = \frac{pM_y}{b}\mathrm{d}Y_1, \mathrm{d}S_1 = \mathrm{d}G, \mathrm{d}(\mathrm{d}D)_1 = (1 - \overline{q} - q_1) \cdot P \cdot \mathrm{d}G,\\
&\mathrm{d}CU_1 = q_1 \cdot P \cdot \mathrm{d}G, \mathrm{d}L_1 = \beta \cdot (1-\rho) \cdot (1 - \overline{q} - q_1) \cdot P \cdot \mathrm{d}G \text{ and}\\
&\mathrm{d}I_1 = \beta \cdot (1-\rho) \cdot (1 - \overline{q} - q_1) \cdot \mathrm{d}G
\end{aligned}$$

The increase in investment demand in the first round will set off the multiplier process and raise Y in the second round by $\mathrm{d}Y_2 = \frac{\beta \cdot (1-\rho) \cdot (1-q-q_1) \cdot \mathrm{d}G}{1-c}$, and e in the second round will go up by $\mathrm{d}e_2 = \frac{pM_y}{b}\mathrm{d}Y_2$. Similarly,

$$\begin{aligned}
&\mathrm{d}S_2 = (1-c)\mathrm{d}Y_2, \mathrm{d}(\mathrm{d}D)_2 = (1 - \overline{q} - q_1)(1-c)P\mathrm{d}Y_2, \mathrm{d}CU_2 = q_1(1-c)P\mathrm{d}Y_2,\\
&\mathrm{d}L_2 = \beta \cdot (1-\rho) \cdot (1 - \overline{q} - q_1)(1-c)P\mathrm{d}Y_2 \text{ and } \mathrm{d}I_2 = \beta \cdot (1-\rho) \cdot (1 - \overline{q} - q_1)(1-c)\mathrm{d}Y_2
\end{aligned}$$

In the same way, third round changes are given by

$$\mathrm{d}Y_3 = \frac{[\beta \cdot (1-\rho) \cdot (1 - \overline{q} - q_1)]^2}{1-c} \cdot \mathrm{d}G, \mathrm{d}e_3 = \frac{pM_y}{b}\mathrm{d}Y_3,$$

$$\begin{aligned}
&\mathrm{d}S_3 = (1-c)\mathrm{d}Y_3, \mathrm{d}(\mathrm{d}D)_3 = (1 - \overline{q} - q_1)(1-c)P\mathrm{d}Y_3,\\
&\mathrm{d}CU_3 = q_1(1-c)P\mathrm{d}Y_3, \mathrm{d}L_3 = \beta \cdot (1-\rho) \cdot (1 - \overline{q} - q_1)(1-c)P\mathrm{d}Y_3 \text{ and}\\
&\mathrm{d}I_3 = \beta \cdot (1-\rho) \cdot (1 - \overline{q} - q_1)(1-c)\mathrm{d}Y_3
\end{aligned}$$

This process of expansion will continue until the increase in Y that takes place in each successive round eventually falls to zero. Total changes in Y, e, $\mathrm{d}D$ and CU are given, respectively, by

$$\begin{aligned}
\mathrm{d}Y &= \frac{1}{1-c}\cdot \mathrm{d}G + \frac{[\beta\cdot(1-\rho)\cdot(1-\overline{q}-q_1)]}{1-c}\cdot \mathrm{d}G + \frac{[\beta\cdot(1-\rho)\cdot(1-\overline{q}-q_1)]^2}{1-c}\cdot \mathrm{d}G + \cdots \\
&= \frac{1}{(1-c)[1-\beta\cdot(1-\rho)\cdot(1-\overline{q}-q_1)]}\cdot \mathrm{d}G \\
&= \frac{1}{(1-c)[1-\beta\cdot(1-\rho)\cdot(1-\overline{q}-q_1)]}\cdot \mathrm{d}\left(\frac{\mathrm{d}H}{P}\right) \qquad (6.25)
\end{aligned}$$

$$\mathrm{d}e = \frac{pM_y}{b}\mathrm{d}Y \qquad (6.26)$$

$$\begin{aligned}
&\mathrm{d}(\mathrm{d}D) = (1-q-q_1)(1-c)P\mathrm{d}Y, \mathrm{d}CU = q_1(1-c)P\mathrm{d}Y, \\
&\mathrm{d}M^s = \mathrm{d}M^d = \mathrm{d}(\mathrm{d}D) + \mathrm{d}CU = (1-q-q_1)(1-c)P\mathrm{d}Y \qquad (6.27)
\end{aligned}$$

In (6.27), M^d denotes money demand (demand for money for holding saving). One can easily check that (6.25), (6.26), and (6.27) tally with (6.20), (6.21), and (6.22), respectively.

6.3 Recession, Banks, and Bank Regulation

We shall now use the model developed above to examine how recessions affect banks and what the government's policy intervention should be in such a scenario. This is of considerable importance as, following the onset of recession in India since 2011–12, banks got into trouble as its stock of non-performing assets increased and became subject to close official scrutiny and concern (see Tables 6.1 and 6.2). To accomplish this task, we have to incorporate in our model the fact that N depends upon the state of the economy indicated by Y and on such factors as the degree of supervision and monitoring, norms specified by the central bank for identifying non-performing assets, etc. We denote these latter factors, which are exogenously given here, by ϕ. An increase in ϕ indicates an increase in the degree of strictness in supervision, monitoring, etc. We, therefore, make N a decreasing function of Y and an increasing function of ϕ. Government and the central bank in India, as we have already mentioned, took alarm at the growth of non-performing assets and punished the banks by putting many of the nationalized banks in a category that requires Prompt Corrective Action (PCA). Obviously, this kind of punitive measure that brings disrepute to the punished banks adversely affecting their business and threatening their survival (for no fault of theirs, when the rise in non-performing assets is due to recession), makes all the banks extremely nervous and makes them extremely cautious about their lending. We can capture this by making β a sharply decreasing function of N. Incorporating this in (6.19), we rewrite it as

$$Y = c\cdot Y + I_0(r(r_p), \varepsilon_0)$$

$$+\beta\left(\underset{-}{N}\left(\underset{-}{Y},\underset{+}{\phi}\right)-\frac{\mathrm{d}\overline{H}}{P}\right)\cdot\left[(1-\rho)(1-\overline{q}-q_1)(1-c)Y-I_0\left(r\left(r_p\right),\varepsilon_0\right)\right]+\frac{\mathrm{d}H}{P} \quad (6.28)$$

In (6.28), $\frac{\mathrm{d}\overline{H}}{P}$ denotes the stock of real balance created by the central bank to buy up the non-performing assets. Using (6.28), we shall now examine how the effect of an adverse exogenous shock to the economy gets magnified manifold on account of the government's obsession with the non-performing assets of the banks. We assume here that on account of exogenous reasons, there takes place a fall in ε_0, which indicates a deterioration in the expectations of the quality investors regarding the future. We derive its impact here by taking total differential of (6.28) treating all exogenous variables other than ε_0 as fixed and, then solving for $\mathrm{d}Y$. This yields the following:

$$\mathrm{d}Y = c\cdot\mathrm{d}Y + I_{0\varepsilon_0}\mathrm{d}\varepsilon_0 + \beta_N N_Y\cdot(1-\rho)(1-\overline{q}-q_1)(1-c)Y\mathrm{d}Y$$
$$+\beta(1-\rho)(1-\overline{q}-q_1)(1-c)Y - \beta I_{0\varepsilon_0}\mathrm{d}\varepsilon_0 \Rightarrow$$

$$\mathrm{d}Y = \frac{(1-\beta)I_{0\varepsilon_0}\mathrm{d}\varepsilon_0}{1-[c+\beta_N N_Y\cdot(1-\rho)(1-\overline{q}-q_1)(1-c)Y+\beta(1-\rho)(1-\overline{q}-q_1)(1-c)]} < 0,$$
$$\text{when } \mathrm{d}\varepsilon_0 < 0 \quad (6.29)$$

From (6.29), it is clear that the extra caution that the banks have to adopt with the increase in their stock of non-performing assets on account of government regulations makes the multiplier much larger than $\frac{1}{1-[c+\beta(1-\rho)(1-\overline{q}-q_1)(1-c)]}$, the value that it otherwise would have assumed. This will be clear, if we explain the expression on the RHS of (6.29). The numerator gives the fall in aggregate investment at the initial equilibrium Y following the deterioration in the quality investors' expectations. Thus, there emerges an excess supply given by the absolute value of the numerator at the initial equilibrium Y. To remove this, producers reduce Y. Per unit fall in Y, excess supply falls by unity. However, the unit fall in Y also reduces demand raising excess supply thereby. A unit fall in Y reduces consumption demand by c. It reduces saving and, thereby, potential supply of bank loan by $(1-c)$ and $(1-\rho)(1-\overline{q}-q_1)(1-c)$, respectively. Hence, aggregate loan disbursement of banks and aggregate investment go down by $\beta(1-\rho)(1-q-q_1)(1-c)$. Therefore, in the net, per unit decline in Y, excess supply falls by $1-[c+\beta(1-\rho)(1-q-q_1)(1-c)]$ (note in this connection that, as Y falls, e adjusts so that net export remains zero. Hence, the fall in Y has no impact on net export). However, governments' efforts at arresting the growth of non-performing assets forces banks to be extra cautious and reduces loan disbursement and investment further by $\beta_N N_y(1-\rho)(1-\overline{q}-q_1)(1-c)Y$. Therefore, per unit decline in Y, excess supply instead of falling by $1-[c+\beta(1-\rho)(1-\overline{q}-q_1)(1-c)]$ falls by a smaller quantity given by $1-\left[c+\beta(1-\rho)(1-\overline{q}-q_1)(1-c)+\beta_N N_y(1-\rho)(1-q-q_1)(1-c)Y\right]$. Hence, the multiplier becomes much larger. This explains (6.29). This yields the following proposition:

Proposition 6.1 *If the central bank and the government impose tighter lending norms on banks following an increase in their stock of non-performing assets or if the* *banks tighten lending norms following an increase in their stock of non-performing assets to avoid punitive action on the part of the central bank or the government, the effect of an exogenous decline in aggregate demand will get magnified manifold bringing about a deep recession.*

6.3.1 Appropriate Counter-Recessionary Policy of the Government

Instead of taking the banks and the firms to task for recession that is completely beyond their control, the government should adopt the following stabilization measure to resolve the problem. The government can tackle the situation by raising G by a suitable amount and financing it by creating money. We can show the impact of this policy by taking total differential of (6.28), and setting $-(1-\beta)I_{0\varepsilon}\mathrm{d}\varepsilon_0 = \mathrm{d}G = \mathrm{d}(\frac{\mathrm{d}H}{P})$. This yields

$$\mathrm{d}Y = c\cdot\mathrm{d}Y + (1-\beta)I_{0\varepsilon}\mathrm{d}\varepsilon_0 + \beta_{\overline{N}}N_Y I_0\mathrm{d}Y + \beta_{\overline{N}}N_Y\cdot[(1-\rho)(1-\overline{q}-q_1)(1-c)Y]\mathrm{d}Y$$
$$+\beta[(1-\rho)(1-\overline{q}-q_1)(1-c)\mathrm{d}Y] + \mathrm{d}\left(\frac{\mathrm{d}H}{P}\right) \Rightarrow \mathrm{d}Y = 0$$

From the above it follows that if the government raises G by the amount of the autonomous decline in investment demand and finances it by money creation, Y will be restored to its initial level and the economy, banks, and investors will again become healthy. Otherwise, the economy will slip into a deep recession and the banks and the investors will plunge into deep trouble. This gives us the following proposition:

Proposition 6.2 *If there takes place au autonomous decline in aggregate demand for exogenous reasons plunging the economy into a recession, the best way of tackling it is to raise government expenditure by the same amount as the autonomous fall in aggregate demand and finance it by money creation. It will restore the economy, banks, and the firms back to health.*

From the above, it follows that a recession should be tackled by an appropriate stabilization policy at the macro level. If instead, firms and banks are taken to task for the losses they make on account of factors, which are completely beyond their control and which stem from the very nature of a capitalist economy, the recession and plight of the firms and banks will deepen instead of the other way round (Fig. 6.2).

6.3.2 Illustration in a Dynamic Set-Up

To illustrate the impact that the government's regulations produce on banks as their stock of non-performing assets increases with the onset of recession, we dynamize

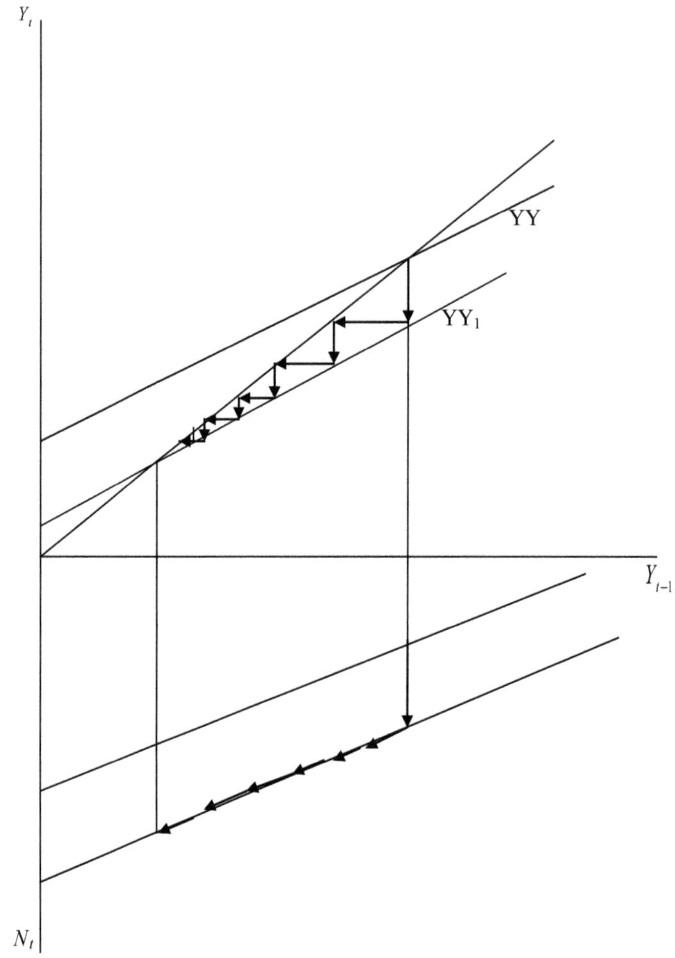

Fig. 6.2 Effect of an autonomous fall in investment demand

the model presented above. We make the stock of non-performing assets of period t a decreasing function of Y_{t-1} and $\frac{\mathrm{d}\overline{H}}{P}$ and an increasing function of ϕ. Thus,

$$N_t = n \cdot \left(\overline{Y} - Y_{t-1}\right) + \phi - \frac{\mathrm{d}\overline{H}}{P}; n > 0, \quad \phi > 0 \tag{6.30}$$

In (6.30), $\overline{Y}$ is a constant and it denotes the full employment level of output. Using (6.30), we rewrite (6.19) (making some simplifications for algebraic convenience) as

$$Y_t = cY_t + \overline{I} + \beta \cdot \left[(1-\rho) \cdot (1 - \overline{q} - q_1) \cdot (1-c)Y_t - \overline{I}\right]$$

$$-\varphi \cdot \left[n \cdot \left(\overline{Y} - Y_{t-1}\right) + \phi - \frac{\mathrm{d}\overline{H}}{P}\right] + \frac{\mathrm{d}H}{P} \quad n > 0, \ \ \varphi > 0 \tag{6.31}$$

In (6.31), aggregate investment is given by

$$\overline{I} + \beta \cdot \left[(1-\rho) \cdot (1-\overline{q}-q_1) \cdot (1-c)Y_t - \overline{I}\right] - \varphi \cdot \left[n \cdot \left(\overline{Y} - Y_{t-1}\right) + \phi - \frac{\mathrm{d}\overline{H}}{P}\right].$$

We have assumed that the quality investors' investment is exogenously given and denoted it by $\overline{I}$, regarded β as fixed and captured the deleterious impact of an increase in the stock of non-performing assets on credit supply and investment due to government regulations by means of the term $\varphi \cdot \left[n \cdot \left(\overline{Y} - Y_{t-1}\right) + \phi - \frac{\mathrm{d}\overline{H}}{P}\right]$. All this has been done for simplicity.

We rewrite (6.31) as

$$\begin{aligned} Y_t = & \frac{(1-\beta)\overline{I} + \frac{\mathrm{d}H}{P} - \varphi\left(n\overline{Y} + \phi - \frac{\mathrm{d}\overline{H}}{P}\right)}{1 - [c + \beta \cdot (1-\rho) \cdot (1-q-q_1)]} \\ & + \frac{\varphi n}{1 - [c + \beta \cdot (1-\rho) \cdot (1-q-q_1)]} Y_{t-1} \end{aligned} \tag{6.32}$$

We assume that the first term on the RHS of (6.32) is positive. We also assume for the sake of existence and stability of the steady state that the coefficient of Y_{t-1} lies between 0 and 1. The line *YY* in Fig. 6.1 represents (6.32). The steady-state value of *Y* corresponds to the point of intersection of *YY* and the 45° line. Now, suppose there takes place a deterioration in the quality investors' morale for exogenous reasons and this brings about a fall in $\overline{I}$ by $\mathrm{d}\overline{I}$. Following this, the *YY* shifts downward bringing about a cumulative decline in *Y* and, therefore, a cumulative increase in the stock of non-performing assets. These cumulative changes have been indicated by arrows. The process may be briefly explained as follows. Following an exogenous decline in quality investors' investment in period 0 by $\mathrm{d}\overline{I}$, the multiplier process operates and in period 0, *Y* goes down by $\frac{(1-\beta)\mathrm{d}\overline{I}}{1-c+\beta\cdot(1-\rho)\cdot(1-\overline{q}-q_1)(1-c)}$. Let us explain this expression. Following the fall in output by $(1-\beta)\mathrm{d}\overline{I}$, aggregate consumption falls by $c \cdot (1-\beta)\mathrm{d}\overline{I}$. On the other hand, aggregate saving and bank deposits decline by $(1-c)(1-\beta)\mathrm{d}\overline{I}$ and $(1-\overline{q}-q_1)(1-c)(1-\beta)\mathrm{d}\overline{I}$, respectively. Hence, disbursement of bank loans and, therefore, investment fall by $\beta(1-\rho)(1-\overline{q}-q_1)(1-c)(1-\beta)\mathrm{d}\overline{I}$. Accordingly, aggregate demand and, therefore, aggregate output go down by $[c + \beta(1-\rho)(1-\overline{q}-q_1)(1-c)](1-\beta)\mathrm{d}\overline{I}$. This multiplier process of contraction will continue, and at the end of the process aggregate output will fall by $\frac{(1-\beta)\mathrm{d}\overline{I}}{1-[c+\beta\cdot(1-\rho)\cdot(1-q-q_1)(1-c)]}$. In the absence of government's obsessive concern with non-performing assets of banks and the efforts it makes to arrest the growth of non-performing assets by forcing banks to follow stricter norms of bank lending, the contraction in GDP would have stopped here. But the latter factors lead to further rounds of contraction in GDP. In the next period, period 1, because of the contraction in GDP in period 0, banks' stock of non-performing assets rises by $n \cdot \frac{(1-\beta)\mathrm{d}\overline{I}}{1-[c+\beta\cdot(1-\rho)\cdot(1-q-q_1)(1-c)]}$. It forces banks to adhere to stricter lending norms stipulated by the central bank and, as a result, bank lending falls further by $\varphi n \frac{(1-\beta)\mathrm{d}\overline{I}}{1-[c+\beta\cdot(1-\rho)\cdot(1-q-q_1)(1-c)]}$, which, through the multiplier process described above, reduces GDP in period 1 by $\varphi n \frac{(1-\beta)\mathrm{d}\overline{I}}{\{1-[c+\beta\cdot(1-\rho)\cdot(1-q-q_1)(1-c)]\}^2}$. This leads to further increase in the stock of non-performing assets by $\varphi n^2 \frac{(1-\beta)\mathrm{d}\overline{I}}{\{1-[c+\beta\cdot(1-\rho)\cdot(1-q-q_1)(1-c)]\}^2}$ in period 2 and reduces GDP by $(\varphi n)^2 \frac{(1-\beta)\mathrm{d}\overline{I}}{\{1-[c+\beta\cdot(1-\rho)\cdot(1-q-q_1)(1-c)]\}^3}$. This process of contraction will continue until the new steady state is reached. The contraction in Y that takes place from period 1 is quite substantial and is entirely due to government's policies toward banks' non-performing assets. Since non-quality borrowers comprising the small and medium borrowers are rationed, when lending norms are tightened, concentration and inequality increase along with the deepening of recession. The above analysis yields the following proposition:

Proposition 6.3 *Stricter lending norms imposed on banks following an onset of recession and the consequent increase in the stock of non-performing assets of banks to arrest the growth of their non-performing assets substantially deepen recession and exacerbate the problem of non-performing assets. They also significantly increase degree of concentration and inequality.*

Clearly, the situation calls for suitable policy intervention on the part of the central bank to avert the crisis. It is quite clear from (6.32) that, if the government raises $G = \frac{\mathrm{d}H}{P}$ by the same amount as the fall in $(1-\beta)\overline{I}$, the *YY* schedule in Fig. 6.1 will remain unaffected and the fall in Y and the increase in non-performing assets can be averted. Thus, instead of taking to task the victims of recession, the government should adopt appropriate, well-informed anti-recessionary policies to keep banks and other economic agents healthy. Otherwise, recession and inequality and along with them economic woes of banks and other economic agents will deepen.

6.4 The Case Where Capital Adequacy Ratio Acts as a Constraint on Loan Supply

In this case, investment is given by (6.17). Substituting (6.2), (6.3), and (6.17) into (6.1), we rewrite it as follows:

$$Y = c \cdot Y + I_0\big(r(r_p), \varepsilon_0\big) + \beta \cdot \big[\theta q(1-c)Y - I_0\big(r(r_p), \varepsilon_0\big)\big] + \frac{\mathrm{d}H}{P} \tag{6.33}$$

We can solve (6.33) for the equilibrium value of Y. We can now examine how an increase in the capital adequacy ratio affects Y and the stock of non-performing assets.

Effect of an Increase in the Capital Adequacy Ratio

Taking total differential of (6.33) treating all variables other than Y and θ as fixed and, then, solving for dY, we get

$$\mathrm{d}Y = \frac{-\beta q(1-c)Y(-\mathrm{d}\theta)}{1-c-\beta\theta q(1-c)} < 0 \quad \because \ \mathrm{d}\theta < 0 \tag{6.34}$$

Let us now explain (6.34). An increase in the capital adequacy ratio means a fall in θ by dθ. At the initial equilibrium Y, supply of new loans to the small and medium producers falls by $\beta q(1-c)Y(-\mathrm{d}\theta)$ lowering their investment by the same amount. In response, producers reduce Y. A unit fall in Y, given demand, will lower excess supply by 1 unit. However, the unit fall in Y will also reduce demand. Consumption demand will fall by c. Saving and, therefore, demand for equity will go down by $(1-c)$ and $q(1-c)$, respectively. Hence, banks' supply of new credit to small and medium producers will go down by $\beta\theta q(1-c)$ lowering their investment by the same amount. Thus, a unit fall in Y lowers aggregate demand by $[c+\beta\theta q(1-c)]$ (note that as Y falls, e adjusts to keep net export at zero. Thus, the fall in Y produces no impact on net export.). Therefore, in the net, excess supply falls by $1-[c+\beta\theta q(1-c)]$. Hence, Y goes down by the expression on the RHS of (6.34). Successive Basel Accords have consistently increased capital adequacy ratios. This, as we have shown, produces strong recessionary impact jeopardizing banks' health and raising their stock of non-performing assets. The finding of our analysis may be presented in the form of the following proposition:

Proposition 6.4 *An increase in the capital adequacy ratio reduces GDP substantially and, thereby, severely jeopardizes banks' health and raises their stock of non-performing assets significantly. Successive Basel norms, which seek to improve the solvency of the banks, have consistently raised capital adequacy ratio of the banks. Hence, they have worsened significantly banks' solvency instead of doing the opposite.*

Recession leads to a shrinkage in bank's business, raises default rate and, thereby, brings about a deterioration in the profitability of banks. Recession also makes equity investment unprofitable. Since Y is an index of recession, we shall make q an increasing function of Y. Incorporating it in (6.33), we rewrite it as follows:

$$Y = c\cdot Y + I_0\left(r\left(r_p\right), \varepsilon_0\right) + \beta\cdot\left[\theta q\left(\underset{+}{Y}\right)(1-c)Y - I_0\left(r\left(r_p\right), \varepsilon_0\right)\right] + \frac{\mathrm{d}H}{P} \tag{6.35}$$

We shall show that, in this scenario an adverse exogenous shock such as an exogenous increase in the capital adequacy ratio produces a much stronger recessionary impact. To prove this, we shall take total differential of (6.35) treating all variables other than Y and θ as fixed and, then, solve for dY. This yields the following

$$\mathrm{d}Y = -\frac{\beta q(1-c)Y(-\mathrm{d}\theta)}{1-[c+\beta\theta q(1-c)+\beta\theta q'(1-c)Y]} < 0 \tag{6.36}$$

Let us now explain (6.36). Following a cut in θ by $\mathrm{d}\theta$, Y, as before, goes down by $\mathrm{d}Y_1 = -\frac{\beta q(1-c)Y(-\mathrm{d}\theta)}{1-[c+\beta\theta q(1-c)]} < 0$ in the first round. Unlike what happens in the previous case, the contraction in Y does not stop here. The fall in Y makes equity holding risky and induces the people to sell off $q'(1-c)Y\mathrm{d}Y_1$ worth of equity to the banks (recall our assumption that buyers of equities can sell their equities back to the banks at the prices at which they bought them). Hence, banks will have to reduce their supply of new loans to the small and medium producers by $\beta q'(1-c)Y\mathrm{d}Y_1$ reducing their investment by the same amount. This will set off the multiplier process, and Y in the second round will fall by $\mathrm{d}Y_2 = -\frac{\beta q'(1-c)Y}{1-[c+\beta\theta q(1-c)]}\mathrm{d}Y_1 < 0$. This second round contraction in Y leads to a further fall in the equity holding of the people by $q'(1-c)Y\mathrm{d}Y_2$, which, in turn, reduces supply of new bank loans to small and medium producers and their investment by $\beta q'(1-c)Y\mathrm{d}Y_2$. Y in the third round will, therefore, fall by $\mathrm{d}Y_3 = -\frac{\beta q'(1-c)Y}{1-[c+\beta\theta q(1-c)]}\mathrm{d}Y_2 = -\left[\frac{\beta q'(1-c)Y}{1-[c+\beta\theta q(1-c)]}\right]^2\mathrm{d}Y_1 < 0$. This process of contraction will continue until the fall in demand that takes place in each successive round eventually falls to zero. Thus, the total contraction in Y is given by (putting the value of $\mathrm{d}Y_1$)

$$\begin{aligned}\mathrm{d}Y &= \mathrm{d}Y_1 - \frac{\beta q'(1-c)Y}{1-[c+\beta\theta q(1-c)]}\mathrm{d}Y_1 - \left[\frac{\beta q'(1-c)Y}{1-[c+\beta\theta q(1-c)]}\right]^2\mathrm{d}Y_1 - \cdots \\ &= -\frac{\beta q(1-c)Y(-\mathrm{d}\theta)}{1-[c+\beta\theta q(1-c)+\beta q'(1-c)Y]}\end{aligned} \tag{6.37}$$

Clearly, (6.37) tallies with (6.36). Our above discussion yields the following proposition:

Proposition 6.5 *An increase in the capital adequacy ratio will lead to a very large and cumulative contraction in Y bringing about a sharp deterioration in the financial health of the banks and the small and medium producers.*

6.5 Conclusion

Banks perform very important social functions. They mobilize savings of the savers and transfer them to the borrowers. Banks cannot perform these functions effectively if they are commercial organizations, whose objective is to make profit and whose viability depends upon whether they are able to make profit. As enshrined in Indian Constitution and, as should be the responsibility of every civilized society, to provide equal opportunity to everyone, every individual should have access to a safe avenue for holding their savings. Banks cannot achieve this, if they are commercial organizations. If they are commercial organizations, they may not consider it profitable to make themselves accessible to every saver. Moreover, they will be subject to vagaries of capitalist market forces. Hence, their liabilities will not be fully safe. They will, therefore, not be able to fully mobilize all the savings of the savers. In fact, the kind of instabilities that a capitalist economy is usually subject to and given the performance of banks in advanced capitalist economies in recent years and also in the past, banks are unlikely to have any access to the major part of savings of the savers. Thus, for banks to be able to effectively mobilize savings generated in the economy, they have to be social institutions owned by the government and protected by the government fully from the vagaries of market forces. Again, an economy, to perform efficiently and equitably, should meet all the genuine credit needs of people and firms—credit needs that arise out of the necessity of producing and/or consuming essential goods. However, when banks are commercially organized, they will disburse credit on the basis of profit criteria. Hence, they will ration small and medium producers, even when they are engaged in the production of essential goods, while credit needs of quality borrowers, even when they use the credit to produce luxury goods, are fully met [see in this connection Bernanke et al. (1996)]. This may lead to severe macroeconomic instability giving rise to shortages of food and other mass consumption goods and large imports of components required for luxury production. Since a poor country like India has an extremely limited export capacity, these large non-essential imports may cause severe balance of payments (BOP) deficit leading to a steep increase in the exchange rate raising domestic price level and, thereby, worsening trade balance further. Shortages of mass consumption goods coupled with sharp increases in the exchange rate generate strong inflationary and recessionary forces. Thus, when banks are commercially organized in a poor and dependent country like India, they fail to meet genuine credit needs of the economy and credit allocation made by profit-driven banks may generate strong destabilizing inflationary and recessionary forces. Banks should be treated as social institutions owned and protected by the government from the vagaries of market forces. They should mobilize saving to the fullest possible extent by providing every individual with a fully safe avenue of saving and utilize the savings to meet all genuine essential credit needs of the economy. Private profit-driven banks/financial institutions perpetrate the kind of disasters that we witnessed in 1991 in Japan, in 2007 in the USA, in 2008 in Europe, and also many times in the past. We shall take up these issues in Chap. 9 of the book.

Commercially organized banks, as pointed out above and as amply evidenced by the disastrous experiences of the advanced capitalist countries, give rise to severe macroeconomic instability through gross misallocation of bank credit (see in this connection Blinder and Zandi (2010a, b), Mishkin (2011), Koo et al. (2008)).

Commercially organized banks, public or private, are subject to vagaries of market forces and, as argued in the present chapter, government's effort at arresting the growth of their non-performing assets following an onset of recession may deepen the recession significantly.

Government, therefore, should regard banks as social institutions that work not for profit, but for maximizing the welfare of the masses. Such banks will provide stability to the economy and help it realize its full development potential. Commercially organized banks driven by profit motive are a source of instability, inequality, and economic disaster.

Commercially organized profit-driven financial institutions help create an island of immense opulence in the midst of country-wide unemployment and poverty and regularly cause crises, which gravely exacerbate economic woes of the masses. We shall seek to substantiate this point in the next chapter. In the next chapter, we shall also examine the implications of FRDI Bill and corruption on the banks and the economy.

References

Bernanke, B., Gertler, M., & Gilchrist, S. (1996). The financial accelerator and the flight to quality. *The Review of Economics and Statistics, 78*(1), 1–16.

Blinder, A. S., & Zandi, M. (2010a). *How the great recession was brought to an end*. Available at www.dismal.com/mark-zandi/documents/End'of-Great-Recession.pdf.

Blinder, A. S., & Zandi, M. (2010b). *Stimulus worked, finance and development* (pp. 14–17), December 2010.

Koo, R. (2008). *The Holy Grail of macroeconomics: Lessons from Japan's great recession*. Wiley.

Mishkin, F. (2011). Over the cliff: From the subprime to the global financial crisis. *Journal of Economic Perspectives, 25*(1), 49–70 (Winter).

Chapter 7
Democracy and Corruption in a Capitalist Economy

Abstract A capitalist society is characterized by extreme inequality and multiparty democracy. In a capitalist society, a small number of giant capitalists have in their command the major part of the country's wealth and income. This chapter argues that the system of private funding of political parties enables the giant capitalists to form and run political parties to usurp state power. They need it to protect their enormous wealth from the masses. The political parties compete with one another for the favors of the giant capitalists and work feverishly to help them increase their command over the society's income and wealth both legally and illegally. On the illegal side, political parties allow giant capitalists to evade taxes, invest their savings in foreign assets in tax havens, and defraud the banks, among others. We have shown in this chapter that these illegal favors or corrupt practices generate strong recessionary forces and slow down drastically the rate of growth of output and employment. In the wake of recessions and bank frauds, which lead to a sharp increase in the non-performing assets of banks and other financial institutes, the political parties pass laws or seek to pass laws such as Financial Regulation and Deposit Insurance Bill (FRDI Bill) in India that empowers the financial institutions to confiscate the savings of the people held with them to tide over the crisis. We have shown here that such a measure is likely to bring about a collapse of the financial institutions and the economy. Of the legal favors granted to the capitalists, we have considered two. Government and the central bank often specify lending norms of banks and other financial institutions in such a manner that they favor the giant capitalists at the expense of the small and medium producers. They also often confiscate land of the small and medium producers and give it away to the giant capitalists. To examine the implications of these legal favors, we have divided the economy into the organized sector and the unorganized sector. The former consists of large firms owned by the giant capitalists, while the latter consists of firms owned by small and medium producers. We have shown here that the legal favors mentioned here will in all probability lead to a cumulative expansion of the organized sector matched by a cumulative contraction of the unorganized sector. Both of these will bring about a sharp deterioration in the standard of living of the workers.

C. Ghosh and A. N. Ghosh, *Keynesian Macroeconomics Beyond the IS-LM Model*, https://doi.org/10.1007/978-981-13-7888-1_7

7.1 Introduction

Capitalism is characterized by democracy, where more than one party competes for power. A high degree of inequality, and high levels of poverty and unemployment are also important features of capitalism. Even in advanced capitalist countries, most of the people do not have access either to higher education or to health care at least on an adequate scale. In a capitalist society, while most of the people live in poverty and unemployment, the major part of the society's income goes into the hands of just a handful of giant capitalists. These giant capitalists also own almost the whole of the society's wealth. In India, for example, 76% of total wealth is owned by just 1% of Indians (Oxfam India 2018). Obviously, this estimate has been made on the basis of declared wealth alone. If undeclared assets were taken into account, the inequality in the distribution of wealth would have been much greater. The inequality in the distribution of wealth also reflects the inequality in the distribution of income. Surprisingly, this extreme inequality in the distribution of income and wealth persists despite the fact that in democracy every adult citizen has one vote. Still no political party in a capitalist society seeks to confiscate the properties of the 1% of people and distribute it among the remaining 99% of the people. Political parties in capitalist societies, in fact, do just the opposite. They confiscate properties of the poor and give them away to the rich. In other words, one-man-one-vote-based democracy in a capitalist society instead of threatening capitalists and capitalism facilitates expansion of the empire of the giant capitalists. Clearly, the coexistence of extreme economic inequality and political equality constitutes a grave puzzle. How does one explain it? In what follows, we seek to give an answer.

The answer lies in the fact that political parties in a democracy under capitalism do not have any source of income of their own. However, they need enormous amounts of fund to campaign for their programmes and policies. The larger the amount of fund at their disposal, the more is their ability to hire workers, services of media, etc., and, hence, the greater is their competitive strength. The giant capitalists, who are just a few in number, own the major part of country's wealth and also have in their command the major part of the country's income. Hence, the giant capitalists have the ability to form and run political parties. They form, fund, and run political parties and, thereby, usurp state power to protect their enormous wealth and income from the masses and also to increase their income and wealth legally and illegally. Political parties, therefore, work for the giant capitalists. Giant capitalists use the following strategy to control them. They make the political parties compete with one another for donations/fund from the giant capitalists. Accordingly, political parties have to compete with one another to work in giant capitalists' favor. If a political party does not work in their favor, they divert their donations from the erring party to other parties. This weakens the erring party and makes the other parties stronger. The system of private funding of political parties makes democracy a farce; it puts them completely in the control of the giant capitalists. Dependence of political parties on private fund, in our view, is at the root of the emergence of corruption in a capitalist economy. Political parties work to enable the giant capitalists increase their income and wealth both legally and illegally. On the legal side, parties in power seek to keep tax rates on the capitalists' income at the minimum possible level and try to use indirect taxes as the principal source of tax revenue. Since capitalists are net borrowers and workers are net lenders, the governments in capitalist countries seek to reduce interest rates to the minimum possible levels. They also facilitate exploitation of workers by relaxing labor laws and by allowing the capitalists to incorporate labor-saving technological and managerial changes. They also seek to remove restrictions on the activities of the capitalists and give them a free hand in managing the economy in their interest. They also specify lending norms for banks and other financial institutions in such a manner that they favor giant capitalist at the expense of small and medium producers. They also forcibly acquire land from poor producers and hand them over to the giant capitalists free of cost. On the illegal side, governments allow the capitalists to evade taxes, to use their income and wealth to buy illegally foreign financial and physical assets, to get away with fraudulent practices, etc. In this chapter, we shall develop simple models to capture the macroeconomic implications of some of the donation-induced legal and illegal favors given to the giant capitalists by the government. The mainstream (neoclassical) literature on corruption in economics and social sciences does not regard corruption as a necessary consequence of democracy under capitalism. It regards corruption as an attribute of self-interest-driven individuals enjoying state power and does not link it to the kind of democracy capitalist societies have. More precisely, this strand of literature argues that self-interest-driven rent-seeking politicians and bureaucrats create regulations to maximize collection of rent (bribes) and private agents bypass the regulations by paying bribes. According to this literature, payments of bribes increase efficiency as they neutralize the distortions created by the regulations (see, e.g., Aidt (2003), Bardhan (1997), Chang (2002), Jain (2001), Nye (1967), Shleifer and Vishney (1993), Hopkins (2002) and Warren (2004) in this connection). Neoclassical theory of corruption, therefore, in consonance with the major thrust of neoclassical economics, regards government as a self-seeking autonomous entity that creates regulations in order to extort as much rent as possible. Obviously, it calls for policies that minimize the government and its regulations. Neoclassical theory does not recognize the fact that corruption is the inevitable outcome of the resolution of the contradiction that lies in the coexistence of extreme economic inequality and political equality in a democratic capitalist society.

We plan this chapter as follows. First, we focus on the corruption that political donations give rise to. Political donations make the political parties turn a blind eye to large-scale tax evasion by giant capitalists. Political parties also allow the giant capitalists to park their savings in foreign assets in tax havens. Political parties also help giant capitalists get away with large-scale defaults and bank frauds. To keep the banks afloat in the wake of these defaults and bank frauds, they pass laws that empower the banks to confiscate depositors' deposits to make up for their losses. Thus, first the giant capitalists rob the workers of their savings through fraudulent practices and defaults and, then, the banks confiscate the rest to make up for their losses. In the first part of this chapter, we develop models to derive the macroeconomic implications of the donation protected illegal activities of the giant capitalists mentioned above.

The system of private funding also induces the political parties in power to heap legal favors on the giant capitalists. Through laws, they help the giant capitalists increase their command over the resources of the economy. They specify lending norms of banks and other financial institutions in such a manner that they lend most of their loanable fund to the giant capitalists at the expense of small and medium producers. Political parties in power also forcibly acquire land from poor and medium producers and give them away free of cost to the giant capitalists. In the latter part of this chapter, we develop models to examine the macroeconomic implications of these legal favors on giant capitalists.

7.2 Political Donations, Tax Evasion, and Illegal Parking of Saving in Foreign Assets

Political donations, as we have just pointed out, give rise to various kinds of corruption. Two of the commonest forms of corruption are large-scale tax evasion and illegal parking of savings in foreign assets by giant capitalists. In exchange for donations, political parties allow the capitalists to evade taxes and park their savings illegally in foreign assets. In this section, we shall examine the macroeconomic implications of these illegal activities in a country like India using a suitable model.

7.2.1 *The Model*

We develop a Keynesian model where aggregate output or GDP denoted by Y is demand determined. The goods market equilibrium condition is given by

$$Y = C\left(\left(1 - \alpha\left(\underset{-}{D}\right)t\right)Y\right) + I\left(\underset{-}{r}, \underset{-}{e}\right) + G + \mathrm{NX}\left(\underset{+}{\frac{P^*e}{P}}, \underset{-}{I\left(\underset{-}{r}, \underset{-}{e}\right)}, \underset{-}{C\left(\left(1 - \alpha\left(\underset{-}{D}\right)t\right)Y\right)}; \underset{+}{Y^*}\right) \quad (7.1)$$

In (7.1), D denotes donations to political parties and $\alpha(D)$ gives the fraction of the tax rate t that the capitalists are unable to evade. $\alpha(D)t$, therefore, represents the tax rate that the taxpayers effectively face. It is a decreasing function of D. We regard political parties as households and donations to political parties, therefore, constitute a transfer from one section of households to another. Hence, payment and receipt of donations do not affect the aggregate disposable income of the households given by $(1 - \alpha(D)t)Y$. Investment, as standard, is made a decreasing function of the interest rate. However, in India there are strong reasons to believe that it is a decreasing function of the nominal exchange rate, denoted e, as well. In case of

Table 7.1 Growth rate of GDP, net FDI, foreign portfolio investment, government consumption, and gross fiscal deficit (GFD)

Year	Growth rate of GDP at factor cost (at constant prices base 2004–05)	Rate of GDCF[a]	Rate of NDCF
2000–01	5.3	24.6	16.7
2001–02	5.5	24.6	16.5
2002–03	5.0	25.4	17.3
2003–04	8.1	27.3	19.5
2004–05	7.0	32.8	25.5
2005–06	9.5	34.9	27.8
2006–07	9.6	36.2	29.2
2007–08	9.6	39.0	32.2
2008–09	6.7	35.6	27.9
2009–10	8.4	38.4	30.9
2010–11	8.4	39.8	32.5
2011–12	6.5	38.8	31.1
2012–13	4.5	38.9	30.9
2013–14	4.7		

Source RBI [a]Gross domestic capital formation

India, an important determinant of the cost of investment is the exchange rate as a large part of investment demand represents demand for imported capital goods. So, an increase in e raises the cost of investment and, hence, given expectations, reduces investment demand for Y. India's production is also highly import-intensive. An increase in e, therefore, generates a strong cost-push. The corporate sector in India, which derives its income principally from the domestic economy in domestic currency, is heavily indebted to foreigners. An increase in e raises debt service charges on external loans in domestic currency substantially. All these adverse supply shocks demoralize the investors and dampen investment demand. Data on exchange rates, growth rates, and capital formation given in Tables 7.2 and 7.1 show that in all the years of recession (2011–12 to 2013–14), exchange rate increased substantially indicating a strong inverse relationship between the exchange rate, rate of capital formation, and growth rate in India. [For details, one may go through Ghosh and Ghosh (2016)]. For all these reasons, we think that investment is highly sensitive to exchange rate in India. Hence, we have incorporated e as a determinant of investment and made it a decreasing function of e.

Net export (NX), as standard, is made an increasing function of the real exchange rate, $\frac{P^*e}{P}$, where P^* denotes the foreign price level in foreign currency and P is the domestic price level in domestic currency. It is also an increasing function of Y^*, which denotes foreign GDP. We consider here a small open economy. Hence, both Y^* and P^* are given to the domestic economy. Besides these two, net export is also decreasing functions of consumption and investment demand, which represent demand not only for domestic goods but also for foreign goods. The same applies to G. However, for simplicity, we assume that G represents demand for domestic goods only. A capitalist economy is usually extremely unequal. This is true of India as well. Hence, the major part of Y accrues to the capitalists, whose consumption propensity for import is very high. We have already pointed out that the import intensity of investment in India is also substantially high.

In India, government seeks to strictly adhere to fiscal deficit targets. This is the norm all through the capitalist world. To capture this here in the simplest possible framework, we assume that the government seeks to achieve a target of zero-budget deficit. Therefore,

$$G = \alpha(D)tY \tag{7.2}$$

Let us now focus on the financial sector.

Financial Sector

The financial sector consists only of the central bank and the commercial banks. The latter do not hold any excess reserve, only households save and they hold their entire saving as bank deposit. Commercial banks are the only source of loans to the firms. Firms borrow from the domestic commercial banks to finance their entire investment expenditure. The central bank lends to the commercial banks at a policy rate denoted by r_c. The commercial banks set their lending rate r on the basis of r_c. Therefore,

$$r = r\left(\underset{+}{r_c}\right) \tag{7.3}$$

The central bank sets r_c at such a level that r remains at a target level and lends to the commercial banks as much as they want to borrow at the given r_c. Supply of new loans by the commercial banks denoted L^S is given by

$$L^S = (1-\rho)\left[\left\{Y - C\left((1-\underset{+}{\alpha(D)}t)Y\right)\right\} - k(D) + b\right] \tag{7.4}$$

In (7.4), ρ denotes the CRR, the new deposit received by the commercial banks is the saving of the households given by $\left\{Y - C\left((1-\underset{+}{\alpha(D)}t)Y\right)\right\}$. $k(D)$ gives the amount of saving the capitalists in the given period are able to illegally invest in foreign assets. This is an increasing function of D. b denotes the amount of new loans taken by the commercial banks from the central bank. The commercial banks meet all the demand for credit that comes forth at $r = r(r_c)$ by choosing an appropriate value of b. Thus, in the situation we consider here, firms, who are by assumption the only borrowers of the commercial banks, are able to fulfill all their planned demand for credit at $r(r_c)$. There is, thus, no rationing of credit in the present case.

Incorporating (7.3) and (7.2) into (7.1), we rewrite it as

$$\begin{aligned} Y = {} & C\left(\left(1-\alpha\left(\underset{-}{D}\right)t\right)Y\right) + I\left(\underset{-}{r(r_c)}, \underset{-}{e}\right) + \alpha(D)tY \\ & + \mathrm{NX}\left(\underset{+}{\frac{P^*e}{P}}, \underset{-}{I\left(\underset{-}{r(r_c)}, \underset{-}{e}\right)}, \underset{-}{C\left(\left(1-\alpha\left(\underset{-}{D}\right)t\right)Y\right)}; \underset{+}{Y^*}\right) \end{aligned} \tag{7.5}$$

Finally, from the exchange rate data of the Indian economy given in Table 7.2, it should be clear that the exchange rate is flexible in India. Hence, in equilibrium

$$\mathrm{NX}\left(\underset{+}{\frac{P^*e}{P}}, \underset{-}{I\left(\underset{-}{r}, \underset{-}{e}\right)}, \underset{-}{C\left(\left(1-\alpha\left(\underset{-}{D}\right)t\right)Y\right)}; \underset{+}{Y^*}\right) + K = 0 \tag{7.6}$$

In (7.6), K denotes net inflow of capital. In India, there are stringent restrictions on Indians purchasing foreign physical and financial assets such as land or bank deposits in foreign countries. Political donations make it possible for the capitalists to invest, as we have pointed out above, $k(D)$ amount of their savings (legal and illegal) illegally in foreign assets. We also assume for reasons explained in Chap. 5 that the rest of the net inflow of capital is exogenously given and denote its exogenously given value by $\bar{K}$. Thus, the BOP equilibrium condition is written as (substituting $r(r_c)$ for r)

$$\mathrm{NX}\left(\underset{+}{\frac{P^*e}{P}}, \underset{-}{I\left(\underset{-}{r(r_c)}, \underset{-}{e}\right)}, \underset{-}{C\left(\left(1-\alpha\left(\underset{-}{D}\right)t\right)Y\right)}; \underset{+}{Y^*}\right) + \bar{K} - k\left(\underset{+}{D}\right) = 0 \tag{7.7}$$

We assume that the producers set P on the basis of cost. As India's production is highly import-intensive, e is an important determinant of cost of production. Assuming other determinants of cost such as the money wage rate to be fixed in the short run, we shall make P an increasing function of e.

Thus, we have

$$P = P\left(\underset{+}{e}\right) \tag{7.8}$$

The specification of our model is now complete. It consists of three key Eqs. (7.5), (7.7), and (7.8) in three endogenous variables Y, e, and P. We solve these equations for the equilibrium values of the endogenous variables as follows. Substituting (7.8) into (7.7), we get

Table 7.2 Exchange rate of the Indian rupee vis-a-vis the US dollar (monthly average)

Year/month	US $ average	Year/month	US $ average	Year/month	US $ average	Year/month	US $ average
2008		Oct	46.7211	Jul	44.4174	Apr	54.4971
Jan	39.3737	Nov	46.5673	Aug	45.2788	May	55.1156
Feb	39.7326	Dec	46.6288	Sep	47.6320	Jun	58.5059
Mar	40.3561	2010		Oct	49.2579	Jul	60.0412
Apr	40.0224	Jan	45.9598	Nov	50.8564	Aug	64.5517
May	42.1250	Feb	46.3279	Dec	52.6769	Sep	64.3885
June	42.8202	Mar	45.4965	2012		Oct	61.7563
Jul	42.8380	Apr	44.4995	Jan	51.3992	Nov	62.7221
Aug	42.9374	May	45.8115	Feb	49.1671	Dec	61.7793
Sep	45.5635	June	46.5670	Mar	50.3213	2014	
Oct	48.6555	Jul	46.8373	Apr	51.8029	Jan	62.1708
Nov	48.9994	Aug	46.5679	May	54.4735	Feb	62.3136
Dec	48.6345	Sep	46.0616	June	56.0302	Mar	61.0021
2009		Oct	46.7211	Jul	55.4948	Apr	60.3813
Jan	48.8338	Nov	46.5673	Aug	48.3350	May	59.3255
Feb	49.2611	Dec	46.6288	Sep	54.3353	June	59.7143
Mar	51.2287	2011		Oct	52.8917	Jul	60.0263
Apr	50.0619	Jan	45.3934	Nov	54.6845	Aug	60.9923
May	48.5330	Feb	45.4358	Dec	54.6439		
June	47.7714	Mar	44.9914	2013			
Jul	48.4783	Apr	44.3700	Jan	54.3084		
Aug	48.3350	May	44.9045	Feb	53.7265		
Sep	48.4389	June	44.8536	Mar	54.5754		

Source RBI

$$\text{NX}\left(\underset{+}{\frac{P^*e}{P(e)}},\ \underset{-}{I\left(\underset{-}{r(r_c)},\ \underset{-}{e}\right)},\ \underset{-}{C\left(\left(1-\alpha\left(\underset{-}{D}\right)t\right)Y\right)};\ \underset{+}{Y^*}\right)+\bar{K}-k\left(\underset{+}{D}\right)=0 \quad (7.9)$$

Some observations regarding (7.9) are in order. Note that, a ceteris paribus increase in e brings about a substantial increase in P. Hence, a ceteris paribus increase in e produces just a small increase in the real exchange rate. Thus, the impact of a ceteris paribus increase in e on net export through its effect on the real exchange rate is insignificant. It raises net export mainly by lowering investment, which is highly import-intensive. We can solve (7.9) for the equilibrium value of e as a function of Y and D. It is given by

$$e = e\Big(\underset{+}{Y};\ \underset{+}{D}\Big) \tag{7.10}$$

Let us derive the signs of the partial derivatives of (7.10) using (7.9). Taking total differential of (7.9) treating all variables other than e and Y as fixed and, then, solving for $\frac{de}{dY}$, we get

$$\frac{de}{dY} = \frac{(-NX_C)C' \cdot \Big(1 - \alpha\Big(D\Big)t\Big)}{NX_p \cdot \frac{P*}{P}\left(1 - \frac{e}{P}P_e\right) + (-NX_I)(-I_e)} > 0 \tag{7.11}$$

Let us explain (7.11). Focus on the expression on the RHS of (7.11). The numerator measures the fall in net export due to the increase in consumption demand induced by a unit increase in Y. Since the major part of the additional unit of Y accrues to the capitalists, the major part of the additional consumption that it induces is capitalists' consumption. Hence, $(-NX_C)$ is fairly large. Thus, a unit increase in Y creates BOP deficit. To remove this, i.e., to restore net export to its initial value, e has to rise. The denominator gives the increase in net export that a unit increase in e brings about. The first term of the denominator which measures the rise in net export due to the increase in the real exchange rate alone brought about by a unit increase in e is, as we have already pointed out, quite small. This is because P_e is very large so that $\left(\frac{e}{P}P_e\right)$ is close to unity. The second term in the denominator gives the rise in net export due to the fall in import induced by the fall in I caused by a unit increase in e. Note that $(-NX_I)$, though fairly large, is a proper fraction. $(-I_e)$, as pointed out earlier, is large too.

Again, taking total differential of (7.9) treating all variables other than e and D as fixed and, then, solving for de, we get

$$\frac{de}{dD} = \frac{(-NX_C)C' \cdot (-\alpha')tY + k'}{NX_p \cdot \frac{P*}{P}\left(1 - \frac{e}{P}P_e\right) + (-NX_I)(-I_e)} > 0 \tag{7.12}$$

Let us explain the numerator of the expression on the RHS of (7.12). It gives the fall in net export that a ceteris paribus increase in D brings about. A unit increase in D allows a higher degree of tax evasion raising disposable income of the capitalists. Hence, their consumption demand rises by $C' \cdot \left(-\alpha'\right)tY$. This lowers net export by $(-NX_C)C' \cdot \left(-\alpha'\right)tY$. Again, a unit increase in D allows capitalists to invest a larger amount of their saving illegally in foreign assets. This is given by k'. Thus, the numerator gives the increase in BOP deficit or the fall in $(NX + K)$ that a unit increase in D causes, given the values of Y, e and all the exogenous variables.

Substituting (7.9) into (7.5), we rewrite it as

$$Y = C\Big(\Big(1 - \alpha\Big(\underset{-}{D}\Big)t\Big)Y\Big) + I\Big(\underset{-}{r(r_c)}, \underset{-}{e}\Big) + \alpha(D)tY - \bar{K} + k(D) \tag{7.13}$$

Substituting (7.10) into (7.13), we rewrite it as

$$Y = C\left(\left(1 - \alpha\left(\underset{-}{D}\right)t\right)Y\right) + I\left(r(r_c), e(\underset{-}{Y}, \underset{-}{D})\right) + \alpha(D)tY - \bar{K} + k(D) \quad (7.14)$$

Equation (7.14) contains only one endogenous variable. We can solve it for the equilibrium value of Y.

7.2.2 *Impact of Political Donation-Induced Tax Evasion and Illegal Parking of Saving in Foreign Assets in the Absence of Credit Rationing*

We shall examine here how a given increase in D affects the equilibrium value of Y. Taking total differential of (7.14) treating all exogenous variables other than D as fixed and, then, solving for dY, we get

$$\mathrm{d}Y = \frac{-[(1 - C')\alpha' tY + \{(-I_e)e_D - k'\}]\mathrm{d}D}{1 - \left[C' \cdot \left(1 - \alpha\left(\underset{-}{D}\right)t\right) + \alpha t - (-I_e)e_Y\right]} \quad (7.15)$$

Let us now derive the values of $(-I_e)e_D$ and $(-I_e)e_Y$. We shall do this using (7.12) and (7.11), which give the values of e_D and e_Y respectively. Now,

$$(-I_e)e_D = (-I_e)\frac{(-\mathrm{NX}_C)C' \cdot (-\alpha')tY + k'}{\mathrm{NX}_p \cdot \frac{P^*}{P}\left(1 - \frac{e}{P}P_e\right) + (-\mathrm{NX}_I)(-I_e)} \quad (7.16)$$

We have already pointed out that the first term in the denominator is very small. For the purpose of illustration, suppose it is zero. Then, (7.16) reduces to

$$(-I_e)e_D = (-I_e)\frac{(-\mathrm{NX}_C)C' \cdot (-\alpha')tY + k'}{(-\mathrm{NX}_I)(-I_e)}$$
$$= \frac{(-\mathrm{NX}_C)C' \cdot (-\alpha')tY + k'}{(-\mathrm{NX}_I)} > k' \quad 0 < (-\mathrm{NX}_I) < 1 \quad (7.17)$$

Let us explain the expression on the RHS of (7.17). In this case, the BOP deficit that emerges on account of a ceteris paribus unit increase in D, which is given by the numerator, is removed entirely through a fall in I. Hence, I has to fall by an amount, which is a large multiple of the numerator and the multiplier is given by $\frac{1}{(-\mathrm{NX}_I)}$. Thus, the fall in I is substantially larger than k'. Thus, if the first term in the denominator of the expression on the RHS of (7.16) is sufficiently small, which is likely to be the case in India for reasons we have explained earlier, $(-I_e)e_D$ will be much larger than k'.

Now, using (7.11), we get

$$(-I_e)e_Y = (-I_e)\frac{(-\mathrm{NX}_C)C' \cdot (1 - \alpha(D)t)}{\mathrm{NX}_p \cdot \frac{P^*}{P}\left(1 - \frac{e}{P}P_e\right) + (-\mathrm{NX}_I)(-I_e)} > 0 \tag{7.18}$$

From (7.18) it is clear that, following a unit increase in Y, e goes up lowering I. Following a unit increase in Y, as we have already mentioned, net export falls at the initial equilibrium e on account of the increase in capitalists' consumption creating a BOP deficit. Hence, e rises to raise net export by the amount given by $(-\mathrm{NX}_C)C' \cdot (1 - \alpha(D)t)$ in the numerator. The denominator gives the increase in net export that takes place per unit increase in e. Since, as we have already pointed out, the first term in the denominator is likely to be very small, the increase in e will raise net export mainly by lowering I. Since $(-\mathrm{NX}_I)$ is likely to be much less than unity, the increase in e that restores BOP equilibrium is likely to lower I by an amount which is larger than the requisite increase in net export.

Let us now focus on (7.15). Consider the numerator. We have already argued that $(-I_e)e_D$ is likely to be much larger than k'. Hence, the numerator is negative and its absolute value is likely to be quite large. The denominator of the expression on the RHS of (7.15) is positive, and we assume it to be less than unity. Thus, Y falls substantially following a given increase in D.

Let us now explain the process of contraction. Following an increase in D, capitalists are able to evade more taxes. Income tax revenue at the initial equilibrium (Y, e) falls by $\alpha' tY\mathrm{d}D$ raising aggregate disposable income by the same amount. Hence, aggregate consumption expenditure rises by $C'\alpha' tY\mathrm{d}D$ and government's consumption falls by $\alpha' tY\mathrm{d}D$. In the net, therefore, aggregate personal and public consumption together falls by $\left(1 - C'\right)\alpha' tY\mathrm{d}D$. The increase in D also allows the capitalists' to use more of their saving to invest illegally in foreign assets. Hence, outflow of capital will rise by $k'\mathrm{d}D$. Again, quite a large part of the increase in consumption demand represents additional demand for imported consumption goods. Thus, demand for imported consumption goods goes up by $-\mathrm{NX}_C \cdot C'\alpha' tY\mathrm{d}D$. Thus, at the initial equilibrium (Y, e), there emerges BOP deficit of $\left(-\mathrm{NX}_C \cdot C'\alpha' tY + k'\right)\mathrm{d}D$. e will, therefore, rise to raise net export by the same amount. However, an increase in e also raises P substantially. Hence, its impact on the real exchange rate is small or insignificant, given the import intensity of India's production. An increase in e, however, substantially reduces I. Hence, an increase in e raises net export mainly by lowering I, which reduces import demand. Thus, as e rises to raise net export by $\left(-\mathrm{NX}_C \cdot C'\alpha' tY + k'\right)\mathrm{d}D$, I falls by a much larger amount since only a fraction of I represents demand for imports. As e rises and restores BOP equilibrium, net export at the initial equilibrium Y increases in the net by $\left(-\mathrm{NX}_C \cdot C'\alpha' tY + k'\right)\mathrm{d}D - \left(-\mathrm{NX}_C \cdot C'\alpha' tY\mathrm{d}D\right) = k'\mathrm{d}D$. Thus, at the initial equilibrium Y, while net export is larger than its initial equilibrium value by only $k'\mathrm{d}D$, I is less than its initial equilibrium value by a much larger amount given by $(-I_e)e_D\mathrm{d}D$. At the initial equilibrium Y, therefore, there emerges a large excess supply of $\left[\left(1 - C'\right)\alpha' tY + (-I_e)e_D - k'\right]\mathrm{d}D$. Producers will respond to this excess supply by reducing their output by $\mathrm{d}Y_1 = \left[\left(1 - C'\right)\alpha' tY + (-I_e)e_D - k'\right]\mathrm{d}D$. This fall in Y reduces aggregate personal and public consumption together by $\left(1 + C'\right)\alpha t\mathrm{d}Y_1$. The fall in personal consumption reduces import demand creating BOP surplus. e will fall by $e_Y \mathrm{d}Y_1$ to restore net export to its initial value and, in the process, will raise I by $(-I_e)e_Y \mathrm{d}Y_1$. The decrease in Y in the first round by $\mathrm{d}Y_1$, therefore, lowers aggregate demand again by $\left[(1 + C')\alpha t - (-I_e)e_Y\right]\mathrm{d}Y_1$ inducing the producers to reduce Y in the second round by $\mathrm{d}Y_2 = \left[(1 + C')\alpha t - (-I_e)e_Y\right]\mathrm{d}Y_1$. Similarly, in the third round, Y will fall by $\mathrm{d}Y_3 = \left[(1 + C')\alpha t - (-I_e)e_Y\right]\mathrm{d}Y_2 = \left[(1 + C')\alpha t - (-I_e)e_Y\right]^2\mathrm{d}Y_1$. This process of contraction will continue until the fall in demand that takes place in each successive round eventually falls to zero. Thus, the total decline in Y in absolute value is given by

$$\begin{aligned} \mathrm{d}Y &= \mathrm{d}Y_1 + \left[(1 + C')\alpha t - (-I_e)e_Y\right]\mathrm{d}Y_1 + \left[(1 + C')\alpha t - (-I_e)e_Y\right]^2\mathrm{d}Y_1 + \cdots \\ &= \frac{\mathrm{d}Y_1}{1 - [(1 + C')\alpha t - (-I_e)e_Y]} \end{aligned} \tag{7.19}$$

Clearly, (7.19) explains (7.15). The above discussion yields the following proposition:

Proposition 7.1 *The system of private donations to political parties in a democracy characterizing a capitalist economy allows, among others, large-scale tax evasion by the giant capitalists and illegal parking of their savings in foreign assets. These manifestations of corruption generate strong recessionary forces that slow down the growth of capitalist economies.*

So far, we considered the case, where borrowers are not credit-rationed. This is, however, seldom the case in reality. In what follows, we shall consider the case where borrowers are credit-rationed.

7.2.3 Impact of Political Donation-Induced Tax Evasion and Illegal Parking of Saving in Foreign Assets in the Presence of Credit Rationing

We now consider the case where banks ration credit at the interest rate $r(r_c)$. Normally, they ration credit. They usually meet all the credit demand of the large corporations, but do not meet the credit demand of the small and medium enterprises. We refer to the former as quality borrowers and the latter as non-quality borrowers. We assume that only firms take loans from commercial banks and they do so only to finance their investment expenditure. We assume that $\bar{I}(r, e)$ is the investment function of the quality borrowers and they finance their investment with new loans from commercial banks and $\bar{K}$. We assume that, as happens in reality, external loans are available only to quality investors. Thus, quality investors' demand for new bank loans at $r(r_c)$ given by $\left[\bar{I}(r(r_c), e) - \bar{K}\right]$ is fully met by the banks, but non-quality investors' demand for new bank credit is not fully met. The amount of investment that non-quality investors can undertake is determined by the amount of new loans that they get from the commercial banks. The amount of new loans that commercial banks plan to supply is given by (7.4). Of this, the amount that the commercial banks use to supply the non-quality borrowers with loans is given by

$$(1-\rho)\left[\left\{Y - C\left((1-\underset{+}{\alpha(D)}t)Y\right)\right\} - k(D) + b\right] - \left(\bar{I}(r(r_c), e) - \bar{K}\right).$$

However, for reasons explained in detail in Chap. 5, the banks give only a fraction, β, of this amount to non-quality borrowers. Since the banks are unable even to disburse their own loanable fund as loan, we shall take b to be zero. Aggregate investment in the economy is, therefore, given by

$$\begin{aligned} I &= \bar{I}(r(r_c), e) + \beta\cdot\left((1-\rho)\left[\left\{Y - C\left((1-\underset{+}{\alpha(D)}t)Y\right)\right\} - k(D)\right] - \left(\bar{I}(r(r_c), e) - \bar{K}\right)\right) \\ &= (1-\beta)\bar{I}(r(r_c), e) + \beta\cdot\left((1-\rho)\left[\left\{Y - C\left((1-\underset{+}{\alpha(D)}t)Y\right)\right\} - k(D)\right] + \bar{K}\right) \end{aligned} \quad (7.20)$$

Incorporating (7.20) into (7.14), we get

$$\begin{aligned} Y &= C\left(\left(1-\alpha\left(\underset{-}{D}\right)t\right)Y\right) + (1-\beta)\bar{I}\left(r(r_c), e(\underset{-}{Y}; \underset{-}{D})\right) \\ &\quad + \beta\cdot[(1-\rho)\{Y - C((1-\alpha(D)t)Y) - k(D)\}] + \beta\bar{K} + \alpha(D)tY - \bar{K} + k(D) \end{aligned} \quad (7.21)$$

To derive the impact of an autonomous increase in D on Y, we shall take total differential of (7.21) treating all variables other than Y and D as fixed and, then, solve for $\mathrm{d}Y$. This yields the following:

$$\mathrm{d}Y = \frac{-[(1-C')\alpha' tY + \{(1-\beta)(-\bar{I}_e)e_D - k'\} + \beta(1-\rho)(C'\alpha' tY + k')]\mathrm{d}D}{1 - \left[C'\cdot\left(1-\alpha\left(\underset{-}{D}\right)t\right) + \alpha t + \beta(1-\rho)(1 - C'(1-\alpha t)) - (-I_e)e_Y\right]} < 0 \quad (7.22)$$

If we compare the expression on the RHS of (7.22) to that of (7.15), we shall show shortly that the absolute value of the numerator of the former is much larger than that of the latter. At the same time, the denominator of the former is much smaller than that of the latter and the contraction in Y is, therefore, substantially larger. We shall seek to explain this point, while describing the adjustment process.

Following an increase in D by $\mathrm{d}D$, public consumption falls and personal consumption increases and, in the net, aggregate public and personal consumption increases as before by $(1-C')\alpha' tY$ at the initial equilibrium (Y, e). Most of the additional consumption expenditure represents additional demand for imported consumption goods. Moreover, the increase in D also allows the capitalists to illegally transfer a part of their saving from domestic bank deposits to foreign assets. Both of these will create BOP deficit and raise e at the initial equilibrium Y. The increase in e will raise net export by the amount of the BOP deficit and, thereby, remove it. However, the increase in net export will come about, for reasons we have already explained, principally by lowering investment. Investment will have to fall by a much larger amount than the requisite increase in net export, since import intensity of investment is much less than unity. In the present case of credit rationing, the increase in e will only lower quality borrowers' investment $\bar{I}$. However, per unit fall in $\bar{I}$, aggregate investment falls only by $(1-\beta)$, since loan supply to non-quality investors increases by β (see 7.20). Therefore, to raise net export by the requisite amount, the fall in $\bar{I}$ must be such that, as follows from (7.17), which gives the value of $I_e e_D \mathrm{d}D$,

$$(1-\beta)\bar{I}_e e_D \mathrm{d}D = I_e e_D \mathrm{d}D \Rightarrow$$

$$\bar{I}_e e_D \mathrm{d}D = \frac{1}{(1-\beta)} I_e e_D \mathrm{d}D \tag{7.23}$$

Substituting (7.23) into (7.22), we rewrite it as

$$\mathrm{d}Y = \frac{-[(1-C')\alpha' tY + \{(-I_e)e_D - k'\} + \beta(1-\rho)(C'\alpha' tY + k')]\mathrm{d}D}{1-\left[C'\left(1-\alpha\left(\underline{D}\right)t\right) + \alpha t + \beta(1-\rho)(1-C'(1-\alpha t)) - (-I_e)e_Y\right]} < 0 \tag{7.24}$$

Now, it is clear that the absolute value of the numerator of the expression on the RHS of (7.24) is much larger than that of (7.15).

Let us now go back to investment. Since, as follows from the above discussion, net export rises by the amount of the BOP deficit principally through the fall in investment and since import intensity of investment is much less than unity, investment is likely to fall by an amount that is much larger than the increase in net export. Hence, the term $((-I_e)e_D - k')$ in the numerator of (7.24) is highly like to be positive as before. In the present case of credit rationing, aggregate investment at the initial equilibrium Y will fall further following a given increase in D for another reason also. Following a given increase in D, consumption at the initial equilibrium Y rises and, therefore, aggregate saving falls by $C'\alpha' tY\mathrm{d}D$. Moreover, the capitalists are able to transfer a part of their saving given by $k'\mathrm{d}D$ from domestic bank deposits to foreign assets. New deposits of commercial banks go down by $(C'\alpha' tY + k')\mathrm{d}D$. Hence, their supply of new loans to non-quality borrowers falls by $\beta \cdot (1-\rho)(C'\alpha' tY + k')\mathrm{d}D$ reducing their investment by the same amount. Thus, at the initial equilibrium Y, aggregate demand falls creating an excess supply of an amount given by the numerator, which we shall denote by N. Producers will respond to it by reducing Y setting off a multiplier process. Y in the first round will go down by $\mathrm{d}Y_1 = \frac{N}{1-[C'\cdot(1-\alpha t)+\alpha t-(-I_e)e_Y]} = \frac{N}{d}$, where $d \equiv 1-\left[C'\cdot(1-\alpha t)+\alpha t-(-I_e)e_Y\right]$. In the absence of credit rationing, the value of the multiplier is $\frac{1}{d}$ and, therefore, the contraction would have ended there (see 7.15). However, in the presence of credit rationing, the process of contraction will continue further. The fall in Y by $\mathrm{d}Y_1$ will reduce aggregate personal saving, given by $[(1-\alpha t)Y - C((1-\alpha t)Y)]$, by $(1-C')(1-\alpha t)\mathrm{d}Y_1$. This will reduce the amount of new bank deposit by the same amount. Hence, the supply of new bank credit will fall by $\theta \mathrm{d}Y_1$, where $\theta \equiv \beta(1-\rho)(1-C')(1-\alpha t)$, reducing aggregate investment by the same amount. Hence, in the second round, Y will go down by $\mathrm{d}Y_2 = \frac{\theta}{d}\mathrm{d}Y_1$. The fall in Y in the second round by $\mathrm{d}Y_2$ will again reduce personal saving. Hence, supply of new bank deposit and new bank credit will fall. The latter will decline by θdY_2 reducing aggregate investment by the same amount. Hence, in the third round, Y will fall by $dY_3 = \frac{\theta}{d}dY_2 = \left(\frac{\theta}{d}\right)^2 dY_1$. This process of contraction will continue until the fall in investment demand that takes place in each successive round eventually falls to zero. Thus, the total fall in Y is given by

$$dY = dY_1 + \frac{\theta}{d}dY_1 + \left(\frac{\theta}{d}\right)^2 dY_1 + \cdots = \left(\frac{d}{d-\theta}\right)dY_1 = \left(\frac{d}{d-\theta}\right)\cdot\left(\frac{N}{d}\right) = \frac{N}{d-\theta} \quad (7.25)$$

One can easily check that (7.25) tallies with (7.24) and (7.22). The contraction in Y is, therefore, substantially larger in the present case. This yields the following proposition:

Proposition 7.2 *The contraction in Y that takes place following a given increase in D on account of the rise in tax evasion and illegal parking of saving in foreign assets is substantially larger under credit rationing than what occurs in the case where there is no credit rationing.*

Political donations have many other ramifications. Bank fraud is one of them. Giant capitalists are defrauding the banks of huge sums of money leading to large increases in banks' non-performing assets. In what follows, we shall dwell on this issue in detail.

7.3 Political Donations and Bank Fraud

According to RBI's Financial Stability Report 2018 (RBI 2018), large borrowers accounted for 58.8% of gross advances and 85.6% of gross non-performing assets of banks. Clearly, in our view, the political patronage that large borrowers buy with their political donations allows them to get away with not servicing their loans. We shall examine here the macroeconomic implications of political donation-induced increase in bank frauds. There are two major reasons for non-performing assets of banks, namely recession indicated by the level of Y and bank frauds, which are usually induced by political donations. Denoting non-performing assets by N, we have

$$N = N\left(\underset{-}{Y}, \underset{+}{D}\right) \quad (7.26)$$

An increase in the stock of non-performing assets reduces the profitability of banks. It also induces the central bank and the government to take the banks to task for failing to arrest the growth in their non-performing assets. Both these make the banks nervous, when their stock of non-performing assets increases. The central bank forces the banks to tighten their lending norms, and the brunt of this action is borne, ironically, not by the large borrowers but by the small and medium businesses whom we refer to as non-quality borrowers. Thus, an increase in N induces the banks to lower the value of β, which denotes the fraction of the banks' loanable fund net of quality borrowers' demand for new bank credit that the banks lend out to non-quality borrowers (see 7.20). We therefore make β a decreasing function of N. Thus, we have

$$\beta = \beta(N(Y, D)) \equiv \bar{\beta}\left(\underset{+}{Y}, \underset{-}{D}\right) \tag{7.27}$$

An increase in the stock of non-performing assets drives the banks into financial trouble. They find it difficult to meet depositors' claims. To keep the banks going, the government has to provide them with funds by buying their equities and bonds. We denote the fund that the government has to give to the banks to bail them out by B and make it an increasing function of N. Thus, we have

$$B = B\left(\underset{+}{N}\right) = B(N(Y, D)) \equiv \bar{B}\left(\underset{-}{Y}, \underset{+}{D}\right) \tag{7.28}$$

Incorporating (7.28) in the government's budget constraint given by (7.2), we rewrite it as

$$G = \alpha(D)tY - \bar{B}\left(\underset{-}{Y}, \underset{+}{D}\right) \tag{7.29}$$

Substituting (7.27) and (7.29) into (7.21), we rewrite it as

$$\begin{aligned} Y = {} & C\left(\left(1 - \alpha\left(\underset{-}{D}\right)t\right)Y\right) + \left(1 - \bar{\beta}\left(\underset{+}{Y}, \underset{-}{D}\right)\right)\bar{I}\left(r\underset{-}{(r_c)}, e(Y; \underset{-}{D})\right) \\ & + \bar{\beta}\left(\underset{+}{Y}, \underset{-}{D}\right) \cdot [(1 - \rho)\{Y(1 - \alpha(D)t) - C((1 - \alpha(D)t)Y) - k(D)\}] \\ & + \bar{\beta}\left(\underset{+}{Y}, \underset{-}{D}\right)\bar{K} + \alpha(D)tY - \bar{B}\left(\underset{-}{Y}, \underset{+}{D}\right) - \bar{K} + k(D) \end{aligned} \tag{7.30}$$

To derive the impact of an increase in D on Y, we shall take total differential of (7.30) treating all variables other than Y and D as fixed and, then, solving for $\mathrm{d}Y$ and using (7.23), we get

$$\mathrm{d}Y = \frac{-[(1 - C')(-\alpha')tY + \{(-I_e)e_D - k'\} + \beta(1 - \rho)(C'(-\alpha')tY + k') + \{(-\bar{\beta}_D\bar{L}) + \bar{B}_D\}]\mathrm{d}D}{1 - \left[\left\{C' \cdot \left(1 - \alpha\left(\underset{-}{D}\right)t\right) + \alpha t + \beta(1 - \rho)(1 - C'(1 - \alpha t)) - (-I_e)e_Y\right\} + (\beta_Y\bar{L} + (-\bar{B}_Y))\right]} < 0$$

$$\bar{L} \equiv \beta.\left[(1 - \rho)\{Y - C((1 - \alpha(D)t)Y) - k(D)\} - \left(\bar{I}(r(r_c), e(Y, D)) - \bar{K}\right)\right] \tag{7.31}$$

Comparing the expressions on the RHSs of (7.24) and (7.31), we find that the absolute value of the numerator of (7.31) is larger than that of (7.24) by the term $\{(-\bar{\beta}_D\bar{L}) + \bar{B}_D\}\mathrm{d}D$ and the denominator of (7.31) is smaller than that of (7.24) on account of the term $(\beta_Y\bar{L} + (-\bar{B}_Y))$. Let us now explain why the contraction in Y is larger in the present case.

First note that, following an increase in D in the present case, at the initial equilibrium Y, aggregate consumption (personal and public) and aggregate investment go down as before by $\left[(1-C')(-\alpha')tY+\{(-I_e)e_D-k'\}+\beta(1-\rho)(C'\alpha'tY+k')\right]\mathrm{d}D$. In addition, the given increase in D lowers β by $\bar{\beta}_D$ and, thereby, reduces investment by $-\bar{\beta}_D\bar{L}\mathrm{d}D$ in absolute value at the initial equilibrium Y. Thus, bank fraud by giant capitalists reduces loan supply to the small and medium producers. The increase in the stock of non-performing assets due to bank fraud also induces the government to infuse capital into the banks by the amount $\bar{B}_D\mathrm{d}D$. This lowers government's consumption expenditure by the same amount. As a result of the fall in aggregate demand by the absolute value of the numerator, which we shall denote by $\bar{N}$, there emerges an excess supply of the same amount at the initial equilibrium Y. This sets off a multiplier process bringing about a cumulative contraction in Y. In the first round, Y falls by $\mathrm{d}\tilde{Y}_1=\frac{\bar{N}}{\bar{d}}$, where $\bar{d}$ denotes the denominator of the expression on the RHS of (7.24). This fall in Y will lower profit and increase losses. As a result, default rate will rise bringing about an increase in the stock of non-performing assets of the banks. Banks in response will lower β reducing loan supply to non-quality investors by $\bar{\beta}_Y\bar{L}\mathrm{d}Y_1$. Hence, aggregate investment will go down by $\bar{\beta}_Y\bar{L}\mathrm{d}Y_1$. Again, the increase in the stock of non-performing assets will put the banks in trouble and the government has to infuse funds into them by the amount $\bar{B}_Y\mathrm{d}Y_1$ to get them going. This reduces government consumption by the same amount. Thus, there again emerges an excess supply of $(\bar{\beta}_Y\bar{L}+\bar{B}_Y)\mathrm{d}Y_1$ and again, through the multiplier process, Y in the second round will go down by $\mathrm{d}\tilde{Y}_2=\frac{(\bar{\beta}_Y\bar{L}+\bar{B}_Y)\mathrm{d}Y_1}{\bar{d}}$. The same process will be repeated in the third round, and Y in the third round will fall by $\mathrm{d}\tilde{Y}_3=\frac{(\bar{\beta}_Y\bar{L}+\bar{B}_Y)\mathrm{d}Y_2}{\bar{d}}=\left[\frac{(\bar{\beta}_Y\bar{L}+\bar{B}_Y)}{\bar{d}}\right]^2\mathrm{d}Y_1$. This process will continue until the contraction in demand that takes place in each successive round eventually falls to zero. Thus, the total fall in Y is given by

$$\mathrm{d}Y=-\left[\mathrm{d}Y_1+\frac{(\bar{\beta}_Y\bar{L}+\bar{B}_Y)}{\bar{d}}\mathrm{d}Y_1+\left[\frac{(\bar{\beta}_Y\bar{L}+\bar{B}_Y)}{\bar{d}}\right]^2\mathrm{d}Y_1+\cdots\right]=-\left[\frac{\bar{d}}{\bar{d}-(\bar{\beta}_Y\bar{L}+\bar{B}_Y)}\right]\mathrm{d}Y_1$$

$$=-\left[\frac{\bar{d}}{\bar{d}-(\bar{\beta}_Y\bar{L}+\bar{B}_Y)}\right]\frac{\bar{N}}{\bar{d}}=-\frac{\bar{N}}{\bar{d}-(\bar{\beta}_Y\bar{L}+\bar{B}_Y)} \tag{7.32}$$

It is clear that (7.32) tallies with (7.31). Thus, political donation-induced bank frauds substantially strengthens the recessionary forces unleashed by tax evasion and illegal investment of savings in foreign assets made possible by the system of political donations. This yields the following proposition:

Proposition 7.3 *Political donations give rise to bank frauds, and they strengthen manifold the recessionary forces generated by tax evasion and illegal investment of savings in foreign assets made possible by the system of private funding of political parties.*

Since bailing out banks puts pressure on government's budget, governments in capitalist countries have suggested an important measure. We shall discuss it below.

7.4 Financial Responsibility and Deposit Insurance (FRDI) Bill

Large-scale bank frauds and speculative activities of financial institutions in capitalist countries often lead to bankruptcies of banks and other financial institutions. This happened in the USA and in many European countries in 2008. This happened in Japan in 1992 and in the East Asian countries in the late nineties. When banks and other financial institutions become bankrupt, governments have to bail them out. Given the stringent restrictions that the governments put on their borrowing, expenditure on bailout of financial institutions put a lot of pressure on governments' budgets. This has led them to find a way out. They have proposed that in case a bank becomes insolvent, depositors will be made to bear the brunt of bank bailout instead of the government. This means that, if a bank becomes insolvent, it will be under no obligation to meet depositors' claims and depositors will simply lose their deposits. Government of India sought to pass a law to this effect recently. For this purpose, it introduced Financial Responsibility and Deposit Insurance Bill in the parliament for its approval. It is now awaiting parliament's approval. In what follows, we shall examine the macroeconomic implications of this policy.

It is clear that, if governments pass such bills, people will lose their trust in the both the government and the financial institutions. They will search for safe avenues for keeping their savings. Government cannot provide them with safe assets on an adequate scale, given the restrictions on its borrowing. Hence, they will have to hold their saving in the form of gold and other precious metals, gems and jewelry, land and currency. They are unlikely to hold their saving in houses, as houses depreciate fast and new houses come up all the time in most localities making old houses lose their value substantially. In India, gold and other precious metals and gems and jewelry are imported as their domestic production is inadequate. Since prices of gold, etc., fluctuate a great deal, it may be highly risky to hold them, given the possibility of large capital losses. Hence, people may hold their saving in currency as well. Government can also provide the people with safe assets to invest their savings in despite the restrictions on its borrowing. This the government can do by holding its borrowings as deposit with the central bank. In this case, its borrowing will be offset by a safe asset of equal value. Hence, its net borrowing will be zero. It cannot hold its borrowings as deposits with financial institutions. This is because if the financial institutions get into trouble, the government will also be in deep difficulty servicing its own debt, given the independence of the central bank. We assume, therefore, that the government parks the sales proceeds from the sales of its safe financial assets with the central bank as deposit. We shall club together safe government assets, land, and currency as one kind of asset and denote it by J, as these assets do not generate any demand for produced goods and services. We shall assume that the savers hold q_1 fraction of their saving in the form of J and q fraction of their saving in the form of imported assets such as gold, and they hold the rest of their saving in the form of bank deposits. We make q and q_1 sharply increasing functions of government's measures that indicate withdrawal of government's support to banks.

We shall denote such measures by Q, and assume that an increase in Q indicates weakening of government's support to the financial institutions. In order to bring out the impact of an increase in Q in sharp relief and also for simplicity, we shall henceforth leave out the terms involving D. Thus, denoting the amount of saving that people hold in the form of new bank deposit by S_b, we have

$$S_b = \left[1 - q\left(\underset{+}{Q}\right) - q_1\left(\underset{+}{Q}\right)\right] \cdot [(1-t)Y - C((1-t)Y)] \tag{7.33}$$

We work under the assumption of credit rationing here. Banks meet all the demand for new credit of the quality borrowers and ration non-quality borrowers. Leaving out all the terms involving D and also $\bar{K}$ for simplicity and incorporating (7.33), we rewrite (7.20) as

$$I = (1-\beta)\bar{I}(r(r_c), e) + \beta \cdot (1-\rho)K \cdot \left[1 - q\left(\underset{+}{Q}\right) - q_1\left(\underset{+}{Q}\right)\right] \cdot [(1-t)Y - C((1-t)Y)] \tag{7.34}$$

Since q fraction of households' saving is held in the form of imported goods, incorporating it and leaving out $\bar{K}$ for simplicity, we rewrite (7.9) as

$$\mathrm{NX}\left(\underset{+}{\frac{P^*e}{P(e)}}, \underset{-}{I}\left(\underset{-}{r(r_c)}, \underset{-}{e}\right), \underset{-}{C((1-t)Y)};\ \underset{+}{Y^*}\right) - q(Q)[(1-t)Y - C((1-t)Y)] = 0 \tag{7.35}$$

Solving (7.35), we get e as a function of Y and Q, among others. Thus, we get

$$e = e\left(\underset{+}{Y};\ \underset{+}{Q}\right) \tag{7.36}$$

Let us now derive the signs of the partial derivatives of $e(\cdot)$. Taking total differential of (7.35) treating all variables other than e and Y as fixed, we get

$$\frac{\mathrm{d}e}{\mathrm{d}Y}(\equiv e_Y) = \frac{(-\mathrm{NX}_C)C' \cdot (1-t) + q(Q)(1-t)\left(1-C'\right)}{\mathrm{NX}_p \cdot \frac{P^*}{P}(1-\eta_P) + (-\mathrm{NX}_I)(-I_e)} > 0 \quad \eta_P \equiv \frac{e}{P}P_e \tag{7.37}$$

In (7.37), $\eta_P \equiv$ exchange rate elasticity of P. It is likely to be close to unity.

$$\frac{\mathrm{d}e}{\mathrm{d}Q}(\equiv e_Q) = \frac{q' \cdot [(1-t)Y - C((1-t)Y)]}{\mathrm{NX}_p \cdot \frac{P^*}{P}(1-\eta_P) + (-\mathrm{NX}_I)(-I_e)} > 0 \quad \eta_P \equiv \frac{e}{P}P_e \tag{7.38}$$

Let us first focus on (7.38). Following an increase in Q by $\mathrm{d}Q$, the amount of households' saving held in the form of imported assets will increase by $q' \cdot [(1-t)Y - C((1-t)Y)]$ at the initial equilibrium (Y, e) creating a BOP deficit.

Hence, e will rise at the initial equilibrium Y to raise net export by the amount of the BOP deficit and, thereby, remove it. However, the increase in net export will come about, for reasons we have already explained, principally by lowering investment. Investment will have to fall by a much larger amount than the requisite increase in net export, since import intensity of investment in much less than unity. The amount of fall in investment that will raise net export by the requisite amount is given by

$$I_e e_Q = I_e \frac{q' \cdot [(1-t)Y - C((1-t)Y)]}{\mathrm{NX}_p \cdot \frac{P*}{P}(1-\eta_P) + (-\mathrm{NX}_I)(-I_e)} \cong \frac{q' \cdot [(1-t)Y - C((1-t)Y)]}{(-\mathrm{NX}_I)} < 0 \quad (7.39)$$

In the present case of credit rationing, the increase in e will only lower quality borrowers' investment $\bar{I}$. However, per unit fall in $\bar{I}$, aggregate investment falls only by $(1-\beta)$, since loan supply to non-quality investors increases by β (see 7.34). Therefore, to raise net export by the requisite amount, the fall in $\bar{I}$ must be such that I falls by the amount given by (7.39). Thus, we must have

$$(1-\beta)\bar{I}_e e_Q \mathrm{d}Q = I_e e_Q \mathrm{d}Q \quad (7.40)$$

Similarly, following a ceteris paribus change in Y, the fall in I that occurs on account of the rise in e is given by

$$\begin{aligned} \bar{I}_e e_Y &= \bar{I}_e \frac{(-\mathrm{NX}_C)C' \cdot (1-t) + q(Q)(1-t)\left(1-C'\right)}{\mathrm{NX}_p \cdot \frac{P*}{P}(1-\eta_P) + (-\mathrm{NX}_I)(-I_e)} \\ &\cong -\frac{(-\mathrm{NX}_C)C' \cdot (1-t) + q(Q)(1-t)\left(1-C'\right)}{(-\mathrm{NX}_I)} < 0 \end{aligned} \quad (7.41)$$

In the present case of credit rationing, as we have pointed out above, following a ceteris paribus unit increase in Y and the increase in e that it gives rise to, aggregate investment falls by $(1-\beta)\bar{I}_e e_Y$, which should be equal to the value of $I_e e_Y$ as given by (7.41). Thus, we have

$$(1-\beta)\bar{I}_e e_Y = I_e e_Y \quad (7.42)$$

Leaving out all terms involving D and $\bar{K}$ for simplicity and incorporating (7.36) and (7.34), we rewrite (7.30) as

$$\begin{aligned} Y = C((1-t)Y) + (1-\beta) \cdot \bar{I}\left(\underset{-}{r(r_c)}, \underset{-}{e(Y;Q)}\right) \\ + \beta \cdot [(1-\rho)(1-q(Q)-q_1(Q))\{Y(1-t) - C((1-t)Y)\}] + tY \end{aligned} \quad (7.43)$$

To derive the impact of an increase in Q on Y, we take total differential of (7.43) treating all variables other than Y and Q as fixed and, then, solving for $\mathrm{d}Y$. This gives us

$$\mathrm{d}Y = \frac{-\left[\beta(1-\rho)\left(q' + q_1'\right)(Y(1-t) - C((1-t)Y)) + (1-\beta)\left(-\bar{I}_e\right)e_Q\right]\mathrm{d}Q}{1 - \left[\left\{C'(1-t) + t - (1-\beta)\left(-\bar{I}_e\right)e_Y\right\}\right] - \beta(1-\rho)(1-q-q_1)(1-C')(1-t)} < 0 \tag{7.44}$$

Using (7.40) and (7.42), we rewrite the above equation as

$$\mathrm{d}Y = \frac{-\left[\beta(1-\rho)\left(q' + q_1'\right)(Y(1-t) - C((1-t)Y)) + (-I)_e e_Q\right]\mathrm{d}Q}{1 - [\{C'(1-t) + t - (-I_e)e_Y\}] - \beta(1-\rho)(1-q-q_1)(1-C')(1-t)} < 0 \tag{7.45}$$

Let us now explain (7.45). Following a given increase in Q, people lose confidence in banks and transfer their saving from bank deposits to other assets. Hence, new bank deposits go down by $\left(q' + q_1'\right)(Y(1-t) - C((1-t)Y))\mathrm{d}Q$. As a result, supply of new loans to non-quality borrowers and, therefore, aggregate investment goes down by $\beta \cdot (1-\rho)\left(q' + q_1'\right)(Y(1-t) - C((1-t)Y))\mathrm{d}Q$ at the initial equilibrium (Y, e). Since a part of the new saving is transferred from the bank deposits to the imported goods, there will emerge BOP deficit of $q'(Y(1-t) - C((1-t)Y))$ at the initial equilibrium (Y, e). e will rise to raise net export by the amount of the BOP deficit. The increase in e will lower I by $(-I_e)e_Q\mathrm{d}Q$ whose value is given by (7.39). q' and q_1' are likely to be very large. Hence, there will emerge a substantial excess supply at the initial equilibrium Y setting off a cumulative contraction in Y. Hence, Y will fall. The multiplier process will operate, and it will fall in the first round by $\mathrm{d}\tilde{Y}_1 = \frac{\left[\beta(1-\rho)\left(q'+q_1'\right)(Y(1-t)-C((1-t)Y))+(1-\beta)\bar{I}_e e_Q\right]\mathrm{d}Q}{1-\left[\left\{C'(1-t)+t-(1-\beta)\left(-\bar{I}_e\right)e_Y\right\}\right]} \equiv \frac{\tilde{N}\mathrm{d}Q}{\tilde{d}}$. The fall in Y by $\mathrm{d}\tilde{Y}_1$ will reduce aggregate saving by $\left(1-C'\right)(1-t)\mathrm{d}\tilde{Y}_1$. This will reduce new bank deposit by $(1-q-q_1)\left(1-C'\right)(1-t)\mathrm{d}\tilde{Y}_1$. Hence, supply of new loans to the non-quality borrowers and, therefore, aggregate investment will fall by $\beta(1-\rho)(1-q-q_1)\left(1-C'\right)(1-t)\mathrm{d}\tilde{Y}_1 \equiv \varphi$. This will again set off the multiplier process, and Y in the second round will decline by $\mathrm{d}\tilde{Y}_2 = \frac{\varphi}{\tilde{d}}$. The fall in Y in the second round will again reduce supply of new loans to non-quality borrowers and aggregate investment by $\varphi \cdot \mathrm{d}\tilde{Y}_2$ lowering Y in the third round by $\mathrm{d}\tilde{Y}_3 = \frac{\varphi \cdot \mathrm{d}\tilde{Y}_2}{\tilde{d}} = \left(\frac{\varphi}{\tilde{d}}\right)^2 \mathrm{d}Y_1$. This cumulative process of contraction will continue until the fall in demand that takes place in each successive round eventually falls to zero. Thus, the total fall in Y is given by

$$\mathrm{d}Y = \mathrm{d}\tilde{Y}_1 + \left(\frac{\varphi}{\tilde{d}}\right)\mathrm{d}Y_1 + \left(\frac{\varphi}{\tilde{d}}\right)^2 \mathrm{d}Y_1 + \cdots = \frac{\tilde{d}}{\tilde{d}-\varphi}\mathrm{d}Y_1 = \frac{\tilde{d}}{\tilde{d}-\varphi}\frac{\tilde{N}\mathrm{d}Q}{\tilde{d}} = \frac{\tilde{N}\mathrm{d}Q}{\tilde{d}-\varphi} \tag{7.46}$$

It is clear that (7.46) tallies with (7.45). If we had made β an increasing function as Y, as we had done earlier, the contraction would have been many times more. (Exercise: Work it out yourself).

The above discussion suggests the following. Political donations give rise to bank frauds. If following a spate of large-scale bank frauds, as has happened in India in recent years, and onset of recession, the stock of non-performing assets of banks increases and the government seeks to get the FRDI Bill approved by the parliament, people will get extremely nervous. They will transfer their savings from banks deposits to currency and other safe government assets and also to precious metals, gems, jewelry, etc., which are all imported. These changes will severely curtail banks' ability to lend, bring about a sharp increase in the exchange rate and, thereby, drive the economy into a deep recession. Clearly, this will lead to a very large increase in the stock of non-performing assets of banks. Banks and other financial institutions will be saddled with very large losses, and the financial system will collapse perpetrating a deep economic crisis. We can summarize this conclusion in the form of the following proposition:

Proposition 7.4 *If the government succeeds in getting the FRDI Bill approved by the parliament, people will lose confidence in banks. They will transfer their savings from bank deposits to currency, safe government assets, and precious metals and stones which are all imported. This will drive the economy into a deep recession, the banks' business will shrink drastically, and they will be in deep financial troubles. In sum, both the financial institutions and the economy will collapse.*

7.5 Political Donations, Allocation of Credit, and Jobless Growth

Political donations allow the giant capitalists to increase their command over resources legally and illegally. One extremely adverse consequence of their absolute control over political parties and the government is the relentless incorporation of labor-saving technological and managerial changes in production. This has led to the phenomenon of jobless growth in the capitalist countries including India. This helps the giant capitalists increase their share in the GDP at the expense of workers. The giant capitalists through the political parties also induce the government and the central bank to specify lending norms in such a manner that the banks and other financial institutions lend to the giant capitalists a larger proportion of their loanable funds than they otherwise would. This helps the giant capitalists grab a larger portion of the scarce resources at the expense of the others. In support of our claim, we cite the following evidence. According to RBI's Financial Stability Report 2018 (RBI 2018), large borrowers accounted for 58.8% of gross advances and 85.6% of gross non-performing assets of banks. Thus, substantially larger percentages of loans given to the large borrowers turn non-performing compared to the small and medium borrowers. Despite this evidence, the major part of the loanable fund of the banks is given to the large borrowers. This points to a close nexus between the government/central bank and the large borrowers. Despite the telltale piece of evidence cited above, the government or the central bank does nothing to stop the large borrowers from bagging most of the credit supply. We shall explore the implications of this bias in the allocation of credit in the context of a country like India. In India, besides the people being divided into two classes, the capitalists and workers, the economy is also divided into two segments: the organized sector and the unorganized sector. The organized sector consists of large companies subject to company laws, while the unorganized sector consists of small production units. The largest segment of the unorganized sector is agriculture. The feature that distinguishes the two sectors is that production in the unorganized sector is constrained by supply-side factors, while the output of the organized sector is demand determined. One important factor that acts as a constraint on the output of the unorganized sector is credit. We shall explore the implications of this constraint here. In what follows, we shall describe the organized and the unorganized sectors. We focus on the organized sector first.

Organized Sector

We denote the output of the organized sector by y, which, as we have pointed out already, is demand determined. It is produced with labor, imported intermediate inputs, intermediate inputs supplied by the unorganized sector and capital. It is a short-run model. So, the stock of capital is given. From Table 7.3, we find that the organized sector has grown at quite a high rate in the post-reform period. However, employment in the organized sector has not grown at all. Hence, we shall assume the stock of labor employed in the organized sector to be fixed. We denote it by $\bar{L}$. The organized sector uses imported goods and also the output of the unorganized sector as intermediate inputs. The requirement of the unorganized sector's output as intermediate input per unit of y is denoted by n. Demand for Y comes from the capitalists (producers in the organized sector) for purposes of consumption and investment. We disregard workers' consumption demand for Y for simplicity. The reasons are the following. The major part of workers' consumption expenditure is spent on the unorganized sector's output, and the marginal propensity to consume organized sector's output of the capitalists is much higher than that of workers. Hence, omission of workers' consumption demand for organized sector's output will not affect our results qualitatively. Producers of the unorganized sector use the output of the organized sector as intermediate input. We assume that m amount of y is required to produce 1 unit of the output of the unorganized sector, which is denoted by x. Foreigners also demand organized sector's output. Substitutes of y are also imported. Hence, we write the equilibrium condition of the organized sector as follows:

$$y = c_c \cdot \left(\left(\left(1 - n\frac{P^x}{P^y} - \bar{m}\frac{P^*e}{P^y} \right) y - \frac{W}{P^y}\bar{L} \right) (1 - t) \right) + I(r) + mx + G$$
$$+ \bar{N}\bar{X}\left(\underset{+}{\frac{P^*e}{P^y}}, \underset{-}{y}; \underset{+}{Y^*} \right) \tag{7.47}$$

In (7.47), c_c denotes the fixed average and marginal propensity to consume of the capitalists, P^x denotes price of x, W denotes the money wage rate, and we assume it to be fixed in the short run. P^y denotes price of the organized sector's output, $\bar{m}$ denotes the fixed amount of imported intermediate input needed to produce one unit of y, and t is the tax rate on both capitalists' and workers' income. $\bar{N}\bar{X}(\cdot)$ is the net export function of the organized sector, and it is quite standard. The meanings of the rest of the notations have been explained in the previous sections. Even though C, I, and

Table 7.3 Employment in the organized sector (in million)

Year	Growth rate of GDP at constant (2004–05) prices	Number of workers employed
1994–95	6.4	27.53
2000–01	5.3	27.79
2001–02	5.5	27.20
2003–04	8.1	26.45
2004–05	7.0	26.46
2005–06	9.5	26.96
2006–07	9.6	27.24
2007–08	9.6	27.55
2008–09	6.7	28.18
2009–10	8.4	29.00
2010–11	8.4	29
2011–12	5.3	29.65

Sources RBI

G represent demand for both domestic and foreign goods, we have not incorporated them in the net export function for simplicity. We have made net export, as standard in text books, an increasing function of the real exchange rate relevant for the y-sector, a decreasing function of y and an increasing function of foreign GDP, Y^*. Since the economy considered here is a small one, both Y^* and P^* are given. We shall now consider the unorganized sector.

Unorganized Sector

As we have already mentioned, we denote the output of the unorganized sector by x. We assume for simplicity that x is produced with land, capital, labor, and intermediate inputs purchased from the organized sector. Stocks of land and capital are fixed. Labor and intermediate input requirements per unit of x are denoted by l and m, respectively. Producers of the unorganized sector use a part of their output for self-consumption and sell the rest. However, we assume for simplicity and without any loss of generality that the whole of x is marketed. Workers of the unorganized sector spend their whole income on x for purposes of consumption. Demand for x also comes from the organized sector. Workers of the organized sector buy it for purposes of consumption, while the producers use it as an intermediate input. Thus, in equilibrium, the following condition must be satisfied

$$\left(1 - \frac{w}{P_x} l\right) x = c_w \cdot \frac{W}{P_x} \bar{L}(1 - t) + ny \tag{7.48}$$

In (7.48), w denotes the money wage rate in the unorganized sector. c_w denotes the fixed average and marginal propensity to consume of the organized sector workers and n denotes per unit requirement of x as an intermediate input in the production of y.

We assume for simplicity that the producers of the unorganized sector hold their sales proceeds in the form of currency, use a part of it to meet their debt service charges, which are on past debts and, therefore, fixed in the period under consideration. They save the rest in the form of currency. The assumption that they hold their saving in the form of currency is made for simplicity.

BOP Equilibrium

We now focus on the BOP equilibrium condition of our model. Since we assume the exchange rate regime to be flexible, this is given by

$$\bar{N}\bar{X}\left(\underset{+}{\frac{P^{*}e}{P_{y}}}, y, \underset{+}{Y^{*}}\right) = 0 \tag{7.49}$$

Let us now consider the financial sector.

Financial Sector

The financial sector consists of banks only. The financial sector is oligopolistic. Oligopolistic interdependence makes the interest rate rigid. We assume that banks set their interest rate on the basis of the policy rate of the central bank. We denote it by r_{c}. The central bank lends to the commercial banks at r_{c}. Therefore, r is an increasing function of r_{c}. Thus, we have

$$r = r\left(\underset{+}{r_{\mathrm{c}}}\right) \tag{7.50}$$

At the given r, banks ration credit. Banks lend to the organized and the unorganized sectors. They allocate their loanable fund between the organized sector and the unorganized sector. On the basis of an assessment of the relative risks and returns of lending to the two sectors, they decide on the allocation of their loanable fund between the two sectors. Let us now discuss how banks' loanable fund is determined. We assume here that only workers of the organized sector hold their saving in bank deposit. Capitalists of the organized sector use their saving to finance their investment. Producers of the unorganized sector hold their saving, as we have already mentioned, in currency. Given these assumptions, the loanable fund of the financial sector denoted L^{b} is given by

$$L^{b} = (1-\rho)\left[(1-c_{w})\frac{W}{P_{y}}\bar{L}(1-t)\right] \tag{7.51}$$

We assume that the banks lend a fraction β of L^{b} to the organized sector. Even though β should depend upon the performances of the y-sector and x-sector, we assume that political donations play an overriding role in determining the value of β and make it an increasing function of D. Thus, the amount of loan the organized sector gets, which we denote by L^{by} is given by

$$L^{by} = \beta\left(\underset{+}{D}\right)\left[(1-\rho)\left\{(1-c_w)\frac{W}{P^y}\bar{L}(1-t)\right\}\right] \tag{7.52}$$

The remaining part of the loanable fund is given to the unorganized sector. Denoting it by L^{bx}, we get

$$L^{bx} = \left[1-\beta\left(\underset{+}{D}\right)\right]\cdot\left[(1-\rho)\left\{(1-c_w)\frac{W}{P^y}\bar{L}(1-t)\right\}\right] \tag{7.53}$$

Since investors in the organized sector are rationed, capitalists, as we have already mentioned, use their saving also to finance investment. Thus, investment in the organized sector denoted I^y is given by

$$\begin{aligned} I^y = {} & \beta\left(\underset{+}{D}\right)\left[(1-\rho)\left\{(1-c_w)\frac{W}{P^y}\bar{L}(1-t)\right\}\right] \\ & + (1-c_c)\left(\left(1-n\frac{P^x}{P^y}-\bar{m}\frac{P^*e}{P^y}\right)Y-\frac{W}{P^y}\bar{L}\right)(1-t) \end{aligned} \tag{7.54}$$

Of course, the capitalists need some fund to service their past debt also. However, since the amount of debt service charges is fixed in the period under consideration, we have not considered them explicitly here.

We assume for simplicity that the unorganized sector requires the loans principally to meet their working capital requirements, i.e., to purchase labor and the intermediate inputs. Producers in the unorganized sector are credit-constrained. Their ability to produce x depends upon the amount of credit they are able to secure to purchase labor and intermediate inputs. Since w is given, we make x an increasing function of L^{bx}.

$$x = a\cdot\left[1-\beta\left(\underset{+}{D}\right)\right]\cdot\left[(1-\rho)\left\{(1-c_w)\frac{W}{P_y}\bar{L}(1-t)\right\}\right] \tag{7.55}$$

Substituting (7.54) and (7.55) into (7.47), we rewrite it as

$$\begin{aligned} y = {} & c_c\cdot\left(\left(\left(1-n\frac{P^x}{P^y}-\bar{m}\frac{P^*e}{P}\right)y-\frac{W}{P_y}\bar{L}\right)(1-t)\right) \\ & + \beta(D)\left[(1-\rho)\left\{(1-c_w)(1-t)\frac{W}{P^y}\bar{L}\right\}\right] \\ & + (1-c_c)\left(\left(1-n\frac{P^x}{P^y}-\bar{m}\frac{P^*e}{P}\right)y-\frac{W}{P_y}\bar{L}\right)(1-t)+G \\ & + \bar{N}\bar{X}\left(\underset{+}{\frac{P^*e}{P^y}}, y, \underset{+}{Y^*}\right) + ma[1-\beta(D)]\left[(1-\rho)\left\{(1-c_w)(1-t)\frac{W}{P^y}\bar{L}\right\}\right] \end{aligned} \tag{7.56}$$

Again, substituting (7.55) into (7.48), we get

$$\left(1-\frac{w}{P_x}l\right)a\cdot\left[1-\beta\left(\underset{+}{D}\right)\right]\cdot\left[(1-\rho)\left\{(1-c_w)(1-t)\frac{W}{P_y}\bar{L}\right\}\right]=c_w\cdot\frac{W}{P_x}\bar{L}+ny \tag{7.57}$$

Finally, we make the assumption that P^y is set on the basis of cost. The most important determinants of the cost of the organized sector is W, P^x, and P^*e, since production of the organized sector in highly import-intensive. As we assume W and P^* to be fixed, we make P^y an increasing function of e and P^x.

Thus, we get

$$P^y=P^y\left(\underset{+}{e},\underset{+}{P^x}\right) \tag{7.58}$$

Substituting (7.58) into (7.49), we rewrite it as

$$\bar{N}\bar{X}\left(\frac{P^*e}{\underset{+}{P^y(P^x,e)}},y,\underset{+}{Y^*}\right)=0 \tag{7.59}$$

We can solve (7.59) for e as a function of y and P^x, among others. Thus, we get

$$e=e\left(\underset{+}{P^x},\underset{+}{y}\right) \tag{7.60}$$

We explain the signs of the partial derivatives of $e(\cdot)$ using Fig. 7.1, where the NX schedule plots the values of net export [given by the LHS of (7.59)] corresponding to different values of e for given values of P^x and y. We assume that, following a ceteris paribus increase in e, the real exchange rate rises despite the increase in P^y and this raises net export. Clearly, the increase in net export per unit increase in e is likely to be quite small. Hence, the NX schedule is quite flat. A ceteris paribus increase in y raises import demand and, thereby, lowers net export corresponding to every given e. Thus, the NX schedule in Fig. 7.1 shifts downward raising the equilibrium value of e. Similarly, a ceteris paribus increase in P^x raises P^y and, thereby, substantially lowers net export corresponding to any given e. Hence, equilibrium value of e will rise by a large amount. This explains the signs of the partial derivatives of (7.60). One can easily derive the signs of the partial derivatives of (7.60) mathematically.

Substituting (7.60) into (7.58), we rewrite it as

$$P^y=P^y\left(\underset{+}{e}(P^x,y),\underset{+}{P^x}\right)\equiv\bar{P}^y\left(\underset{+}{P^x},\underset{+}{y}\right) \tag{7.61}$$

Incorporating (7.61) into (7.57), we get

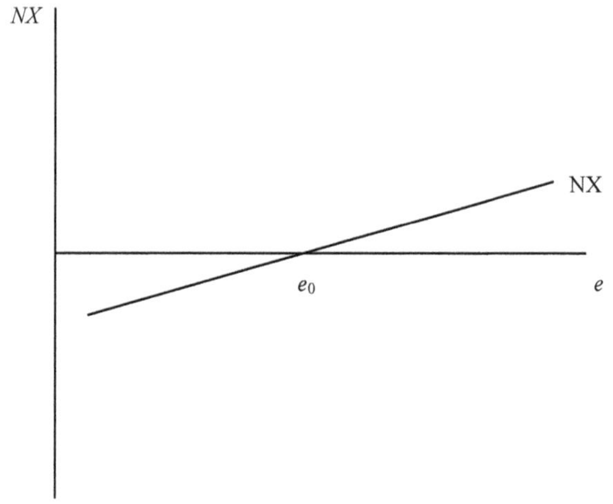

Fig. 7.1 Derivation of the equilibrium value of *e*

$$\left(1-\frac{w}{P_x}l\right)\cdot a\cdot\left[1-\beta\left(\underset{+}{D}\right)\right]\cdot\left[(1-\rho)\left\{(1-c_w)\frac{W}{\bar{P}^y(P_x,y)}\bar{L}(1-t)\right\}\right]$$
$$=c_w\cdot\frac{W}{P_x}\bar{L}(1-t)+ny \tag{7.62}$$

We can solve (7.62) for P^x as a function of, among others, y, D and $\bar{L}$. Thus, we have

$$P^x=P^x\left(\underset{+}{y};\underset{+}{D},\bar{L}\right) \tag{7.63}$$

We shall explain the signs of the partial derivatives of (7.63) using Fig. 7.2, where the equilibrium values of P^x and x correspond to the point of intersection of x^S and x^D schedules representing the LHS and RHS of (7.62), respectively, in the (x, P^x) plane. x^D schedule is clearly negatively sloped. Even though an increase in P^x exerts two opposite effects on the supply of x, we assume for simplicity and without any loss of generality that the supply of x rises following a ceteris paribus increase in P^x. Hence, x^S schedule is upward sloping. Following a ceteris paribus increase in y, x^S schedule shifts to the left, since supply of x corresponding to every P^x falls on account of the increase in P^y it induces. Again, a ceteris paribus increase in y leads to a rightward shift of the x^D schedule. Hence, equilibrium P^x rises. A ceteris paribus increase in D leads to a fall in the supply of x corresponding to any given value of P^x. Hence, x^S schedule shifts to the left, while x^D schedule remains unaffected. Hence, P^x rises. Following a ceteris paribus increase in $\bar{L}$, both demand for x and supply of x increase corresponding to any given P^x. If the increase in the supply of x corresponding to any given P^x is larger than that of the demand for x, P^x will fall. In the opposite case, it will increase.

Substituting (7.63) into (7.61), we get

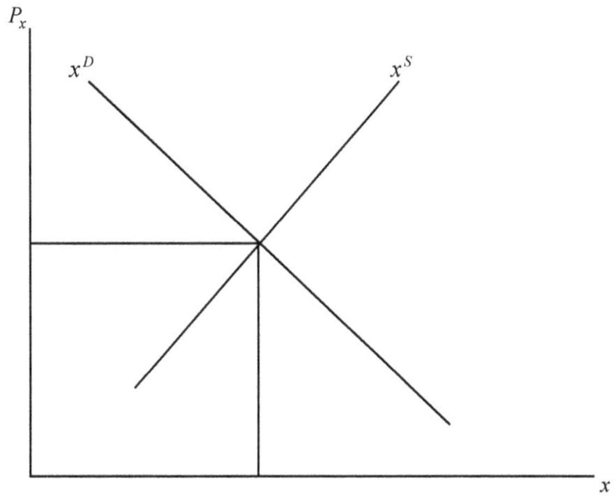

Fig. 7.2 Derivation of the equilibrium value of P_x

$$P^y = \bar{P}^y\left(P^x\left(\underset{+}{y};\ \underset{+}{D},\ \bar{L}\right),\ y\right) \equiv \tilde{P}^y\left(\underset{+}{y};\ \underset{+}{D},\ \bar{L}\right) \tag{7.64}$$

Substituting (7.63) into (7.60), we get

$$e = e\left(\underset{+}{P^x\left(\underset{+}{y},\ \underset{+}{D},\ \bar{L}\right)},\ \underset{+}{y}\right) \equiv \bar{e}\left(\underset{+}{y},\ \underset{+}{D},\ \bar{L}\right) \tag{7.64a}$$

Substituting (7.49), (7.63), (7.64), and (7.64a) into (7.57), we rewrite it as

$$\begin{aligned} y = c_c \cdot &\left(\left(\left(1 - n\theta - \bar{m}\hat{\theta}\right)y - \frac{W}{P^y(y;\ D,\ \bar{L})}\bar{L}\right)(1-t)\right) \\ &+ \beta(D)\left[(1-\rho)\left\{(1-c_w)(1-t)\frac{W}{P^y(y;\ D,\ \bar{L})}\bar{L}\right\}\right] \\ &+ (1-c_c)\left(\left(1 - n\theta - \bar{m}\hat{\theta}\right)y - \frac{W}{P^y(y;\ D,\ \bar{L})}\bar{L}\right)(1-t) \\ &+ G + ma[1-\beta(D)]\left[(1-\rho)\left\{(1-c_w)(1-t)\frac{W}{P^y(y;\ D,\ \bar{L})}\bar{L}\right\}\right] \end{aligned} \tag{7.65}$$

In (7.65), $\theta \equiv \frac{P^x(y;D,\bar{L})}{\tilde{P}^y(y,D,\bar{L})}$ and $\hat{\theta} \equiv \frac{P^*\bar{e}(y;D,\bar{L})}{\tilde{P}^y(y,D,\bar{L})}$. Following an increase in either y, D, or $\bar{L}$, both P^x and P^y change in the same direction. Hence, their ratio is likely to change by a very small amount. We shall not lose anything, if we assume the ratio to be fixed for simplicity. We make the same assumption regarding $\frac{P^*\bar{e}(\cdot)}{P^y(\cdot)}$ and assume it to be equal to $\bar{\theta}$. (7.65) contains only one endogenous variable y. We can, therefore, solve it for its equilibrium value. We are now in a position to examine how a given increase in D is likely to affect Y. We derive this below:

7.5.1 *Effect of an Increase in Political Donations to Secure a Larger Fraction of the Available Credit*

To derive the impact of an increase in D on Y, we take total differential (7.65) treating all variables other than D and Y as fixed and then solve for dY. This gives

$$\mathrm{d}Y = \frac{\begin{array}{c}(1-ma)\beta'\left[(1-\rho)\left\{(1-c_w)(1-t)\frac{W}{P^y}\bar{L}\right\}\right]\mathrm{d}D+ \\ [1-(\beta+ma(1-\beta))(1-\rho)(1-c_w)(1-t)]\frac{W}{(P^y)^2}\bar{L}\tilde{P}^y_D\mathrm{d}D\end{array}}{1-\left[\{c_c(1-n\theta-\bar{m}\bar{\theta})(1-t)\}+\{1-(\beta+ma(1-\beta))(1-\rho)(1-c_w)(1-t)\}\frac{W}{(P^y)^2}\bar{L}\tilde{P}^y_y\right]} \quad (7.66)$$

Let us now explain the expression on the RHS of (7.66). Focus on the numerator first. It gives the amount of excess demand for y that emerges at the initial equilibrium y following an increase in D by dD. Let us explain. Following an increase in D by dD, supply of new credit to the organized sector rises by $\beta' \cdot \left[(1-\rho)\left\{(1-c_w)(1-t)\frac{W}{P^y}\bar{L}\right\}\right]\mathrm{d}D$. The whole of this will be used to finance additional investment demand for y. However, supply of new credit to the unorganized sector will fall by the same amount. Since the unorganized sector uses new credit to purchase not only organized sector's output but also labor, the fall in the unorganized sector's demand for y will be less than the fall in the supply of new credit to the unorganized sector. This means that ma is less than unity and, in the net aggregate demand for y rises. This is given by the first term of the numerator. The fall in the supply of new credit to the unorganized sector reduces supply of x creating an excess demand for x at the initial equilibrium P^x. P^x will, therefore, rise and equilibrate the unorganized sector. The increase in P^x will raise P^y and lower organized sector's workers' disposable income in terms of y by $(1-t)\frac{W}{(P^y)^2}\bar{L}\tilde{P}^y_D\mathrm{d}D$. Capitalists' disposable income will rise exactly by the same amount, and they will spend the whole of it to raise their consumption and investment demand for y. The fall in organized sector workers' disposable income will reduce their saving and, therefore, supply of new credit by $[(1-\rho)\{(1-c_w)\}](1-t)\frac{W}{(P^y)^2}\bar{L}\tilde{P}^y_D\mathrm{d}D$. This, in turn, will reduce demand for y by $(\beta+ma(1-\beta))[(1-\rho)\{(1-c_w)\}](1-t)\frac{W}{(P^y)^2}\bar{L}\tilde{P}^y_D\mathrm{d}D$, which is just a small fraction of the fall in the disposable income of the organized sector workers. Hence, on account of the rise in P^x at the initial equilibrium y, aggregate demand for y will increase in the net by $[1-(\beta+ma(1-\beta))(1-\rho)(1-c_w)](1-t)\frac{W}{(P^y)^2}\bar{L}\tilde{P}^y_D\mathrm{d}D$, which is the second term of the numerator. Thus, at the initial equilibrium y, there emerges an excess demand for y given by the numerator denoted by N^o. This will induce the producers of y to raise y setting off a multiplier process. Since a unit increase in y at the initial equilibrium P^y raises consumption demand for y by

$c_c \cdot \left(1 - n\theta - \bar{m}\hat{\theta}\right)(1-t)$, y in the first round will go up by $\mathrm{d}y_1 = \frac{N^o}{d^o}$, where $d^o \equiv 1 - c_c \cdot \left(1 - n\theta - \bar{m}\hat{\theta}\right)(1-t)$. However, this increase in y will lower net export creating a BOP deficit at the initial equilibrium e. The increase in y will also generate an excess demand for x at the initial equilibrium P^x. The BOP deficit will raise e so that net export rises to its initial equilibrium value. The excess demand for x will raise P^x so that equilibrium is restored in the unorganized sector. Both these increases in e and P^x will raise P^y. It will go up by $\tilde{P}^y_y \mathrm{d}y_1$. The increase in P^y will lower organized sector workers' disposable income in terms of y by $(1-t)\frac{W}{(P^y)^2}\bar{L}\tilde{P}^y_D \mathrm{d}D$. Capitalists' disposable income will rise exactly by the same amount, and they will spend the whole of it to raise their consumption and investment demand for y. The fall in organized sector workers' disposable income will reduce their saving and, therefore, supply of new credit in terms of y by $[(1-\rho)\{(1-c_w)\}](1-t)\frac{W}{(P^y)^2}\bar{L}\tilde{P}^y_y \mathrm{d}y_1$. This, in turn, will reduce demand for y by $(\beta + ma(1-\beta))[(1-\rho)\{(1-c_w)\}](1-t)\frac{W}{(P^y)^2}\bar{L}\tilde{P}^y_y \mathrm{d}y_1$, which is just a small fraction of the fall in the disposable income of the organized sector workers. Hence, on account of the rise in P^x and e induced by the increase in y by dy_1, aggregate demand for y will increase in the net by $[1 - (\beta + ma(1-\beta))(1-\rho)(1-c_w)](1-t)\frac{W}{(P^y)^2}\bar{L}\tilde{P}^y_y \mathrm{d}y_1 \equiv \bar{d}^o \mathrm{d}y_1$. This will again start the multiplier process and raise y in the second round by $\mathrm{d}y_2 = \frac{\bar{d}^o}{d^o}\mathrm{d}y_1$. This will again raise e and P^x and, thereby, P^y by $P^y_y \mathrm{d}y_2$ redistributing income from the workers to the capitalists in the organized sector. This will again, as before, create an excess demand for y of $\bar{d}^o \mathrm{d}y_2$ setting off a multiplier process. Hence, in the third round, y will increase by $\mathrm{d}y_3 = \frac{\bar{d}^o}{d^o}\mathrm{d}y_2 = \left(\frac{\bar{d}^o}{d^o}\right)^2 \mathrm{d}y_1$. This process of cumulative expansion in y will continue until the increase in demand that takes place in each successive round eventually falls to zero. Thus, the total increase in y is given by

$$\mathrm{d}y = \mathrm{d}y_1 + \frac{\bar{d}^o}{d}\mathrm{d}y_1 + \left(\frac{\bar{d}^o}{d}\right)^2 \mathrm{d}y_1 + \cdots = \frac{d^o}{d^o - \bar{d}^o}\mathrm{d}y_1 = \frac{N^o}{d^o - \bar{d}^o} \tag{7.67}$$

One can easily check that (7.67) tallies with (7.66).

Let us now focus on the economic condition of the workers, which is given by their consumption level. It is given by the output of the unorganized sector net of the part that is used as intermediate input of the organized sector. The consumption level of the workers, denoted by CW, is, therefore, given by

$$\mathrm{CW} = a \cdot \left[1 - \beta\left(\underset{+}{D}\right)\right] \cdot \left[(1-\rho)\left\{(1-c_w)\frac{W}{\tilde{P}^y\left(y;\, D, \bar{L}\right)}\bar{L}(1-t)\right\}\right] - ny \tag{7.68}$$

Taking total differential of (7.68) taking all variables other than D and y as fixed, we get

$$\mathrm{d(CWCW)} = -\left\{\begin{array}{c} a \cdot \beta' \cdot \left[(1-\rho)\left\{(1-c_w)\dfrac{W}{\tilde{P}^y(y;D,\bar{L})}\bar{L}(1-t)\right\}\right] + \\ a(1-\beta) \cdot \left[(1-\rho)\left\{(1-c_w)\dfrac{W}{(P^y)^2}\bar{L}(1-t)\right\}\tilde{P}_D^y\right] \end{array}\right\} \mathrm{d}D$$
$$-\left[a(1-\beta)\cdot\left[(1-\rho)\left\{(1-c_w)\frac{W}{(P^y)^2}\bar{L}(1-t)\right\}\right]\tilde{P}_y^y + n\right]\mathrm{d}y \tag{7.69}$$

Substituting (7.67) into (7.69), we rewrite it as

$$\mathrm{d(CW)} = -\left\{\begin{array}{c} a \cdot \beta' \cdot \left[(1-\rho)\left\{(1-c_w)\dfrac{W}{\tilde{P}^y(y;D,\bar{L})}\bar{L}(1-t)\right\}\right] + \\ a(1-\beta) \cdot \left[(1-\rho)\left\{(1-c_w)\dfrac{W}{(P^y)^2}\bar{L}(1-t)\right\}\tilde{P}_D^y\right] \end{array}\right\} \mathrm{d}D$$
$$-\left[a(1-\beta)\cdot\left[(1-\rho)\left\{(1-c_w)\frac{W}{(P^y)^2}\bar{L}(1-t)\right\}\right]\tilde{P}_y^y + n\right]\left(\frac{N^o}{d^o-\tilde{d}^o}\right) \tag{7.70}$$

Let us consider the expression on the RHS of (7.70). Following a ceteris paribus increase in D, supply of new credit to the unorganized sector falls reducing its output at the initial equilibrium (y, P^x, P^y). The excess demand for x that emerges at the initial equilibrium P^x induces an increase in P^x to restore equilibrium. This, however, leads to an increase in P^y reducing organized sector's workers' income in terms of y. This lowers supply of new credit to the unorganized sector in terms of y further bringing about a contraction in the supply of x. This leads to an increase in P^x and, thereby, that in P^y again at the initial equilibrium y. Thus, there will occur a cumulative increase in P^x and P^y bringing about a cumulative contraction in x at the initial equilibrium y. The cumulative contraction in x that occurs at the initial equilibrium y on account of the factors mentioned above is given by the first term of the expression on the RHS of (7.70). Besides this, as given by (7.66) and (7.67), the cumulative increase in y that takes place following a ceteris paribus increase in D through the process described in detail earlier lowers drastically the amount of x available for workers' consumption. This is given by the second term of the expression on the RHS of (7.70). Thus, there takes place a substantial decline in workers' consumption level. It is often said that, even though the organized sector grows without creating jobs, its growth brings about an expansion in the demand for employment-intensive unorganized sector's output. We show that such additional demand for x leads to a contraction in x and takes away resources from the production of workers' consumption goods. Both of these bring about a sharp deterioration in the economic condition of the workers. This yields the following proposition:

Proposition 7.5 *An increase in D that induces the government and the central bank to change the lending norms of banks in favor of the organized sector and against the* *unorganized sector has the following outcome. It leads to a cumulative expansion of the organized sector's output and a cumulative contraction in the output of the unorganized sector. Both of these lead to a sharp deterioration in the economic condition of the workers. The growth in the organized sector creates demand for the unorganized sector's output. But this, instead of improving the lot of the workers, diverts resources away from the production of mass consumption goods and, thereby, brings about a sharp deterioration in the living condition of the workers.*

7.6 Political Donations, Forcible Acquisition of Land, Employment, and the Common Man

In the previous section, we examined the implications of political donations aimed at securing a larger proportion of the available credit for the organized sector. Here, we shall examine how workers will fare if donation-driven political parties forcibly acquire land from the unorganized sector and give them away to the giant capitalists of the organized sector. To put the issue in sharp relief, we shall assume that the organized sector's investors are not credit-rationed and the only constraint that operates on the organized sector's investment is the amount of land they get from the government. On the other hand, unorganized sector producers are both credit-constrained and also land-constrained. We assume that the producers of the unorganized sector use land, labor, and intermediate inputs to produce x and they need credit to buy intermediate input and labor. An increase in the availability of land raises unorganized sector's production even with unchanged supply of credit. This happens because producers are heterogeneous. Not all producers are credit-constrained. There are credit-constrained producers with underutilized family labor. Even with no extra credit available, they can utilize the land for production using traditional techniques. There are many firms where production is carried out with family labor without the use of intermediate inputs bought from the organized sector. Moreover, for many producers, availability of credit depends upon the amount of land they own. Therefore, an increase in the stock of land owned by the producers of the unorganized sector will augment its output, and this will happen even if supply of credit remains unchanged. However, for simplicity, we shall capture the effect of an increase in the stock of land in the possession of the unorganized sector on its output through the assumption that it increases supply of credit to the unorganized sector. Taking these factors into account, we rewrite the equilibrium condition of the organized sector, (7.47), as follows:

$$y = \left(\left(\left(1 - n\frac{P^x}{P^y} - \bar{m}\frac{P^*e}{P^y}\right)y(1-t) - \frac{W}{P^y}\bar{L}\right)(1-t)\right) + I\left(\underset{-}{r}, \underset{+}{N^g(D)}\right) + mx$$
$$+ G + \bar{N}\bar{X}\left(\underset{+}{\frac{P^*e}{P^y}}, \underset{-}{y}; \underset{+}{Y^*}\right) \quad (7.71)$$

Let us explain (7.71). Let us first note the difference between (7.47) and (7.71). The difference between (7.47) and (7.71) is that in the latter investment is an increasing function of $N^g(D)$, which denotes the amount of land the government takes away from the producers of the unorganized sector and gives to the capitalists for industrialization. We further assume for simplicity that $I(r, N^g(D))$ represents the part of investment that the capitalists finance with new bank credit. Over and above this, they also use their saving for purposes of investment. This makes investment an increasing function of profit as well. Therefore, aggregate investment is given by $I(r, N^g(D)) + (1 - c_c)\pi^y$, where $\pi^y \equiv \left[\left(1 - n\frac{P^x}{P^y} - \bar{m}\frac{P^*e}{P^y}\right)y - \frac{W}{P^y}\bar{L}\right](1 - t)$. Hence, aggregate demand for y is given by

$$c_c\pi^y + I\big(r, N^g(D)\big) + (1 - c_c)\pi^y + mx + G + \bar{N}\bar{X}(\cdot) = \pi^y + I(\cdot) + mx + G + \bar{N}\bar{X}(\cdot).$$

This explains (7.71).

Equation (7.48) gives the equilibrium condition of the unorganized sector as before. The BOP equilibrium condition is still given by (7.49). Equations describing the financial sector, however, become somewhat different. Equation (7.50) still holds. One major difference is that the capitalists of the organized sector are not rationed in the credit market. Only producers of the unorganized sector are rationed. Supply of new bank credit to them is given by

$$L^{bx} = \alpha \cdot \left[(1 - \rho) \cdot (1 - c_w)\frac{W}{P^y}\bar{L}(1 - t) - I\big(r, N^g(D)\big)\right] \tag{7.72}$$

In (7.72), the fraction of loan that the banks give to the producers of the unorganized sector is denoted by α. Using (7.72) and (7.50), we rewrite (7.55) as

$$x = a \cdot \alpha \cdot \left[(1 - \rho) \cdot (1 - c_w)\frac{W}{P^y}\bar{L}(1 - t)\right] - I\big(r(r_c), N^g(D)\big) \tag{7.73}$$

Regarding prices, Eqs. (7.58), (7.60), and (7.61) still hold. Using them and (7.73), we write the equilibrium condition of the unorganized sector as follows:

$$\left(1 - \frac{w}{P^x}l\right) \cdot a \cdot \alpha \cdot \left[(1 - \rho)\left\{(1 - c_w)\frac{W}{\bar{P}^y(P^x, y)}\bar{L}(1 - t)\right\} - I\big(r(r_c), N^g(D)\big)\right]$$
$$= c_w \cdot \frac{W}{P^x}\bar{L}(1 - t) + ny \tag{7.74}$$

We can solve (7.74) for P^x as a function of y and D, among others. Thus, we get

$$P^x = \bar{P}^x\Big(\underset{+}{y};\ \underset{+}{D}\Big) \tag{7.75}$$

Let us derive the signs of the partial derivatives of (7.75). Taking total differential of (7.74) treating all variables other than y and P^x as fixed and, then, solving for $\frac{\mathrm{d}P^x}{\mathrm{d}y}$, we get

$$\frac{\mathrm{d}P^x}{\mathrm{d}y} = \frac{(\Delta_y - S_y)\mathrm{d}y}{S_{P^x} - \Delta_{P^x}} > 0 \tag{7.76}$$

In (7.76), Δ denotes organized sector's demand for x given by the RHS of (7.74) and S denotes supply of x to the organized sector given by the LHS of (7.74).

$$\Delta_y = n > 0 \tag{7.77}$$

$$\Delta_{P^x} = -c_w \cdot \frac{W}{(P^x)^2}\bar{L}(1-t) < 0 \tag{7.78}$$

$$S_y = -\left(1 - \frac{w}{P^x}l\right) \cdot a \cdot \alpha \cdot \left[(1-\rho)\left\{(1-c_w)\frac{W}{(P^y)^2}\bar{L}(1-t)\right\}\bar{P}^y_y\right] < 0 \tag{7.79}$$

$$\begin{aligned} S_{P^x} &= \frac{Wl}{(P^x)^2}ax - \left[\left(1 - \frac{W}{P^x}l\right)a \cdot \alpha \cdot (1-\rho)(1-c_w)\frac{W}{(P^y)^2}\bar{L}(1-t)\bar{P}^y_{P_x}\right] \\ &\equiv \bar{A} - \bar{B}\bar{P}^y_{P_x} \end{aligned} \tag{7.80}$$

Even though the sign of S_{P^x}, which measures the increase in the supply of x to the organized sector (denoted by S) induced by a unit increase in P^x, is ambiguous, we shall assume it to be positive for simplicity. A unit increase P^x produces two opposite effects on S. On the one hand, it reduces unorganized sector's workers' real income in terms of x and, thereby, lowers their demand of x by the same amount. At the given x, therefore, S also rises by the same amount. This is given by the first term of the expression on the RHS of (7.80). However, a unit increase in P^x raises P^y. This reduces the real value of the new credit supplied to the unorganized sector in terms of y. Hence, producers of the unorganized sector have to lower their output. This lowers S. This is given by the second term of the expression on the RHS of (7.79). We assume that the first term is larger than the second term. Even if we do not make this assumption, the denominator of (7.76) has to be positive for stability. Hence, the assumption made here does not affect our results qualitatively.

We are now in a position to explain (7.76). Following a ceteris paribus increase in y, demand for x of the organized sector rises, while supply of x to the organized sector falls creating an excess demand for x at the initial equilibrium P^x. This excess demand is given by the numerator of the expression on the RHS of (7.76). P^x, therefore, rises to clear the market for x. Per unit increase in P^x, excess demand for x falls by the amount given by the denominator of the expression on the RHS of (7.76). This explains (7.76).

Let us now derive the impact of a given increase in D on P^x. Again, taking total differential of (7.74) treating all variables other than P^x and D as fixed and, then, solving for $\frac{\mathrm{d}P^x}{\mathrm{d}D}$, we get

$$\frac{\mathrm{d}P^x}{\mathrm{d}D} = \frac{-S_D}{S_{P^x} - \Delta_{P^x}} > 0 \tag{7.81}$$

$$S_D = -\left[\left(1 - \frac{w}{P^x}l\right)a\left\{\alpha I_{N^g} N^{g'}\right\}\right] < 0 \tag{7.82}$$

It is quite easy to explain the expression on the RHS of (7.81). Following an increase in D and the consequent transfer of land from the unorganized sector to the organized sector, banks divert credit supply from the producers of the unorganized sector to those of the organized sector. This will lower x creating an excess demand of $-S_D$ at the initial equilibrium P^x. Hence, given the meaning of the denominator we have explained earlier, P^x will go up by the expression on the RHS of (7.81). In fact, the increase in P^x will be quite large and cumulative. Let us explain the process. Following a unit increase in D, there will emerge an excess demand for x of $-S_D$. P^x will rise to clear the x-market. Given P^y, P^x in the first round will go up by $\mathrm{d}P^{x1} = \frac{-S_D}{\bar{A}-\Delta_{Px}}$ (see 7.79, 7.80, and 7.82). This increase in P^x will raise P^y by $P^y_{P_x}\mathrm{d}P^{x1}$. This will reduce supply of x and create an excess demand for x of $\bar{B}P^y_{P_x}\mathrm{d}P^{x1}$(see 7.80). P^x will, therefore, rise again. It will rise in the second round by $\mathrm{d}P^{x2} = \frac{\bar{B}P^y_{P_x}\mathrm{d}P^{x1}}{\bar{A}-\Delta_{P_x}} \equiv \gamma \mathrm{d}P^{x1}$. This will, again, raise P^y by $P^y_{P_x}\mathrm{d}P^{x2}$ creating an excess demand for x of $\bar{B}P^y_{P_x}dP^{x2}$. This will raise P^x in the third round by $\mathrm{d}P^{x3} = \frac{\bar{B}P^y_{P_x}\mathrm{d}P^{x2}}{\bar{A}-\Delta_{Px}} \equiv \gamma \mathrm{d}P^{x2} = \gamma^2\mathrm{d}P^{x1}$. This process will continue until the excess demand that is created in each successive round eventually falls to zero. It is clear that for the process to be convergent γ has to be less than unity. Thus, the total increase in P^x is given by

$$\mathrm{d}P^x = \mathrm{d}P^{x1} + \gamma\mathrm{d}P^{x1} + \gamma^2\mathrm{d}P^{x1} + \cdots = \frac{1}{1-\gamma}\mathrm{d}P^{x1} = \frac{-S_D}{\bar{A} - \bar{B}P^y_{Px} - \Delta_{Px}}$$

From the above, it follows that following a given increase in D, there will take place a large and cumulative increase in both P^x and P^y.

Substituting (7.75) into (7.61), we rewrite it as

$$P^y = \bar{P}^y\left(\bar{P}^x\left(\underset{+}{y};\underset{+}{D}\right), \underset{+}{y}\right) \equiv \tilde{P}^y\left(\underset{+}{y}, \underset{+}{D}\right) \tag{7.83}$$

Again, substituting (7.75) into (7.60), we rewrite it as

$$e = e\left(\underset{+}{\bar{P}^x\left(\underset{+}{y}, \underset{+}{D}\right)}, \underset{+}{y}\right) \equiv \tilde{e}\left(\underset{+}{y}, \underset{+}{D}\right) \tag{7.83a}$$

Substituting (7.49), (7.73), (7.75), (7.83), and (7.83a) into (7.71), we rewrite it as follows:

$$y = \left(\left(\left(1 - n\frac{\bar{P}^x(y, D)}{\tilde{P}^y(y, D)} - \bar{m}\frac{P^*\tilde{e}(y, D)}{\tilde{P}^y(y, D)}\right)y - \frac{W}{\tilde{P}^y(y, D)}\bar{L}\right)(1-t)\right) + I\left(\underset{-}{r(r_c)}, \underset{+}{N^g(D)}\right)$$

$$+ma\cdot\alpha\cdot\left[(1-\rho)(1-c_w)\frac{W}{\tilde{P}^y(y,D)}\bar{L}(1-t)-I\big(r(r_c),N^g(D)\big)\right]+G \tag{7.84}$$

Since, following given changes in y and D, P^y and P^x change in the same direction, the change in their ratio is likely to be quite small. Hence, for simplicity, we assume the ratio to be fixed and denote it by $\bar{\theta}$. The same argument holds for $\frac{P^*\tilde{e}(\cdot)}{\tilde{P}^y(\cdot)}$. Hence, we assume it to be fixed and denote it by $\tilde{\theta}$. Incorporating these in (7.84), we rewrite it as

$$\begin{aligned} y = .&\left(\left(\left(1-n\bar{\theta}-\bar{m}\tilde{\theta}\right)y-\frac{W}{\tilde{P}^y(y,D)}\bar{L}\right)(1-t)\right)+I\Big(\underset{-}{r(r_c)},\underset{+}{N^g(D)}\Big)\\ &+ma\cdot\alpha\cdot\left[(1-\rho)(1-c_w)\frac{W}{\tilde{P}^y(y,D)}\bar{L}(1-t)-I\Big(\underset{-}{r(r_c)},\underset{+}{N^g(D)}\Big)\right]+G \end{aligned} \tag{7.85}$$

To derive the impact of an increase in D on y, we take total differential of (7.85) treating all variables other than y and D as fixed and, then, solving for dy, we get

$$\mathrm{d}y=\frac{\left[\begin{array}{l}\left\{I_{N^g}N^{g'}-ma\left(\alpha I_{N^g}N^{g'}\right)\right\}+\\ \left\{(1-ma\alpha(1-\rho)(1-c_w))\frac{W}{(P^y)^2}\bar{L}(1-t)P_D^y\right\}\end{array}\right]\mathrm{d}D}{1-\left(1-n\bar{\theta}-\bar{m}\tilde{\theta}\right)(1-t)-\left\{(1-ma\alpha(1-\rho)(1-c_w))\frac{W}{(P^y)^2}\bar{L}(1-t)P_y^y\right\}} \tag{7.86}$$

Following an increase in the donation-induced forcible acquisition of land and the transfer of such land to the capitalists of the organized sector, investment in the organized sector gets a boost. On the other hand, output of the unorganized sector will shrink due to fall in credit supply reducing demand for the output of the organized sector. However, the whole of the additional credit given to the organized sector will be spent on the output of the organized sector, while quite a large part of the credit given to the unorganized sector is used to pay for labor and inputs secured from within the unorganized sector. Moreover, the fall in credit supply to the unorganized sector is much less than the increase in credit supply to the organized sector, since α is usually quite small. Thus, $ma\alpha$ is substantially less than unity and demand for y in the net will increase by a large amount. This increase in demand for y is given by the first term in the numerator. Let us now come to the second term in the numerator. The reduction of x creates excess demand for x at the initial equilibrium (P^x, y). There will, therefore, take place a large and cumulative increase in P^x and P^y, as described above at the initial equilibrium y. This will redistribute income from the organized sector workers to the capitalists. Capitalists will spend the whole of their additional profit for purposes of consumption and investment. However, the increase in P^y will reduce the value of new credit supply to the unorganized sector in terms of y by only a small fraction of the increase in profit in terms of y, since $\alpha(1-\rho)(1-c_w)$ is substantially less than unity. This will, therefore, reduce unorganized sector's demand for y by a small fraction of the increase in profit in terms of y. In the net, therefore, demand for y will rise substantially. This increase in demand for y due to the rise in P^y at the initial equilibrium y is given by the second term of the numerator. It is positive and large since 1 is much larger than $ma\alpha(1-c_w)$ for reasons we have already explained.

Thus, there is likely to emerge a large excess demand for y at the initial equilibrium y given by the numerator of the expression on the RHS of (7.86), which we shall denote by N_l. Producers of y will, therefore, begin to raise y setting off a multiplier process. In the first round, y will go up by $\mathrm{d}y^{(1)} = \frac{N_l}{1-c_c\left(1-\bar{\theta}n-\tilde{m}\tilde{\theta}\right)(1-t)} \equiv \frac{N_l}{\lambda_1}$. The increase in y will raise demand for x creating an excess demand in the x-market. This will set off a cumulative process of increase in P^x, and P^y described earlier. The rise in P^y will redistribute income from the organized sector workers to the capitalists raising their consumption and investment demand by the amount of the whole of the additional profit. The rise in P^y will also lower the value of the supply of new credit to the unorganized sector in terms of y. However, this fall in the supply of new credit to the unorganized sector in terms of y, as we have already explained, is just a small fraction of the increase in profit in terms of y. This will reduce unorganized sector's demand for y by a small fraction of the increase in capitalists' spending on y. In the net, therefore, demand for y will go up by $(1-ma\alpha(1-c_w))\frac{W}{(P^y)^2}\bar{L}(1-t)P_y^y\mathrm{d}y^{(1)} \equiv \lambda\mathrm{d}y^{(1)}$. This is likely to be positive and large for reasons we have already explained. Hence, y in the second round will increase by $\mathrm{d}y^{(2)} = \frac{\lambda}{\lambda_1}\mathrm{d}y^{(1)}$. Similarly, the increase in y in the second round will again bring about a large and cumulative increase in P^y creating again an excess demand for y of $\lambda\mathrm{d}y^{(2)}$. Hence, y in the third round will go up by $\mathrm{d}y^{(3)} = \frac{\lambda}{\lambda_1}\mathrm{d}y^{(2)} = \left(\frac{\lambda}{\lambda_1}\right)^2\mathrm{d}y^{(1)}$. This process will continue until the excess demand for y created in each successive round eventually falls to zero. Thus, the total increase in y is given by

$$\mathrm{d}y = \mathrm{d}y^{(1)} + \frac{\lambda}{\lambda_1}\mathrm{d}y^{(1)} + \left(\frac{\lambda}{\lambda_1}\right)^2\mathrm{d}y^{(1)} + \cdots = \frac{\lambda_1}{\lambda_1-\lambda}\mathrm{d}y^{(1)} = \frac{N_l}{\lambda_1-\lambda} \tag{7.87}$$

It is clear that (7.87) tallies with (7.86). This cumulative increase in y that takes place brings about a large increase in demand for x for being used as an intermediate input in the organized sector. This increase in demand is accommodated through reduction in workers' consumption brought about through the increase in P^x. Thus, the expansion in the organized sector creates additional demand for the output of the employment-intensive unorganized sector. However, such increase in demand instead of relaxing the constraints operating on the supply of x tightens them and diverts resources away from workers' consumption. Output of the unorganized sector not only contracts, a larger part of it also gets utilized to meet the intermediate input demand of the organized sector. Both of these lead to a sharp decline in the level of workers' consumption and living standard. We can sum up our above discussion in the form of the following proposition:

Proposition 7.6 *Following a political donation-driven forcible acquisition of land from the unorganized sector and its transfer to the organized sector, there is a strong possibility that there will take place a large and cumulative expansion in the output of the organized sector accompanied by a large and cumulative contraction in the output of the unorganized sector. The growth in the output of the organized sector will generate additional demand for the output of the unorganized sector for being used as intermediate input in the organized sector. Both the shrinkage in the output of the unorganized sector and the increase in its demand for being used as intermediate input in the organized sector are accommodated through a steep rise in the prices that bring about a sharp fall in the consumption levels of workers of both the sectors. The expansion of the organized sector, though creates additional demand for the employment-intensive unorganized sector, generates inflation and worsens workers' living conditions sharply.*

7.7 Conclusion

A capitalist society is characterized by private funding-based multiparty democracy. The giant capitalists who have in their command most of the country's wealth and income fund these political parties, control them, and make them work in their favor to protect and expand their business empire. Thus, democracy is a sham in a capitalist society. Political parties in power help the giant capitalists increase their command over the country's resources legally and illegally. Accordingly, private funding of political parties is at the root of all corruption and the woes of common man in a capitalist society. In this chapter, we have explored the macroeconomic implications of some of the illegal and legal favors given by the political parties in power to the capitalists. Illegal favors that we have taken into account are tax evasion, illegal parking of savings in foreign assets, and bank frauds. We have found that these illegal activities generate strong recessionary forces substantially lowering the country's growth rate of output and employment. Recessions and bank frauds lead to a sharp increase in banks' and other financial institutions' non-performing assets driving them into deep financial trouble. To keep the financial institutions and, thereby, the economy afloat, the government has to infuse large amounts of fund into them. This puts a lot of pressure on the government's budget. To reduce the pressure on government's budget, the governments pass or seek to pass laws that empower the financial institutions to confiscate the savings kept with them and use them to tide over the crisis. India seeks to pass FRDI Bill with this end in view. We have shown in the chapter that such a measure will lead to collapse of both the financial institutions and the economy.

Legally, the political parties in power seek to pass laws that help the capitalists increase their command over resources. The governments pass laws so that capitalists can incorporate labor-saving technological and managerial changes without any hindrance. This gives rise to the phenomenon of jobless growth. Governments and central bank specify lending norms for banks and other financial institutions in such a manner that they favor large borrowers despite substantially higher default rate on the part of large borrowers compared to small and medium borrowers. Governments in capitalist countries also pass laws to confiscate land forcibly from small and medium producers and give them away free of cost to giant capitalists. We have examined the macroeconomic implications of these laws and norms in this chapter. For this purpose, we have divided the economy into two sectors, the organized sector and the unorganized sector. The former consists of large companies subject to company laws. It also displays jobless growth. The unorganized sector consists of small and medium firms and is labor-intensive. We have shown that, if, induced by donations from giant capitalists, the government modifies lending norms of banks in favor of the large producers of the organized sector at the expense of small and medium producers of the unorganized sector, or if the government confiscates land from the producers of the unorganized sector and gives it away to those of the organized sector, there is a strong likelihood that the impact will be devastating for the working class. To be more specific, there is a strong possibility that there will take place a cumulative expansion of the organized sector matched by a cumulative contraction of the unorganized sector. The cumulative expansion of the organized sector will lead to a cumulative increase in its demand for the unorganized sector's output. This will drastically reduce resources available within the unorganized sector for the production of mass consumption goods. Both these cumulative contraction in the output of the unorganized sector and the cumulative increase in the demand of the organized sector for the unorganized sector's output will reduce the consumption level of the workers making them substantially worse-off.

The practice of private funding of political parties in capitalist societies characterized by multiparty democracy gives the giant capitalists complete control over political parties. Through them, the giant capitalists usurp state power and use it to corner through both legal and illegal means as much productive resources of the society as possible. The workers as a result live in considerable poverty, with large-scale and growing unemployment, no bargaining strength, and bad and worsening work conditions. Income disparity widens rapidly and relentlessly. Unless the workers become aware of the reason for their plight, unemployment and poverty, get united and force the government to stop private funding of political parties, there is no hope for them. To wrest the political parties from the clutches of the giant capitalists, to make them represent the causes of the masses, the government should be made to stop private funding of political parties. The government should be made to build infrastructure to give all political parties equal opportunities for airing their views free of charge. Unless workers unite and force the governments to do this, there is no hope for them.

References

Aidt, T. S. (2003, November). Economic analysis of corruption: A survey. *Economic Journal, 113*(8), F-632–F-652.

Bardhan, P. K. (1997, September). Corruption and development: A review of the issues. *Journal of Economic Literature, 35*(3), 587–605.

Chang, H. (2002, September). Breaking the mould: An institutional political economy alternative to the neo-liberal theory of the market and the state. *Cambridge Journal of Economics, 26*(5), 359–559.

Ghosh, C., & Ghosh, A. (2016). *Indian Economy: A macro-theoretic analysis*. Delhi: PHI Learning Private Limited.

Hopkins, J. (2002, August). States, markets and corruption: A review of some recent literature. *Review of International Political Economy, 9*(3), 574–590.

Jain, A. K. (2001, February). Corruption: A review. *Journal of Economic Surveys, 15*(1), 71–120.

Nye, J. S. (1967, June). Corruption and political development: A cost-benefit analysis. *American Political Science Review, 61*(2), 417–427.

Oxfam India. (2018). *India Inequality Report*, Delhi.

Reserve Bank of India. (2018). *Financial stability report*, June 26, 2018. https://rbi.org.in/Scripts/PublicationReportDetails.aspx?UrlPage=&ID=906.

Shleifer, A., & Vishney, R. W. (1993, August). Corruption. *Quarterly Journal of Economics, 108*(3), 599–617.

Warren, M. E. (2004, April). What does corruption mean in a democracy? *American Journal of Political Science, 48*(2), 328–343.

Chapter 8
The Greek Crisis

Abstract The Greek economy went through a period of unprecedented boom during 1996–2007. However, it plunged into a deep recession since 2008. The contraction of the Greek economy since 2008 drove the Greek Government into a sovereign debt crisis in 2010. The Greek Government sought the assistance of the European Commission, European Central Bank, and the IMF, henceforth referred to as the troika, to service its debt. The troika obliged, but in exchange imposed on Greece stringent austerity measures. The objective of this chapter is to explain the above-mentioned booms and recessions in the Greek economy and the cause of the sovereign debt crisis in Greece. It also carefully analyzes the implications of the austerity measures and attributes the perpetuation and deepening of the recession in the Greek economy since 2010 to them. It also suggests the measures that would have raised Greece's growth rate to a high level and resolved Greece's sovereign debt crisis.

8.1 Introduction

Before World War I, western capitalists colonized the whole world to expand their business empire and the state of the ordinary toiling masses was miserable. However, the greed of the capitalists led them into two world wars where they fought bitterly with one another and became considerably weak. This allowed the ordinary people to wrest power after World War I in Tsarist Russia, which eventually expanded into Soviet Union, and also, after World war II, in China, Cuba, and many other places. Many of the colonies after World War II gained independence, and some of them including India pursued socialist goals and adopted Soviet model of planned economic development. Thus, in the post-World War II period, the world was divided into two blocs, the socialist and the capitalist. The former was led by the Soviet Union and the latter by the USA. There was a balance in the world economic order. Socialist parties and ideas and workers' movements became quite strong even in capitalist countries and the capitalists were forced to build up a large welfare state and provide considerable concessions to the working class. However, Soviet Union lost the Cold War to the vastly richer capitalist bloc and collapsed making the socialist bloc considerably weaker. The world became unipolar again. Capitalism and capitalists

C. Ghosh and A. N. Ghosh, *Keynesian Macroeconomics Beyond the IS-LM Model*, https://doi.org/10.1007/978-981-13-7888-1_8

are now at the zenith of their power and are ruling the world today. Capitalists in the capitalist bloc have become united in their fight against socialism and the working class. They are devising different strategies to weaken the socialist bloc and the workers. They are also reducing the concessions provided to the working class including the size of the welfare state. We exemplify our claim by focusing on the case of Greece, which the capitalists have got completely under their control and are forcing it to destroy its large welfare state.

Remarkably, following the collapse of the Soviet Union in 1991, the capitalist world is going through a prolonged period of recession (see Table 8.1). Japan is in recession since 1992. USA and Europe are in recession since 2001 and 2008, respectively. In all these cases, recessions followed collapse of huge asset price bubbles. Stock and real estate price bubbles collapsed in Japan in 1991. A huge dot-com bubble crashed in USA in 2001. In many European countries, real estate bubbles burst in 2008. In the USA, the recession that started in 2001 deepened into a severe crisis in the wake of a crash in a huge house price bubble (see Table 8.1). Speculative activities of global financial capital (global financial institutions) are at the root of all these troubles. The latest victim is Greece, which plunged into a severe recession since 2008. The purpose of this paper is to explain how Greece plunged into a severe crisis since 2008, making lives miserable for its common people, who lost jobs on a large scale and suffered drastic cuts in wages and welfare spending including retirement and unemployment benefits.

The dominant view explaining Greek crisis in the literature is the following: In the wake of the formation of Eurozone, there took place large inflows of capital from the center of the Eurozone (consisting of Germany, France, Netherlands, and Austria) to Greece, as exchange rate risk disappeared. Borrowing cost as a result went down in Greece inducing the Greek Government and private economic agents to borrow on a large scale. These borrowings made Greece's debt very large. This led to a sharp deterioration in the risk perception of the foreign investors regarding Greece and induced them to stop investing in its assets. With the drying up of foreign capital inflows, government and private spending declined substantially creating a severe recession in Greece. For a detailed exposition of this view, one may go through, for example, Gibson et al. (2014), Krugman (2013), Lane (2012), Dellas and Tavlas (2013) et al.). The problem with this literature is that it did not develop its argument rigorously within an explicit theoretical framework. We shall subject this line of thought to close scrutiny in light of the available evidences, identify the factors responsible for the Greek crisis, and present our argument in a rigorous theoretical framework. A careful analysis of data reveals that the Greek crisis is on account of not just one but two factors. Besides the large inflow of capital, the recession in other European nations and the USA due to the collapse in the real estate bubbles also contributed to the crisis.

The recession significantly reduced income of the Greek Government. Along with that, loan supply stopped. These two together made it impossible for the Greek Government to service its debt. Loan supply stopped at a time the Greek Government needed it the most to tide over the crisis caused by recession. Greece appealed to European Central Bank, European Commission, and IMF for assistance. They paid

Table 8.1 Annual growth rate of GDP annual percentage growth rate of GDP at market prices based on constant local currency. Aggregates are based on constant 2005 US dollars

	1991	92	93	94	95	96	97	98	99	2000
China	9.3	14.3	13.9	13.1	11.0	9.9	9.2	7.9	7.6	8.4
France	1.0	1.6	−0.6	2.3	2.1	1.4	2.3	3.6	3.4	3.9
Germany	5.1	1.9	−1.0	2.5	1.7	0.8	1.8	2.0	2.0	3.0
Greece	3.1	0.7	−1.6	2.0	2.1	2.9	4.5	3.2	3.1	4.2
Ireland	1.9	3.3	2.7	5.8	9.6	9.3	11.2	8.9	10.8	10.2
Italy	1.5	0.8	−0.9	2.2	2.0	1.3	1.8	1.6	3.7	1.8
Japan	3.3	0.8	0.2	0.9	1.9	2.6	1.6	−2.0	−0.2	2.3
KoreaRep (South)	9.7	5.8	6.3	8.8	8.9	7.2	5.8	−5.7	10.7	8.8
Malaysia	9.5	8.9	9.9	9.2	9.8	10.0	7.3	7.4	6.1	8.9
Portugal	4.4	1.1	−2.0	1.0	4.3	3.5	4.4	4.8	3.9	3.8
Spain	2.5	0.9	−1.0	2.4	2.8	2.7	3.7	4.3	4.5	5.3
Thailand	8.6	8.1	8.3	8.0	8.1	5.7	−2.8	−7.6	4.6	4.5
UK	−1.2	0.4	2.6	4.0	4.9	2.7	3.1	3.4	3.1	3.8
USA	−0.1	3.6	2.7	4.0	2.7	3.58	4.5	4.4	4.7	4.1
	2001	02	03	04	05	06	07	08	09	10
China	8.3	9.1	10.6	10.1	11.4	12.7	14.2	9.6	9.2	10.6
France	2.0	1.1	0.8	2.8	1.6	2.4	2.4	0.2	−2.9	2.0
Germany	1.7	0.0	−0.7	1.2	0.7	3.7	3.3	1.1	−5.6	4.1
Greece	4.1	3.9	5.8	5.1	0.6	5.7	3.3	−0.3	−4.3	−5.5
Ireland	5.8	5.9	3.8	4.4	6.3	6.3	5.5	−2.2	−5.6	0.4
Italy	1.8	0.3	0.2	1.6	0.9	2.0	1.5	−1.0	−5.5	1.7
Japan	0.4	0.3	1.7	2.4	1.3	1.7	2.2	−1.0	−5.5	4.7
KoreaRep (South)	4.5	7.4	2.9	4.9	3.9	5.2	5.5	2.8	0.7	6.5
Malaysia	0.5	5.4	5.8	6.8	5.3	5.6	6.3	4.8	−1.5	7.4
Portugal	1.9	0.8	−0.9	1.8	0.8	1.6	2.5	0.2	−3.0	1.9
Spain	4.0	2.9	3.2	3.2	3.7	4.2	3.8	1.1	−3.6	0.0
Thailand	3.4	6.1	7.2	6.3	4.2	5.0	5.4	1.7	−0.7	7.5
UK	2.8	2.5	3.3	2.5	3.0	2.7	2.6	−0.5	−4.2	1.5
USA	1.0	1.8	2.8	3.8	3.3	2.7	1.8	−0.3	−2.8	2.5

	2011	12	13	14	15
China	9.5	7.8	7.7	7.3	
France	2.1	0.2	0.7	0.2	
Germany	3.7	0.4	0.3	1.6	
Greece	−9.1	−7.3	−3.2	0.7	
Ireland	2.6	0.2	1.4	5.2	
Italy	0.6	−2.8	−1.7	−0.4	
Japan	−0.5	1.8	1.6	−0.1	

(continued)

Table 8.1 (continued)

	2011	12	13	14	15
KoreaRep (South)	3.7	2.3	2.9	3.3	
Malaysia	5.3	5.5	4.7	6.0	
Portugal	−1.8	−4.0	−1.1	0.9	
Spain	−1.0	−2.6	−1.7	1.4	
Thailand	0.8	7.3	2.8	0.9	
UK	2.0	1.2	2.2	2.9	
USA	1.6	2.3	2.2	2.4	

Source World Bank

off Greece's creditors and, thereby, transferred all of Greece's debts to themselves. However, they did not write off these debts. Nor did they allow Greece to devise its own strategy to pay off its debt. Instead, they imposed on Greece stringent austerity measures consisting in drastic reductions in welfare spending, hikes in tax rates, and sell-off of government assets. These measures have led to severe contraction of Greek economy, which compounded its debt problem manifold instead of alleviating it. In what follows, we shall develop a suitable model to identify the cause of Greece's crisis, examine the impact of austerity measures, and suggest policies that may lift Greece out of its crisis.

8.2 The Model

We divide the economy into two sectors: the real sector and the financial sector. We focus on the real sector first.

The Real Sector

We first consider the government. During the period of time under consideration (from 1996 to 2010), Greek Government's expenditure was subject to stringent fiscal deficit target. Therefore, Greek Government's budget may be written as

$$G + d_g\tilde{r} + B - tY - \tilde{t}Y = aY \quad (8.1)$$

where G denotes government consumption expenditure, d_g stands for government's outstanding debt, $\tilde{r}$ denotes the average interest rate applicable to the outstanding public debt, B stands for the amount that the government has to spend to bail out the banks, t and $\tilde{t}$ denote income tax rate and indirect tax rate, respectively, while Y denotes GDP and aY gives government's new borrowings. Note that the loans constituting the outstanding public debt were taken in the past at interest rates that prevailed in the past periods. $\tilde{r}$ is, therefore, given in the current period. a denotes the fiscal deficit target of the government, i.e., the targeted ratio of government's new borrowings to GDP. Equation (8.1) states that government finances its expenditure with tax revenue and new borrowings. More precisely, given t, $\tilde{t}$, a and Y, government chooses G in such a manner that (8.1) is satisfied, since $\tilde{r}d_g$ and B are given to the government. Following Keynes, we assume that the aggregate output or GDP is demand-determined. The goods market equilibrium condition is written as

$$Y = C\cdot\left(1-\tilde{t}\right)Y(1-t) + I(r) + G + \mathrm{NX}\left(\frac{P^*}{P(w)}\left(1-\tilde{t}\right), Y; Y^*\right)$$

$$C \equiv \left(C_w\cdot\left(w\cdot l_y\right)\frac{1}{P(w)}\right) + C_c\cdot\left(\left(1-w\cdot l_y\right)\frac{1}{P(w)}\right) \tag{8.2}$$

Let us explain (8.2). In (8.2), $C_w \equiv$ fixed average/marginal propensity to consume of workers, $w \equiv$ money wage rate of the workers, $l_y \equiv$ labor requirement per unit of output, $P \equiv$ domestic price level, which is made an increasing function of the money wage rate, and $C_c \equiv$ fixed average and marginal propensity to consume of capitalists. There is an indirect tax at the rate τ on the production or sales of Y so that producers have to pay a tax of $P\tau$ from every unit of Y produced. Thus, while producers receive the price P, buyers pay the price $P(1+\tau)$ for every unit of Y purchased. Total indirect tax collection of the government is $P\tau Y$, which in real terms is $\frac{P\tau Y}{P(1+\tau)} \equiv \frac{\tau}{(1+\tau)}Y \equiv \tilde{t}Y$. Real wage income of the workers per unit of Y is given by $\frac{wl_y}{P(w)}\cdot\frac{1}{(1+\tau)} \equiv \frac{wl_y}{P(w)}\left(1-\tilde{t}\right)$. We have ignored workers' interest income, which is fixed in the short run, for simplicity. Similarly, real income of the capitalists per unit of Y is given by $\frac{P-wl}{P}\cdot\frac{1}{(1+\tau)} \equiv \left(1-\frac{wl}{P(w)}\right)\left(1-\tilde{t}\right)$. Workers and capitalists pay income tax at the rate t. Hence, their disposable real incomes per unit of Y are given respectively by $\frac{wl}{P(w)}\left(1-\tilde{t}\right)(1-t)$ and $\left(1-\frac{wl}{P(w)}\right)\left(1-\tilde{t}\right)(1-t)$. Hence, $C\cdot\left(1-\tilde{t}\right)(1-t)Y$ gives the aggregate consumption demand of the economy, $I(r)$ gives the aggregate investment demand, while NX denotes the net export function. Both these functions are standard. Here, we have assumed that Greece trades only with other Eurozone countries for simplicity. Hence, the exchange rate is fixed and equal to 1. Note that, even though Greece joined Eurozone in 2001, it pegged its currency to European Currency Unit (ECU) in 1996. Therefore, exchange rate of Greece's currency vis-à-vis that of other Eurozone countries was fixed from 1996. Hence, they may be taken to be unity for simplicity and without any loss of generality from 1996. Thus, the exchange rate regime assumed here is applicable to Greece from 1996.

The Financial Sector

We shall now describe the financial sector. We assume that the only kind of financial intermediaries that exist are banks. We assume for simplicity that people hold all their savings as domestic bank deposits. We assume in consonance with reality that the interest rate charged by banks on their new loans is rigid. We denote this fixed interest rate on new bank loans by $\bar{r}$. Denoting the new deposits received by the commercial banks by D, we have

$$D = (1 - C)(1 - t)\left(1 - \tilde{t}\right)Y \tag{8.3}$$

Banks' potential supply of new loans is given by $(1 - \rho)(1 - C)(1 - t)\left(1 - \tilde{t}\right)Y$, where ρ denotes the reserve–deposit ratio of the banks. We assume it to be exogenously given for simplicity. However, banks normally cannot disburse all its potential loan supply. At the given interest rate, they meet all the demand for new loans of quality borrowers consisting of large corporate houses with substantial financial standing and the government. However, it rations the non-quality borrowers consisting mainly of small and medium enterprises (see Bernanke and Blinder (1988) in this context). Let us elaborate. Keeping deposits idle over and above the part, which the banks consider optimal to be held in the form of cash, is not profitable for banks. However, the dilemma of the banks stems from the fact that extension of loans to non-quality borrowers raises not only banks' expected income but also the amount of risk the banks assume. Thus, by raising the fraction of its loanable funds given out as loan to non-quality borrowers, banks raise both their expected income and risk. Therefore, on the basis of banks' preferences over risk and expected income, banks, a la Tobin (1958), choose what fraction of their loanable funds to be given out as loans to non-quality borrowers. We denote this fraction by β. We make β a decreasing function of N, which denotes the stock of nonperforming assets of the banks. We also make β an increasing function of ϕ, which indicates government's policy stance. The more expansionary the government's policies, the higher is the value of ϕ. Policy parameters of the government, as follows from (8.1), are t, $\tilde{t}$ and a, while G is an endogenous variable. Clearly, ϕ should be made a function of a, t and $\tilde{t}$. Thus,

$$\phi = \phi\left(\underset{-}{t}, \underset{-}{\tilde{t}}, \underset{+}{a}\right) \tag{8.4}$$

We denote quality investors' investment demand by $\bar{I}$ and make it a decreasing function of r and an increasing function of E_Q, which denotes expectations of quality investors. Hence, their investment function is given by $\bar{I}\left(r, E_Q\right)$. Besides domestic banks, foreign lenders also lend to domestic borrowers. However, foreign lenders lend only to quality borrowers and the government. Given these assumptions, non-quality investors get new bank loans of the amount Z, which is given by

$$Z = \beta\left(\underset{-}{N}, \underset{+}{\phi(t, \tilde{t}, a)}\right)\left[(1 - \rho)(1 - C)\cdot(1 - t)(1 - \tilde{t})Y - \left\{\bar{I}(\bar{r}, E_Q) + aY - \bar{K}\right\}\right] \tag{8.5}$$

In (8.5), $\bar{K}$ gives the amount of new loans extended by foreigners to the domestic government and the domestic quality borrowers. We assume $\bar{K}$ to be exogenously given for simplicity. Non-quality investors' investment is, accordingly, given by (8.5). Aggregate effective investment demand of the domestic investors, denoted $\tilde{I}$, is, therefore, given by

$$\tilde{I} = \bar{I}\left(\bar{r}, E_Q\right) + \beta\left(\underset{-}{N}, \underset{+}{\phi}\right)\left[(1 - \rho)(1 - C)\cdot(1 - t)(1 - \tilde{t})Y - \left\{\bar{I}(\bar{r}, E_Q) + aY - \bar{K}\right\}\right] \tag{8.6}$$

We further assume that

$$N = N\left(\underset{-}{Y}\right) \tag{8.7}$$

and

$$B = B\left(\underset{+}{N}\right) \tag{8.8}$$

Substituting (8.7) into (8.8), we rewrite it as

$$B = \bar{B}\left(\underset{-}{Y}\right) \tag{8.9}$$

Similarly, using (8.4), we get

$$\beta = \beta\left(\underset{-}{N}, \underset{+}{\phi(t, \tilde{t}, a)}\right) = \beta\left(N\left(\underset{-}{Y}\right), \underset{+}{\phi(\cdot)}\right) \equiv \bar{\beta}\left(\underset{+}{Y}, \underset{+}{\phi(\cdot)}\right) \tag{8.10}$$

We also assume that E_Q depends positively on Y^* and $\bar{K}$, as they generate expansionary impact through an increase in export demand and supply of new foreign loans. It also depends positively on ϕ. Thus, we have

$$E_Q = E\left(\underset{+}{Y^*}, \underset{+}{\bar{K}}, \underset{+}{\phi(a, t, \tilde{t})}\right) \tag{8.11}$$

Using (8.11), we rewrite quality investors' investment function as

$$\bar{I} = \bar{I}(\bar{r}, E(Y^*, \bar{K}, \phi(\cdot))) = \hat{I}\left(\underset{-}{\bar{r}}, \underset{+}{\overset{*}{Y}}, \underset{+}{\bar{K}}, \underset{+}{\phi(\cdot)}\right) \tag{8.12}$$

Substituting (8.10) and (8.12) into (8.6), we rewrite it as

$$\begin{aligned} \tilde{I} = {} & \left(1 - \bar{\beta}\left(\underset{+}{Y}, \underset{+}{\phi(\cdot)}\right)\right)\hat{I}(\bar{r}, Y^*, \bar{K}, \phi) \\ & + \bar{\beta}\left(\underset{+}{Y}, \underset{+}{\phi(\cdot)}\right)\left[(1-\rho)(1-C).(1-t)(1-\tilde{t})Y - \left\{aY - \bar{K}\right\}\right] \end{aligned} \tag{8.13}$$

Substituting (8.1) and (8.13) into (8.2), we rewrite it as

$$Y = C \cdot (1 - \tilde{t})(1 - t)Y + \left(1 - \bar{\beta}\left(\underset{+}{Y}, \underset{+}{\phi(a, t, \tilde{t})}\right)\right)\hat{I}(\bar{r}, Y^*, \bar{K}, \phi)$$

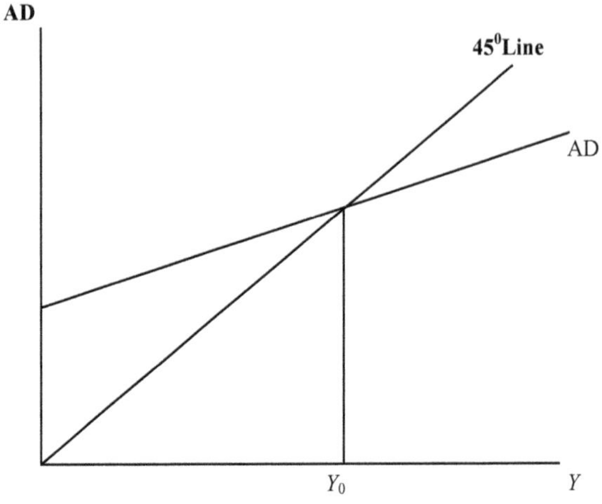

Fig. 8.1 Determination of Y

$$+\bar{\beta}\Big(\underset{+}{Y},\underset{+}{\phi(\cdot)}\Big)\big[(1-\rho)(1-C)\cdot(1-t)\big(1-\tilde{t}\big)Y-\big\{aY-\bar{K}\big\}\big]$$
$$+\big(\tilde{t}+t+a\big)Y-\tilde{r}\cdot d_g-B\Big(\underset{-}{Y}\Big)+\mathrm{NX}\Big(\frac{P^*}{P(w)}\big(1-\tilde{t}\big),Y;Y^*\Big) \quad (8.14)$$

The specification of our model is now complete. Equation (8.14) is the key equation, which contains only one endogenous variable Y. We can solve it for the equilibrium value of Y. The solution is shown in Fig. 8.1, where the AD schedule represents the RHS of (8.14), which we denote by AD (aggregate demand). The slope of this schedule denoted by α is given by

$$\alpha=\big\{C\cdot\big(1-\tilde{t}\big)(1-t)-(-\mathrm{NX}_Y)\big\}+\beta\big[(1-\rho)(1-C)\big(1-\tilde{t}\big)(1-t)-a\big]$$
$$+\beta_Y\big[(1-\rho)(1-C)\big(1-\tilde{t}\big)(1-t)Y-\big\{\bar{I}(\cdot)+aY-\bar{K}\big\}\big]+\big[\tilde{t}+t+a+\big(-B'\big)\big]<1 \quad (8.15)$$

Let us explain α. It gives the increase in aggregate demand that a unit increase in Y gives rise to. The first term within second brackets gives the increase in consumption demand for domestic goods. The second term gives, given the value of β, the increase in investment demand of non-quality borrowers due to the increase in the supply of new loans to them on account of the increase in aggregate saving of the households. The third term also gives the increase in the supply of new loans to non-quality borrowers due to the increase in the value of β induced by the fall in the stock of nonperforming assets. The fourth term gives the increase in government's consumption demand that a unit increase in Y gives rise to. Thus, a unit increase in Y causes a large increase in aggregate planned demand. However, we assume it to be less than unity.

8.3 Economic Performance of Greece and Greek Crisis

We shall now use the model developed above to explain the growth performance of the Greek economy in the pre-crisis era and the outbreak of crisis in Greece. The model is applicable to Greece, as we have already pointed out above, from 1996. From the data presented in Tables 8.2 and 8.5, we find that there took place a decisive break in the growth performance of Greece in 1997. During the period 1991–1996, annual average growth rate of Greece's GDP was around 1.5%. It more than doubled to around 3.83% during 1997–2002 and rose further to around 4.1% during 2003–2007. How do we explain this jump in Greece's growth performance? We get some clue regarding this from the data of Tables 8.1, 8.2, and 8.4. Let us focus on the period 1997–2002 first. We find from Tables 8.1 and 8.4 that during 1997–2002, many European countries and the USA experienced large increases in their growth rates. Of the set of countries considered in Tables 8.1 and 8.4, average annual growth rates of Spain, Portugal, Ireland, France, and the USA increased substantially during the period under consideration. In terms of our model, therefore, Y^* grew at a high rate during 1997–2002. Table 8.4 shows that during the latter period 2003–07, growth rates of almost all the countries declined, but, as we find from Table 8.2, net capital inflow into Greece grew at a very high rate during the period under consideration. In fact, net capital inflow into Greece was non-existent till 1998. It was negative in 1999. It became positive, but stagnant during 2000–02. However, it grew at a very high rate during 2003–2007. Thus, in the latter period, growth rate of Y^* declined, but that of K increased remarkably. We shall now examine how an increase in Y^* and $\bar{K}$ affects the growth rate of GDP in our model.

8.3.1 *Effect of an Increase in Y**

Here, we shall examine the impact of an increase in Y^* using Fig. 8.2, where the equilibrium level of Y labeled Y_0 corresponds to the point of intersection of the AD schedule and the 45° line. Following a ceteris paribus increase in Y^* by $\mathrm{d}Y^*$, net export rises by $\mathrm{NX}_{Y*}\mathrm{d}Y^*$. (Data of Table 8.5 corroborate this. It shows that annual average growth rate of export rose from 4.33% during 1991–96 to 11.17% during 1997–02.) Quality investors' expectations also improved raising their investment demand by $\bar{I}_{Y*}\mathrm{d}Y^*$. (Table 8.5 shows that average annual growth rate of investment rose from 1.65% during 1991–96 to 6.43% during 1997–02.) Hence, corresponding to every Y, as follows from (8.14), aggregate demand goes up by $\left[\mathrm{NX}_{Y*} + (1-\beta)\hat{I}_{Y*}\right]\mathrm{d}Y^*$ shifting the AD schedule upward by the same amount. Hence, equilibrium Y rises. The new equilibrium Y is labeled Y_1 in Fig. 8.2. Let us now explore the implications of this result. The purpose of the kind of models developed here is to explain the actual growth performance of an economy. Let us explain. The equations of the model represent an economy in a given period of time. In the period under consideration, the level of Y of the previous period is given. Therefore, determination of Y in the

Table 8.2 Net inflow of capital, unemployment, and growth rates of GDP and government consumption expenditure of Greece

Year	GDP growth (annual %)	General govt final consumption exp (annual % growth)	Unemployment, total (% of total labor force)	Portfolio equity, net inflows (BOP, current US $)	Growth rate of net inflow of capital
1981	−1.553	6.817	3.4	–	
1982	−1.132	−2.046	4.9	–	
1983	−1.078	3.597	7.8	–	
1984	2.010	2.681	8.1	–	
1985	2.509	3.836	7.8	–	
1986	0.517	−1.094	7.4	–	
1987	−2.258	0.22	7.6	–	
1988	4.287	−5.499	7.5	–	
1989	3.8	5.4	7	–	
1990	0	0.6	7.7	–	
1991	3.1	−1.5	7.7	–	
1992	0.7	−3	7.8	–	
1993	−1.6	2.6	8.6	–	
1994	2	−1.099	8.9	–	
1995	2.099	5.60	9.1	–	
1996	2.862	5.268	9.7	–	
1997	4.484	−3.16	9.6	–	
1998	3.894	2.59	10.8	–	
1999	3.072	3.57	11.8	−2,600,000,000	
2000	3.919	3.63	11.2	+1,640,000,000	
2001	4.131	4.76	10.5	+1,830,000,000	11.58
2002	3.922	2.72	10	+1,400,000,000	−23.5
2003	5.794	2.98	9.4	+2,570,000,000	83.57
2004	5.060	4.07	10.3	+4,290,000,000	66.93
2005	0.599	4.09	10	+6,290,000,000	46.62
2006	5.652	6.80	9	+7,530,000,000	19.71
2007	3.273	5.39	8.4	+10,900,000,000	44.75
2008	−0.335	−2.33	7.8	−5,300,000,000	−104.86
2009	−4.300	2.023	9.6	+764,000,000	114.42
2010	−5.479	−4.16	12.7	−1,500,000,000	−296.33
2011	−9.132	−7.020	17.9	−350,000,000	
2012	−7.3	−5.99	24.4	−66,000,000	

(continued)

Table 8.2 (continued)

Year	GDP growth (annual %)	General govt final consumption exp (annual % growth)	Unemployment, total (% of total labor force)	Portfolio equity, net inflows (BOP, current US $)	Growth rate of net inflow of capital
2013	−3.241	−6.449	27.5	+3.130000000	
2014	0.739	−1.36	26.5	+11,300,000,000	
2015	−0.290	1.23	24.9	+7,000,000,000	
2016	−0.244	−1.46	23.5	+554,000,000	

Source World Bank

period under consideration amounts to determining the growth rate of Y from the previous period to the given period. Thus, we can state our result in the following way. Given the values of all other exogenous variables, the higher the growth rate of foreign GDP from the previous period to the given period, the greater is the growth rate of domestic GDP from the previous period to the given period. Thus, our model yields the result that the high growth in other European countries and USA during 1997–2002 is the likely cause for the high growth in Greece during the same period. We shall now derive the result mathematically.

Taking total differential of (8.14) treating all exogenous variables other than Y^* as fixed, and solving for $\mathrm{d}Y$, we get

$$\mathrm{d}Y = \frac{\left(\mathrm{NX}_{Y^*} + (1-\beta)\bar{I}_{Y^*}\right)\mathrm{d}Y^*}{1-\alpha} \quad \text{(see 8.15)} \tag{8.16}$$

Let us now explain (8.16). Following an increase in Y^* by $\mathrm{d}Y^*$, export demand and aggregate investment go up by $\left[\mathrm{NX}_{Y^*} + (1-\beta)\bar{I}_{Y^*}\right]\mathrm{d}Y^*$ at the initial equilibrium Y setting off the multiplier process. Hence, Y in the first round will go up by $\mathrm{d}Y_1 = \frac{\left[\mathrm{NX}_{Y^*}+(1-\beta)\bar{I}_{Y^*}\right]\mathrm{d}Y^*}{\theta}$ $\theta \equiv 1 - \left[C\cdot(1-t)\left(1-\tilde{t}\right) - (-\mathrm{NX}_Y)\right]$. The expansion, however, will not stop here, as happens in the IS-LM-based Keynesian models. People will save out of $\mathrm{d}Y_1$ the amount given by $(1-C)(1-t)\left(1-\tilde{t}\right)\mathrm{d}Y_1$ and put it in banks as new deposits raising banks' potential supply of new loans by $(1-\rho)(1-C)(1-t)\left(1-\tilde{t}\right)\mathrm{d}Y_1$. On the other hand, the increase in Y enables the government to increase its borrowing from banks by $(a\mathrm{d}Y_1)$. Therefore, banks' potential supply of loans to non-quality borrowers rises by $\left[(1-\rho)(1-C)(1-t)\left(1-\tilde{t}\right) - a\right]\mathrm{d}Y_1$. Again, the increase in Y lowers default rates reducing the stock of nonperforming assets of banks. This improves banks' risk perception raising the value of β. For all these reasons, banks' loan supply to non-quality borrowers will go up by $\left\{\beta\cdot\left[(1-\rho)(1-C)(1-t)\left(1-\tilde{t}\right) - a\right] + \beta_Y L_{sm}\right\}\mathrm{d}Y_1 \equiv \bar{\theta}\mathrm{d}Y_1$, where $L_{sm} \equiv (1-\rho)(1-C)(1-t)\left(1-\tilde{t}\right) - \left(\hat{I}(\cdot) + aY - \bar{K}\right)$. Hence, aggregate investment of non-quality borrowers will increase by $\bar{\theta}\mathrm{d}Y_1$. Moreover, government's revenue goes

Table 8.3 Growth rates of export, import, and gross investment in Greece

Year	Exports of goods and services (annual % growth)	Imports of goods and services (annual % growth)	Gross capital formation (annual % growth)
1991	4.123	5.836	9.805
1992	10.021	1.076	−8.243
1993	−2.596	0.628	−4.388
1994	7.384	1.500	−0.643
1995	2.999	8.945	5.461
1996	4.084	8.936	7.879
1997	23.102	8.437	2.857
1998	4.514	18.161	17.133
1999	24.444	14.486	−0.463
2000	22.183	20.180	12.363
2001	0.120	0.991	4.465
2002	−7.324	−3.432	2.233
2003	−0.734	7.393	18.604
2004	18.550	4.417	−0.653
2005	3.339	0.854	−10.638
2006	5.212	13.309	23.881
2007	10.618	15.499	8.531
2008	3.472	1.320	−9.214
2009	−18.519	−20.353	−26.883
2010	4.861	−3.430	−10.770
2011	0.027	−9.448	−21.824
2012	1.173	−9.099	−24.076
2013	1.510	−2.392	−9.915
2014	7.749	7.677	6.650
2015	3.09	0.404	−9.035
2016	−1.820	0.253	7.419

Source World Bank
Gross capital formation: Annual growth rate of gross capital formation based on constant local currency. Aggregates are based on constant 2010 US dollars. Gross capital formation (formerly gross domestic investment) consists of outlays on additions to the fixed assets of the economy plus net changes in the level of inventories. Fixed assets include land improvements (fences, ditches, drains, and so on); plant, machinery, and equipment purchases; and the construction of roads, railways, and the like, including schools, offices, hospitals, private residential dwellings, and commercial and industrial buildings. Inventories are stocks of goods held by firms to meet temporary or unexpected fluctuations in production or sales, and "work in progress." According to the 1993 SNA, net acquisitions of valuables are also considered capital formation

Table 8.4 Average growth rates of GDP during the periods 1991–96, 1997–02, 2003–07, and 2008–10[a]

	1991–96	1997–02	2003–07	2008–10	2011–14
Greece	1.5	3.83	4.1	−3.37	−4.725
Spain	1.72	4.11	3.62	−0.83	−0.98
Portugal	2.05	3.27	1.16	−0.3	−1.5
UK	2.23	3.11	2.82	−1.06	2.08
Ireland	5.43	8.8	5.26	−2.47	2.35
France	1.3	2.72	2.0	−0.23	1.55
Italy	1.15	1.83	1.24	−1.6	−0.72
Germany	1.83	1.62	1.64	−0.03	1.5
USA	2.15	4.01	2.88	−0.35	2.13

[a]Simple arithmetic mean of the annual growth rates given in Table 8.1

Table 8.5 [a]Average annual growth rates of GDP, export, G and I of Greece

Period	Average annual growth rate of GDP	Average annual growth rate of export	Average annual growth rate of *G*	Average annual growth rate of I
1991–96	1.5	4.33	1.31	1.65
1997–02	3.83	11.17	2.35	6.43
2003–07	4.1	7.397	4.66	7.95
2008–10	−3.37	−3.4	−1.49	−15.62
2011-14	−4.73	2.614	−3.32	−12.29

[a]Simple arithmetic mean of figures given in Table 8.3

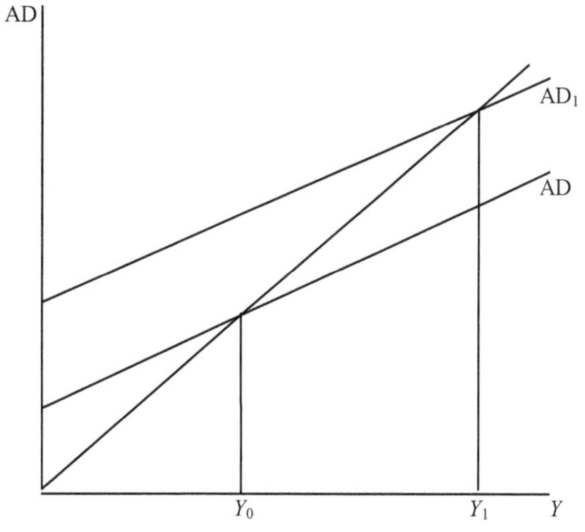

Fig. 8.2 Effect of an Increase in Y^* on Y

up by $(t + \tilde{t})\mathrm{d}Y_1$. The increase in Y also lowers banks' stock of nonperforming assets reducing government's expenditure on bank bailout by $\bar{B}'\mathrm{d}Y_1$. Thus, government's consumption expenditure will go up by $\left[(t + \tilde{t} + a) + (-B')\right]\mathrm{d}Y_1$. This will again set into motion the multiplier process and raise income in the second round by $\mathrm{d}Y_2 = \frac{\bar{\theta}\mathrm{d}Y_1 + [t+\tilde{t}+a+(-B')]\mathrm{d}Y_1}{\theta} \equiv \frac{\tilde{\theta}\mathrm{d}Y_1}{\theta}$. Out of this additional income, people will save $(1 - C)(1 - t)(1 - \tilde{t})\mathrm{d}Y_2$ and put it in banks as new deposits raising banks' potential supply of new loans by $(1 - \rho)(1 - C)(1 - t)(1 - \tilde{t})\mathrm{d}Y_2$ and, just the way it happened in round 2, aggregate investment and government's consumption expenditure together will go up by $\tilde{\theta}\mathrm{d}Y_2$ raising aggregate output in the third round by $\mathrm{d}Y_3 = \frac{\tilde{\theta}\mathrm{d}Y_2}{\theta} = \left(\frac{\tilde{\theta}}{\theta}\right)^2 \mathrm{d}Y_1$. This process of expansion will continue until the additional demand generated in each successive round falls to zero. Thus, total increase in Y is given by (using the value of $\mathrm{d}Y_1$)

$$\mathrm{d}Y = \mathrm{d}Y_1 + \frac{\tilde{\theta}}{\theta}\mathrm{d}Y_1 + \left(\frac{\tilde{\theta}}{\theta}\right)^2 \mathrm{d}Y_1 + \cdots = \frac{\theta}{\theta - \tilde{\theta}}\mathrm{d}Y_1 = \frac{\left[\mathrm{NX}_{Y^*} + (1 - \beta)\bar{I}_{Y^*}\right]\mathrm{d}Y^*}{1 - \alpha} \tag{8.17}$$

One can easily check that $\theta - \tilde{\theta} \equiv 1 - \alpha$.

The above discussion brings out clearly the role the banks play in the transmission of the effect of an exogenous demand shock. In the absence of banks or financial intermediation, the increase in Y would have been only $\mathrm{d}Y_1$. However, because of the financial intermediation by the banks, the increase in Y is many times more. In fact, the greater the faith of the banks in the government's ability to keep the economy stable, the greater the assurance that the government will make up for banks' losses, which are not on account of banks' faults, the lower will be the value of β making the value of the multiplier larger. In fact, if people have no faith in banks or financial intermediaries, they will hold all their savings in currency. In such a scenario, again, the increase in Y would be $\mathrm{d}Y_1$ only. The above discussion yields the following proposition:

Proposition 8.1 *Following an increase in the growth rate of the trading partners of Greece, growth rate in Greece goes up. The operation of the banking sector magnifies the impact of this favorable demand shock and makes the increase in Greece's growth rate substantially large.*

8.3.2 *Effect of an Increase in $\bar{K}$*

Let us now focus on the period 2003–07. During this period, as we find from Table 8.4, growth rates of major trading partners of Greece dropped a little reducing the annual average growth rate of export from 11.17% during 1996–2002 to 7.397%. However, the annual average growth rate of GDP rose from 3.83% during 1996–02 to 4.1%

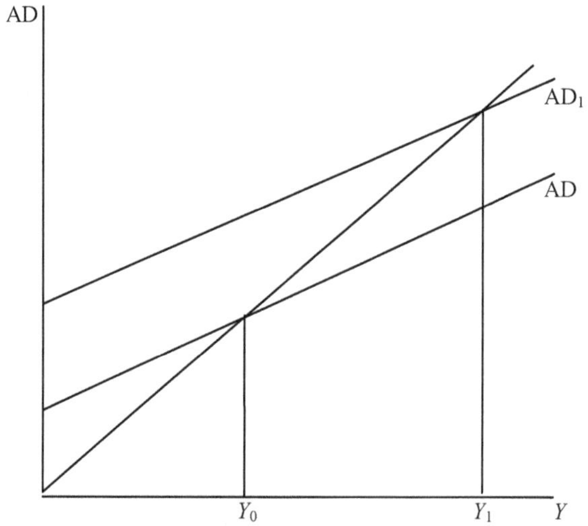

Fig. 8.3 The effect of an autonomous increase in the net inflow of capital on Y

during 2003–07. How does one, then, explain the jump in the growth rate of GDP? We get the answer from the data of Table 8.2, which shows that during 2003–07, annual growth rate of net inflow of capital, which was non-existent or stagnant earlier, became very high. We shall, therefore, examine how an autonomous increase in $\bar{K}$ affects Y in our model.

We shall first derive the impact of an exogenous increase in $\bar{K}$ using Fig. 8.3, where the initial equilibrium level of Y labeled Y_0 corresponds to the point of intersection of the AD schedule representing the RHS of (8.14) and the 45° line. With larger inflow of capital, more loans become available giving rise to an expectation of a boom. The improvement in quality borrowers' expectations raises their investment demand. The availability of more loans makes it possible for the banks to extend larger amounts of loans to non-quality borrowers. This raises their investment demand also. From (8.14), we find that, following an exogenous increase in $\bar{K}$ by $\mathrm{d}\bar{K}$, aggregate investment demand and aggregate demand corresponding to any given Y increase by $\left[(1-\beta)\hat{I}_{\bar{K}}+\beta\right]\mathrm{d}\bar{K}$. Hence, AD schedule in Fig. 8.3 shifts upward by the same amount. Hence, equilibrium Y and, therefore, growth rate of Y from the previous period to the given period increase. Let us now derive the result mathematically. Taking total differential of (8.13) treating all exogenous variables other than $\bar{K}$ as fixed and, then, solving for $\mathrm{d}Y$, we get

$$\mathrm{d}Y = \frac{\left[(1-\beta)\hat{I}_{\bar{K}}+\beta\right]\mathrm{d}\bar{K}}{1-\alpha} \tag{8.18}$$

The adjustment process may be explained as follows:

Following the exogenous increase in $\bar{K}$ by $\mathrm{d}\bar{K}$, aggregate investment demand goes up by $\left[(1-\beta)\hat{I}_{\bar{K}}+\beta\right]\mathrm{d}\bar{K}$ at the initial equilibrium Y setting off the multiplier process. Hence, in the first round, Y will go up by $\mathrm{d}Y_1 = \frac{\left[(1-\beta)\hat{I}_{\bar{K}}+\beta\right]\mathrm{d}\bar{K}}{\theta}$; $\theta \equiv 1 - \left(C\cdot\left(1-\tilde{t}\right)(1-t) - \mathrm{NX}_Y\right)$. In the IS-LM model, the expansion in Y would have stopped here. But, in this model, the expansion goes on much further. From $\mathrm{d}Y_1$, as before, people will save the amount given by $(1-C)(1-t)\left(1-\tilde{t}\right)\mathrm{d}Y_1$ and put it in banks as new deposits raising banks' potential supply of new loans by $(1-\rho)(1-C)(1-t)\left(1-\tilde{t}\right)\mathrm{d}Y_1$. On the other hand, the increase in Y enables the government to increase its borrowing from banks by $(a\mathrm{d}Y_1)$. Therefore, banks' potential supply of loans to non-quality borrowers rises by $\left[(1-\rho)(1-C)(1-t)\left(1-\tilde{t}\right)-a\right]\mathrm{d}Y_1$. Again, the increase in Y lowers default rates reducing the stock of nonperforming assets of banks. This improves banks' risk perception raising the value of β. For all these reasons, banks' loan supply to non-quality borrowers will go up by $\left\{\beta\cdot\left[(1-\rho)(1-C)(1-t)\left(1-\tilde{t}\right)-a\right]+\beta_Y L_{sm}\right\}\mathrm{d}Y_1 \equiv \bar{\theta}\mathrm{d}Y_1$, where $L_{sm} \equiv (1-\rho)(1-C)(1-t)\left(1-\tilde{t}\right)-\left(\hat{I}(\cdot)+aY-\bar{K}\right)$. Hence, aggregate investment of non-quality borrowers will increase by $\bar{\theta}\mathrm{d}Y_1$. Moreover, government's revenue goes up by $\left(t+\tilde{t}\right)\mathrm{d}Y_1$. The increase in Y also lowers banks' stock of nonperforming assets reducing government's expenditure on bank bailout by $\bar{B}'\mathrm{d}Y_1$. Thus, government's consumption expenditure will go up by $\left[\left(t+\tilde{t}+a\right)+\left(-B'\right)\right]\mathrm{d}Y_1$. This will again set into motion the multiplier process and raise income in the second round by $\mathrm{d}Y_2 = \frac{\bar{\theta}\mathrm{d}Y_1+\left[t+\tilde{t}+a+\left(-B'\right)\right]\mathrm{d}Y_1}{\theta} \equiv \frac{\tilde{\theta}\mathrm{d}Y_1}{\theta}$. Out of this additional income, people will save $(1-C)(1-t)\left(1-\tilde{t}\right)\mathrm{d}Y_2$ and put it in banks as new deposits raising banks' potential supply of new loans by $(1-\rho)(1-C)(1-t)\left(1-\tilde{t}\right)\mathrm{d}Y_2$ and, just the way it happened in round 2, aggregate investment and government's consumption expenditure together will go up by $\tilde{\theta}\mathrm{d}Y_2$ raising aggregate output in the third round by $\mathrm{d}Y_3 = \frac{\tilde{\theta}\mathrm{d}Y_2}{\theta} = \left(\frac{\tilde{\theta}}{\theta}\right)^2\mathrm{d}Y_1$. This process of expansion will continue until the additional demand generated in each successive round falls to zero. Thus, total increase in Y is given by (using the value of $\mathrm{d}Y_1$)

$$\mathrm{d}Y = \mathrm{d}Y_1 + \frac{\tilde{\theta}}{\theta}\mathrm{d}Y_1 + \left(\frac{\tilde{\theta}}{\theta}\right)^2\mathrm{d}Y_1 + \cdots = \frac{\theta}{\theta-\tilde{\theta}}\mathrm{d}Y_1 = \frac{\left[\mathrm{NX}_{Y^*}+(1-\beta)\bar{I}_{Y^*}\right]\mathrm{d}Y^*}{1-\alpha} \tag{8.19}$$

One can easily check that $\theta - \tilde{\theta} \equiv 1 - \alpha$.

From the above, it follows that in reality the multiplier is much larger than what the IS-LM model shows. This yields the following proposition:

Proposition 8.2 *An exogenous increase in net capital inflow raises aggregate investment, which produces a significantly large positive multiplier effect on Y, raising the growth rate of Y from the previous period to the given period substantially.*

Thus, during 2003–07, despite the drop in the growth rates of the major trading partners of Greece and the consequent decline in the growth rate of export, the very high growth rate of net inflow of capital more than compensated for the loss due the lower growth rate of export and brought about an increase in the growth rate of Greece.

8.3.3 Greek Crisis

Greece entered into a crisis since 2008. After growing at unprecedented high rates during 1997–2007, Greece's GDP began to contract since 2008 and the contraction is going on unabated till now. What are the factors responsible for this continuous and massive contraction in Greek economy? We shall focus on this issue here. We shall first focus on the period 2008–10 for reasons that will be clear shortly. During this period, there took place a large contraction in the Greek economy. The annual growth rates of Greece' GDP in 2008, 2009, and 2010 were −0.335%, −4.3%, and −5.48%, respectively (see Table 8.2). To explain this sudden large contraction in the Greek economy, we have to turn to the events that unfolded in the US economy. In the second half of 2007, house prices began to crash in the USA driving it into a recession, which turned into a severe crisis in 2008. The crisis in the USA had a strong contagion effect on Europe and most of the European countries also contracted during the period 2008-10. Average annual growth rates of GDP of all the countries recorded in Table 8.4 were negative during 2008–10. Thus, for Greece, there took place a massive decline in Y^* so much so that the growth rate of Y^* was negative. The contraction in Y^* brought about a decline in Greek export. From Table 8.5, we find that average annual growth rate of Greek export was −3.4% during 2008–10. In addition to the drastic fall in Y^*, there also took place massive outflows of capital from Greece. From Table 8.2, we find that in 2008 and in 2010 annual growth rates of net inflow of capital were −104% and −296.33%, respectively. In 2009, there took place just a small amount of capital inflow. Thus, during 2008–10, there took place a massive contraction in $\bar{K}$ in the Greek economy. We have already shown that a contraction in Y^* and $\bar{K}$ will bring about large contractions in Y—see (8.16) and (8.18). Therefore, we can attribute the large contraction in Greece's GDP to the substantial contractions in Y^* and $\bar{K}$.

Sovereign Debt Crisis in Greece

In 2010, the Greek economy was plagued by sovereign debt crisis, i.e., the Greek Government found that it was not in a position to meet its debt service charges. We can explain this using the government's budget constraint (8.1). During 1997–2007, Greek GDP grew at unprecedented high rates. Every year, the Greek Government borrowed a fixed fraction of GDP, which we have denoted by a in our model. Therefore, Greek Government's debt (d_g) also grew at an unprecedented high rate during 1997–2007 and became very large in 2008. During 2008–10, there took place substantial contraction in Greek GDP so much so that the resources at the command of the government given by $(\tilde{t} + t + a)Y$ became very small. At the same time, the massive contraction in Greek GDP led to large losses of Greek firms and they defaulted on a large scale on their loans. Hence, there took place a sharp increase in the stock of nonperforming assets of banks. Hence, the amount of fund Greek Government needed to bail out Greek banks (denoted B here) increased steeply. In terms of (8.1), $\tilde{r}d_g$ and B became so large relative to $(\tilde{t}+t+a)Y$ that after meeting the minimum level of government consumption expenditure and the bailout expenses for rescuing Greek banks, it was not possible for the Greek Government to meet its debt service obligations given by $\tilde{r}d_g$. This led to the sovereign debt crisis of Greece in 2010. Since Greece had no authority to print Euro, which was just a foreign currency to them, it had to seek the assistance of European Central Bank (ECB), European Commission (EC), and IMF. We shall henceforth refer to these institutions as troika. The troika obliged; they bought off all of Greek Government's debts from private lenders. Thus, Greek Government's debts got transferred to the troika. They did not write off these debts. Nor did they allow Greece the time to recover from the deep crisis it was in. Instead, it thrust on Greece a slew of extremely contractionary and onerous measures, called the austerity measures, to force Greece to pay off its debts. The austerity measures, as we shall presently show why, deepened Greece's woes and caught it in a perpetual debt trap instead of alleviating its economic and debt problems.

8.4 Austerity Measures

The troika imposed on Greece stringent austerity measures since 2010. These austerity measures consisted in massive cuts in government consumption consisting of wages and salaries and pensions of government employees and steep hikes in indirect and direct tax rates. The objective of these measures was to generate budget surplus, which the government would use to pay off its debt. However, these measures led to a massive increase in the rate of contraction of the Greek GDP and a very large increase in the rate of unemployment from 9.6% in 2009 to 23.5% in 2016 (see Table 8.2). The massive contraction of Greek GDP that took place following the adoption of the austerity measures led to perpetuation of large budget deficits exacerbating government's debt problem instead of alleviating it. In what follows, we shall explain why austerity measures increased the rate of contraction of Greek economy and, thereby, worsened Greek Government's debt problem.

Prior to the adoption of austerity measures, G was an endogenous variable determined by (8.1). In the regime that obtained under austerity measures, G became a policy variable determined by the government's austerity program. Under the austerity regime, government sought to lower G to the maximum possible extent and raise t and $\tilde{t}$ to the maximum possible extent so that the budget surplus of the government denoted BS and given by the following equation was maximized:

$$BS = (t+\tilde{t})Y - \bar{G} \tag{8.20}$$

Accordingly, we have to rewrite (8.14) as

$$\begin{aligned} Y = {} & C\cdot(1-\tilde{t})(1-t)Y + \Bigg(1-\beta\bigg(\underset{+}{Y}, \underset{+}{\bar{\phi}(G,t,\tilde{t})}\bigg)\Bigg)\hat{I}(\bar{r}, Y^*, \bar{K}, \bar{\phi}(\cdot)) \\ & + \beta\bigg(\underset{+}{Y}, \underset{+}{\bar{\phi}(\cdot)}\bigg)\big[(1-\rho)(1-C)\cdot(1-t)(1-\tilde{t})Y + \bar{K}\big] \\ & + \bar{G} + \mathrm{NX}\bigg(\frac{P^*}{P(w)}(1-\tilde{t}), Y; Y^*\bigg) \end{aligned} \tag{8.21}$$

Austerity measures, as we have already pointed out, consisted in drastic cuts in G and steep hikes in t and $\tilde{t}$ so that the government can increase budget surplus as much as possible. In what follows, we shall examine the impact of each of these using (8.21). Note that announcement of austerity measures creates an apprehension of severe recession bringing about a large fall in ϕ.

A Cut in $\bar{G}$

We shall examine here how a cut in $\bar{G}$ affects Y using (8.21). Taking total differential of (8.21) treating all exogenous variables other than $\bar{G}$ as fixed, and, then, solving for $\mathrm{d}Y$, we get

$$\mathrm{d}Y = \frac{\big(1+\big[(1-\beta)\bar{I}_\phi + \beta_\phi L'_{sm}\big]\bar{\phi}_G\big)\mathrm{d}\bar{G}}{1-\alpha'} < 0 \quad \therefore d\bar{G} < 0 \tag{8.22}$$

In (8.22),

$$\begin{aligned} \alpha' \equiv \frac{\partial(AD')}{\partial Y} = {} & \{C\cdot(1-\tilde{t})(1-t) - (-\mathrm{NX}_Y)\} + \beta\big[(1-\rho)(1-C)(1-\tilde{t})(1-t)\big] \\ & + \beta_Y\Big[(1-\rho)(1-C)(1-\tilde{t})(1-t)Y - \Big\{\hat{I}(\cdot) - \bar{K}\Big\}\Big] < 1 \end{aligned} \tag{8.23}$$

where AD' denotes the RHS of (8.21).

$$L'_{sm} \equiv (1-\rho)(1-C)(1-t)(1-\tilde{t}) - \Big(\hat{I}(\cdot) - \bar{K}\Big) \tag{8.24}$$

Let us now explain (8.22). Following the cut in $\bar{G}$ by $\mathrm{d}\bar{G}$ and the fall in ϕ by $\bar{\phi}_G\mathrm{d}\bar{G}$ induced by the adoption of the austerity measure, government's consumption and investment at the initial equilibrium Y fall by $\mathrm{d}\bar{G} + \Big[(1-\beta)\hat{I}_\phi + \beta_\phi L'_{sm}\Big]\bar{\phi}_G\,\mathrm{d}\bar{G}$. Explain this expression yourself. This sets off the multiplier process and Y in the first round decreases by

$$\mathrm{d}Y_1 = \frac{\big(1+\big[(1-\beta)\bar{I}_\phi + \beta_\phi L'_{sm}\big]\phi_G\big)\mathrm{d}\bar{G}}{\theta}; \quad \theta \equiv C\cdot(1-t)(1-\tilde{t}) - (-\mathrm{NX}_Y) \tag{8.25}$$

In the IS-LM model, the contraction in Y would have stopped here. But, in reality, as we show here, the contraction would be much larger. The contraction in Y reduces people's saving by $\big[1 - C\cdot(1-t)\cdot(1-\tilde{t})\big]\mathrm{d}Y_1$, which lowers bank deposits by the same amount. This lowers banks' potential supply of new loans by $(1-\rho)\left[1-C\cdot(1-t)\cdot\left(1-\tilde{t}\right)\right]\mathrm{d}Y_1$. Hence supply of new loans to and, therefore, investment of non-quality borrowers falls by $(1-\rho)\beta\left[1-C\cdot(1-t)\cdot\left(1-\tilde{t}\right)\right]\mathrm{d}Y_1$. Moreover, the fall in Y lowers β and, thereby, reduces supply of new loans to the non-quality borrowers further by $\beta_Y L'_{sm}$. Therefore, aggregate investment of non-quality borrowers goes down by $\left[\beta(1-\rho)\left[1-C\cdot(1-t)\cdot\left(1-\tilde{t}\right)\right]+\beta_Y L'_{sm}\right]\mathrm{d}Y_1 \equiv \hat{\theta}\mathrm{d}Y_1$. Hence, in the second round, through the operation of the multiplier process, Y falls by

$$\mathrm{d}Y_2 = \frac{\hat{\theta}\mathrm{d}Y_1}{\theta} < 0 \tag{8.26}$$

Again, the decline in Y in the second round, just the way it did in the second round, lowers Y in the third round by

$$\mathrm{d}Y_3 = \frac{\hat{\theta}\mathrm{d}Y_2}{\theta} = \left(\frac{\hat{\theta}}{\theta}\right)^2 \mathrm{d}Y_1 < 0 \tag{8.27}$$

This process of contraction will continue until the contraction in Y that takes place in each successive round eventually falls to zero. When that happens, the economy achieves a new equilibrium.

Thus, the total contraction in Y is given by

$$\begin{aligned}\mathrm{d}Y &= \mathrm{d}Y_1 + \frac{\hat{\theta}}{\theta}\mathrm{d}Y_1 + \left(\frac{\hat{\theta}}{\theta}\right)^2 \mathrm{d}Y_1 + \cdots = \frac{\theta}{\theta-\hat{\theta}}\mathrm{d}Y_1 \\ &= \frac{\left(1+\left[(1-\beta)\bar{I}_\phi + \beta_\phi L'_{sm}\right]\phi_G\right)\mathrm{d}\bar{G}}{1-\alpha'} < 0\end{aligned} \tag{8.28}$$

Thus, a cut in $\bar{G}$ will produce a very large contraction in Y. This yields the following proposition:

Proposition 8.3 *A ceteris paribus cut in $\bar{G}$ brings about a very large contraction in Y. The multiplier is much larger than what is predicted by the IS-LM model. This is due to the operation of financial intermediaries, which mobilize saving into investment.*

An Increase in the Income Tax Rate t

Let us now focus on how a hike in the income tax rate t will affect Y. Its announcement will also make the investors nervous and bring about a fall in ϕ by $\phi_t\mathrm{d}t$. Taking total differential of (8.21) treating all exogenous variables other than t as fixed and, then, solving for $\mathrm{d}Y$, we get

$$\mathrm{d}Y = \frac{-\left\{\left[C\left(1-\tilde{t}\right)\cdot Y + \beta(1-\rho)(1-C)(1-\tilde{t})Y\right] + \left[(1-\beta)\hat{I}_\phi + \beta_\phi L'_{sm}\right]\phi_t\right\}\mathrm{d}t}{1-\alpha'} < 0 \quad \because \mathrm{d}t > 0 \tag{8.29}$$

Explanation of (8.29) is quite simple. Following a ceteris paribus increase in t by $\mathrm{d}t$, as follows from (8.21), consumption demand goes down by $C \cdot \left(1 - \tilde{t}\right) Y\,\mathrm{d}t$ at the initial equilibrium Y, people's saving and, therefore, new bank deposits go down by $(1 - C) \cdot \left(1 - \tilde{t}\right) Y\,\mathrm{d}t$ at the initial equilibrium Y. Hence, supply of new bank credit to the non-quality borrowers falls by $\beta \cdot (1 - \rho)\,(1 - C) \cdot \left(1 - \tilde{t}\right) Y\,\mathrm{d}t$ at the initial equilibrium Y. ϕ also goes down by $\phi_t \mathrm{d}t$, which leads to a deterioration in quality investors' confidence lowering aggregate investment by $(1 - \beta)\hat{I}_\phi \phi_t\,\mathrm{d}t$ at the initial equilibrium Y. Again, banks' apprehension regarding lending to non-quality borrowers increases reducing β and, thereby, lending to non-quality borrowers by $\beta_\phi \phi_t\,\mathrm{d}t$ and $\beta_\phi L'_{sm} \phi_t\,\mathrm{d}t$, respectively, at the initial equilibrium Y. Thus, as follows from (8.21), aggregate demand at the initial equilibrium Y falls by the numerator of the expression on the RHS of (8.29). This sets off the multiplier process, and just the way it happened in the case of a given cut in $\bar{G}$, there would take place a large and cumulative contraction in Y. This yields the following proposition:

Proposition 8.4 *A hike in income tax rates leads to a very large contraction in Y and the multiplier is much larger than that in the IS-LM model or the simple Keynesian model on account of the operation of the financial intermediaries, which have to reduce their lending following a fall in saving induced by the contraction in Y.*

An Increase in the Indirect Tax Rate $\tilde{t}$

We shall now examine how a hike in the indirect tax rate affects Y using (8.21). Taking total differential of (8.21) treating all exogenous variables other than $\tilde{t}$ as fixed and, then, solving for $\mathrm{d}Y$, we get

$$\mathrm{d}Y = \frac{-\left\{[C(1-t)\cdot Y + \beta(1-\rho)(1-C)(1-t)Y] + \left[(1-\beta)\hat{I}_\phi + \beta_\phi L'_{sm}\right]\phi_{\tilde{t}} + \mathrm{NX}_p\right\}\mathrm{d}\tilde{t}}{1-\alpha'} < 0 \quad \because \mathrm{d}\tilde{t} > 0 \tag{8.30}$$

Interpretation of (8.30) is similar to that of (8.29). However, there is one important difference. It raises domestic price level and, thereby, adversely affects net export. Hence, the contractionary effect of a hike in indirect tax rate will be larger than that of a direct tax rate.

Proposition 8.5 *A hike in indirect tax rates leads to a very large contraction in Y and the multiplier is much larger than that in the IS-LM model or the simple Keynesian model on account of the operation of the financial intermediaries, which have to reduce their lending following a fall in saving induced by the contraction in Y. The effect of a hike in the indirect tax rate is much more contractionary than that of the direct tax rates. This is because the former, unlike the latter, adversely affects net export.*

From Propositions 8.3, 8.4, and 8.5, it is clear why the austerity measures so massively increased the rate of contraction of the Greek economy. Such large contractions in Y created substantial deficits in government's budget despite large cuts in G and steep hikes in direct and indirect tax rates.

8.5 Appropriate Policies for Resolving the Debt Problem of the Greek Government

It is clear from the above discussion that the best way of tackling Greek Government's problem is to raise G and finance it by raising income tax collection at the initial equilibrium Y so that

$$\mathrm{d}\bar{G} = Y\,\mathrm{d}t \tag{8.31}$$

We shall derive the impact of this policy below. Since here $\mathrm{d}t$ is determined by $\mathrm{d}G$, for simplicity and without any loss of generality, we make ϕ an increasing function of G alone so that $\phi = \tilde{\phi}\left(\underset{+}{G}\right)$. Substituting it in (8.21), we rewrite it as

$$\begin{aligned} Y = {} & C\cdot\left(1-\tilde{t}\right)(1-t)Y + \left(1-\beta\left(\underset{+}{Y}, \underset{+}{\tilde{\phi}(\bar{G})}\right)\right)\hat{I}\left(\bar{r}, Y^{*}, \bar{K}, \tilde{\phi}(\bar{G})\right) \\ & + \beta\left(\underset{+}{Y}, \underset{+}{\tilde{\phi}(\bar{G})}\right)\left[(1-\rho)(1-C)\cdot(1-t)\left(1-\tilde{t}\right)Y + \bar{K}\right] \\ & + \bar{G} + \mathrm{NX}\left(\frac{P^{*}}{P(w)}\left(1-\tilde{t}\right), Y; Y^{*}\right) \end{aligned} \tag{8.32}$$

Taking total differential of (8.32) treating all exogenous variables other than $\bar{G}$ and t as fixed, setting $Y\,\mathrm{d}t = \mathrm{d}\bar{G}$, and solving for $\mathrm{d}Y$, we get

$$\mathrm{d}Y = \frac{\left[1-\left\{C\cdot\left(1-\tilde{t}\right)+\beta(1-\rho)(1-C)\left(1-\tilde{t}\right)\right\}\right]\mathrm{d}\bar{G} + \left[(1-\beta)\hat{I}_{\phi}\tilde{\phi}_{G}\right]\mathrm{d}\bar{G} + \left[\beta_{\phi}\cdot\left(\bar{L}_{sm}-\hat{I}\right)\tilde{\phi}_{G}\right]\mathrm{d}\bar{G}}{1-\left[C\cdot(1-t)\left(1-\tilde{t}\right)+\mathrm{NX}_{Y}+\beta\cdot(1-\rho)(1-C)\left(1-\tilde{t}\right)+\beta_{Y}\left(\bar{L}_{sm}-\hat{I}\right)\right]} > 0 \tag{8.33}$$

In (8.33), $\bar{L}_{sm} \equiv (1-\rho)(1-C)(1-t)\left(1-\tilde{t}\right)Y + \bar{K}$. Let us now explain (8.33). Focus on the numerator of the expression on the RHS of (8.33). Following an increase in $\bar{G}$ and income tax collection at the initial equilibrium Y by $\mathrm{d}\bar{G}$, disposable income at the initial equilibrium Y falls by $\left(1-\tilde{t}\right)\mathrm{d}\bar{G}$ reducing consumption and saving by $C\cdot\left(1-\tilde{t}\right)\mathrm{d}\bar{G}$ and $(1-C)\cdot\left(1-\tilde{t}\right)\mathrm{d}\bar{G}$, respectively. The reduction in saving lowers supply of credit to non-quality borrowers and, therefore, investment demand by $\beta(1-\rho)$ $(1-C)\cdot\left(1-\tilde{t}\right)\mathrm{d}\bar{G}$. Thus, in the net, aggregate demand at the initial equilibrium Y goes up by the first term of the numerator. The expansionary policy is likely to give a boost to quality investors' morale. This will raise aggregate investment by the second term of the numerator. The expansionary policy is also likely to improve banks' perception regarding the risk of lending to the non-quality borrowers. This will raise supply of new credit to the non-quality borrowers raising their investment. This is given by the third term of the numerator. Thus, the numerator of the expression on the RHS of (8.33) gives the excess demand that emerges in the goods market at the initial equilibrium Y following the adoption of the given policy. Producers will increase Y to meet this excess demand setting off the multiplier process. In the first round, Y will go up by

$$\mathrm{d}Y_1 = \frac{N}{\lambda} \tag{8.34}$$

In (8.34), N denotes the numerator of the expression on the RHS of (8.33) and $\lambda \equiv 1 - \left[C \cdot \left(1 - \tilde{t}\right)(1 - t) + \mathrm{NX}_Y\right]$. However, the expansion in Y does not stop here. Out of $\mathrm{d}Y_1$, people save $\tilde{\lambda}\mathrm{d}Y_1$, where $\tilde{\lambda} \equiv 1 - C \cdot (1 - t)\left(1 - \tilde{t}\right)$. They put this additional saving in banks as new deposits. Hence, banks supply new loans of $\beta(1 - \rho)\tilde{\lambda}\mathrm{d}Y_1$ to non-quality borrowers. The increase in Y emboldens the banks and, thereby, induces them to increase β. This will raise supply of new loans to non-quality borrowers further by $\beta_Y\left(\bar{L}_{sm} - \hat{I}\right)\mathrm{d}Y_1$. Hence, aggregate investment will go up by $\beta(1 - \rho)\tilde{\lambda}\mathrm{d}Y_1 + \beta_Y\left(\bar{L}_{sm} - \hat{I}\right)dY_1 \equiv \bar{\lambda}\mathrm{d}Y_1$ setting off the multiplier process, and in the second round, Y will go up by $\mathrm{d}Y_2 = \frac{\bar{\lambda}\mathrm{d}Y_1}{\lambda}$. The increase in saving in the second round will again generate new saving, new bank deposit, and new bank credit raising aggregate investment. Hence, in the third round, Y will go up by $\mathrm{d}Y_3 = \left(\frac{\bar{\lambda}}{\lambda}\right)^2 \mathrm{d}Y_1$. This process of expansion will continue until the increase in Y that takes place in each successive round eventually falls to zero. When that happens, the economy attains a new equilibrium. Thus, the total increase in Y, using (8.34), is given by

$$\mathrm{d}Y = \mathrm{d}Y_1 + \frac{\bar{\lambda}}{\lambda}\mathrm{d}Y_1 + \left(\frac{\bar{\lambda}}{\lambda}\right)^2 \mathrm{d}Y_1 + \cdots = \left(\frac{\lambda}{\lambda - \bar{\lambda}}\right)\mathrm{d}Y_1 = \left(\frac{\lambda}{\lambda - \bar{\lambda}}\right)\frac{N}{\lambda} = \frac{N}{\lambda - \bar{\lambda}} \tag{8.35}$$

One can easily check that (8.35) tallies with (8.33). From the above, it follows that the policies suggested here produce a large expansion in Y and generate additional tax revenue over and above $\mathrm{d}\bar{G}$ of $\left(t + \tilde{t}\right)\mathrm{d}Y = \left(t + \tilde{t}\right) \cdot \frac{N}{\lambda - \bar{\lambda}}$. This, the government can use to pay off its debt. The government should set $d\bar{G}$ at such a level that Y rises to its full employment level. The additional income tax should be collected from the rich, who can afford to pay the tax. Their loss will be compensated for by the large increase in Y the bulk of which will go into their hands. Moreover, the prospect of a very large increase in Y and substantial improvement in government's budget is likely to dispel the gloom and gives a boost to the morale of investors and financial institutions making $\tilde{\phi}_G$ in (8.33) substantially large. This yields the following proposition:

Proposition 8.6 *To resolve Greece's sovereign debt problem, the troika should have asked the Greek Government to raise its consumption expenditure and finance it by raising additional income tax from the rich at the initial equilibrium Y. The policy generates a very large increase in Y and, thereby, raises substantially government's tax revenue over and above the increase in G. To improve government's budget to the* *maximum possible extent, the government should raise its consumption expenditure to such a level that Y rises to the full employment level.*

8.6 Conclusion

Our above analysis suggests that the Greek crisis is due to the speculative activities of the global financial institutions that operate in the asset markets of different countries globally. They started lending to Greek Government and Greek investors on a massive scale during 2003-07 creating an unprecedented boom. Greek GDP grew at a very high rate during the given period. Eurozone countries have to abide by strict fiscal deficit target (government borrowing) norms. Under these norms, government of a Eurozone country has to keep its borrowings as a percentage of GDP at or below a target level. Thus, throughout the boom period Greek Government kept its borrowing at the targeted percentage of GDP. As a result, Greek Government's borrowing and, thereby, its debt grew at very high rates. It became very large at the end of 2007. Along with it, Greek Government's debt service charges also became very large. Besides the global investors' entry into Greece on a massive scale, financial institutions created massive bubbles in the share prices of Internet companies in the USA and prices of real estate in both USA and many European countries during 1996–2007 creating a boom in the USA and the European countries including Greece. In fact, Greece experienced a boom during 1996–2002 also on account of the boom in many European countries and the USA. The high growth of Greek GDP during 1996–2002 also contributed to the growth in Greek Government's debt. While the bubble in the stock prices of Internet companies in the USA, called the dot-com bubble, burst in 2001, the real estate bubble collapsed in 2008 driving both the USA and the European countries into a deep recession. Right at that time, the global financial institutions not only stopped lending to Greece but also started withdrawing funds from Greece. The deep recession in the rest of Europe and the USA led to a large contraction in export demand. The outflow of capital led to a severe cut in the supply of credit. Both these factors led to drastic cuts in investment and government spending and also to a sharp deterioration in investors' morale. Greek economy went into a very severe recession. Government's revenue fell to such low levels that it was not possible to service its debt after meeting other essential expenditure commitments. Greece had to appeal to the troika for a bailout.

Clearly, the Greek crisis created by deep recession could be resolved only through the adoption of expansionary policies that would have lifted the economy out of recession and brought it back to health. Instead, the troika thrust on Greece a set of austerity measures, which were extremely contractionary and devastated Greece. They perpetuated deep recession and, thereby, large deficits in government's budget forcing Greece into a perpetual debt trap. They hurt the working class the most by raising the unemployment rate to around 24 percent in 2016 from around 7 percent in 2008. There took place massive cuts in wages and pensions, layoffs of workers on a large scale and substantial dilution of labor laws safeguarding the interest of the workers.

Table 8.6 Budget deficit of Greek Government as a percentage of GDP

Year	BD/GDP	Year	BD/GDP
2000	−4.1	09	−15.1
01	−5.5	10	−11.2
02	−6	11	−10.3
03	−7.8	12	−8.9
04	−8.8	13	−13.2
05	−6.2	14	−3.6
06	−5.9	15	−5.7
07	−6.7	16	0.6
08	−10.2	17	0.8

Source World Bank

There also took place privatization of government organizations and sell-off of government's assets on a large scale. From the above, it is clear that Greece is another example of a country, which the giant global capitalists have conquered through their investments in Greece. The objective is to destroy the bargaining strength of the workers, acquire government's assets, and take the government completely under their control (Table 8.6).

References

Bernanke, B. S., & Blinder, A. S. (1988). Credit, money and aggregate demand. *The American Economic Review, 78*(2), 435–439.

Dellas, H., & Tavlas, G. S. (2013). The gold standard, the euro and the origins of the Greek sovereign debt crisis. *Cato Journal, 33*(3), 491–520.

Gibson, H. D., Palivos,T., & Tavlas, G. S. (2014) The crisis in the euro area. *Journal of Macroeconomics, 38*(B), 233–460.

Krugman, P. (2013) Revenge of the optimum currency area. *NBER Macroeconomic Annual 2012*, 27: 439–448.

Lane, P. R. (2012). The European sovereign debt crisis. *Journal of Economic Perspectives, 26*(3), 49–68.

Tobin, J. (1958, February). Liquidity preference as behaviour towards risk. *Review of Economic Studies, 25*(2), 65–86.

Chapter 9
The Crisis in the US Economy

Abstract A huge house price bubble formed in the US economy in the late nineties, and it collapsed in 2006 plunging the economy into a deep recession. The objective of this chapter is to identify the causes of the formation of the house price bubble and its collapse. After carefully analyzing the available evidences, it concludes that the giant capitalists who control the giant financial institutions created the bubble and burst it. They did it to have the workers savings parked with the financial institutions transferred to themselves in the form of speculative capital gains. They also made sure that the remaining part of the workers' savings become available to them at the minimum possible interest rate and the small and medium producers get competed out. Policies of the US Government and Fed also facilitated the plan of the giant capitalists and helped them keep the economy under their control.

9.1 Introduction

The last twenty years witnessed the formation and collapse of two massive bubbles in quick succession in the US economy: the bubble in the stock prices of dot-com companies and that in the price of houses. The dot-com bubble formed in 1997 and swelled during 1997–2000. This was a period of boom—see Table 9.1. The dot-com bubble collapsed in 2001 plunging the economy into a recession—see Table 9.1. The housing bubble started in 1998. It gathered momentum since the collapse of the dot-com bubble in 2001 and finally collapsed in 2006 with devastating effect—see Table 9.1. The whole of the US financial sector went into a deep crisis, with most of the major financial institutions in considerable trouble. The US economy went into a severe recession the like of which it never experienced since its recovery from the Great Depression. The recession is continuing even today. The US economy is not an exception. All the major crises in recent history the world over are due to formation and collapse of asset price bubbles. Take, for example, the case of Japan. A massive bubble formed in the prices of its stocks and real estate in the mid-eighties, and it collapsed in 1991 drawing the Japanese economy into a deep recession in 1992. Japan is yet to recover from it. Collapse of real estate bubble in 1997 in the Southeast Asian countries drove them into a severe recession. Many European countries plunged into

C. Ghosh and A. N. Ghosh, *Keynesian Macroeconomics Beyond the IS-LM Model*, https://doi.org/10.1007/978-981-13-7888-1_9

Table 9.1 House price inflation, consumer price inflation, and interest rates

Year	HPI[a]	CPI	r^b	R^c	Y^d
1994	2.83	2.6	7.15	8.35	4.0
1995	1.11	2.8	8.83	6.15	2.7
1996	2.83	3.0	8.27	5.84	3.8
1997	2.73	2.3	8.44	5.99	4.5
1998	5.66	1.6	8.35	5.13	4.5
1999	7.41	2.2	8.00	5.43	4.7
2000	6.62	3.4	9.23	6.26	4.1
2001	6.49	2.8	6.91	3.83	1.0
2002	8.76	1.6	4.67	2.64	1.8
2003	8.72	2.3	4.12	1.65	2.8
2004	10.98	2.7	4.34	2.38	3.8
2005	10.16	3.4	6.19	3.85	3.3
2006	0.86	3.2	7.96	4.82	2.7
2007	−4.64	2.8	8.05	4.36	1.8
2008	−10.27	3.8	5.09	2.01	−0.3
2009	−0.5	−0.4	3.25	0.96	−2.8
2010	−4.68	1.6	3.25	0.7	2.5
2011	−2.7	3.2	3.25	0.45	1.6
2012	7.28	2.9	3.25	0.28	2.2
2013			3.25	0.31	1.5

[a]House price inflation, [b]average majority prime rate charged by banks on short-term loans to business, [c]contract rate on 30-year fixed rate conventional home mortgage commitments, [d]percentage increase in real GDP from the previous year
Source HPI has been computed from the house price index published by Freddie Mac; data of CPI and percentage change in real GDP are taken from US Bureau of Economic; analysis; data on interest rates have been taken from the Board of Governors of the Federal Reserve System

a deep recession in 2008 following the collapse of real estate bubbles. It is, therefore, extremely important to know how or why bubbles in asset prices form and why or how they collapse. The objective of this chapter is to shed light on this issue.

The endeavor is worthwhile because the existing literature cannot satisfactorily explain why bubbles form in asset prices or why they collapse. The price of an asset contains a bubble, when it exceeds the level that is warranted by the true worth of the asset. The excess of the price of the stock of a company from the level that is warranted by the true income-yielding capacity of the company is referred to as bubble. Similarly, the excess of the price of a house from its cost of production plus a reasonable profit margin is referred to as bubble. Thus, if the rate of inflation in house prices exceeds the rate of inflation in the general price level, there is a bubble in house prices as they are growing at a faster rate than the cost of production of houses. Given the enormous importance of asset price bubbles in perpetrating crises in different countries the world over, it is of paramount importance to know how bubbles in asset prices form and how they collapse. The existing literature on the US house price bubble attributes the formation and collapse of the house price bubble to the conditions prevailing in the credit market. One common explanation for the formation of the house price bubble in the USA is that easily available credit, perhaps caused by a 'global savings glut,' led to low real interest rates that boosted housing demand (Himmelberg et al. 2005; Mayer and Sinai 2005; Taylor 2009). Others have suggested that easy credit market terms, including low down payments and high mortgage approval rates, allowed many people to act at once and helped generate large, coordinated swings in housing markets (Khandani et al. 2009). However, Glaeser et al. (2010) dispute these claims. Many other economists also do not agree with the view presented above. For example, Case and Shiller (2003) and Shiller (2006) have argued that mass psychology is more important than any of the mechanisms suggested by the research cited above.

From the data given in Table 9.1, it seems that the credit market explanation of the formation of bubbles cited above, which constitutes the only major explanation of the formation of house price bubbles in the USA, is untenable for the following reasons. First, if we compare the rates of house price inflation and the CPI, we find that they were more or less equal till 1997. The former jumped up and exceeded the latter by a substantial amount in 1998. Since then, the gap between the two went on increasing until the collapse of the bubble in 2006. However, between 1997 and 1998, as should be clear from the data on interest rates, there did not take place any softening of credit market conditions (see Table 9.1). In fact, credit market softened only since 2001, when, following the collapse of the dot-com bubble in 2001, the Fed cut down its policy rates to tackle the ensuing recession. Thus, the remarkable jump in (more than doubling of) the rate of house price inflation from 1997 to 1998 and its sustenance at such high levels in the next two years (1999–2000) in the face of unchanged inflation rate and interest rates cannot in any way be linked to a softening of credit market conditions. During these three years, 1998, 1999, and 2000, the rate of house price inflation and the interest rates were so close to one another that they did not warrant any speculative purchase of houses let alone mass speculative exuberance. Such opportunities emerged starkly since 2001, when interest rate declined substantially, while the rate of house price inflation remained at its high level. Such a situation continued until 2006. Thus, the scope for large gains from the speculative purchase of houses opened up and it came into the view of the people only in 2001. Thus, the mass exuberance for the speculative purchase of houses could have started only after that. How does one explain then the remarkable high rate of inflation in the house prices during 1998–2000. The only plausible explanation of this phenomenon is that the jump in the house price inflation was caused by those speculators who foresaw the marked decline in the interest rate that would take place since 2001. They kept the rate of house price inflation at a high rate for some years preceding 2001 so that once the rate of interest dropped, ordinary people could clearly perceive (or could be made to clearly perceive) the scope for large speculative gains from house purchases and jump into the trap. Since the media is in the hands of the large financial institutions to a large extent (both being controlled by the same group of giant capitalists), the people were made to perceive the huge opportunities for speculative gains in the housing sector through the media. This means that these speculators created the dot-com bubble and had it burst in 2001. They knew that following the collapse of the dot-com bubble, the economy would enter into a recession and the Fed would reduce rates to contain it. These speculators, obviously a group of large financial institutions with tremendous financial might, purchased dot-come stocks and created the dot-com bubble and when prices of dot-com stocks reached their peaks riding on public speculative frenzy, offloaded their stock of dot-com stocks, and burst the bubble at a huge profit. From the above, it follows that the speculators who created and burst the dot-com bubble were also responsible for the formation and collapse of the house price bubble. This line of thought seems to be the only explanation for the remarkable jump in the rate of house price inflation in 1998 and its sustenance at such a high level in the next three years. In what follows, we shall develop a very simple model to capture the modus operandi of these speculators and the impact their activities produce in the economy.

9.2 The Model

We shall develop a simple model to explain how economic crisis occurred in the USA. We divide the real sector into two segments: one producing an asset such as houses and the other producing all other produced goods and services. The former and the latter are referred to as the A-sector and the Y-sector, respectively. We denote the outputs of the A-sector and the Y-sector by A and Y, respectively. Let us focus on the Y-sector first.

Y-Sector

We assume that Y is demand-determined. The equilibrium of the Y-sector in period t is given by

$$Y_t = C\left((1-\tau)Y_t, \underset{+}{\left(\frac{P_{at}}{P_{yt}}\tilde{A}_{ht} - d_{ht}\right)}\right) + I\left(\underset{-}{r}\right)\bar{G} \tag{9.1}$$

In (9.1), $\tau \equiv$ direct tax rate, $P_{at} \equiv$ price of the asset produced by the A-sector in period t, $P_{yt} \equiv$ price of the goods and services produced by the Y-sector in period t, $\tilde{A}_{ht} \equiv$ the stock of the asset held by the households in period t, and $d_{ht} \equiv$ outstanding net debt of the households in period t expressed in terms of Y. In (9.1), C is a function not only of disposable income but also of the value of households' net worth in terms of Y defined as households' outstanding stock of the asset A in terms of Y net of the outstanding debt of the households in terms of Y. Note that in this model households hold their wealth not only in the form of the asset A but also in the form of bank deposits. Accordingly, d_{ht} denotes the stock of outstanding loan of the households in period t net of the outstanding stock of bank deposits of the households. It is quite standard to assume that aggregate consumption is an increasing function of households' aggregate wealth or net worth. An increase in the net worth of the households raises their credit-worthiness and, thereby, allows those that are credit-constrained to secure more credit—[see in this connection Bernanke et al. (1996)]. We have avoided these complications in case of investment for simplicity and made it a function only of interest rate in period t, which we denote by r_t. We assume that government's consumption expenditure is given at all t and denote it by $\bar{G}$. Again, for simplicity and without any loss of generality, we shall assume P_{yt} to be fixed for all values of t and assume it to be equal to unity.

The rate of inflation in P_a in period t denoted by Π_{at} is given by

$$\Pi_{at} = \frac{P_{at} - P_{at-1}}{P_{at-1}} = \frac{P_{at}}{P_{at-1}} - 1 \tag{9.2}$$

From (9.2), it follows that

$$P_{at} = (1 + \Pi_{at})P_{at-1} \tag{9.3}$$

Since P_y is assumed to be unity, substituting (9.3) into (9.1), we rewrite it as

$$Y_t = C\Big((1 \underset{+}{-} \tau)Y, (1 + \Pi_{at})\underset{+}{P_{at-1}}\tilde{A}_{ht} - d_{ht}\Big) + I\Big(\underset{-}{r}\Big) + \bar{G} \tag{9.4}$$

Given the situation we shall try to explain, a situation where households' net worth was determined principally by the price of the asset, it may be sensible to assume for simplicity and without any loss of generality that households' net worth, $(1 + \Pi_{at})P_{at-1}\tilde{A}_{ht} - d_{ht}$, is an increasing function of P_{at} alone and is given by $g((1 + \Pi_{at})P_{at-1})$. Incorporating it in (9.4), we rewrite it as

$$Y_t = C\Big((1 \underset{+}{-} \tau)Y_t, g((1 + \underset{+}{\Pi_{at}})P_{at-1})\Big) + I\Big(\underset{-}{r}\Big) + \bar{G} \tag{9.5}$$

A-Sector

Let us now focus on the market for the asset A. Regarding its supply, we postulate that the higher is P_a relative to P_y, the larger is the profitability of producing A. So, we make supply of A, denoted A^S, an increasing function of $\frac{P_a}{P_y}$. Thus, using (9.3) and the assumption that P_y is unity, we write

$$A_t^S = S\Big(\Big(1 \underset{+}{+} \Pi_{at}\Big)P_{at-1}\Big) \tag{9.6}$$

Demand for the asset A has three components. The asset has a use value. So, it has a demand for its use value. We make this component of demand a decreasing function of

P_a and the interest rate. However, we drop r for simplicity. We denote this component of demand by D_1 and write it as $D_{1t} = D_1\left(\underset{-}{(1 + \Pi_{at})P_{at-1}}\right)$. Besides this, the asset has a speculative demand component. We denote this component of demand by D_2 and make it an increasing function of the difference between the expected rate of inflation and r. If people's expected rate of inflation (denoted Π_a^e) exceeds r, they expect to make profit by buying the asset with loans or with their savings and selling it at a later date. When $\Pi_a^e - r = 0$, speculative demand for the asset is zero. When $\Pi_a^e - r < 0$, there is a rush to sell off the speculative stock, if there is any, made in the past to minimize losses. So, speculative demand for the asset is negative in such situations. We assume that individuals' expectations are adaptive. The present and past values of Π_a play an important role in determining their expectation regarding the future value of Π_a. Moreover, individuals' expectations differ. Through $D_2(\cdot)$, we seek to capture the behavior of individuals when they were caught in a speculative frenzy. When Π_a exceeded r and people got the impression through the media and other means such as hearsay spread through party cadres that the situation was going to last in future, many people were convinced, formed the expectation that way, and took the plunge in the speculative purchases of the asset. Clearly, the larger the excess of Π_a over r, the stronger is the reason to be convinced regarding the persistence of the gainful opportunity. Hence, a larger number of people are likely to join the speculative fray. Again, when Π_a dropped below r, many people became panicky and apprehended losses from holding on to the asset, while others might have hoped for a reversal and held on to their stock of the asset or might have even bought the asset in the hope that Π_a would soon rise above r. Clearly, the less the Π_a relative to r, the greater is the panic and the larger is the number of people deciding to sell off the asset. We, therefore, make D_2 an increasing function of $\Pi_a - r$. Moreover, the longer a situation persists, the greater is the conviction among the people that the situation will persist further. Thus, if in any given period $\Pi_a - r > 0$, then in the next period more people will be convinced that the situation will persist in future and, therefore, will take to speculative purchase of the asset. Similarly, if $\Pi_a - r < 0$ in any given period, in the next period more people will be gripped by panic and will want to sell off the asset. Thus, we posit

$$D_{2t} = D_2\left(\underset{+}{\Pi_{at} - r_t}; t\right); \quad \frac{\partial D_2}{\partial t} > 0 \text{ when } \Pi_{at} - r_t > 0$$
$$\text{and } \frac{\partial D_2}{\partial t} < 0 \text{ when } \Pi_{at} - r_t < 0 \tag{9.7}$$

There is also an autonomous component of the domestic demand for the asset, which we denote by $\bar{D}$. This autonomous component of demand comes from the financial institutions, which purchase or sell the asset to manipulate the price of the asset. Thus, aggregate demand for the asset, denoted A^D, is given by

$$A_t^D = D_1\left(\underset{-}{(1 + \Pi_{at})P_{t-1}}, \underset{-}{r}\right) + D_2\left(\underset{+}{\Pi_{at} - r_t}; t\right) + \bar{D}_t \tag{9.8}$$

From (9.8), we find that a ceteris paribus increase in Π_{at} lowers D_1 and raises D_2. Hence, the direction of change in the aggregate demand for the asset is ambiguous. Here, we shall consider two cases: in one, speculative demand for the asset is absent, while in the other, speculative purchase/sale of the asset far outstrips the purchase of the asset for its ordinary use. Hence, in the former case, aggregate demand for the asset falls with an increase in Π_a, while in the latter case, aggregate demand for the asset rises with an increase in Π_a.

The market for the asset is in equilibrium when

$$S((1+\Pi_{at})P_{at-1}) = D_1\left(\underset{-}{(1+\Pi_{at})P_{t-1}}, \underset{-}{r}\right) + D_2\left(\underset{+}{\Pi_{at} - r_t}; t\right) + \bar{D}_t \tag{9.9}$$

Financial Sector

The financial sector consists only of the central bank and the commercial banks. The latter do not hold any excess reserve, only households save, and they hold their entire saving as bank deposit. Commercial banks are the only source of loans to the firms and households. Firms borrow from the domestic commercial banks to finance their entire investment expenditure. Households borrow from the commercial banks to finance their purchase of the asset. The government finances its deficit by borrowing from the commercial banks. In case it runs a budget surplus, it holds it as deposit with the commercial banks. The central bank lends to the commercial banks at a policy rate denoted by r_c. The commercial banks set their lending rate r on the basis of r_c. Therefore,

$$r = r\left(\underset{+}{r_c}\right) \tag{9.10}$$

The central bank sets r_c at such a level that r remains at a target level and lends to the commercial banks as much as they want to borrow at the given r_c. Supply of new loans by the commercial banks denoted L^S is given by

$$L_t^s = (1-\rho)\left[\left\{Y_t - C\left(\underset{+}{(1-\tau)Y_t}, \underset{+}{g((1+\Pi_{at})P_{at-1})}\right)\right\} + b_t\right] \tag{9.11}$$

In (9.11), ρ denotes the CRR; the new deposit received by the commercial banks is the saving of the households given by

$$\left[Y_t - C\left(\underset{+}{(1-\tau)Y_t}, \underset{+}{g((1+\Pi_{at})P_{at-1})}\right)\right]$$

and b_t denotes the amount of new loans taken by the commercial banks from the central bank in period t. The commercial banks meet all the demand for credit that comes forth at $r = r(r_c)$ in period t by choosing an appropriate value of b_t. Thus, in the situation we consider here households, firms and the government are able to fulfill all their planned demand for consumption, investment and the asset as specified in (9.5) and (9.8) at $r = r(r_c)$ in every period.

Substituting (9.10) into (9.5) and (9.9), we rewrite them as follows:

$$Y_t = C\Big(\underset{+}{(1-\tau)Y_t}, \underset{+}{g((1+\Pi_{at})P_{at-1})}\Big) + I\Big(\underset{-}{r(r_c)}\Big) + \bar{G} \tag{9.12}$$

and

$$S((1+\Pi_{at})P_{at-1}) = D_1\Big(\underset{-}{(1+\Pi_{at})P_{t-1}}\Big) + D_2\Big(\underset{+}{\Pi_{at} - r(r_c)}; t\Big) + \bar{D}_t \tag{9.13}$$

The specification of our model is now complete. It consists of two key Eqs. (9.12) and (9.13). We shall use these two equations to capture the behavior of the US economy.

9.3 The Period Prior to the Mass Speculative Frenzy (1998–2000)

We shall first consider the situation where the speculative component of the demand for the asset was absent. This was the situation that prevailed during the period prior to 2001, when Π_a was below or equal to $r(r_c)$ so that there was no basis for luring the masses into speculation. In this situation, therefore, $D_2(\cdot)$ is zero and the asset market equilibrium condition (9.13) is rewritten as

$$S((1+\Pi_{at})P_{at-1}) = D_1\Big(\underset{-}{(1+\Pi_{at})P_{t-1}}\Big) + \bar{D}_t \tag{9.14}$$

We can solve (9.14) for the equilibrium value of Π_{at}, given the values of P_{at-1} and $\bar{D}_t$. The solution of Π_a in this situation is shown in Fig. 9.1. In Fig. 9.1, DD_0 represents demand for the asset A as given by the RHS of (9.14), and A^S schedule represents the LHS of (9.14). The equilibrium value of Π_{at} labeled Π_{at0} corresponds to the point of intersection of the two schedules. Before 1998, Π_{at0} was equal to the inflation rate in the general price level (see Table 9.1). Since in our model P_y is taken to be fixed, we make Π_{at0} equal to zero. It was much below $r(r_c)$. In 1998, suddenly the rate of inflation in the price of the asset jumped up far above the inflation rate in the general price level. As in 1998 there was no basis for luring the masses into speculation, the giant financial institutions owned by the giant capitalists, who have the financial might to create asset price bubble anywhere in the world, must have created the bubble in 1998 knowing fully well that they would engineer a recession a few years later by bursting the dot-com bubble giving the central bank an excuse to lower interest rates substantially. Until then, the giant capitalists planned to keep the inflation rate in the price of the asset at the high level. Once the central

Fig. 9.1 Determination of the equilibrium value of Π_a

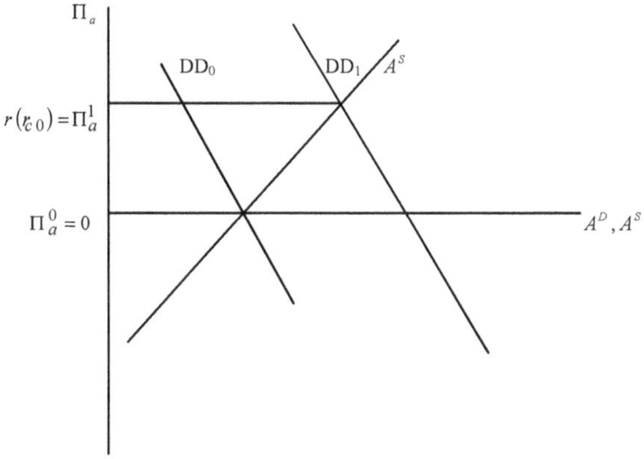

bank cut interest rates substantially to a level much below the rate of inflation in the price of the asset, they would lure the masses into a speculative frenzy and, thereby, make speculative profit by selling from their stock of the asset, which they started building since 1998. This is the only possible explanation of the trebling of the house price inflation rate in 1998. Thus, in 1998, the financial institutions either directly or through their agents raised $\bar{D}_t$ shifting the DD schedule in Fig. 9.1 rightward from DD_0 to DD_1 raising Π_a to Π_{at1}, which was equal to $r(r_c)$. Let us now examine, for reasons that will be clear shortly, how the financial institutions have to change the value of $\bar{D}$ in the next period, period $t+1$, to keep Π_{at+1} at $r(r_c)$. Now, $P_{at} = (1+\Pi_{at1})P_{t-1} = (1+r(r_c))P_{t-1} > P_{at-1}$. In period $t+1$, A^S schedule is given by $S((1+\Pi_{at+1})P_{at})$. Corresponding to any given Π_{at+1}, therefore, P_{at+1} and supply of A-good will be larger in period $t+1$ bringing about a rightward shift in the A^S schedule in Fig. 9.1. Again, in period $t+1$, the DD schedule will be given by $D_1((1+\Pi_{at+1})P_{at}) + \bar{D}_{t+1}$. Thus, in period $t+1$, corresponding to any given Π_{at+1} and $\bar{D}_{t+1} = \bar{D}_t$, P_{at+1} will be larger and demand for the asset A will be less. Thus, in period $t+1$, for $\bar{D}_{t+1} = \bar{D}_t$, the DD schedule will be to the left of DD_1 schedule in Fig. 9.1. Hence, the equilibrium value of Π_{at+1} will be much less than $r(r_c)$, when $\bar{D}_{t+1} = \bar{D}_t$. Therefore, to keep Π_{at+1} at $r(r_c)$, $\bar{D}_{t+1}$ has to be made much larger than $\bar{D}_t$.

During 1998–2001, the financial institutions made $\bar{D}_t$ grow in such a manner that Π_{at} remained at $\Pi_{at1} = r(r_c)$. Assuming the year 1997 to be period zero, the time path of $\bar{D}_t$ during 1998–2001 is given, as follows from (9.14), by the following equation:

$$\bar{D}_t = S\big((1+r(r_c))^t P_{a0}\big) - D_1\Big(\underset{-}{(1+r(r_c))^t P_{a0}}\Big) \tag{9.15}$$

From (9.15), it is clear that as t rises, $S(\cdot)$ becomes larger and $D_1(\cdot)$ becomes less, and hence, $\bar{D}_t$ rises.

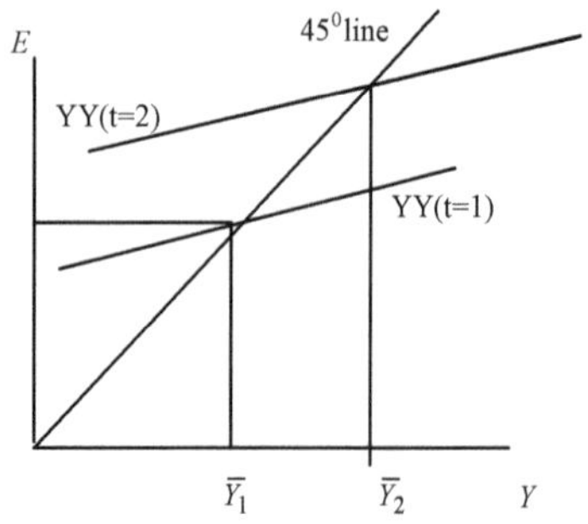

Fig. 9.2 Determination of the equilibrium value of Y

To get a specific solution of $\bar{D}_t$, we take simple forms of $S(\cdot)$ and $D_1(\cdot)$ and rewrite (9.15) as

$$s \cdot \left((1 + r(r_c))^t P_{a0}\right) = \bar{d} - d \cdot \left((1 + r(r_c))^t P_{a0}\right) + \bar{D}_t \tag{9.16}$$

Solving (9.16), we get

$$\bar{D}_t = (d + s)(1 + r(r_c))^t P_{a0} - \bar{d} \tag{9.17}$$

To capture the behavior of Y during 1998–2001, we rewrite (9.12) as follows:

$$Y_t = C\left(\underset{+}{(1 - \tau)Y_t}, \underset{+}{g\left((1 + r(r_c))^t P_{a0}\right)}\right) + I\left(\underset{-}{r(r_c)}\right) + \bar{G} \tag{9.18}$$

Corresponding to any given value of t, we can solve (9.18) for Y_t. The solution of (9.18) is shown in Fig. 9.2. The $YY(t = 1)$ schedule represents the RHS of (9.18) for $t = 1$. The equilibrium Y in period $t = 1$ corresponds to the point of intersection of the 45° line and $YY(t = 1)$ schedule. As t rises from 1 to 2, the value of the RHS corresponding to any given Y rises. Hence, $YY(t = 2)$ schedule will lie above $YY(t = 1)$ schedule. Hence, the equilibrium value of Y in period 2 will be larger. This is shown in Fig. 9.2, where Y rises from $\bar{Y}_1$ in period 1 to $\bar{Y}_2$ in period 2. Let us explain this result. On account of the inflation in the asset price at the rate r_c, the price of the asset rises from $P_{a0}(1 + r_c)$ in period 1 to $[P_{a0}(1 + r_c)]^2$ in period 2. This raises the value of the stock of the asset net of debt of the households raising their consumption level corresponding to any given Y. Thus, at $Y = \bar{Y}_1$, there emerges excess demand for Y setting off the multiplier process. Hence, equilibrium occurs at a larger Y in period 2. Thus, the higher rate of inflation in the price of the asset led to a higher growth rate of Y.

To get explicit solution of Y_t, we assume a simple specific form of the consumption function and rewrite (9.18) as

$$Y_t = C_y \cdot (1-\tau)Y_t + C_a \cdot g\big((1+r(r_c))^t P_{a0}\big) + I\Big(\underset{-}{r(r_c)}\Big) + \bar{G} \tag{9.19}$$

Solving (9.19), we get

$$Y_t = \frac{C_a \cdot g\big((1+r(r_c))^t P_{a0}\big) + I\Big(\underset{-}{r(r_c)}\Big) + \bar{G}}{1 - C_y \cdot (1-\tau)} \tag{9.20}$$

From (9.20), it is clear that Y grows as t increases and the higher the rate of inflation, given by $r(r_c)$ here, the greater will be the growth rate in Y. Thus, during 1998–2001, the giant financial institutions owned by the giant capitalists artificially raised the inflation rate in the asset price at a high level and kept it there. This increase in the inflation rate in the asset price also raised the growth rate of GDP. This is consistent with data of growth rate given in Table 9.1, which shows that annual rates of growth of GDP during 1998–2000 were quite high relative to those in the preceding years.

9.4 The Period of Mass Speculative Frenzy (2001–2010)

Let us now focus on the period 2001–2010 during which the mass speculative frenzy for the purchase of houses started and collapsed. The US economy went into a recession in 2001 following the collapse of the dot-com bubble and the sharp fall in the prices of the stocks of the Internet companies. In terms of our model, P_a declined steeply in 2001 reducing drastically households' net worth. As a result, as shown above, the economy plunged into a recession. The Fed cut r_c substantially to counter it. Consequently, $r(r_c)$ dropped significantly below its initial value. Since the financial institutions kept Π_a at the level equal to the initial value of $r(r_c)$, the fall in $r(r_c)$ much below its initial value to, say, $r(r_{c1})$ created a basis for expecting large speculative gains in future from speculative purchase of houses. The financial institutions, which so long kept Π_a at the initial value of $r(r_c)$, succeeded in creating this expectation among the masses through various means including the media. Driven by this expectation, the masses got into a speculative frenzy. Aided by Fed, which lowered r_c to a very low level and was prepared to meet all the loan demand that would come forth from the financial institutions at the lower r_c, the financial institutions diluted credit standards substantially and facilitated the mass speculative frenzy by extending as much loan as the masses wanted. Expectations generated among the masses, thus, turned self-fulfilling, and Π_a started soaring even from its initial high value. We shall capture this frenzy using (9.13). Corresponding to any given value of t, we can solve it for Π_{at}. Since during the period under consideration, speculative demand for the asset A dominated overwhelmingly its ordinary demand, we shall assume D_1 in (9.13) to be substantially small relative to D_2 so that following a ceteris paribus increase in Π_a, aggregate demand for the asset rises instead of falling. The

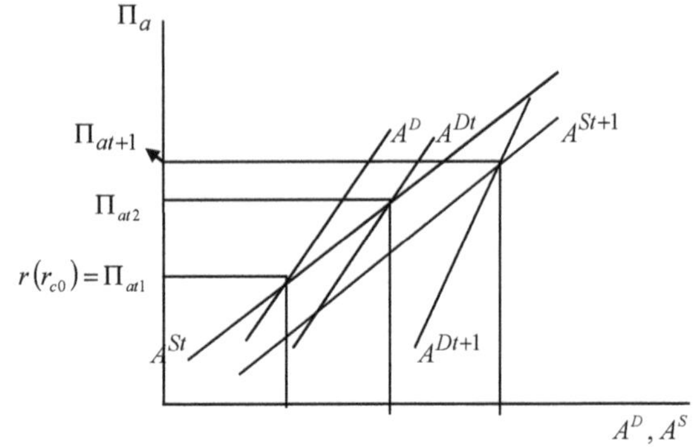

Fig. 9.3 Effect of a cut in the policy rate on asset price inflation

situation is shown in Fig. 9.3, where the A^D schedule representing the RHS of (9.13) is positively sloped and the equilibrium Π_{at} corresponds to the point of intersection of the A^D and A^{St} schedules. The latter represents the LHS of (9.13). We have made A^D schedule flatter than the A^S schedule for reasons of stability. Initially, the equilibrium Π_{at} was $\Pi_{at1} = r(r_{c0})$, where r_{c0} denotes the initial value of r_c and there was no speculative demand for the asset except for $\bar{D}_t$. In 2002, however, Fed cut r_c substantially from r_{c0} to r_{c1} reducing r from $r(r_{c0})$ to $r(r_{c1})$. Hence, corresponding to any given Π_{at}, $(\Pi_{at} - r)$ increased substantially from $(\Pi_{at} - r(r_{c0}))$ to $(\Pi_{at} - r(r_{c1}))$ shifting the A^D schedule rightward by a large amount. The new A^D schedule is labeled A^{Dt} in Fig. 9.3. The mass speculative frenzy began, and Π_a rose. It rose from Π_{at1} to Π_{at2} in Fig. 9.3. Let us link our finding to actual experiences. Following the substantial cut in the interest rate in 2002, Π_a exceeded r by a large amount. As Π_a remained equal to $\Pi_{at1} = r(r_{c0})$ during 1998–2000, it was easy to convince the people through the media and other means that Π_a would remain at the higher level in future. This caught the masses in a speculative frenzy. Demand for the asset A increased substantially raising Π_a by a large amount. From the data given in Table 9.1, we find that the house price inflation rate increased from 6.49% in 2001 to 8.76% in 2002.

Let us now examine how the increase in Π_{at} affects Y_t. Upon substituting the equilibrium value of Π_{at} into (9.12), we can solve it for the equilibrium value of Y_t. The solution of (9.12) is shown in Fig. 9.4, where the initial equilibrium Y_t labeled Y_{t1} corresponds to the point of intersection of the $YY(\Pi_{at1})$ line representing the RHS of (9.12), when Π_{at} is fixed at Π_{at1}, and the 45° line. From (9.12), it follows that following an increase in Π_{at} from Π_{at1} to Π_{at2}, the level of consumption demand and, therefore, that of aggregate demand rise corresponding to every Y_t. Hence, the YY line shifts upward from $YY(\Pi_{at1})$ to $YY(\Pi_{at2})$ raising the equilibrium value of Y_t. Thus, the increase in the rate of asset price inflation contributed to the growth rate of Y. From Table 9.1, we find that the rate of growth of GDP increased steadily from 1% in 2001 to 3.3% in 2005.

Let us now examine how Π_a is likely to change in period $t+1$ using (9.13). Rewriting it for period $t+1$, we get

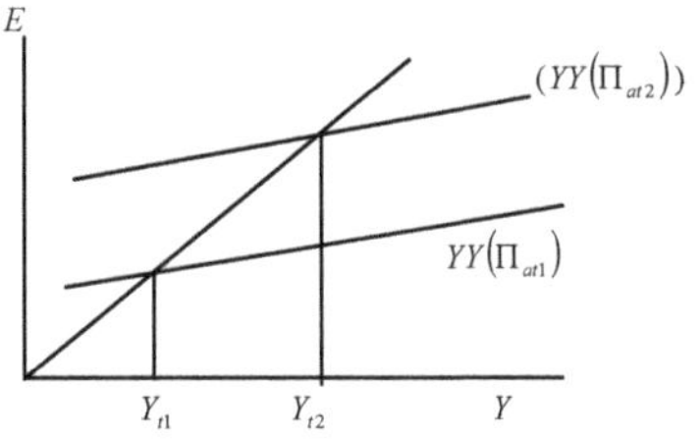

Fig. 9.4 Effect of an increase in the asset price inflation rate on Y

$$S((1+\Pi_{at+1})P_{at}) = D_1\Big(\underset{-}{(1+\Pi_{at+1})P_{at}}\Big) + D_2\Big(\Pi_{at+1} \underset{+}{-} r(r_{c1}); t+1\Big) + \bar{D}_{t+1} \tag{9.21}$$

Now,

$$P_{at} = (1+\Pi_{at2})P_{at-1} > P_{at-1} \tag{9.22}$$

Substituting (9.22) into (9.21), we rewrite it as follows:

$$S((1+\Pi_{at+1})(1+\Pi_{at2})P_{at-1}) = D_1\Big((1+\Pi_{at+1})\underset{-}{(1}+\Pi_{at2})P_{at-1}\Big)$$
$$+ D_2\Big(\Pi_{at+1} \underset{+}{-} r(r_{c1}); t+1\Big) + \bar{D}_{t+1} \tag{9.23}$$

We can solve (9.23) for the equilibrium value of Π_{at+1}. Let us first focus on the LHS. Since P_{at} is much larger than P_{at-1}, corresponding to any Π_a, the supply of asset A will be much larger in period $t+1$ than that in period t. Thus, the A^S schedule in period $t+1$, labeled A^{St+1}, will be to the right of the A^{St} schedule in Fig. 9.3. Let us now consider the RHS. Focus on D_1 first. Since P_{at} is much larger than P_{at-1}, corresponding to any Π_a, D_1 for asset A will be smaller in period $t+1$ than that in period t. Focus on D_2 now. In period t, many people engaged in speculative purchase of the asset in the expectation of Π_a remaining much above $r(r_{c1})$ in future. Their expectation turned self-fulfilling as Π_a rose from $\Pi_{at1} = r(r_{c0})$ to a much higher level Π_{at2}. Clearly, this encourages the people to engage on a larger scale in the speculative purchase of the asset in period $t+1$. Emboldened by the success of the speculators in period t, more people in period $t+1$ join the speculative fray and the old speculators increase their speculative purchases. The speculative enthusiasm of the people was facilitated by the financial institutions making loans available to everyone who asked for it at $r(r_{c1})$. Thus, as t increased to $t+1$, value of D_2 corresponding to any given Π_a becomes much larger than that in period t so much so that aggregate demand for the asset in period $t+1$ corresponding to any given Π_a becomes much larger than that in period t. The increase in D_2 corresponding to every Π_a in period $t+1$ is likely to become so large that financial institutions need not engage in any speculative purchase of the asset to stop Π_a from falling from the level it attained in period t. Thus, A^{Dt+1} schedule representing the RHS of (9.23) is likely to be to the right of the A^{Dt} schedule, even with $D_{t+1} = 0$. It is obvious that on account of the Fed- and financial-institution-aided mass speculative frenzy, the rightward shift in the A^D schedule from period t to period $t + 1$ will be much larger than the rightward shift in the A^S schedule, even with $D_{t+1} = 0$. Hence, equilibrium value of Π_a will rise in period $t + 1$ from what it was in period t.

This speculative frenzy would have continued indefinitely because the expectation that the inflation rate would remain much above the interest rate was self-fulfilling, given the easy credit market conditions which made credit supply abundant to all and sundry at low interest rates. Thus, with the passage of time, every individual engaged in speculation became bolder and increased the purchase of the asset and more and more individuals emboldened by the success of the speculators started joining the game. Of course, the giant speculators who built up a stock of the asset during 1998–2000 would sell from the stock to make profit, but in their own interest they would regulate their sale in such a manner that the speculative frenzy did not get disrupted. This they did by selling from their stock only when the price of the asset in a given period rose to the desired level. In fact, as production of the asset on such a huge scale as was required to meet the demand thrown up by the mass speculative frenzy was not possible, the giant speculators had to sell from their stock to meet the demand of the mass speculators at the appropriately high price in each period. Thus, there was no reason why the speculative frenzy would come to an end. However, the speculative frenzy that started in 2001 instead of continuing indefinitely ended abruptly in 2006, when the house price inflation rate suddenly crashed from 10.16% in 2005 to 0.86% in 2006 (see Table 9.1). Clearly, the frenzy would not have ended without any exogenous intervention. Only two factors could have ended it. Either the financial institutions (or their agents), which built up a huge stock of the asset during 1998–2000, intentionally offloaded the remaining part of their stock precipitating a crash in the asset price (for reasons that we shall explain shortly) or the financial institutions raised the interest rate creating a panic or both. The latter did not happen. As we find from Table 9.2, the long-term interest rate, which is the relevant interest rate here, did not change in the period under consideration. The only explanation of the collapse of the speculative frenzy, therefore, consists in the financial institutions dishoarding the remaining stock of the asset. In terms of our model, in 2006, $\bar{D}$ dropped by a very large amount from zero precipitating the crisis. Assuming 2006 to be period $t + 2$, $\bar{D}_{t+2}$ dropped by a very large amount from zero, which was its value in the previous period. We shall now examine its impact using Fig. 9.5.

In Fig. 9.5, the initial equilibrium value of Π_a labeled Π_{at+1} corresponds to the point of intersection of A^{St+1} and A^{Dt+1} schedules representing the LHS and RHS of (9.23), with $\bar{D}_{t+1} = 0$. This is the situation that obtained in period $t + 1$. The asset market equilibrium condition in period $t + 2$ is given by

$$S((1 + \Pi_{at+2})P_{at+1}) = D_1\left((1 + \underset{-}{\Pi_{at+2}})P_{at+1}\right)$$

Table 9.2 Growth rate of GDP (Y), unemployment rate (U), labor force participation rate (L) (in percent)

Year	Y	U	L	P
1991	−0.1	6.9	65.06	1.33
1992	3.6	7.6	65.33	1.38
1993	2.7	7.0	65.24	1.32
1994	4.0	6.2	65.62	1.22
1995	2.7	5.7	65.74	1.19
1996	3.8	5.5	65.92	1.16
1997	4.5	5.0	66.23	1.2
1998	4.5	4.6	66.31	1.16
1999	4.7	4.3	66.37	1.15
2000	4.1	4.1	66.43	1.11
2001	1.0	4.8	66.06	0.99
2002	1.8	5.9	65.71	0.92
2003	2.8	6.1	65.31	0.86
2004	3.8	5.6	65.04	0.92
2005	3.3	5.2	65.06	0.92
2006	2.7	4.7	65.17	0.96
2007	1.8	4.7	64.99	0.95
2008	−0.3	5.9	64.98	0.94
2009	−2.8	9.4	64.32	0.87
2010	2.5	9.7	63.58	0.83
2011	1.6	9.0	63.01	0.74
2012	2.2	8.2	62.89	0.75
2013	1.5	7.4	62.51	0.71
2014	2.4	6.2	62.21	0.75
2015	2.8	5.3	62.01	0.75
2016	1.4	5.3	62.16	0.73
2017	2.2	4.4	61.89	0.71

Source World Bank

$$+ D_2\left(\Pi_{at+2} \underset{+}{-} r(r_{c1}); t+2\right) + \bar{D}_{t+2} \tag{9.24}$$

We can solve (9.24) for the equilibrium value of Π_{at+2}, given the value of $\bar{D}_{t+2}$.

Let us first focus on the LHS of (9.24). $P_{at+1} = (1 + \Pi_{at+1})P_{at} > P_{at}$. Hence, corresponding to any positive value of Π_a, P_a will be larger in period $t+2$ than that in period $t+1$. Hence, corresponding to any given $\Pi_a > 0$, supply of the asset A in period $t+2$ will be larger than that in period $t+1$. Hence, A^{st+2} schedule representing

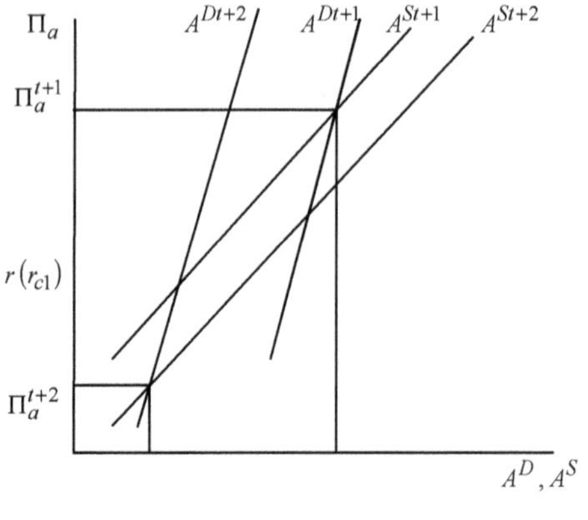

Fig. 9.5 Collapse of the speculative euphoria

the LHS of (9.24) will be to the right of the A^{st+1} schedule. Let us now consider the RHS of (9.24). Focus on D_1. Since P_{at+1} is larger than P_{at}, corresponding to any positive value of Π_a, P_a will be larger in period $t + 2$ than that in period $t + 1$. Hence, corresponding to any given Π_a, D_1 will be smaller in period $t + 2$ than that in period $t + 1$. However, D_2 is likely to be much larger in period $t + 2$ than what it was in period $t + 1$, and its increase is much larger than the fall in D_1. The reasons may be explained as follows. Persistence of Π_a far above $r(r_{c1})$ in both period t and period $t + 1$ should make the individuals bolder and substantially contribute to their speculative euphoria. Every ordinary speculator must have planned a much larger amount of purchase of the asset than what they planned to sell. Thus, as t increases from $t + 1$ to $t + 2$, D_2 goes up by a very large amount corresponding to any given Π_a in period $t + 2$. Clearly, if $\bar{D}$ had remained the same in period $t + 2$ as it was in period $t + 1$, A^{Dt+2} schedule representing the RHS of (9.24) would have intersected the A^{st+2} schedule at a point that would correspond to a Π_a, which is larger than Π_{at+1}. It is clear, then, that the speculative euphoria was ended through a drastic cut in $\bar{D}_{t+2}$ from zero so that A^{Dt+2} schedule intersected A^{st+2} schedule at a point that corresponded to a Π_a, labeled Π_{at+2}, that was much less than $r(r_{c1})$. This is shown in Fig. 9.5.

As Π_a plummeted far below $r(r_{c1})$, many people, particularly the financially weak ones who borrowed on a large scale to make speculative purchase of the asset A, became panicky and made a rush to sell off their stock of the asset in period $t + 3$ to minimize their loss. In terms of our model, as t increased from $t + 2$ to $t + 3$, D_2 corresponding to any given Π_a declined drastically so much so that Π_a in period $t + 3$ went even below Π_{at+2} (Work out the details and the diagrammatic illustration yourself.). From the above, it is clear that the panic on the part of a large number of speculators that Π_a will remain below $r(r_{c1})$ is self-fulfilling. Thus, as Π_a drops further below $r(r_{c1})$, the panic spreads and the rush for selling off the speculative stock of the asset as quickly as possible to minimize losses grips the masses. As a result, Π_a goes on falling over time until the speculative stock of the asset with the masses is exhausted. From Table 9.1, we find that the house price inflation rate dropped from 0.86% in 2006 to −4.64% in 2007 and further down to −10.27% in 2008.

We can examine the impact of the decline in Π_a on Y using (9.12). Taking simple linear form of the consumption function, we rewrite (9.12) as follows:

$$Y_t = c_y \cdot (1 - \tau)Y_t + c_a \cdot g(P_{at}) + I\left(\underset{-}{r(r_c)}\right) + \bar{G} \tag{9.25}$$

Solving (9.25) for Y_t, we get

$$Y_t = \frac{c_a \cdot g\left(\underset{+}{P_{at}}\right) + I\left(\underset{-}{r(r_c)}\right) + \bar{G}}{1 - c_y \cdot (1 - \tau)} \tag{9.26}$$

From (9.26), it follows that the rate of growth of Y depends crucially on the rate of inflation in P_a. The higher the rate of inflation in P_a, the higher is the growth rate of the autonomous component of consumption due to the higher growth rate of wealth, and therefore, the higher is the growth rate of Y. In 2006, Π_a declined drastically from 10.16 to 0.86%. Accordingly, growth rate of Y also dropped from 3.3 to 2.7%. Again in 2007, Π_a dropped from 0.86 to −4.64%. Accordingly, growth rate of Y also fell from 2.7 to 1.8%. In 2008, Π_a fell from −4.64 to −10.27%. Accordingly, the growth rate of Y fell from 1.8 to −0.3%. However, in 2009, even though Π_a rose from −10.27 to −0.5%, the growth rate of Y dropped from −0.3 to −2.8%. The reason is not far to seek. The very large fall in the asset price led to large-scale bankruptcy of the households. They defaulted on their loans. This, in turn, drove the financial institutions into deep trouble. The steep decline in consumption demand together with the sharp deterioration in the solvency of the financial institutions and the contraction in GDP in 2008 led to a collapse in investors' confidence. Thus, along with consumption, investment declined substantially too plunging the economy into a deep crisis in 2009.

9.5 Counter-Recessionary Measures and Motivation for Perpetrating the Crisis

To get the economy out of the crisis, the US Government and Fed adopted a number of measures (one may go through Blinder and Zandi 2010 for details). The US Government adopted expansionary fiscal policy in 2010. The Fed on the other hand adopted both conventional and unconventional monetary policy. The latter consisted in buying up all the non-performing assets of the financial institutions at remunerative prices so that their losses were fully made up. This brought the financial institutions back to health and restored people's confidence in them. The conventional monetary policy consisted in the Fed cutting down the policy rate, r_c, drastically to zero. To capture the impact of the counter-recessionary policies and also to bring out the motivation of bursting the speculative bubble, we shall use the following goods market equilibrium condition:

$$Y = C_w \cdot \left(\frac{wl}{P}\right) Y(1-\tau) + C_c \cdot \left(1 - \frac{wl}{P}\right) Y(1-\tau) + \bar{I}\left(\underset{-}{r(r_c)}\right) + \tilde{I}\left(\underset{-}{r(r_c) + \gamma}\right) + G \tag{9.27}$$

Let us explain (9.27). We have divided the population into two classes: workers and capitalists. C_w and C_c denote fixed average consumption propensities of workers and capitalists, respectively. Since workers are much poorer than the capitalists, C_w is much greater than C_c. With the exhaustion of the speculative stock of the asset, it is no longer necessary for our purpose to consider wealth as a determinant of consumption. Hence, we make workers' and capitalists' consumption a function of only their respective incomes. Workers' aggregate real income is given by $\frac{wl}{P}Y$, where w is the money wage rate, l is the fixed amount of labor required per unit of Y, and P is the price level. We assume both w and P to be fixed for simplicity. We have also ignored workers' income from their saving for simplicity. Capitalists get the rest of the GDP. τ denotes the tax rate. $\bar{I}(\cdot)$ is the investment function of the giant corporations controlled by the giant capitalists. We call them quality investors. It is a decreasing function of $r(r_c)$. $\tilde{I}(\cdot)$ is the investment function of the non-quality borrowers comprising mainly the small and medium enterprises. The interest rate they face is not $r(r_c)$ but $r(r_c) + \gamma$, where γ is the risk premium charged by the financial institutions. Their investment is a decreasing function of $r(r_c) + \gamma$. We have not considered foreign trade here because it is not relevant for our purpose. We can solve (9.27) for the equilibrium value of Y. It is given by

$$Y = \frac{\bar{I}\left(\underset{-}{r(r_c)}\right) + \tilde{I}\left(\underset{-}{r(r_c) + \gamma}\right) + G}{1 - \left[C_w\left(\frac{wl}{P}\right) + C_c \cdot \left(1 - \frac{wl}{P}\right)\right](1-\tau)} \tag{9.28}$$

Equation (9.28) identifies three major determinants of growth rate, namely, growth rates of $\bar{I}$, $\tilde{I}$, and G. We shall now use (9.28) to explain how the US economy fared in the post-2009 period.

Following the deepening of the crisis in 2009, the Fed cut r_c to zero. The commercial banks could borrow as much as they wanted at $r_c = 0$. The Fed also announced that it would keep r_c at zero till 2014. The banks lowered their lending rates to the minimum possible level. However, they made loans available at this low rate only to the quality investors. In the pretext of the deep recession the USA was in, they increased the risk premium very steeply on the loans to the non-quality borrowers. As a result, the interest rates faced by the non-quality borrowers became much higher than those in the pre-crisis period (see Mishkin (2011) in this context). The high interest rate coupled with the large excess capacity of the non-quality borrowers led to a collapse of their investment. In 2010, therefore, the growth initiative rested with quality investors and the government. In 2010, G increased substantially financed with loans from financial institutions. $\bar{I}$ must have increased too. As a result of these factors, GDP in the USA recorded a positive growth rate of 2.5% (see Table 9.1). However, the government withdrew its expansionary fiscal program from 2011 onward leaving the growth initiative entirely to the quality investors. The giant capitalists, in their turn, regulated the growth rate in the US economy in such a manner that it remained in a desired state of recession. The reason why they kept the economy in a desired state of recession is the following: First, the risk premium on loans to non-quality borrowers would remain high so that they would have no incentive to expand allowing the quality investors to grab their market share and also full control of the economy. Second, they wanted to slow down the rate of growth of employment to create vast pools of unemployed persons to destroy the bargaining strength of the workers. This they did to keep wages low and to incorporate all kinds of labor saving technological and managerial changes to reduce l and, thereby, increase their share in total output. Thus, the giant capitalists made huge speculative gains by selling their speculative stock they built during 1998–2000 at much higher prices during the period of the mass speculative frenzy. Along with that, they wrested full control of the economy so that they could keep the economy in a desired state of recession and thereby, for reasons explained above, increase their share in GDP at the cost of the rest of the people. One may argue in this connection that unemployment rate did fall in the USA from 9.4% in 2009 to 4.4% in 2017 despite low growth rate of GDP (see Table 9.2). However, one can argue that this decline in the unemployment rate may not indicate a higher rate of growth of employment but a lower rate of growth of labor force. Let us explain. First, note that population growth rate declined steadily in the USA (see Table 9.2). During the period of boom, 1991–2000, population growth rate dropped by 16.54%. During 2001–2009, it declined by 12.12% and in the next 8 years 2010–2017, it fell by 14.45%. Therefore, the rate of growth of working age population also declined steadily. More intriguing is the behavior of the labor participation rate. During the boom period, 1992–2000, it increased steadily from 65.331 to 66.431% (see Table 9.2). However, with the onset of recession in 2001, it began to drop. It dropped from 66.066% in 2001 to 64.32% in 2009—a fall of 2.6%. The decline continued. It fell from 64.32% in 2009 to 61.89% in 2017—a drop of 3.8%. From the data, it is clear that the labor force participation rate is highly sensitive to employment scenario. When employment grows at a high rate relative to the rate of growth of working age population, more people belonging to the working age group get the incentive to join the labor force and look for work. However, when employment grows slowly relative to the growth rate of the working age population, people become despondent and quit looking for work and, thereby, drop out of labor force. Thus, despite the steadily falling rate of growth of the working age population, the rate of growth of employment was so low during 2009–2017 that people gave up searching for work and dropped out of the labor force so much so that labor force grew at a lower rate than employment bringing about a fall in the unemployment rate. We can explain this point as follows. Consider the following equation

$$U = \frac{L - N}{L} = 1 - \frac{N}{L} \tag{9.29}$$

In (9.29), U, L, and N denote unemployment rate, the number of persons in the labor force, and the number of employed persons, respectively. Evidences strongly point to the possibility that in the post-crisis period, low growth rate of N induced an even lower growth rate of L bringing about a rise in (N/L) and, thereby, a decline in U.

9.6 Labor Saving Technological Changes, Marx's Underconsumption Crisis, and Capitalists' Counter-Strategy

Just like incorporation of labor saving technological changes, an increase in the share of large corporations in GDP at the expense of small and medium enterprises also reduces labor requirement per unit of output, since small and medium enterprises are much more labor-intensive than the large corporations. We can examine the impact of this decline using (9.28), which give the equilibrium value of Y. Let us focus on the denominator of the expression on the RHS of (9.28). Focus on the term $C_w \cdot \left(\frac{wl}{P}\right) + C_c \cdot \left(1 - \frac{wl}{P}\right)$, which we denote by c. This gives the average consumption propensity of the economy out of the aggregate disposable income $(1 - \tau)Y$. Following a decrease in l, share of workers in GDP given by $\left(\frac{wl}{P}\right)$ falls, while capitalists' share in GDP given by $\left(1 - \frac{wl}{P}\right)$ increases by the same amount. Since C_w is much larger than C_c, c falls raising the value of the denominator. Hence, equilibrium Y goes down. The point is that, following a decline in l, aggregate consumption demand at the initial equilibrium Y falls by $Y(1 - t)\frac{\partial c}{\partial l}dl$ creating excess supply at the initial equilibrium Y. Hence, there will take place a cumulative contraction in Y. Marx argued that competition among the capitalists to cut costs will lead to continuous fall in l and, thereby, in Y. This will make many firms bankrupt. Bankruptcy on the part of a large number of firms will also make a large number of financial institutions bankrupt. The latter event will make the savers lose their faith in the financial institutions. Hence, the financial institutions will not be able to make new loans available to the producers and investors. Hence, investment and, therefore, Y will fall drastically exacerbating the already adverse scenario and precipitating a crisis. Marx called this the crisis of underconsumption or overproduction. To counter the problem, capitalists spend on a massive scale on R&D. These expenditures create demand for goods and services, but do not create any productive capacity for consumption and investment goods. They produce blueprints of new technology that open up vast opportunities for investment: investments that will not add to capacities for producing the same kind of goods in the same manner but investments that will modernize existing capacities by incorporating higher degree of automation and/or by enabling them to produce new superior substitutes of existing products or completely new products altogether. Thus, the capitalists can undertake as much investment as they want in R&D to bring about a decline in l and to produce superior substitutes of existing products or new items of luxury consumption in future. This enables the capitalists to regulate the growth rate of a capitalist economy despite the continuous fall in the labor requirement of production and, thereby, avoid the crisis of underconsumption of Marx. If the capitalists keep a capitalist economy in a desired level of recession, the central bank of the country will get an excuse to keep r_c at zero so that loans become available to the giant capitalists at the minimum possible interest rate. This may be another reason why the giant capitalists will want to keep a capitalist economy at a desired level of recession.

The continuous expulsion of labor, principally low-skilled labor, will lead to shrinkage of the mass consumption goods sector, and this will be matched by expansion of the R&D sector and the luxury consumption good sector catering to needs of the capitalists and their entourage of highly skilled workers. Imagine a world, which is inhabited and owned by just a few giant capitalists. All production is carried out with robots, and there is a class of highly skilled workers controlling these robots and working on ways of making the robots more productive and more docile. This world is now a possibility and economically quite viable.

9.7 Nexus Between the Giant Capitalists and the US Government and Fed

Obviously, if common people perceived the asset price bubble and made frenzied contribution to it before being its victim, it definitely came to the notice of the US Government and Fed and they willingly allowed the bubble and the frenzy to continue, even though they pretended to have been caught unawares after the bubble had collapsed plunging the economy into a deep crisis. The pretense is all the more stark, since what happened in the USA is nothing new. Such events happened earlier in Japan at the beginning of nineties, in the East Asian countries in the late nineties, and also in many other places with devastating effects. Europe's experience was more or less the same as that of the USA. Thus, the conclusion that seems unexceptionable is that the giant capitalists, who control the large financial institutions that operate globally, in connivance with the governments of the major capitalist countries of the world, are perpetrating crises in country after country through their operations in the asset markets. It should be noted here that, when a financial institution makes losses or becomes bankrupt, its directors (the persons who run the company) need not necessarily make any losses. Financial institutions are joint stock companies where liabilities of the owners are limited to the value of the shares of the company they hold. This means that if a joint stock company suffers losses and becomes bankrupt, a shareholder's only loss is the loss in the value of his shares. He is under no obligation to pay back the loans of the company along with the interest. Financial institutions hold one another's shares. They buy one another's shares with the money common people deposit with them. More than fifty percent of the shares of a financial institution may be held by other financial institutions. It is, therefore, quite possible that the financial institutions vote one another's promoters on to the boards of their respective financial institutions. In such a scenario, the directors who run the company may not hold any share in the company. Thus, it is quite likely that, when a financial institution becomes bankrupt, it is not its directors who lose; it is the ordinary people who kept their money with the financial institution lose their savings. Directors of financial institutions draw astronomical sums in salaries and bonuses at the expense of the ordinary shareholders of the financial institutions. Thus, the giant capitalists who control the giant financial institutions rob the workers of all their savings in the following way. They build up a huge speculative stock of an asset and, thereby, create an asset price bubble. Through various means at their disposal, they induce the masses into a speculative frenzy. Financial institutions aided by the central bank of the country make loans available at low interest rate and extremely soft conditions to all and sundry. As the price of the asset soars riding on the mass speculative wave, the giant capitalists start selling off from their stock and, thereby, get the workers' savings parked with the financial institutions to themselves and at an opportune moment sell off the remaining part of their stock bursting the bubble. The collapse of the asset price bubble drives the economy into a deep recession. The government rescues the economy from the deep recession through fiscal expansion and unconventional and conventional monetary policies and then hands over the control of the economy to the giant capitalists, who keep the economy at a desired level of recession so that workers' labor and new saving become available to them at the minimum possible wages and interest rates. In a democracy, political parties need enormous amounts of fund to sustain themselves and to compete with one another. They have to hire workers and services of the media to make their programs and policies popular. They have to lure people to be their workers with job offers. Obviously, they get these funds and jobs for their workers from the giant capitalists, who have almost the whole of the production process of the economy in their control. Hence, political parties work for the giant capitalists. If any party does not abide by the dictates of the giant capitalists, they divert their jobs and funds to other political parties making them stronger. Thus, in a multiparty democracy, political parties are just like other business enterprises of the giant capitalists. They control and run these political parties in their interest. Giant capitalists are just a few in number, but they own the major part of the country's wealth and earn the major part of the country's aggregate income. To protect their enormous business empire from the masses, expand it, and keep the mass of workers under control, they need state power. Hence, they fund and run the political parties. This explains the close nexus between the giant capitalists and the US Government including the Fed.

9.8 Conclusion

A capitalist society divides its population into two classes: the capitalists and the workers and sets them against one another. The capitalists secure from the workers their labor and their saving and devise all sorts of ways of keeping the workers under control and getting their labor and savings at lowest possible prices. They run the political parties and the government to help them in their venture. After carefully analyzing the evidences, we have come to the conclusion that the crisis that occurred in the USA in 2008–09 did not happen the way natural calamities such as earthquakes or typhoons happen. Instead of being an event caused by impersonal market forces, the crisis was preplanned. It was perpetrated by the giant capitalists, and the policies of the US Government and Fed facilitated their program. The objective was to take away the workers' savings in the form of massive speculative gains. A capitalist economy is controlled and planned by the giant capitalists who keep it in a desired state of recession to keep wages and interest rate at the lowest possible levels. They relentlessly incorporate labor saving technological changes to create vast pools of unemployment to eliminate the bargaining strength of the workers. Most of the workers live in poverty without access to basic necessities of life in adequate quantities. The collapse of the Soviet Union has substantially weakened the socialist bloc and the workers' movements everywhere. The capitalists now reign supreme. Unless the workers identify their true exploiters, unite and assert their rights, and seek to wrest the political parties and the government from the clutches of the giant capitalists, there is no hope for the workers.

References

Bernanke, B., Gertler, M., & Gilchrist, S. (1996). The financial accelerator and the flight to quality. *The Review of Economics and Statistics, 78*(1), 1–15.

Blinder, A. S., & Zandi, M. (2010). *How the great recession was brought to an end*. Available at www.dismal.com/mark-zandi/documents/End'of-Great-Recession.pdf.

Case, K. E., & Shiller, R. J. (2003). Is there a bubble in the housing market? *Brookings Papers on Economic Activity, 2,* 299–342 (Fall).

Glaeser, E. L., Gottlieb, J. D., & Gyourko, J. (2010). *Can cheap credit explain the housing bubble?* NBER Working Paper 16230, July.

Himmelberg, C., Mayer, C., & Sinai, T. (2005). Assessing high house prices: Bubbles, fundamentals and misperceptions. *Journal of Economic Perspectives, 19*(4), 67–92.

Khandani, A., Lo, A. W., & Merton, R. C. (2009). *Systemic risk and the refinancing Ratchet effect.* NBER Working Paper 15362, September.

Mayer, C., & Sinai, T. (2005). Bubble trouble? Not likely. *Wall Street Journal* editorial, September 19, 2005.

Mishkin, F. (2011). Over the cliff: From the subprime to the global financial crisis. *Journal of Economic Perspectives, 25*(1), 49–70 (Winter).

Shiller, R. J. (2006). Long-term perspectives on the current boom in home prices. *The Economists' Voice, 3*(4), 4.

Taylor, J. B. (2009). *Getting off track: How government actions and interventions caused, prolonged, and worsened the financial crisis*. Hoover Institution Press.

Index

C. Ghosh and A. N. Ghosh, *Keynesian Macroeconomics Beyond the IS-LM Model*, https://doi.org/10.1007/978-981-13-7888-1

Lightning Source UK Ltd.
Milton Keynes UK
UKHW020851120421
381772UK00003BA/317